Tabeau's Narrative
of Loisel's Expedition to
the Upper Missouri

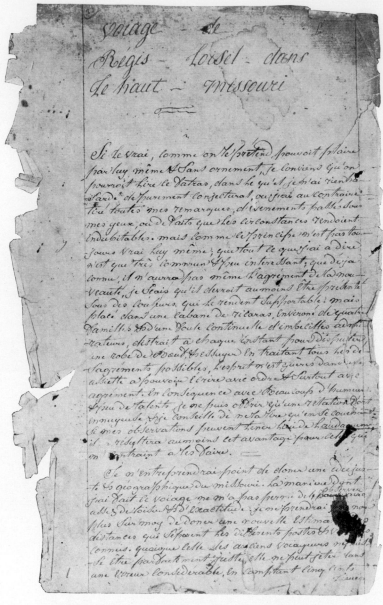

FIRST PAGE OF THE TABEAU NARRATIVE

Washington Version

Tabeau's Narrative
of Loisel's Expedition to the
Upper Missouri

EDITED BY

ANNIE HELOISE ABEL

TRANSLATED FROM THE FRENCH BY

ROSE ABEL WRIGHT

University of Oklahoma Press
Norman, 1939

Copyright 1939

BY THE

UNIVERSITY OF OKLAHOMA PRESS

ALL RIGHTS RESERVED

SET UP AND PRINTED AT NORMAN, OKLAHOMA, U.S.A.

BY THE UNIVERSITY OF OKLAHOMA PRESS

PUBLISHING DIVISION OF THE

UNIVERSITY

First Edition, 1939

To the memory
of our dearly beloved father
George Abel
who was born in the parish of Fintray, Aberdeenshire,
November 9, 1840, and who, after a long
life, lived well and honorably
and for an almost equal length of time in the United
Kingdom, and in the United States of America,
died at Aberdeen, Washington,
February 20, 1934

PREFACE

IT is a far cry, perhaps, from boys' books of adventure to serious recital of a fur trader's life among the red men, such as the narrative here published, yet my personal interest in the North American Indians may be said to date from the time when, as a child in England, I revelled in *The Three Trappers, Afar in the Forest, In the Far, Far West,* the very authors' names of which I have forgotten or, what is more likely, never knew. They and others like them were the particular property of my brothers and, in the jealous fashion of children, their perusal, no doubt, permitted to me only as a rare privilege. A privilege in truth it must have been; for, in the years since, the interest that they, half fact, half fiction, aroused in me has never waned. On the contrary, the interest has increased, inspiring the seeking and reading of innumerable travel narratives that have been their successors.

Regardless of that interest, however, it was never my intention, originally, to undertake the editing of fur-trader journals. I had no wish to be diverted from the task I had already set myself; research into the treatment accorded aborigines by Anglo-Saxon peoples bent upon colonizing; but, having been prevailed upon by friends at the Indian Office to undertake the identification of the so-called Lewis and Clark itinerary map, it was futile to raise objections to the companion studies next presented, the Truteau, the Mackay, the Chardon, and the Loisel-Tabeau.

The work on the Loisel-Tabeau narrative began tentatively years ago at the time when the Nicollet chest that contained it was first unearthed in the Topographical Bureau of the United States War Department. Promising large returns in the shape of distinct contributions to our knowledge of the red men, it was promptly photostated and the photostatic copy handed over to my sister, Dr. Rose Abel-Wright, for translation. That arduous work completed, it was ready for the editing and that I began as soon as I was free to do so, going in turn to Washington, D.C., St. Louis, and, finally, to Ottawa, Ontario, where I practically finished it seven years ago.

Next came thoughts of publishing and there was the rub. Several competent judges had examined the original manuscript and declared it exceedingly interesting and valuable. Among them were Dr. F. W. Hodge of the Museum of the American Indian and Dr. Isaiah Bowman, then Director of the American Geographical Society and now President of Johns Hopkins University; but, for one reason or another, and principally, I believe, because I wanted the French original to be included with the translation no opportunity for publication seemed to be forthcoming. In Canada, prospects seemed brighter and, before very long, the choice of two very excellent plans was given. The one plan meant joining an ambitiously-designed group, *Fur Traders of the West,* the other, constituting a report of the Dominion Archives, which, under the law, must appear in both French and English. The decision was easily made in favor of the second plan and I began at once to recast the *Historical Introduction* so as to give to it, what the material itself naturally had, a French-Canadian slant.

The Loisel manuscript is anonymous. My sister, however, early came to the conclusion, upon comparing it with the Lewis and Clark journals, that its author was very probably the "Mr Anty Tabo," who came from the Arikara Indians to visit the explorers when they arrived at the place where they expected to spend the winter and his full name of *Pierre Antoine* suggested itself when I brought it to her attention that they were seeking among the Indians, a "Mr. Peter Tabeau." The job of identifying him was then greatly simplified.

And soon came a most astonishing confirmation of authorship. From the start, after I had resolved to accept the Deputy Minister's generous offer, various members of his staff, especially Major Gustave Lanctôt, Doctor J. F. Kenney, Miss Margaret A. Robertson, and the late Mr. William Smith, performed many acts of kindness in their individual ways and were always most encouraging. One day, Major Lanctôt, in his enthusiasm over the manuscript, having occasion to go to Montreal, took it with him to exhibit it to his friends there. He returned bringing with him what, in many respects, seemed to be a typewritten copy of its duplicate. This he had obtained from M. Aegidius Fauteux, Librarian then of the Bibliothèque Saint-Sulpice and now of the Montreal Civic Library. The title-page carried the name of *Pierre-Antoine Tabeau,* the author by implication. From that time on I ceased to use *Loisel* as a designation for the document I was editing.

The typewritten copy of the Montreal version came in handy for purposes of comparison. The results I give elsewhere. Residence in Canada made it a somewhat simpler matter than it had been in other places to trace, in some degree, the origin and fortunes of the few men who actually figure in the Tabeau narrative; but there was not much to discover. Obscurely they lived and obscurely died.

Towards the end of my second winter in Ottawa, I went away thinking it would not be long thereafter before publication would begin; but year after year passed and nothing was done. It was the period of the great depression. Occupied with other duties, it was some time before I could personally enquire into the reasons for delay. When I did, I found it was the all too common one, lack of funds sufficient for so large and costly an undertaking. Not a great while thereafter, the whole idea of Canadian governmental publication, Doctor Doughty's own in the beginning, had to be reconsidered and then entirely given up.

But, if there be anything that can truly reconcile me to the thought of abandoning all hope of publishing the French text with the translation thereof, it would be the inclusion of that translation in a series of scholarly treatises on Indian civilization, which is the joyful end now in prospect, the substitute project that may ultimately satisfy the most exacting of well-wishers.

The literary resurrection of Tabeau has had already one very gratifying result. It has given birth apparently in French Canada to an interest in him commensurate with that reserved previously for his nephew and namesake who came so near to becoming Bishop of Montreal. A year ago, or thereabouts, two separate instances of this suddenly awakened interest came to my notice, both of which, through exchange of courtesies, have redounded measurably to my advantage. Through the kind offices of E.-Z. Massicotte, Archivist at the Old Court House in Montreal, I have been able recently to procure a certified copy of Tabeau's will and, through those of Professor Benoît Brouillette of the *Ecole des Hautes Etudes Commerciales,* University of Montreal, a new and more carefully collated copy of the Montreal version of his narrative, one made by Professor Brouillette himself for use in certain geographical researches. One regret I have and that is that I have never yet seen the original text of the version, which is, as I understand, a part of the archives of the Archepiscopal Palace.

Of Doctor Wright's work in any detail I have not yet had opportunity to speak and I do not intend to do so at any length. It stands in a class by itself and speaks for itself, requiring no commendation from me. Mrs. Nettie Beauregard, Archivist of the Missouri Historical Society, read critically the first draft of the translation and made, with reference to it, some helpful suggestions. A later draft Major Lanctōt glanced over and then passed it on for final remarks to the official translator of the Dominion Archives Department.

In making the translation, Doctor Wright had an eye first of all to accuracy and correct transmission of the thought. While not ignoring literary effect but seeking it whenever possible, she never subordinated to it the literal. Exactness established as the rule, her only conscious departure from it was that necessitated by Tabeau's inordinate resort to the historical present. For smoothness of phrase changes occasionally had to be made. Tabeau's spelling of Indian tribal names has been retained and, in some instances, of rivers, also his use, the usual French, of *Savage* as a synonym for Indian.

It was considered advisable to omit certain marginal notes which appeared in the Tabeau manuscripts. This entails no loss, however, since they are topical merely and neither corrective nor explanatory.

In conclusion, I would like to acknowledge my sincere gratitude for every bit of help rendered. The principal sources I have indicated. To particularize further, beyond including Mr. Joseph Tarte of the Parliamentary Library and Miss Stella M. Drumm of the Jef-

PREFACE

ferson Memorial in my list of interested friends would be invidious and, all things considered, impossible. One special kind of help I would in no wise overlook. It was material in a double sense, being both timely and substantial. It took the form of a grant-in-aid from the Social Science Research Council, making possible to an appreciable extent my protracted stay in the Dominion of Canada capital. Engaged upon this study and upon that of Canadian Indian affairs, I was in residence there a few months short of two years.

ANNIE HELOISE ABEL

CONTENTS

ILLUSTRATIONS

HISTORICAL INTRODUCTION

HISTORICAL INTRODUCTION

THE French in early St. Louis had journeyed thither from two principal directions, New Orleans and Canada. For the migrants from the north the regular route was across the Illinois country, a way seemingly long and arduous, yet one that, in its earlier stages at all events, was far from unfamiliar. Much of it had become known during the period of the intercolonial wars to those bent, consciously or unconsciously, upon carrying out the excellent ideas, credited to La Salle, of uniting French territories north and south by peacefully appropriating and occupying the intervening stretch. The rest of it rapidly became known after Britain, by means of the Royal Proclamation of 1763, had thrown open the traffic in furs to all who cared to participate. It was not alone the enterprising Briton, a self-exiled Highlander in the main, who took advantage of the boon.[1] Beside him stood the French-Canadian and he stood there not simply as *coureur de bois, voyageur,* interpreter, or guide, but frequently as a trader on his own account, a capitalist. The trade licenses[2] of the period—certainly those issued at Quebec over the signature of the governor-in-chief—would seem to have been in them-

---

[1] There was an almost mad rush for an entry into the trade after the transfer to British control and it is interesting to observe, from the trade licenses issued at Quebec, how very many French-Canadians shared the enthusiasm and, in this connection, it is interesting also to observe that all who did go into the fur-trading area carried with them an abundance of spirituous liquors, rum, brandy, high wines, etc. Some American writers, seeking to differentiate between British methods and French, have endeavored to throw the onus of responsibility for the introduction of fire water into the trade upon the British; but, if the records tell anything and if they do not tell a quite different story, they at least draw no national or racial line. Moreover, they show that in times, when the traffic by means of rum was out-and-out illicit, the vendors of fire water were more often French than British. The credit — and it is a large one — for such restraint as existed or was imposed under the old régime belongs to the Roman Catholic missionaries and especially to the Jesuits. The influence of the Jesuits once removed — and its removal, though not due in any degree to the coming of the British, was practically coincident with it — the way was open to an all-too-general use of intoxicants.

[2] For specimen licenses, see Appendix III. They were selected from the many as having to do with the Tabeau family.

selves an invitation to penetrate the country more and more; for, though they specified Niagara, Toronto, the Grande Portage, La Baye,[3] Michilimackinac,[4] Detroit, Fort Chartres,[5] or more vaguely sometimes, Lac Ontario, Lac Superior, the Upper Country, Illinois as the destination of a given cargo,[6] they also, by implication, conferred a right of way to parts beyond, wherever might be found to exist a sufficient lure.[7]

The lure, as events would have it, was not invariably of the inanimate variety; for the little French settlements, survivals of that earlier day of keen Anglo-Gallic rivalry, were scattered here and there throughout the Illinois country and offered to the Montreal

[3] Green Bay, *"Baie verte ou des Puants,"* *"La Baye des Puants."*

[4] For variants of the name, see Riddell, William Renwick, *A Pretty Quarrel over Rum in Old Michillimackinac*, Royal Society of Canada *Transactions*, 1928, third Series, 114, n. 1.

[5] A license, granted in 1769 to St. Martin Adhemar, who later seems to have become a resident of the United States (Riddell, Wm. R., *The First Judge at Detroit and His Court*, p. 26) and whose Christian name was occasionally used as a surname (*Index des Registres des Notaires de Detroit*, 1737-1796, Dominion Archives) was for "Niagara & Fort Chartres and from thence to such markets or parts as he shall find most Advantageous for the disposal of the Merchandize, ..." (Dominion Archives).

[6] These were not, by any manner of means, the only places named in the licenses for the various years. Pierre Robichaud received a license, 8 January 1769, permitting him to renew his trade "to any part of this Province on the South side of the River St. Lawrence to the Eastward of the River Chaudiere . . . ." and William Smith, on the sixth of May following, one permitting him "to pass unmolested with One Schooner or Shallop manned with Six Men . . . . to Chaleurs Bay & Ristigouche and from thence to such Markets or Parts as he shall find most advantageous for the disposal of the said Merchandise . . . . Provided always, That nothing herein contained shall be construed to extend to give any Authority to the said Wm. Smith to trade or Traffick with the Indians without the Limits of this Province, or at the Posts of the King's Domain . . . ." Maurice Blondeau was licensed, 27 April 1769, to go to "Michilimackinac & La Mer de l'ouest."

[7] The meaning of this must not be too greatly amplified; for the whole idea behind the licensing system was regulation. General Gage was not alone in thinking that, in any reform adopted, there ought to be a provision that traders should not be allowed to "go anywhere but to the Posts fixed upon for their Trade" (Gage to Johnson, June 24, 1764, quoted from *Gage Letter Book,* in Alvord, Clarence W., and Carter, Clarence E., *Critical Period, 1763-1765*, Illinois Historical *Collections*, X, 268-69). For George Croghan's suggestions to the Lords of Trade, June 8, 1764, see *idem*, pp. 256-63 and, for the inception of the license regulation, see the "Plan for the Future Management of Indian Affairs, July 10, 1764," *idem*, pp. 273-80; *New York Colonial Documents*, VII, 637-41.

traders a reunion, not infrequently, with relatives and friends and, always, an environment most congenial. From Cahokia, from Rocher du Prairie, or even from Kaskaskia — to mention only three of the settlements — it was but a step, so to speak, to the Missouri-Mississippi confluence, while just about five miles from that strategic point was a lure greater than any other, the little town, St. Louis of Illinois, that Pierre Laclede Liguest had founded in 1764, immediately subsequent to the close of the Seven Years' War. Established, not only to exploit the country and to divert the trade, if possible, from the British posts on the eastern side of the Mississippi, but also to permit escape for individual Frenchmen, should they desire it, from Anglo-Saxon control, an adverse fate had made it Spanish. The town lay in Upper Louisiana and by the secret treaty of Fontainebleau, Louis XV had handed all Louisiana over to Spain, the ally of France under the Bourbon Family Compact, by way of compensating her for the loss of Florida, which had been surrendered to Britain in exchange for conquered Havana.

Of the French in and around St. Louis even to the Illinois side of the Mississippi who engaged in the fur trade — and they were ever the great majority of all who did — the more prominent, with a few notable exceptions, were of Canadian origin. Foremost among the exceptions, as foremost among the traders, were the Chouteaus, hailing from New Orleans. Men of the name of Cerré, Papin, Robidou,[8] Sanguinet, Vallée,[9] and various others, appearing sooner or later in Missouri, were all originally from the Province of Quebec. To a great extent the leaders and second rank men belonged to Canada, either by birth or lineage; and this was true of the lesser men, from whom

[8] As evidence of there being a certain degree of intimacy existing between the Robidou and Tabeau families, of probable moment because of Robidou's interest in the Missouri River trade — for instance, he helped to outfit the second D'Eglise expedition (Nasatir, Abraham P., *Anglo-Spanish Rivalry on the Upper Missouri*, Mississippi Valley Historical *Review*, XVI, 367) — note the case of Robidou's calling upon "old Mr. Tabeau, a Canadian resident of this place for many years, who knew your petitioner's family connections" to vouch for it that no members of the Robidou family had "surrendered their souls to the devil" (Billon, F. L., *Annals of St. Louis in Its Early Days under French and Spanish Dominations*, pp. 174-76).

[9] For the Vallée, or Vallé, family, see Tanguay, Mgr. C., *Dictionnaire Généalogique des Familles Canadiennes*, VII, 414-18; Dalton, Mary Louise, *Notes on the Genealogy of the Vallé Family*, Missouri Historical Society *Collections*, II, 54 *et seq.*

5

the engagés generally were recruited, to an even greater extent. Because of his long acquaintance with the Indians, intimate to an unusual degree, and because of his well-nigh perfect adaptability to the wild life of stream and of mountain, of forest and of prairie, the *habitant*[10] was to every single fur-trading company, no matter under what flag operating, an economic asset that it dared not ignore and could never, under any conceivable circumstances, entirely dispense with.[11]

Neither could the Spanish rulers of Louisiana dispense with the French-Canadians. Aside from prominent men like François Vallé at old Ste. Geneviève, there were many more obscure who gave their services loyally and unstintedly to His Catholic Majesty, despite the fact that the French all along the lower Mississippi deeply resented the transfer to his jurisdiction. Spain, in possession of the west bank of the Father of Waters, seemed fully as anxious to rivet her claim territorially and to utilize the natural resources, of which fur at the moment was held to be the chief, as could have been any of her neighbors under similar conditions. Moreover, she was determined to prevent at all cost further encroachment upon her preserves by Anglo-Saxons, whether of British or American connection. The

10 Strictly speaking, of course, the *habitants* were the peasants, the agriculturists, "the people of the colonial seigniories" (Munro, Wm. B., *The Seigniorial System in Canada*, Harvard Historical *Studies*, XIII, 9, 39, n. 2); nevertheless, it was from their ranks that the traders were drawn. It was their young men that answered the call of the wilderness, "succumbed to the fascination of the forest life and, abandoning their lands and families, betook themselves by the score to the roving life of the coureur-de-bois . . . ." (Munro, Wm. B., *Documents Relating to the Seigniorial Tenure in Canada*, Historical Introduction, Champlain Society *Publications*, p. xxxix), and "the seductive charm" that the fur traffic had for them was "the curse of Canadian agricultural interests," the chief obstacle in the way of economic development.

11 This was as true of the American Fur Co. as of any other. For the value that John Jacob Astor, personally, put upon the French-Canadian, see Chittenden, H. M., *History of the American Fur Trade of the Far West*, I, 229. In the eyes of this shrewd German emigrant, it was not merely the French from the north who were of large worth, but Montreal men generally, although after he had severed his own connection with the city that was then the great fur emporium of the New World and had become a citizen of the United States, he manifested an intense prejudice against the British both before and after the War of 1812. He secured the enactment of the Exclusion Act of 1816 as a means of eliminating the British as his competitors, yet he was so dependent upon British subjects for nearly all classes of his employees that he became himself the most notorious violator of the Act.

Americans, being closer at hand and equally aggressive, acquisitive and enterprising, she hated and distrusted more, if that were possible, than she did the British; but, obviously, that was because they were known to covet whatever would give them free access to the outlet of the Mississippi and round off their own possessions to the southward. Florida, hers again since 1783, had been long enough in British hands — two full decades — to allow of considerable economic progress there, including settlement from the upper Atlantic seaboard colonies, and soon its state was, from the viewpoint of Spanish tenure, precarious in the extreme, owing to the expansionist designs of the Americans, politically independent now, colonists no longer.

It was Louisiana, however, that gave to Spain her more immediate concern. The closing eighteenth century saw in Spain a sort of revival of the adventurous spirit that had won for her an overseas empire in the sixteenth. Under its impetus, to lay hold upon western North America, as she had laid hold long since upon Central and South, appeared to her imperative. The pretension to exclusive rights at Nootka was not without significance, particularly as it was almost simultaneous with an unprecedented activity in the vast interior of the continent. At both points it was chiefly with the British that Spain expected to have to measure swords; for they were trading on the upper Missouri, among the Mandans especially[12] and onwards towards the far west, with pack horse or canoe, precisely as they were trading with their ships on the North Pacific.[13]

[12] In the second part of John MacDonell's journal, 1793-1795 (Masson Collection), there are many allusions to a passing back and forth, for purposes of trade, between old Fort Esperance, the North West Company post near the mouth of the *Rivière Qu' Appelle,* and the Mandans. For additional evidence and also for some slight reference to like activity on the part of the Hudson's Bay Company, see Nasatir, A. P., *John Evans, Explorer and Surveyor,* Missouri Historical Review, XXV, 230-34, 585-91.

[13] Doctor Nasatir has been engaged for several years in making a very excellent and exhaustive study of Anglo-Spanish trade rivalry and has published various articles bearing upon different phases of the subject, one or two of considerable length and all intended to be contributory to a book in prospect, which will give, it is to be hoped, the final word on many disputed points. In one of his subsidiary studies he has shown that the rivalry extended even to the lower Missouri and its tributaries, where French-Canadian subjects of Britain endeavored to open up trade with the Osages. See Ducharme's *Invasion of Missouri, an Incident in the Anglo-Spanish Rivalry for the Indian Trade of Upper Louisiana,* Missouri Historical *Review,* XXIV, 3-25, 238-60, 420-

To oust the British from the interior country or to anticipate them should it transpire that they had not yet obtained a foothold; to capture the peltry trade for the denizens of Spain;[14] and, finally, to discover a transcontinental route to the far-famed southern sea, effecting thereby a junction with Mexico and California, became the wish and the determination of Spanish authorities. A company was formed, *La Compagnie de Commerce pour la Découverte des Nations du haut du Missouri,* called, for short, here as elsewhere today, the "Company of Commerce" or, better yet, the "Missouri Company." The idea[15] of such a contrivance as a means to the desired end was broached in the autumn of 1793 about a year to the very month after Jacques D'Eglise, the first Spanish subject to make the ascent of the Missouri — he had set forth in the late summer of 1790 — had returned to St. Louis, brimful of information, good, bad, and indifferent, about the Indians resident along its banks and the extent among them of British commercial activities. It took some time, naturally, for the details of the plan of the operating company to be perfected and the project itself was not formally approved at Madrid until 1796; but long before that its best and, indeed, its only presumptively scientific work had been done, it being inevitable, seemingly, that sooner or later it would degenerate into a purely pecuniary scheme, private altogether.

---

39. A communication of date, July 29, 1797 (*Vasquez Papers,* Missouri Historical Society, hereafter to be designated MHS), accused the Osages of inclining towards the British and the Americans of condoning intrusions upon Spanish possessions.

14 See Carondelet's military report, November 24, 1794 (Robertson, James A., *Louisiana under the Rule of Spain, France, and the United States, 1785-1807,* I, 335); also the James Mackay testimony in the *Cuivre Dardenne* River case, March 7, 1817 ("Published Argument on Behalf of Claimants," *Clamorgan Papers,* MHS), which was one of several cases involving the alleged claims of Clamorgan.

15 Since it has been suggested that the idea may have been inspired from British sources (Wisconsin Historical Society *Collections,* XXII, 16, n. 1), it is interesting to observe that Doctor Nasatir, at the time he wrote his own article, "The Formation of the Missouri Company" (Missouri Historical *Review,* XXV, 10-22), was not prepared, on the basis of his own findings to subscribe to it (see p. 17, n. 14). Others less well qualified to speak might go farther and think the suggestion almost fantastic; for, while it is true that the most prominent of the explorers, James Mackay and John Evans, were British-born, true also that the former had once been at Red River in the employ of the North West Company, there is nothing to show that they had anything to do with the inception of the idea. Moreover, after they had once committed themselves to the interests of Spain, they served her loyally.

Before that time came, however, it bid fair fully to justify itself. So eager was it to begin functioning that, without waiting even for the official sanction of Baron de Carondelet, the Governor-General of Louisiana, it sent out in 1794 its initial expedition, placing it, very wisely from the standpoint of its professed purposes, under the direction of Jean-Baptiste Truteau, an ex-schoolmaster and, therefore, a man presumably far removed from thoughts and things gainful, although, withal, a distant relative of the Lieutenant-Governor, Zenon Trudeau, who, regardless of what his real motives may have been, had fostered the notion of a company from the beginning. D'Eglise was in line for requisition also; for Truteau, thinking, no doubt, that his larger and richer experience could not fail to be helpful, invited him urgently to join the party; but he declined, preferring, we may suppose, to go on rather in the way he had started with material and personal profit his sole excuse for hazardous adventure. D'Eglise, be it remarked, had already made a second trip up the Missouri, unfortunately a frustrated one because of Sioux and Arikara interference, and was even then upon his third, notwithstanding that he had been refused a trade monopoly applied for, it being deemed not compatible with the objects and declared intentions of the infant company.

Besides the Truteau expedition just referred to, which was begun in 1794, the Missouri Company sponsored two others, both in 1795, the Lécuyer in the spring and the Mackay in the summer. In the second of these three major affairs this historical introduction takes great interest for the simple reason that the author of our present narrative was unquestionably the Tabeau that belonged to it and that Mackay, when he heard about his doings in connection with it, scurrilously called "an infamous rascal." The Lécuyer expedition came to grief at the Poncas, pillaged, it is thought, by the Indians; but, beyond the bare fact of that disaster, few of its incidents are known. One thing is certain, though, and that is that the Tabeau complained of was not, as Professor Teggart surmised years since, "one of the renegade whites mentioned by Lewis and Clark and John MacDonnell."[16] A relief party was sent forward to Lécuyer's assistance but

---

[16] If Professor Teggart consulted only that part of MacDonell's Journal published by Masson in his *Les bourgeois de la Campagnie du Nord-ouest*, Vol. I, which was

vainly and, when later on, much later that same summer, Mackay, at the head of his exploring troop, appeared, he was joined by six of Lécuyer's men, from whom he must have heard news so disparaging that it made him write:

"Tabeau, one of the high men in Lecuye's carriage, should not only lose his salary but be severely punished as an example for the

---

obviously the only part that Father Morice, whom he cites, did, it is no wonder that he has an entirely wrong idea as to who the Tabault was who was "de la fourche de la riviere Qu'Appelle." From the complete MacDonell journal, which is in the *Masson MSS* although catalogued erroneously as "The Journal of John MacDonald, 1793-1795," it is apparent that Tabault was within reach of the North West Company establishment, "called by Mr. Robert Grant, when he built it, *Fort Esperance,*" from November 21, 1793 to May 6, 1795; for, on those dates and at irregular intervals in between, MacDonell had occasion to make some reference to him, to him himself, to his daughter, *Otchightche,* or to his adopted son. It seems scarcely possible, therefore, that he could have been the Tabeau of the ill-fated Lécuyer expedition. Moreover, he was, as the following passages, quoted from the MacDonell journal, reveal, not a white man, but an Indian:

21 April 1795 — "Tabaults Band & Self arrived & made the following presents . . . . Gave each of them a large keg & chiefs clothing . . . ."

22 April 1795 — Tabault & his band traded & ascended the Hill to camp & had to wade through two feet water to reach its base . . . ."

MacDonell's "Tabault" was, undoubtedly, the Assiniboine (or Cree?) concerning whom Alexander Henry had something to say:

8 January 1810 — "Early this morning a small Band of Blackfeet arrived, but on being informed that the Asineboine were expected in to day. They traded and I sent them off instantly. At 2 Oclock the Asineboines arrived, 35 men of the Gens de Peid Tribe a most notorious, set of horse thieves. I had a long conversation with them on the subject but like all their Countrymen, it was never any of them present that ever stole horses. Old Tabeau Le Boeuf Blanc and Tourbillion was also along with them. I gave them some Liquor and they continued drinking all night. The two Crees much inclined to be troublesome" (*Coventry Copy of Henry Journal,* II, 892; Coues, *New Light on the Early History of the Greater Northwest,* II, 579).

4 May 1810 — "This afternoon arrived Tabeau with three Asineboines . . . . (*Coventry Copy, op. cit.,* II, 929; Coues, *op. cit.,* II, 597).

2 September 1810 — ". . . . At all events every Body will be happy at the death of the Moose Dung even his own people detested the sight of him, and no later than last Spring, Old Tabeau beged. of me to give him a dose of Poison to kill him &c . . . . (*Coventry Copy, op cit.,* II, 981; Coues, *op. cit.,* II, 623).

Simon Fraser met with an Indian of a name suggestive of Tabeau. It was "Tabot Tho'," "Tabah Tha'," etc., *Report of the Public Archives* (Canada), 1929, pp. 129, 132, 133, 142, 144. For a young Snake Indian, "Tabbobo," "Tebow," "Tabow," see Phillips, Paul C., *Forty Years on the Frontier,* p. 207 and Index.

That Pierre-Antoine Tabeau was not a "renegade white" in the estimation of Captains Lewis and Clark there is no difficulty at all in proving. The citations from

future. He is an infamous rascal. Lecuye, the conductor, who has no less than two women since he arrived among the Poncas, has given away a large number of things belonging to the Company, as you will see in the report which I have received and which I am sending to you."[17]

Thus did James Mackay pronounce sentence but whether justly or no is another matter. The account of the affair, as we at present have it, sounds prejudicial and is assuredly meager. Even the specific nature of the accused man's wrong-doing is withheld from us. That being the case, queries galore force themselves to the attention. In what, for instance, consisted his rascality?[18] Is it not conceivable that Lécuyer's gross licentiousness gave deep offence to some of his men, disgusted them maybe, and destroyed utterly any respect that, in virtue of his position, they might otherwise have entertained for him? Tabeau himself, if we can judge from his none too personally-revealing narrative, was not the sort to be easily susceptible to Indian feminine charms. He gave the red folk, whenever he could, a wide berth and kept his relations with them as much as possible on a

---

their journals (American Historical Association *Report*, 1908, *op. cit.*, I, 190, n. *e*) are very numerous and convey the idea of being cumulative evidence of his rascality, whereas they are really nothing but the index to the instances of Tabeau's being mentioned by either Lewis or Clark, usually because of some service he had rendered. Upon examination, indeed, not a single one of them will be found to contain anything disparaging, quite the reverse. What little the American explorers had to say of Tabeau was good. They entertained him at breakfast on terms of equality; they sought his advice; they trusted him; they took his word as against that of others; and they obtained from him a great deal of information of so valuable a character that they incorporated it, unquestioned, into their own report.

[17] Extract from one of the documents included by Dr. Nasatir in *John Evans, Explorer and Surveyor*, Missouri Historical *Review*, XXV, 440-41. Apparently the date was October 24, 1795 and Mackay writing to Clamorgan and Rheile, directors of the Missouri Company. Doctor Teggart, in his *Notes Supplementary* to *Any Edition of Lewis and Clark*, American Historical Association *Report*, 1908, I, 190, quotes from the French: "Tabeau un des engagés de la voiture de Lecuyer non seulemen doit etre privé de ses gages mais encore devrait être severemen punis pour servir d'exemple a l'avenir; cest un infame coquin." The original seems to a part of the Bancroft-Pinart *Collection*, University of California.

[18] He was certainly not the pillager of the expedition, yet, judging by the index to the first volume of the Annual Report of the American Historical Association for 1908 (see p. 535), it would seem that someone got that impression from the reading, superficial, we admit, of Professor Teggart's article.

strictly business footing. Race conscious to a degree not usual in a Frenchman, proud and high-spirited, did he foment an uprising in protest against Lécuyer's undignified and lascivious goings-on or did he simply pick a private quarrel? No matter what the merits of the quarrel, if it resulted in monetary loss to the company, Mackay, so-licitous only on account of the company, would have been incapable of being impartial. Ignoring the evidence, ignoring the extenuating circumstances, he would inevitably have adjudged the conduct of the fault-finder or, if you will, the mischief-maker exceedingly reprehen-sible. At this distance of time and with such limits to our knowl-edge, there is little more to be said one way or the other. Let us pass on.

The Company of Commerce for the Discovery of the Nations of the Upper Missouri had, as its director, Jacques Clamorgan, who, in accordance with trade regulations previously issued, had been elected to the post of "Syndic of Commerce,"[19] and it was to enjoy, by direct grant from Carondelet, a monopoly of whatever commerce might develop from the expeditions and excursions it devised and expedited. Given so good an opportunity for self-enrichment, Clamorgan took full advantage of it, a no very difficult thing to do, perchance, inas-much as the shareholders of the company were not many and did not include some of the most influential of the St. Louis merchants.[20]

Such as they were, however, Clamorgan's associates being envious, took umbrage,[21] especially after it was divulged that Andrew Todd, an Irish merchant of Montreal, who had been trading for several

[19] See Nasatir, A. P., *Anglo-Spanish Rivalry, op cit.*, Mississippi Valley Historical *Review*, XVI, 370.

[20] What purports to be a complete list of the original members of the company is to be found in the *Houck Transcripts from Spanish Archives*, MHS. "The great majority of the merchants of St. Louis," writes Mrs. Beauregard, "held aloof" from it (Missouri Historical Society *Collections*, IV, 10-12) and Doctor Nasatir accounts for the absence of the Chouteaus and of Gratiot from the number by implying that they had other more important duties, the Chouteaus, for example, being busy with the Osages. See *The Formation of the Missouri Company*, Missouri Historical *Review*, XXV, 16-17.

[21] Among the *Houck Transcripts, op. cit.*, there is a *Memorial*, dated 1796, of St. Louis merchants, Manuel Lisa being one of them, praying that the monopoly held by the company be revoked. In a marginal note, some later scribe has suggested that the date of its presentation was subsequent to that given; but why he has not said.

years at Michilimackinac[22] and who had acquired large land hold-ings even in Pennsylvania, had, through Clamorgan's agency, been granted permission to participate in the operations of the company and worse still had been conceded trade privileges west of the Mis-sissippi that ought, in reason, to have been the peculiar birthright of Spanish subjects.

The entering wedge for Andrew Todd would seem to have been the fact that, in the early days of the Missouri Company, his had been its supply house.[23] It is claimed, indeed, that he individually outfitted the Mackay expedition.[24] At all events, it was in recogni-tion of his services, personal and financial, past and prospective, that, near the beginning of 1796 and through the intercession of Clamor-gan, he was accorded the right to have "an interest in the company of discoveries" and the exclusive trade with the Sacs and Foxes whose lands were on the Mississippi.[25]

A concession such as this to a foreigner was remarkable and all the more so because, on the face of it, it was in direct contravention of what was alleged to be the principal reason for organizing the

[22] Although the only extant trade licenses, on file at Ottawa, issued to Andrew Todd personally, are two in number, both of the 1786 issue, April and June respec-tively, and both for the Michilimackinac trade, he was yet at Michilimackinac or in its neighborhood for several years subsequent thereto. In 1787-88, he figured as a witness in the enquiry into the conduct of Dease and Ainse (*Haldimand Papers*, Michigan Pioneer and Historical *Collections*, XI, 514-620). In the early part of 1791, John Johnston, who claimed him as an old friend (Schoolcraft, H. R., *Memoir of John Johnston, idem*, XXXVI, p. 55), accompanied him to Michilimackinac (Letter of John Johnston, 28 April 1828, *idem*, XXXII, 337). The trade licenses issued to him, as well as his attaching his signature to the *Memorial* drawn up by various merchants of Montreal, 4 April 1786 (*Haldimand Papers, op. cit.*, pp. 483-84) indicate that he regarded himself as a citizen of Lower Canada.

[23] Clamorgan to Carondelet, April 10, 1796, Missouri Historical *Review*, XXV, 456. This is one of the documents included by Doctor Nasatir among those compris-ing his edited article, *John Evans, Explorer and Surveyor*. How close Andrew Todd's business connection with his uncle's firm was I am not prepared to say. From the *Askin Papers* at Ottawa and from a photostat there also of a sort of calendar of *Burton MSS* at Detroit, I have been led to infer that a relation only a little short of an actual partnership existed. Even before his death, Andrew Todd's affairs were the burden of letters passing between Isaac Todd, his uncle, and John Askin. The trade licenses or passes are noncommittal as to the precise personnel of the house of Todd, McGill & Co. at any given time.

[24] Beauregard, Mrs. Nettie H., Missouri Historical Society *Collections*, IV, 13.

[25] Carondelet to Clamorgan, May 11, 1796, *Clamorgan Papers*, MHS.

13

Missouri Company, the checkmating of the British. Let it be remembered, however, that Todd's privileges were limited, he being altogether debarred from trading on the Upper Missouri, and that Spanish suspicions, concentrated justifiably upon the French at the time of the exposure of the activities of Citizen Genét and his emissaries, George Rogers Clark and others, were being drawn thither again, in this very year of 1796, by the expedition of Victor Collot, ex-French general, ex-governor of Guadeloupe.

The real purposes[26] of Collot, in projecting his expedition, are somewhat obscure; but, whatever they were, they had the endorsement of Adet, the new French minister to the United States, and were, in part, inspired by Collot's intense antipathy to the British, who had brought his career in the West Indies to a rather ignominious close, and by his bitter resentment against the Washington government because of its Federalist leanings in their direction as manifested in the rejection of Genét and in the negotiation of the Jay treaty. In his own account[27] of his doings, not published until after his death and thus many years after their occurrence, he outlined a very plausible story of political disinterestedness and professed to have been taken completely by surprise when Carondelet brought his avowedly innocent travels to an abrupt termination.

Those travels had begun in March, when, leaving Philadelphia on the twenty-first, he had shaped his course for the West. The observation he made, as he passed along, of the various French settlements in the Illinois country was most minute as was also that of those in the vicinity of St. Louis, although by no means flattering at

[26] While dissent must be taken from the charge that Collot "was no doubt sent by Genét to spy out the land in furtherance of some design which was never carried out or attempted" (Missouri Historical Society *Collection*, III, 72, n. 3), the following can be wholly subscribed to: "The French designs on Louisiana by no means ceased with the failure of this expedition. Collot's investigations . . . . , undertaken in 1796, at the desire of Adet, ... constitute a link between the project of Clark and the retrocession of Louisiana to Napoleon, and the French archives show a continuity of interest in the plan of regaining Louisiana from 1789 to 1800" (American Historical Association *Report*, 1896, p. 932).

[27] It appeared in 1826 in French and, minus the Appendix, in English also. Two years short of a century later another edition in English came out under the editorship of Jens Christian Bay with a translation of the original Appendix. Included in the *Transactions* of the Illinois Historical Society for 1908, pp. 269-98, are such parts of Collot's narrative as deal with Illinois and with St. Louis and towns adjacent.

times.[28] Arriving in St. Louis, he made his plans for the ascent of the Missouri. How far up he would have gone can only be conjectured; for he was soon brought to a sudden halt, the "excessive indulgence" that Don Zenon Trudeau, perfectly trustworthy himself but far too credulous and kind-hearted, had extended to him, being summarily cancelled.[29] Collot went, as a matter of fact, only as far as the River of the Great Osages and, for all that he found out about the country higher up, had to depend upon the hearsay evidence of the traders he consulted, one of the principal of whom was undoubtedly Jean Baptiste Truteau, who appears to have written for Collot's perusal a brief and very general account of his own experiences while exploring for the Missouri Company. [30]

[28] The picture he drew of Illinois was somber enough (*Journey in North America* . . . . , pp. 232-33), that of Missouri, depressing. This is his account of St. Charles which most travellers found an interesting little settlement, not so Collot:

"St. Charles contains about an hundred or an hundred and twenty ill-constructed houses; the inhabitants do not till the ground, though it be extremely fertile; their ordinary occupations are hunting and trading with the Indians; a few hire themselves out as rowers; and it would be difficult to find a collection of individuals more ignorant, stupid, ugly, and miserable. Such are the sad effects of extreme poverty, with its train of cares and evils, that it destroys not only the beauty of the person but even the intellectual powers, and blunts all those feelings of delicacy and sensibility which belong to a state of ease, and the advantages of a good education" (*idem,* p. 277).

[29] Carondelet to Don Carlos Howard, dated New Orleans, 26 November 1796, Missouri Historical Society *Collections,* III, 84.

[30] This is not the opinion I held when editing Truteau's *Description of the Upper Missouri,* for which, see Mississippi Valley Historical *Review,* VIII, 149-79; but, at that time, I regret to have to acknowledge it did not occur to me to consult Collot's work. I have since done so and have been struck with the close resemblance existing between it and Truteau's, within, of course, the limits of the latter. As a matter of fact, they are practically identical, even to the odd spelling of proper nouns. The distances noted vary a trifle, occasionally, as if Collot checked Truteau's information by that obtained elsewhere. The incident of the knife, marked with the name, *Cook* (Collot, Victor, *A Journey in North America* . . . . p. 289), and sent as incriminating evidence to the Governor of Louisiana — disquieting, we may imagine, in the extreme — did not come from the ex-schoolmaster. Collot, be it remarked, proved far more insistent than was Truteau in voicing the necessity for restricting the British, who ought, in his opinion, to be prevented "from obtaining settlements" among the tribes of the Upper Missouri, all of whom, except the Sioux, appeared to be most mild. If Truteau wrote expressly for Collot's edification, the approximate date of Truteau's narrative is fixed. The use of it by Collot in 1796 did not preclude its use by Perrin du Lac in 1802 and Truteau may still have been Perrin du Lac's *"ancien traiteur de la rivière des Illinois,"* unless, indeed, Pierre-Antoine Tabeau was. Tabeau was then

Collot's presence in St. Louis occasioned not a little commotion among some of the French inhabitants, restive under Spanish dominance, and a *sans-culotte* society sprang into being, possibly by his contrivance. Further than that his plans and schemes went all awry; for, innocent or nefarious, they fell foul of Carondelet and, by him, were completely frustrated. Moving on discomfited towards New Orleans, Collot was mortified and indignant to find himself arrested and his papers, all the careful calculations he had made of military strength and national attachment, confiscated. What must have been his real object being defeated, it could have mattered little to him that the bulk of them were subsequently restored.

Such was the situation in the Louisianas when Andrew Todd, taking time by the forelock, prepared to exercise the monopoly rights conceded to him.[31] These he was destined never actually to enjoy. His preparations took him to New Orleans, where Clamorgan had urged him to establish a branch of the House of Todd for the more convenient serving of the Missouri Company.[32] Unfortunately, it happened to be a time when one of the rather common epidemics was raging there and, to this, Andrew Todd fell an almost immediate victim, dying within a few days. Prognostications[33] as to what

---

only forty-seven years old, having been born in 1755; but he knew well the Illinois country and was old in experience.

[31] That he had gone there, as his friend John Johnston seems to have supposed (Michigan Pioneer and Historical *Collections,* XXXII, 343), because he had been conceded the exclusive trade of the entire province was, of necessity, not the case. It is easy to see, notwithstanding the impossibility of this, that Collot must have entertained much the same idea and must also have identified Andrew Todd with the house of Todd, McGill & Co. (*A Journey in North America, op. cit.,* Part 2, p. 126).

[32] Clamorgan to Carondelet, April 10, 1796, Missouri Historical *Review,* XXV, 456.

[33] What might well be interpreted as prognostications of embarrassment a letter, written shortly after the death of Todd, very interestingly set forth. It is given here as it was published by Mrs. Beauregard (Missouri Historical Society *Collections,* IV, 13-14) and because of the references it contains to the circumstances of Andrew Todd's decease and to his relations with Clamorgan and the Company.

"MOST EXCELLENT SIR:

Among the individuals who have lately had the misfortune to be victims of the epidemic which, in the letter of October 31st, I advised you was afflicting this Province, and which at this time, thanks to the Omnipotent, seems nipped by the rains, although light, and cold spells which we are having, fate struck Don Andrew Todd, to whom His Majesty by Royal Order of June 11th of this year was pleased to grant

his death would signify to the Missouri Company were soon verified, considerable embarrassment coming to Clamorgan personally, because of the litigation which accompanied, as was inevitable, the settlement of the deceased man's estate. Under the will, Isaac Todd was his executor and it took him many years to collect even a portion of the debts due, so enormous were they in variety and amount, so irregular, to some extent, in character.[34]

The largest single account was against the firm of Clamorgan, Loisel and Company, a part of which Andrew Todd had assumed for Jean-Baptiste Vallé of Ste. Geneviève.[35] Exactly when this firm of Clamorgan, Loisel and Company came into being has not been

the exclusive trade with the Indian nations established to the North of the Ohio and Missouri. This young and robust Irishman had come down from Illinois to arrange his accounts with his correspondents in this Capital, to give his orders for the shipment from Europe of the equipment necessary for his traffic, and intended to return immediately towards the North; but before he was in town for fifteen days the contagion attacked him, and within five days he was buried.

His death, if his successors and associates do not obtain the same privilege and carry out the same projects, besides undoing the favorable results which were the cause of the granting of the privilege, is a mortal blow to the Spanish Company of Discoverers to the West of the Missouri. Todd it was who had the greatest number of shares of stock, and who, moreover, on account of the extensive plans to gather and secure all the peltries of that Territory, had advanced to the Company the value of eight thousand dollars in goods adapted to the trade with the Indians; and if his heirs, creditors or companions should demand the payment, the Company would undoubtedly remain without means to continue its operations.

I advise Your Excellency of the foregoing in compliance with my duty and in order that you may not be wanting in the intimate knowledge of the affairs of these countries which you should have so that you may better be able to take such steps as you may judge opportune in view of the best service of the Sovereign.

May our Lord prosper the life of Your Excellency many years.

JUAN VENTURA MORALES.

Exmo. Senor Don Diego de Gardoqui,
New Orleans, December 1, 1796."

[34] The following all have to do with the Andrew Todd estate and are indicative of the protracted settlement: Todd to Askin, 8 June 1799, *Burton MSS, op. cit.,* VI, 88; Same to Same, 15 October 1799, *idem,* VII, 84; Same to Same, 22 January 1800, 2 July 1800, 12 April 1801, *Askin Papers, op. cit.;* Same to Same, 23 January 1802, *Burton MSS,* XI, 95; Askin to Todd, 30 January 1802, *idem,* p. 100; Todd to Askin, 18 April 1802, *idem,* p. 136; Same to Same, 1 March 1805, *idem,* XIII, 113; Same to Same, 23 June 1806, *Askin Papers.*

[35] Isaac Todd to John Askin, 25 April 1799, *Askin Papers, op. cit.;* Same to Same, *Burton MSS, op. cit.,* VI, 154.

ascertained. The impression conveyed by Clamorgan's report to Carondelet, April 10, 1796, was that it was to begin operations the month following; but it was most likely already functioning *sub rosa*,[36] since, for the whole of the period from the beginning of 1796 to 1800 inclusive, its existence can be vouched for by extant accounts of its commercial transactions,[37] many of which were with Vallé as they had been, at the outset, with Andrew Todd, to whose executor they were probably occasion of much exasperation, causing him to exclaim, when writing to his friend, John Askin, in 1799, that of "near 100,000 liwers owing And^w. Todd in that rascally Country of Illanoa I never expect a thousand."[38]

Meanwhile, pending the settlement of the Todd estate, Clamorgan seems to have appropriated to himself, in the name of the de-

[36] From a document in the *Auguste Chouteau Collection*, MHS, dated 8 July 1795, being the account of Régis Loisel with Andrew Todd of Michilimackinac, it would appear that it was not yet in existence, unless *sub rosa;* but that it was prior to the death of Andrew Todd it seems fair to assume from the following extract from one of Lieutenant-Governor Zenon Trudeau's reports, that of January 15, 1798:

"This company (the Spanish Company of Commerce) consisted at the beginning of eight members or associates who risked an equal sum. The greater part of them resigned, ruined, and the company is today represented by the house of [Cla] Morgan, Loisel and Company, which has acquired the shares through the resignation of some and the purchase of the rest. This house was established for its operations in that of Don Andres Todd, who has died in Nueva Orleans . . . ." (Houck, Louis, *Spanish Régime in Missouri*, II, 254).

[37] In the *Pierre Chouteau Collection*, MHS, there are allusions to it for the years from 1796 to 1800. In particular, note the Envelope, labelled, "Accounts, Receipts, &c., 1756-1858," where can be found a document of date, December 1, 1800, signed by Auguste Chouteau and Daniel Clark, Jr., *"Relatif aux affaires de la Maison de Messrs Clamorgan, Loisel & Co., July, 1798 to December, 1800."* In the *Vallé Papers* of the *Minnie Vallé Fairfield Collection*, MHS, and especially in the accounts of François Vallé of Ste. Geneviève included there, are many references to dealings with Régis Loisel. See Appendix IV.

[38] Extract, Letters of 25 April 1799, *Askin Papers, op. cit.* An affair of 1795 had been the beginning of Isaac Todd's grudges and grievances against the section of country where Clamorgan's influence was strong. There had been a seizure of goods at St. Louis and his firm, in conjunction with Forsyth, Richardson & Co., likewise of Montreal, had sought diplomatic intervention in support of a claim for damages. See Secretary of State *Papers*, Internal Correspondence, Lower Canada, 11 September 1795. It was against Post Vincennes that Askin, on one occasion, expressed himself with equal bitterness, condemning it as "the most rascally place in the country" (Letter to James and Andrew McGill & Co., 5 October 1805, *Burton MSS, op. cit.*, XII, 237).

ceased trader, the privileges that Carondelet had granted at his importunity and more besides. He could do this with impunity; inasmuch as, though the Governor's commercial policy, after the Collot adventure had aroused his distrust and strengthened his apprehensions, became restrictive elsewhere, in Clamorgan's direction, it apparently continued liberal. For Clamorgan the times were propitious and when, on March first, 1797, he petitioned for a greater favor than ever, for nothing less, in fact, than a ten year monopoly of the Upper Missouri commerce, his prayer was forthwith granted, provisionally by Trudeau and Carondelet, each in his turn, and, finally, by the King. Clamorgan's reasons were specious. They were both economic and political; for, while expressing a desire to open up the trade, he also promised to acquire information and to ward off foreign intruders. The favor shown him was doubtless attributable to the unwavering confidence that Carondelet had seen fit to repose in his discretion and general trustworthiness throughout the Collot excitement. Such confidence the French merchants of St. Louis were far from sharing. Their envy and distrust of Clamorgan ultimately found expression in a formal protest[39] which the almost obliterated shareholders of the Missouri Company, speaking through Joseph Robidou, one of their number, addressed to Carondelet in 1798. The protest was likewise a petition and its authors prayed that the commercial rights and privileges, which the Director had so definitely usurped, might be withdrawn. Unfortunately for them, the upshot of the affair was not the one the disgruntled shareholders so ardently hoped for. The very desirable reorganization of the Spanish Company of Commerce for the Discovery of the Nations of the Upper Missouri did, indeed, take place; but the forces that emerged triumphant from the process were the very ones complained of and, henceforth, with but a bare interval by way of transition, the firm of Clamorgan, Loisel and Company operated without disguise.

At this point and at the risk of making too wide a digression, one finds it advisable to make some enquiry into the previous history of this firm's junior partner, Régis, or Régistre, Loisel; for the narrative here edited in translation is a narrative of his last and most impor-

---

[39] Billion, *op. cit.*, pp. 283-88.

tant expedition, made while he was yet, ostensibly, Clamorgan's partner and the representative of the erstwhile Missouri Company.

Régis Loisel was a native of Lower Canada. Like a great number of his compatriots, he was of Norman stock, the first emigrant of the name to New France having come from the diocese of Bayeux. This was a certain Louis Loisel, great-grandfather of Régis, who became a soldier of the citadel at Quebec. The descendants of Louis, children and grandchildren of his several sons — he was twice married — are traceable in the parish registers of the lower St. Lawrence and of Chateauguay. His son Jacques married Anne Paradis and François Régis Loisel, one of their many children, became the father of Clamorgan's agent and partner. On his mother's side, Loisel was related to the Vallé family, his mother, Madeleine Massue, being the daughter of another Madeleine, née Vallée, who had married one Nicolas Massue, an emigrant from Orleans and, at Varennes in the District of Montreal, Province of Quebec, an innkeeper of prominence,[40] later still a merchant.

Of Régis Loisel's personal history in Canada little seems to be known except that he was baptized and, therefore, probably born in the Parish of L'Assomption, Montreal.[41] He is said to have arrived in St. Louis in 1793 and, since he must have been a mere youth at the time, scarcely out of his teens, the date of the marriage of his parents being January 28, 1772, he doubtless travelled direct, without, that is, tarrying along the way at one or another of the intervening old French settlements, notwithstanding that people of his name living at places like Detroit and Kaskaskia could not have failed to be his relatives. He must have passed through Illinois, indeed, at a time when the French were deserting rather than lingering in the country they had once regarded as a veritable "terrestrial paradise,"[42] they

[40] For these and other genealogical items relative to the beginnings of the Loisel family in Lower Canada, see Tanguay, *op. cit.,* V, 425. Among the inn and tavern licenses for the sale of spirituous liquors (Dominion Archives, Ottawa), under date of April 29, 1769 and August 13, 1771, is evidence of the fact that Nicholas Massue was proprietor of *The Gray Horse.*

[41] Billon, *op. cit.,* p. 465.

[42] So stated Governor William Franklin of New Jersey in the document he drew up setting forth the reasons why an English colony ought to be founded in the Illinois country (Alvord, C. W., and Carter, C. E., *The New Régime, 1765-1767,* Illinois Historical *Collections,* XI, 248).

having had ample cause for years to be increasingly dismayed on account of the chaotic state of civil and political conditions there.[43] To go whither most of them had gone or were going was the most natural thing for the future partner of Jacques Clamorgan to do, particularly as he was distantly connected with the Vallé family, already influential and deservedly so in the official life of Spanish Louisiana.

How soon, after his arrival in St. Louis, the young Loisel made the acquaintance of Clamorgan has not been ascertained. Their formal partnership most certainly dates from the spring of 1796; but their informal may have started much earlier. In fact, it is not at all unlikely that as soon as Clamorgan began to divert the profits of the Missouri Company to other than their legitimate ends, he used Loisel as a screen for himself and, in his dealings with Andrew Todd, utilized Loisel as a sort of covering agent. Apparently, Loisel was on the Des Moines before he was on the Missouri and, when there, was making a first acquaintance with the Sioux, also, though somewhat unpleasantly, with traders already established among them, with a British subject of the name of Crawford,[44] probably Lewis, and with the Dorions, Pierre and his two valiant sons. He was yet esteemed an authority on trade facilities and rivalries of the Des Moines in 1799.[45]

---

[43] For the confusion in Illinois consult the following: Boggess, A. C., *The Settlement of Illinois,* Chicago Historical Society *Collections,* V, 41; James, J. A., *Life of George Rogers Clark,* pp. 349-50; Allinson, May, *The Government of Illinois, 1790-1799,* Illinois State Historical Society *Transactions,* 1907, pp. 277-92. To the source materials upon which these accounts are severally based may be added two emanating from the United States national records, one, a report, 1791, on *Land Claims of French Settlers in Illinois,* American State Papers, *Public Lands,* I, 18-20; the other, a report, 1810, on *Land Claims in the District of Kaskaskia, idem,* II, 123 *et seq.*

[44] Lewis Crawford became a member of the North West Company. For the energy he displayed in the War of 1812 and the recognition it brought him, see Wisconsin Historical Society *Collections,* XIX, 342, n. 82. Crawford seems to have been among those disaffected spirits who objected to the amalgamation of the Hudson's Bay and North West companies in 1821 and to have thrown in his lot with the dissentients who formed the Columbia Fur Company. See Abel, Annie Heloise, *Fort Clark Journal of Francis A. Chardon,* n. 86, and n. 522. He stayed with its leading men, Kenneth Mackenzie and others, when they, in 1827, united with the American Fur Company to form the Upper Missouri Outfit of its Western Department. He happened to be stationed at Fort Clark at the time of George Catlin's visit in 1832. See Catlin, George, *North American Indians,* I, 200.

[45] In a letter from "Haut du Rapide de la Riviere des Moine," October 16, 1799 (*Pierre Chouteau Collection,* "Envelope, 1764-1904," MHS), Louis Honore Taisont

But even then what were to be larger and more lasting interests on the Upper Missouri had come to intrigue him. They made their appearance, apparently, with the reorganization of the Missouri Company following the upheaval of 1798. Of that new company, which, functioning commercially, was virtually nothing more nor less than the Clamorgan-Loisel partnership, Régis Loisel may possibly have been a full-fledged member[46] and have made, prior to 1800, "considerable sacrifices," as he claimed, in its behalf. With the turn of the century, his position became still better defined; for the firm of Clamorgan, Loisel and Company, which had been so much to the fore previously that it had practically obscured the older corporation without, however, quite accomplishing its extinction,[47] now retired into the background itself and might be thought, after this long interval of time, to have disappeared altogether were it not for the fact that its chief constituent members continued to be identified with the same or closely related enterprises. To disarm their critics and their competitors they would seem to have gone henceforth their separate ways, while having between themselves some definite understanding and leaving their affairs, old and new, inextricably interwoven.

The year 1800 was a decisive one for Régis Loisel. In it occurred his marriage.[48] This was May 27th, the bride being Hélène Chauvin, whose father, Jacques Chauvin,[49] was one of those St. Louis merchants originally approached with reference to the formation of the

---

cited Loisel as well acquainted with the facts in a certain altercation that he (Taisont) had had with the other traders and willing to testify. For an account of the letter-writer, see Coues, Elliott, *Expeditions of Zebulon Montgomery Pike*, p. 222, and n. 2.

[46] The editor of the Ordway Journal inclines to the opinion that Loisel was a member (Wisconsin Historical Society Collections, XXII, 22). His relations with individual members of the company were not always of the friendliest (Billon, *op. cit.*, pp. 314-15; Houck, *Spanish Régime, op. cit.*, II, 159, n. 3).

[47] Doctor Nasatir seems to regard Clamorgan, Loisel and Company as, in reality, the successor of the Missouri Company and asserts that it "had been dispatching agents and merchandise to the Upper Missouri and particularly to the Mandan villages . . . ." (Mississippi Valley Historical *Review*, XVI, 525).

[48] Collot, Oscar W., *Index to St. Louis Cathedral and Carondelet Church Registers and to Records in the Recorder's Office of St. Louis County, Vol. on "Marriages,"* p. 52.

[49] For a sketch of the Chauvin family, inclusive of Jacques, see Billon, *op cit.*, pp. 458-59.

Spanish Company of Commerce. Loisel was still a very young man, about twenty-seven perhaps; but both of his parents were dead and he, with what may have been his last link with French Canada broken, was completely committed to a trading and mercantile career.[50]

In the March preceding his marriage, Loisel made another notable venture and one that was above ordinary importance in its ultimate consequences. Claiming to have made the "considerable sacrifices in the Upper Missouri Company" already hinted at and to be "intending to continue on his own account the commerce which his partners have abandoned in that quarter," he petitioned for the right "to form an establishment in Upper Missouri, where he will build a fort."[51] One month earlier, Clamorgan had made a somewhat similar request; since, while soliciting the privilege of exclusive trade with the "Othoas, Mahas, and Poncas," he likewise asked to be allowed the additional privilege of building a fort "to restrain the Mandans," who, it must not be forgotten, were the Indians with whom the British from the north had so long traded. As a protection against these same British and to prevent their further aggressions, Clamorgan offered "to support 100 militia." Both petitions were granted, it is claimed, without demur and, the year following, on April 27th, Clamorgan asked that his rights be extended so as to comprehend the "Cancas Nation." Again his plea was successful, the concession bearing date, May 2, 1801.[52] The extortionate demands[53] that, in earlier years of the company, Clamorgan had made on the pretext of defraying the expense of garrisoning any posts it might erect had, obviously, though reported upon adversely in 1796 by the

[50] Years after Loisel's death, when the legality of claims under grant from Spain was a subject for investigation, it was argued that a certain grant made to Loisel was of an exceptional nature; since, under the regulations of the then governor-general, no grants could be made to merchants and he was a merchant (*House Executive Documents,* Twenty-fourth Congress, first session, No. 59, p. 7). For a grant of 1480 arpens, made in 1796, see *idem,* No. 270, p. 132; and for other property owned by Loisel, see MHS *Collections,* III, 185; Scharf, J. T., *History of St. Louis City and County,* I, 146).

[51] For text of this petition, see Appendix V.

[52] *Clamorgan Papers,* MHS.

[53] *Houck's Transcripts, op. cit.*

[54] Because of Carondelet's complaints of the multiplicity of his duties, Spain had, in 1794, separated the offices of Governor and Intendant. See Gayarré, Charles, *History of Louisiana,* "Spanish Domination," p. 334.

Intendant[54] *ad interim* of Louisiana, operated neither to his discomfiture nor to his prejudice. Taken in combination, the requests of Clamorgan and Loisel were so all-inclusive that they left little for anyone else. Moreover, the projects that the two men had in contemplation can be interpreted in no other way than to imply that, whatever the Missouri Company may or may not have accomplished in the past, it was to function as a corporate body no longer and that even the Clamorgan-Loisel partnership had, in a measure, disintegrated.[55]

To relate, even were it possible, how much or how little Clamorgan acted upon the concessions made to him is not pertinent to what remains of the present story, which concerns itself more particularly with the upper reaches of the great muddy river and with the comings and goings of Clamorgan's quondam partner, who was not at all dilatory in testing the value of his privileges. Without allowing even his marriage to detain him unduly long, he must have arranged to ascend the Missouri that same summer and, arriving at an eligible point, started the construction of his promised fort. This he did, if we can trust the memory or the veracity of Auguste Chouteau, who, in a later time, gave it as his recollection that it was built this very year of 1800.[56] What more Loisel did can only be surmised from the fact that the summer following he entered into a two-year trade agreement with a certain Hugh Heney,[57] a former inn and general

---

[55] The weakness of this argument is seen in the fact that when, under Act of Congress, March, 1805, a board was created empowered to take testimony in the matter of the alleged Spanish grants, Clamorgan, posing as the assignee of Loisel, who was then dead, set up a claim to an extensive area, including Loisel's island, and produced in evidence of title Loisel's petition of March, 1800, also a concession from Delassus dated 25 March 1800, and a figurative plan (American State Papers, *Public Lands,* II, 567).

[56] American State Papers, *ibid.,* II, 567; Houck, Louis, *A History of Missouri,* I, 252, n. 45.

[57] This man, whose very name, in its correct form, eluded Elliott Coues so long (*New Light on the Early History of the Greater Northwest,* I, 424-25, n. 1), escaping him entirely all the time he was engaged on his edition of the Lewis and Clark journals, was surely no other than the "Hughes Heney" whom the Curé of the Parish of Lachine again and again vouched for. Heney was the keeper of a public alehouse, or victualling house, and, year by year, beginning with 1769, applied for a license to vend spirituous liquors and, on each occasion, the worthy parish priest gave written testimony to the effect that Heney was *"domicilé dans ma parcisse"* and *"en honnête*

storekeeper of Montreal, and the same person undoubtedly as the Monsieur Héné, who also went up the Missouri in 1800, starting in June apparently, and who had the misfortune, so Clamorgan, his employer, claimed, to have his expedition "destroyed by the British."[58] The Loisel-Heney *Convention de Commerce*[59] was drawn up and executed at St. Louis, July 6, 1801, therefore Loisel could have made only a very brief stay upstream but, as to whether or no he returned short of the two years intended because blocked in his operations by the Sioux,[60] as was most certainly the case on a subsequent trip, is a little doubtful. That he did return fairly soon adds weight to the assertion of "Antoine Tiebeau," when giving testimony under oath in August, 1806, that Loisel's trading-post, or fort, was not built in 1800, as Chouteau remembered, or even begun then; but was "built entire" two years afterwards, when Tabeau himself was of the party.[61] Knowing that Tabeau, after Loisel's death, seemed bent upon depreciating Loisel's position and work, we scarcely know what choice to make between his word and Chouteau's. Chouteau[62] witnessed the Loisel-Heney trade agreement and, of course, it is quite conceivable that Loisel, in order to make his prospects as bright as possible, may have represented to his intimates of the summer of

---

homme." See *Tavern Licenses*, Dominion Archives, Ottawa. For additional information as regards Heney, see Appendix VI.

[58] Nasatir, A. P., *Anglo-Spanish Rivalry on the Upper Missouri*, Mississippi Valley Historical *Review*, XVI, 526.

[59] The French original of this trade agreement is among the papers and documents of the *Auguste Chouteau Collection*, MHS. For its reproduction here in translation, the work of Doctor Rose Abel Wright, see Appendix VI. *"La Societe de Loisel & Heney"* was yet in existence in August, 1804, presumably for liquidation purposes (See *Manuel Lisa Papers*, MHS). From Tabeau's narrative, it appears that Heney was "a trader among the Sioux" in 1804; but towards the end of the year he went over to the North West Company.

[60] Nasatir, A. P., Mississippi Valley Historical *Review*, XVI, 527.

[61] American State Papers, *Public Lands*, II, 567. Tabeau, in his narrative, but without giving any intimation that he himself was along, speaks of Loisel's being on the river in 1801. It was then that Loisel discovered the bone of a fish so large that it must have been an antediluvian.

[62] In this connection it might be well to recall that Auguste Chouteau, who closed up Loisel's estate, claimed a part of it, later, as his assignee; but this claim was disallowed. See American State Papers, *Public Lands*, II, 638. A Spanish edition of Loisel's will is in the St. Louis Mercantile Library.

1801 a larger measure of preparedness than was actually the case. Tabeau was obviously not one of that honored group. Had it been otherwise, he would not have testified in 1806 that he had never so much as been aware that Loisel held a concession. Perfect candour in business relations is often wanting; but how Loisel could have deceived Heney, supposing Heney went up the river about the time he did and high enough up to be within range of the British long arm, is a mystery. Under the circumstances, perhaps it is well not to enquire too closely into the accuracy of the basis for Clamorgan's complaint.

An interesting history attaches to the Loisel fort quite apart from the doubt surrounding the time of its construction. Two contemporary descriptions of it have come down to us, Patrick Gass's[63] and John Ordway's,[64] while various maps of the period indicate its location with reasonable precision.[65] It was built, we are told, where wood was abundant and of cedar logs, which was to be expected, since its site was a large cedar island[66] within the area outlined in

[63] *Gass Journal*, 3rd edition, p. 42; Thwaites, R. G., *Original Journals of the Lewis and Clark Expedition*, I, 160 n.; Coues, Elliott, *History of the Lewis and Clark Expedition*, I, 126-27, n. 63.

[64] Wisconsin Historical Society *Collections*, XXII, 135.

[65] On the map, which, to my own satisfaction, I identified years ago as a Lewis and Clark itinerary map (See Geographical *Review*, I, 329-45) and which, because it was found at the Office of Indian Affairs, I ordinarily refer to as the "Indian Office Map," appears the legend, "Mr. Louisells House in the Winter 1803 & 4." It is to be found between "Old Englishman's Island" and "Little Missouri River" (*idem*, between pp. 344 and 345). Clark located "Louisells Fort on Cedar Island" 1226 miles up the Missouri (*Original Journals, op. cit.*, VI, 59).

[66] Bradbury described the island as being "about two miles in length, and mostly covered with fine cedar, and rose and currant bushes considerably overrun with vines" (*Travels . . . .* , edition of 1817, p. 176; Thwaites, R. G., *Early Western Travels*, V, 184). When he passed along, however, Loisel's fort must have been gone; for he wrote, "Great Cedar Island, where a French trader, named L'Oiselle, formerly had a post or trading house" (*idem*). This lends color to the view that Loisel's fort became the Little Beaver's house of the Sioux pictographic records and was destroyed either in the winter of 1808-9 (*Fourth Annual Report of the Bureau of Ethnology*, p. 135) or, as is more likely, in that of 1809-10 (*idem*, p. 106; *Tenth Annual Report . . . .* , pp. 275, 315). There are in all seven different records, five of which are in substantial agreement as to the burning down of the post, while a sixth, the Flame chart so-called, implies that, though the "trapper" was burnt, his house, which it locates on White River, was not. Who Little Beaver was is somewhat of an enigma. According to the Baptiste Good winter count, he was an English trader; accord-

Loisel's petition, between *Riviere du vieux Anglais* and *Riviere de la Cote de Medecine,* and specifically mentioned by him. The island was one of a group called the "Three Sisters," situated above the Grand Detour, or Great Bend of the Missouri, and below the mouth of the Little Missouri, a stream, which Lewis and Clark, when they observed it, re-christened the "Teton" for the reason that the country all around was the range of that particular division of the formidable Sioux family.[67] It is the Bad River of today. With the Teton Sioux Loisel was to open up commerce, his dealings being, in the main, with that section of them known from their darker hue, the Bois Brûlés.[68] He did not, however, meet with the happiest results.

But that was not immediately. If Tabeau be right, Loisel went up the Missouri again in 1802, Tabeau accompanying him. It was on this trip that Loisel built his *Fort aux Cedres*[69] and built it at his own expense. We can safely assume, however, that it was not exclusively with such matters or with trade that he occupied his time. True to the promises he had held out in his petition of 1800, he took cognizance of the dangers besetting Spanish jurisdiction and one wonders if he could have been sanguine as to its being perpetuated. From the Sioux, steadfast friends of the British, he was bound to learn considerable that was not to his liking and, when he returned from this expedition, he promptly reported many disconcerting things to Delassus, the then Lieutenant-Governor at St. Louis, the result being that

---

ing to the Swan chart he was a French trader, which further says that he was blown up by powder on the Little Missouri and says nothing about his house. The Lone Dog record makes Little Beaver out to have been a chief, himself the incendiary and victim. Whoever the man was, of this we can rest assured that, if he perished in the conflagration, he was neither Loisel nor Tabeau, since the one had died in 1805 and the latter lived until 1820.

[67] A very recent authority on Sioux divisions and migrations is Hyde, George E., *Red Cloud's Folk*.

[68] Lewis and Clark were given to understand that the trade of "Mr. Loisell & Co. of St. Louis" was "with the Teton-Bois brule from the mouth of the White River to the Teton with headquarters at the Cedar Island and near the mouth of the Cheyenne R. on the Mo." (Lewis, Meriwether, *Statistical View,* American State Papers, Indian Affairs, I, 712).

[69] Houck is my authority for applying this name to Loisel's fort (See *History of Missouri, op. cit.,* II, 252). The name is appropriate enough; but, since it was applied to one erected for the Missouri Fur Company (*History of the Lewis and Clark Expedition, op. cit.,* I, 122, n. 52), care must be taken not to confound one post with the other.

he was commissioned, in April, 1803, to undertake a thorough investigation and that, not alone of the intrusions upon the territory, but also of its resources and its aboriginal inhabitants.

Once more Régis Loisel went up the Missouri, starting forthwith.[70] The trip was a memorable one, if only from the fact that it was the last he was ever to make; but that, of course, he was not to know. He went direct to the Isle of Cedars and, from thence, with Tabeau again as his companion, journeyed "about sixty-five leagues higher up," where the two of them "made a garden and a large field"; but the ensuing winter Loisel spent at his cedar fort.[71] From that point as a distributing centre, his plan was to send out equipments round-about, to the Fork, for instance; but the Bois Brûlés proved obstreperous and their interference, if Tabeau's narrative is to be trusted, entailed such a pecuniary loss to Loisel and left so much merchandise upon his hands that he was obliged to arrange for his men to make a further stay, while he himself returned to St. Louis, one whole year sooner than he had originally planned. If there was anything additional that impelled him to depart, his reticence then has operated to keep it hidden ever since; but that, when he left, he fully expected to return can be deduced from his admission that he "would have again ascended, however, had it not been for the change which the Government has experienced."[72] It is not likely that, at so early a date, the least inkling of the turn of affairs had reached so remote a spot as the Isle of Cedars. On his way down the river, when he was within, as it proved, about three days' journey of St. Louis, Loisel fell in with Lewis and Clark who had left St. Charles a few days before and, from whom, if previously unaware of the fact, he heard of the formal transfer of Upper Louisiana to the United States the preceding March. It was now the twenty-fifth

[70] The evidence for this prompt start is to be inferred from the Tabeau narrative.

[71] On the Indian Office, or Lewis and Clark itinerary, map, appears this legend, which probably had its source in information furnished either by Loisel himself or Tabeau: "Mr. Louisells House in the Winter 1803&4" (*Geographical Review,* I, 332, n. 10). Moreover, Lewis and Clark in their journals and when they had arrived within range of the Isle of Cedar, wrote, ". . . . on the South Side of this Island Mr Louiselle a trader from St Louis built a fort of Cedar & a good house to trade with the Seaux & Wintered last winter . . . ." (*Original Journals, op. cit.,* I, 160).

[72] See Loisel Memorial, Appendix VII.

of May. In the course of the interview with the explorers-to-be, Loisel, too, communicated news of interest, so they tell us.[73] We can imagine some of it.

In making their preparations for their voyage, Lewis and Clark had not hesitated to secure information from every available source. Citizens of St. Louis were the most helpful and, of one such, they made this record:

"Mr Labaum informs that a Mr Tebaux who is at present with Louasell up the Missouri can give us much infomation in relation to that country."[74] We can readily believe, therefore, that a first question put to Loisel elicited from him the exact whereabouts of the man they sought. About the time of Loisel's own departure downstream, Tabeau had taken up his abode among the Arikara Indians.[75] Lewis and Clark were now undoubtedly so informed and made the following memorandum on their itinerary map:

"Mr. Peter Tabeau" in pencil and underneath in ink,
  Mr. Peter Tabeau
    at the Ricaries"[76]

When Loisel reached St. Louis, Delassus was yet there and, on the twenty-eighth, Loisel addressed to him a memorial,[77] or report, of what he had been able to accomplish in execution of his mission. This document, which has the earmarks of hasty preparation, the former Lieutenant-Governor, with favorable comments of his own and reflected fears, duly transmitted to Casa Calvo, Loisel himself, being made, apparently, its bearer.

[73] Clark's journal entry, recording the meeting, is as follows:
May 25, 1804— ".... (La Charrette) we met with M Louisell, immediately down from the Seeder [Cedar] Isl^d. Situated in the Country of the Sciox [Sioux] 400 Leagues up he gave us a good Deel of information [and] Some letters he informed us that he Saw no Indians on the river below the *Poncrars* [Poncaras] . . . ." (*Original Journals, op. cit.,* I, 29).

[74] *Idem,* VI, 270. This was Louis Labeaume, for an account of whom, see Missouri Historical Society *Collections,* III, 259, n. 43; Bradbury, *Travels* . . . . , p. 253; Billon, *op cit.,* pp. 467-68.

[75] In his narrative, Tabeau mentions the fact that, by the beginning of 1805, he had about eight months' experience in dealing with the Arikaras.

[76] Geographical *Review,* I, 333.

[77] For the complete text of the Memorial and for the text also of Casa Calvo's letter of transmittal, see Appendix VII.

Doubt there may be — considering the time and the circumstances — as to what object the Spanish officials had really had in view when they started Loisel upon his quest, even admitting the original idea to have been his own; but none there can be as to the way his findings affected them, especially when taken in connection with other disquieting occurrences and rumors. To both Delassus at St. Louis and Casa Calvo at New Orleans it seemed only too evident that the Americans, if conceded all their pretensions, would threaten Spanish rights and sources of wealth at Santa Fé and beyond. With this thought uppermost, Casa Calvo, in sending on to Madrid a translation of Loisel's memorial, made the most of the danger and urged that the only way to obviate it was to prevent the United States — and by resort to arms if necessary — from retaining the west bank of the Mississippi. He had talked with Loisel personally, moreover, and, having convinced himself that he was a man to be trusted, now recommended that a suggestion Loisel had embodied in his report be complied with and he appointed agent to the Indian tribes, to the end that their friendship with Spain might be preserved and all tampering with them circumvented.

Casa Calvo's apprehensions were well-founded. There is not the shadow of a doubt of that; but his advice, under existing conditions, was little short of puerile. How the course he proposed could have availed Spain anything must have puzzled the "Prince of the Peace," Godoy, to whom he had dispatched his appeal. Matters had already gone much too far for any such restraint as was advocated to be effectual. Armed intervention to undo a *fait accompli* would have been difficult at the best of times and impossible to Spain in the straits to which she had long since found herself reduced. Powerless she had been to resist Napoleon's demand for Louisiana and powerless to prevent his illegal cession to the United States, illegal because contrary to the express terms of the Treaty of San Ildefonso. And the Indian agency was out of the question within a month of Casa Calvo's writing, at all events so far as it was predicated upon the incumbency of Loisel; for, in October, he died,[78] another victim, most likely, of the

[78] From the *Pierre Chouteau Papers*, MHS, it can be seen that Loisel was yet in St. Louis in June, 1804 and, from the *Manuel Lisa Papers*, MHS, in August. There the record of his movements, as traced, ends, except that Casa Calvo mentions having

vitiated air of New Orleans, since he was yet in his prime as years go, yet, so Casa Calvo had written, "active, young and enterprising." Young he certainly was to meet so untimely a death. He was only thirty-one.[79]

But would Régis Loisel have been, had he lived, quite so suitable a person for a high trust as was supposed? Was he the faithful person that Casa Calvo imagined? These questions give us pause; for there was certainly something rather suspicious in his relations with Hugh Heney, who, if not before Loisel's decease, an employee of the North West Company, lost no time, after it, in becoming one. A "Nor' Wester" he clearly was when Lewis and Clark were at the Mandans in the winter of 1804-5.[80] Could it have been that Régis Loisel was, in reality, serving two masters, playing a waiting game, prepared, if need be, "to run with the hare and hunt with the hounds?" Why was he so ready to continue to serve an alien power in preference to the country of his own forebears? Though no formal transfer had been made, Louisiana was a French possession and known to be such when Loisel first accepted the post of special investigator from Delassus. Finally, was his somewhat equivocal position the explanation of his agent's posthumous attitude towards him, the real reason, that is, why, in preparing a copy of his own narrative for a friend in Montreal, that agent gave not the slightest intimation of the true relation in which he and Loisel stood to each other, no suggestion whatsoever of the source of his own authority? Although Tabeau may not have been in Loisel's confidence, he must surely have had some

---

discussed matters with him after having heard from Delassus, which was in the same month of August. Delassus stayed in St. Louis until October. For the date of Loisel's death, see Billon, *op. cit.,* p. 466.

[79] Loisel was survived by a widow, the bride of three and a half years before, and two infant daughters. A son, Régis, born posthumously, is said to have been the first St. Louison to be ordained a priest. For interesting facts about him, see Rothensteiner, John, *History of the Archdiocese of St. Louis,* I, 442, 501, 636. Loisel's daughters, Josephine and Clementine, married two of the Papin brothers, Hypolite and Sylvestre respectively, which brought them within the circle of the Chouteau family. Loisel's widow married again in 1813, her second husband being François Lebeau of St. Louis. For additional items of genealogical value, see Collot, *op. cit.,* Vols. on "Baptisms," 157, "Marriages," 64; Tanguay, *op. cit.,* III, 46, VI, 206; Billon, *op. cit.,* p. 466.

[80] See Appendix VI.

idea of what his immediate employer was about. At any rate he knew that the two of them were not on the Upper Missouri on equal terms. More of this later.

And to what had Loisel's investigation amounted? Judged by its results alone, it had amounted to very little and his memorial was far from deserving the weight attached to it by Delassus and Casa Calvo, supposing them, in their turn, to have been sincere in their protestations and representations. In it Loisel had divulged nothing that Truteau or Mackay, not to mention D'Eglise[81] and several others, could not have communicated without resorting to a special inquest. The men mentioned were all earlier explorers of the Upper Missouri and were, for anything that can be proved to the contrary, among those holding the full confidence of the Spanish authorities in Upper Louisiana. In conversations, true enough, Loisel may well have revealed more than he penned. Likewise it has to be acknowledged, in justice to him and his memory, that his report was but an earnest of what was to follow; for, when he left the Isle of Cedars, he had admittedly not finished his investigation but had, by his own showing, deputed the task of completing it to his "agent and man of affairs." That was the man Tabeau, with whom Lécuyer had quarrelled and whom Mackay had dubbed "an infamous rascal," a man, forsooth, who, by present rating, except for the one incomprehensible act of disparaging his employer by ignoring him, is to be esteemed far above that same employer, because of the manner in which he did his duty. It is Tabeau's report, or narrative, to which Loisel's own was presumed to be but introductory, that constitutes the text of this editing. More about him is, therefore, in order.

Pierre-Antoine Tabeau[82] was the younger son of Jean-Baptiste Tabeau and of his wife, Marie-Josephe née Vallée,[83] and was born at

81 John Evans would head this list were I not afraid that he must have been dead by this time. Mackay wrote of him, in 1799, as "very ill," though "doing better." See Missouri Historical *Review*, XXV, 238-39. D'Eglise was killed in Mexico in 1809. For the circumstances of his tragic end, see Bloom, Lansing B., *Death of Jacques D'Eglise*, New Mexico Historical *Review*, II, 369-79.

82 For information about the name, see Appendix I.

83 This lady, Tabeau's mother, was the great-granddaughter of Jean Vallée (Tanguay, *op. cit.*, VII, 414-15), whose brother, Louis-Charles, was the direct ancestor of the Vallé family of Ste Geneviève, Missouri (Missouri Historical Society *Collections*, II, 56).

Lachine, January 15, 1755, in the evening.[84] The family from which he was sprung had emigrated from Prignac, France in the person of his great-grandfather, Pierre,[85] in 1669 and had established its domicile within about nine miles of Montreal, exactly where, as the years passed, there proved to be the greatest possible inducement for venturing forth into the unexplored West; for the place, at the base of the rapids, was to become the starting point of all the fur-trading expeditions to the Great Lakes. It was the Lachine of La Salle's selection. It was only to be expected, therefore, that the Tabeau family would furnish its full quota of *voyageurs* and *coureurs du bois,* which it did. To consider three generations of one Christian name alone, it develops that Pierre-Antoine's great uncle, Jean, had wandered as far as the site of the present Detroit, Cadillac's settlement,[86] in 1708; that his own father, Jean-Baptiste,[87] was a *voyageur,* or, more

[84] This information, gleaned from miscellaneous sources, was confirmed by the record of Lachine parish. The following is a translation of so much of a letter, written in response to an application that Major Lanctôt made at my request, as is pertinent:

"I have verified in the registers of the parish of Lachine, the baptism of Pierre Antoine Tabau, on January 16, 1755, born the preceding night, son of Jean-Baptiste Tabau, resident and merchant, and of Marie-Josephe Vallée, his wife.

"The index of withdrawals and assignments does not go farther than 1771, and Mr. Massicotte says that it would be necessary to examine the minutes of thirty notaries to find the assignment of Pierre Antoine Tabeau, if he had any, from 1771 on. . . . ." (Montarville B. de La Bruère to Monsieur the Major Gustave Lanctôt, Archivist of the Dominion, Ottawa, dated Public Archives of Canada, Montreal, February 15, 1930).

It would seem that my enquiry aroused in Mr. Massicotte, Archivist at the Old Court House, Montreal, sufficient interest to cause him to begin a search into the genealogy of the Tabeau family, the results of which have recently appeared in print. See *Notes sur la Famille Tabeau, Le Bulletin des Recherches Historiques,* XLIII, 367-70. For the Tabeau Genealogical Chart I myself prepared, see Appendix II.

[85] Pierre Tabault, the emigrant from Prignac, had three sons, Pierre, Alexis, and Jean. The line of Jean died out in his own generation; for, although he married twice and had two children, both of them died in infancy. Their mother, Jean's first wife, was Angelique Brunét, a younger sister of his brother Pierre's wife, Catherine. Jean Tabault died in 1728 at the age of forty-six; but there is evidence that up to at least two years before his death he was still a *voyageur.* See *Archives de Québec* (1921-22), p. 212.

[86] Burton, C. M., *Cadillac's Village, or Detroit under Cadillac,* p. 34: Jean Tabeaux was not the first of the family to visit Cadillac's settlement. A "Jacques Tabeau" came there as a bargeman, May 30, 1705 (*idem*) and must have been Jean's nephew, the eldest son of his brother Pierre.

[87] He was probably the "Jean Baptiste Tabeau" of Lachine, 15 June 1746 (Ar-

properly, a canoeman, and that his only brother, Jean-Baptiste-Henri, was successively a *voyageur* and trader.[88]

For all three of these, as well as for others of their family, the voyaging life had its irresistible attractions as it was to have, eventually, for Pierre-Antoine, although, at the start, he seemed destined for higher things, if such the intellectual be. To him, possibly because of a delicacy of physique or because of early indications of a literary aptitude, was given more than the customary advantages of an education. From such opportunities as were afforded him at Montreal, he passed to the Seminary at Quebec, now Laval University, and was in residence there for two full years, from the autumn of 1771 to August of 1773.[89] At the end of that time he was about eighteen and a half years of age. The next three years in his life's record are, at

---

chives de Québec [1922-23], p. 223), the "Jean Tabau" of Lachine, 2 April, 1747 (*idem*, p. 225) and, possibly, even the "B. Tabeau" of Pointe Claire, 25 May 1749 (*idem*, p. 241), likewise the "Sieur Tabeau" associated with Courtois, June, 1752, and bound for Detroit (*idem*, p. 263). Though some doubt may exist as to his identity with respect to the last two men, there is none whatever with the "Jn Bte Tabaux" to whom the "Upper Country" trade license of 28 April 1769 was issued (See Appendix III). The grantee could scarcely have been Pierre-Antoine's brother, Jean-Baptiste-Henri; for, at that time, he would have been not yet sixteen years of age, he having been born in the autumn of 1753.

88 This man, the brother of one Pierre-Antoine Tabeau and the father of another, also the trade partner of Étienne Campion, a wintering partner of the North West Company, and honored by being made a member of the Beaver Club, was pretty thoroughly identified with Michilimackinac up to at least 1786. Although apparently not one of the traders that, at the instance of Lieutenant-Governor Sinclair, moved from the mainland to the island (*Haldimand Papers*, B98), it is his name surely that appears with the names of other traders in correspondence with Sinclair, 21 July 1781 (*idem*, Part 2, p. 60). Three years afterwards, he was among several chosen by ballot as a committee, or what the editors of the *Lewis Bond Papers* not inappropriately call "the earliest Board of Trade in Michigan" (Michigan Pioneer and Historical *Collections*, XXXVII, 427), and was probably the same as the Baptiste Tabeau described as an *habitant* of Michilimackinac in 1786 (*Bulletin des Récherchés Historiques*, X, 68). He met his death by drowning near the mouth of the River du Moine. See Bigsby, John J., *The Shoe and Canoe*, I, 159.

89 Upon application, the Seminary of Quebec furnished the following detail as to his education:

"He began his education at Montreal, very probably with Mr. Curalteau, curé at Longue-Pointe.

"In the autumn of 1771, Pierre-Antoine Tabeau entered the second class (Belles-Lettres) at the Seminary of Quebec. He had as professor the Abbé Urbain Boiret, the

this writing and to this writer, a blank; but, in 1776, for a certainty, he went to the West as an engagé in his brother's canoe.[90] From that time forward, with an occasional period of greater or shorter length unaccounted for, his career can be traced for practically three decades. Then descends a veil again and, henceforth, no record at all until the very end.

After once yielding to the fascination of the wandering life it is safe to assume Pierre-Antoine Tabeau never abandoned it so long as his physical strength held out.[91] By 1783, he was a full-fledged trader

---

senior Superior of the Seminary and at that time director of the pupils in the little seminary. This comprised eighteen pupils whose names follow:

P. Victor Archambault, Charles Chauveaux, J. B. Contant, Jacques Cugnet, Louis Décormier, Chs. De Tounancour, Frs. Xavier Dufau, Alexis Fournier, Louis Hubert, Michel Laleine, Pierre Lefrançois, Joseph Maurice, Pierre Huot, Bernard-Claude Panet, future bishop of Quebec, Jacques Panet, brother of the above, Chs. Perrault, Pierre Antoine Tabau, Charles Vincennes.

"The following year, 1772-1773, Pierre-Antoine Tabeau studied Rhetoric and had as professor the Abbé Bailly who was later coadjutor of the bishop of Quebec. The 15th of August, 1773, Tabeau left the Seminary for good.

"We do not have the grades of the pupils of that time. What makes us believe that Tabeau was a good pupil is that after having been of the brotherhood of the Holy Virgin at Montreal, he entered immediately into that of our Seminary and became advisor there, then secretary.

"In 1772-73, Mr. Feligonde, steward of Saint Sulpice, sent the money for the board of Tabeau. Did he himself pay, was he simply the intermediary? I know not. . . . ." (The Reverend Amédée Gosselin of the Seminary of Quebec to Major Lanctôt, February 14, 1930).

[90] I have taken the "Baptiste Tabault," described as the bourgeois to whom a license was granted, July 12, 1776, for one canoe valued at £300 to go to Michilimackinac, to have been Jean-Baptiste-Henri and the canoeman, "Antoine Tabault de la chine," his brother. See Appendix III. In a license granted the selfsame day for the selfsame place to Pierre Chaboillez, one of the men in the three canoes appears as "Antoine tabault de Chataugue." This was License No. 13 and the other, License No. 18. The two engagés of the name Antoine Tabault were, most likely, near relatives. The family of Pierre Tabault, Jr. had established itself at Chateauguay; but, very unfortunately, no Antoine appears in Tanguay among his descendants of the time. His brother Alexis had a son, Antoine, who had a namesake. One or the other may have come to reside at Chateauguay.

[91] The record of his whereabouts, movements, or activities for the years intervening between 1776 and 1783, the duration of the American War of Independence, is a somewhat incomplete one. Some outstanding facts there are. For example, in 1778, after Étienne Campion and other merchants of Michilimackinac had petitioned Sir Guy Carleton that a missionary be permitted to come to the post (*Haldimand Papers;* B97-1, pp. 30-32), he, "P. Anton Tabeaux," and his brother, "Bte Tabeau," were

and went back, in that year, to Michilimackinac jointly licensed with his brother, the two being their own securities and, therefore, most likely free lances, their equipment a considerable one of £3,000 value.[92] Up to about this time there had been numerous independent traders and small, more or less temporary, combinations; but, between this date approximately and 1787, there arose unions on a larger scale and of a more permanent character. Jean-Baptiste-Henri Tabeau, who, from time to time had other seasonal associates[93] besides his brother, finally formed a partnership with Étienne Campion,[94] "Societé de Campion et Tabeau," and, with him, was grad-

---

among those pledging themselves to an annual subscription for his support and maintenance (*idem,* pp. 35, 36), the former, twenty-four # [*sic*] for an indeterminate period, the latter, thirty, for the space of ten years. In considering the amount pledged, cognizance should be taken of the fact that the *franc* had never "constituted the chief circulating medium among the common people of Lower Canada" (Shortt, Adam, *Documents Relating to Canadian Currency, Exchange and Finance during the French Period,* II, 893, n. 1). Only where expressly stated ought it to be applied to the figures put down (Michigan Pioneer and Historical *Collections,* X, 288-90). In all other cases, the *livre* was probably meant. For its value, see Quaife, *Askin Papers,* I, 162, n. 92.

In one other prominent way, Tabeau figured during the years referred to; for "P. An. Tabeau" and "Ette Campion" were among the witnesses to the purchase, May 12, 1781, of Michilimackinac Island from the Chippewas (*Haldimand Papers,* B114, p. 178; *Canada, Indian Treaties and Surrenders,* I, 1). Lieutenant-Governor Patrick Sinclair, having recognized its strategic value, designed making it a site of the military post in lieu of the south shore of the strait.

[92] This is to be understood from the details in the list of trade passes issued for that year. The brothers are cited as, "J. B. & P. A. Tabeau." The following was their manifest of their equipment, valued at £3000:

3 canoes	30 gal. Fusils
202 Battoes	1600 lbs. powder
27 Men	10 cwt. shott
200 gal. Rum	
60 gal. wine	(Dominion Archives, Ottawa).

[93] Pascal Pillet was his partner in 1782, supposing the "J. Bte Tabeau" was the brother and not the father. The father was, however, yet alive in 1781. See Case of J. B. Tabeaux, Pere, of Montreal involving the sale of a house (*Internal Records of Lower Canada,* 1781, Dominion Archives, Ottawa). The "J. B. Tabeault," plaintiff in a suit against Charlotte Tachette, 8 November 1783 (*idem*) would appear to have been the son.

[94] The trade licenses of Étienne Campion apparently begin with 1774 and are extant for 1776, 1781, 1782, 1783, 1786. If better known than his partner, Tabeau, he was also more frequently under fire because of unfair or cruel treatment of the Indians. On August 10, 1787, he with several other merchants of Michilimackinac, his

ually drawn into the service of the North West Company. In 1786-87, he appears to have wintered in the West and, having become a wintering partner thereby, was, in 1787, elected a member of the Beaver Club.[95] Meanwhile, his brother had drifted down to Cahokia, presumably in the employ of the Michilimackinac Company, which, organized about the same time as the North West Company, had, at least as early as 1786, "a large Trading House" there "for the suply of the Savages."[96] Trade interests at Cahokia, however, did not imply for Tabeau all at once a definite residence in the old Sulpician settlement. Michilimackinac was yet the greatest of all the trading posts and the distance between it and Cahokia much traversed so that for a time Tabeau retained his interests at the former place and at Montreal,[97] even after he was sufficiently established at Cahokia

---

brother Alexis, "Bte Tabeau," and "AP. [sic] Tabeau," among them, made formal complaint against certain agents of the Indian Department, particularly Dease and Ainse (Transcripts, Colonial Office Records, being "Canada," Q series, XLVIII, Part I, pp. 127-31) and a Board of Enquiry was instituted. The evidence furnished by both sides was of the incriminating sort and the conduct of Campion towards the Indians at the Falls of St. Anthony was shown to be most unjust (idem, vol. XLVIII, Part 2, pp. 533 et seq.). In 1792, Étienne Campion was arrested with others for the brutal treatment of an Indian, compassing his death (Riddell, W. R., Michigan under British Rule, pp. 454-55).

[95] Although there is no trace of the issuance of a trader's pass or license to Jean-Baptiste-Henri Tabeau in the summer of 1787, he seems, none the less, to have been at Michilimackinac; for he signed the complaint against the Indian agents, August 10th, and was, with his brother, a witness at an interment. See Mackinac Register, "Interments," Wisconsin Historical Society Collections, XIX, 161. For the Beaver Club as a social organization within the North West Company, see Burpee, L. J., The Beaver Club, Canadian Historical Association Report, 1924, pp. 73-92; Masson. Les Bourgeois de la Compagnie du Nord-Ouest, Introduction; Massicotte, E. Z., Hôtelleries, Clubs et Cafés à Montréal de 1760 à 1850, Royal Society of Canada Transactions, 3rd. series (1928), XXII, 43-44; Davidson, G. C., The North West Company, pp. 244-45.

[96] John Edgar to George Rogers Clark, October 23, 1786 (Kaskaskia Records, op. cit., p. 395; British Régime in Wisconsin, op. cit., p. 439).

[97] "Antoine Tabeau" obtained a pass, No. 23, in 1786 and "Pierre Ant. Tabeau" a trader's license for Michilimackinac in 1787. How very much he was there is indicated by his signature to various documents, to the formal complaint of August 10th, 1787, to a burial certificate, and, as a godfather, to a baptismal. For the record of the last, see Mackinac Register, "Baptisms" (Wisconsin Historical Society Collections, XIX, 93). The child, "Sieur Antoine Tabeau" stood sponsor for, on August 15, 1787, was "Amable, 13 years old, natural son of Pierre Grignon and a savage mother."

to take, in 1785, the oath of fidelity to the United States;[98] to be described, in 1789, as a merchant of the bank there;[99] and, in 1790, to be enrolled in the militia of the District of Kaskaskia, which last-named fact entitled him, under Act of Congress, to claim a "donation" grant of one hundred acres of land.[100]

The chaotic state of affairs in the Illinois country generally has already been incidentally referred to. Although less pronounced in Cahokia than elsewhere, it was bad enough everywhere and disgracefully so after the somewhat shadowy authority of Virginia had been withdrawn, following her surrender to the Continental Congress of the title she had advanced to the region and, indeed, to the entire Northwest in virtue, first, of the royal charter granted to the London Company in 1609 and, secondly, of the so-called George Rogers Clark conquest. The proposed Ordinance of 1784 failing of enactment and the accepted one of 1787 of immediate execution, the forces of law and order were at a standstill. The first Territorial

---

[98] The following is a Court Record of Cahokia (Alvord, C. W., Illinois Historical *Collections*, II, 217):

"At a Court the 19th of November, 1785, M. Pierre Antoine Tabeau made oath of fidelity to the United States of America and promised to conform to the edicts and regulations of the government of Virginia, and has signed the said day and year.

"P. A. Tabeau

"J. B. H. La Croix, Pres.

"Labuxiere (Clerk)"

[99] *Idem*, p. 427. For his signature, "Tabeau," attached to documents in 1789, see pp. 422, 423. It would appear, too, that he was the plaintiff in the Louis Gaud case (*idem*, pp. 427-35) and one of the several debtors to the estate of Wm. Kay, late of Montreal (*idem*, p. 523).

[100] On January 2, 1811, Albert Gallatin, as Secretary of the Treasury, communicated to the United States Senate a report, No. 180, on "Land Claims in the District of Kaskaskia" (American State Papers, *Public Lands*, II, 123 *et seq.*). The claim, No. 435 (*idem*, p. 173) was described as having been originally allotted to "Pierre Ant. Tabeau," the present claimant, however, being, as in many similar cases, William Morrison. All such claims as No. 435 were "founded on an act of Congress granting a donation of one hundred acres of land to each militiaman enrolled and doing duty in the Illinois, on the 1st day of August, 1790, within the district of Kaskaskia" (*idem*, p. 166). "Alexis Tabeaux" had also had a claim (*idem*, p. 229), but not one of the same sort, he having died before 1789 (Alvord, C. W., Illinois Historical *Collections*, II, 629, n. 62). It is gratifying to know that the Tabeau claims were among those confirmed; for so great had been the attempted fraud and perjury that the Commissioners were noticeably relieved when they had finished drawing their "melancholy picture of human depravity" (American State Papers, *Public Lands*, II, 126).

Governor, Arthur St. Clair, was tardy in making his appearance, not arriving at Kaskaskia until the spring of 1790. By that time, many of the inhabitants, despairing of relief and, in not a few instances, distrustful of American intentions, apprehensive that the Ordinance of 1787 would bring in its train an interference with their ownership of slaves, had taken their departure. Some, much as they abhorred George Morgan, had yet seen fit to accept the liberal offers he made and had crossed over to his embryo colony at New Madrid. Others did the same when, largely through the machinations of the venal Wilkinson, Morgan's project had collapsed and the Spaniards, succeeding to the enterprise, had adopted his methods and had gone even beyond him in their advertisement of benefits to be bestowed. Among those who may have gone from Cahokia in the later period was Pierre-Antoine Tabeau. Where he went and whether alone or with an unknown family is conjectural. One of his name, however, seems to have arrived at New Madrid fairly early, possibly in the middle nineties.[101] The exact facts will probably remain forever a mystery since New Madrid suffered more than any other place from the earthquake devastations of 1811-12. Its church disappeared and with the church the chief of its vital records.

It is safe to conclude that wherever Pierre-Antoine Tabeau was he was still the trader and, potentially, the *voyageur*. That being the case, it was he, without a doubt, who joined the Lécuyer expedition under the auspices of the Spanish Company of Commerce and, in April or May, 1795, started for the Upper Missouri. Pure love of adventure must have led him to do this unless he had met with reverses; for, evidently, his rank was only that of a rather superior engagé, which, in view of his age and the variety of his experiences, was, to say the least, surprising. No wonder he ran amuck of his superior, that superior *pro tem.* being such an unsuitable person for directing any assignment of consequence. Opportunities could have been so many for friction between them, especially if they were old acquaintances and especially since Tabeau had so moral and religious a background.

Reprehensible though his conduct may have been in this single instance, Tabeau had yet his good points or soon redeemed himself.

---

[101] Houck, *History of Missouri, op. cit.,* II, 153. There is no name at all like

Otherwise he would not have been chosen by the very practical Régis Loisel for a somewhat similar undertaking a few years thereafter and in a much higher capacity and he would not have been recommended to Lewis and Clark by so prominent and estimable a citizen as Louis Labeaume.[102]

When, upon the departure of Loisel for St. Louis, Tabeau took up his quarters among the Arikaras, in that village of theirs, which was situated approximately in the center of a large island about three miles long, "near the L. Side (of the Missouri) & near the foot of Some high bald uneaven hills,"[103] his lodging was with Chief Kakawita, about whom, in his narrative, he had a deal to recount. His stay with the Arikaras was an exceptionally lengthy one, considering that the Loisel expedition seems to have had set to it, originally, a time limit. In fact, Tabeau was almost as long a sojourner among

this, however, in the "Statistical Census of New Madrid of 1797," Houck, *Spanish Régime, op. cit.,* II, 393-97. In fact, many things about Pierre-Antoine Tabeau defy investigation and successfully elude it. For all that has been found with certainty to the contrary, he may have continued to live on the Illinois side and that view is strengthened by his repeated allusion to the Illinois country in his revised version of his narrative, or he may have returned to Canada. The letter, accompanying that revised version, in the form in which it has come into my hands has no date and no place indicated from which it was written. Because of the hiatus in New Madrid records, due to the catastrophe of the earthquake, it has seemed possible that therein lies the explanation for the mystery surrounding the domestic life and the years prior to 1819 of the writer of the Régis Loisel narrative; but it is all of supposition and nothing of proof. A John B. Thibault (Jean Baptiste Tabeau?) was, however, a sufferer from the earthquake shocks of 1811-12 and claimed a land indemnity under the Act of Congress of 17 February 1815 (*House Executive Documents,* Twenty-fourth Congress, first session, No. 197, p. 2). In subsequent years, Archibald Gamble came forward as the assignee of his heirs and representatives, so that he was certainly dead by 1833 (*idem,* pp. 2-3, 4, 5) and could not have been the Jean-Baptiste Tabeau that accompanied John C. Frémont to California in 1843 and was killed by Indians near the Rio Virgen (*Report of the Exploring Expedition to the Rocky Mountains, 1842, and to Oregon and North California, 1943-44,* pp. 105, 160, 268-69; *Memoirs,* pp. 380-81). Sergeant Ordway made a statement in his journal that might be held to signify that Tabeau had a son on the Upper Missouri. It is this:

"we left one of our frenchman with Mr Tabbow & took his Soon in his place" (Wisconsin Historical Society *Collections,* XXII, 149).

102 "Mr Labaum informs that Mr Tebaux who is at present with Louasell up the Missouri can give us much infomation in relation to that country" (*Original Journals, op. cit.,* VI, 270).

103 *Original Journals, op. cit.,* I, 183, 184.

the Arikaras as had been Truteau ten years earlier. Great changes had occurred in the interval and greater yet were at hand; for the Arikaras, "Durtey, Kind, pore & extravigent";[104] but more inoffensive, perhaps, than even the Mandans, were to become the most obnoxious of all to American traders, the most treacherous, many of the traders declared, and the most unfeignedly hostile.

As Labeaume had recommended Tableau to Lewis and Clark and as Loisel could not have done less than tell them that his own trust in him was so implicit that he had left him behind as his representative, they must have been genuinely glad to have him arrive upon the scene, one morning early, in time for "brackfast."[105] Mr. Gravelines was with him, whom they had met two days before, when they first sighted the Arikara island. After holding a council with the assembled Arikaras, the Americans went on to the Mandans where their idea was to spend the winter. There they built a fort and, every once in a while, held communication with Tableau at the Arikaras. In April, he asked[106] to be allowed to embark on a barge that the American captains were preparing to send down to St. Louis and on that he did embark,[107] carrying, no doubt, with him his narrative

---

104 *Idem*, p. 188.

105 October 10, 1804, *idem*, pp. 185-86.

106 7 April 1805 — "a windey day. The Interpreter we Sent to the Villages returned with Chief of the Ricara's & 3 men of that nation, this Chief informed us that he was Sent by his nation to know the despositions of the nations in this neighbourhood in respect to the recara's Settleing near them, that he had not yet made those arrangements . . . . we gave him a certificate of his good Conduct & a Small Medal, a Carrot of Tobacco and a String of Wompom. he requested that one of his men who was lame might decend in the boat to their nation and returned to the Mandans well Satisfied. The name of this Chief of War is *Kah-kah, We-to* — Raven brave. This Cheif delivered us a letter from Mr. Taboe. informing us of the wish of the Grand Chiefs of the Recarras to visit their Great father and requesting the privolage of put'g on board the boat 3000lb. of skins &c. & adding 4 hands and himself to the party. this preposeal we Shall agree to, as that addition will make the party in the boat 15 Strong and more able to defend themselves from the Seoux &c." (*idem*, pp. 285-86).

107 This is a fair inference from the following:

7 *April 1905* — "Having on this day at 4. P. M. completed every arrangement necessary for our departure, we dismissed the barge and crew with orders to return without loss of time to St. Louis, ... ; two Frenchmen and a Ricara Indian also take their passage in her as far as the Ricara Villages, at which place we expect Mr. Tiebeau [Tableau] to embark with his peltry who in that case will make an addition of two, perhaps four men to the crew of the barge. . . . ." (*idem*, p. 283).

in a complete or wellnigh complete form. And there his story ends, except for a few isolated facts. He appeared, for instance, in court for the purpose of giving evidence in the case involving Loisel's possessory right to the Isle of Cedars.[108] That was in August, 1806. In September, 1806, Lewis and Clark returned to St. Louis and, on reaching St. Charles, *en route,* were enthusiastically received by many of the inhabitants.[109] Among those who gave them an exceptionally warm welcome was a Mr. "Taboe."[110] If that were Pierre-

---

[108] American State Papers, *Public Lands,* II, 567; Missouri Land Cases," *House Executive Documents,* Twenty-fourth Congress, first session, No. 16, pp. 184-87. See also n. 85.

[109] *21 September 1806* — ". . . . at 4 P M we arrived in Sight of S[t]. Charles, the party rejoiced at the Sight of this hospita[b]l[e] village plyed thear ores with great dexterity and we Soon arived opposit the Town this day being Sunday we ob⌐ served a number of Gentlemen and ladies walking on the bank, we saluted the Village by three rounds from our blunderbuts and the Small arms of the party, and landed near the lower part of the town. we were met by great numbers of the inhabitants, we found them excessively polite. we received invitations from Several of those Gentlemen a M[r]. Proulx, Taboe, Decett, Tice Dejonah & Quarie and several who were pressing on us to go to their houses, we could only visit M[r]. Proulx and M[r]. Deucett in the course of the evening . . . .

22 September 1806 — "This morning being very wet and the rain Still continueing hard, and our party being all sheltered in the houses of those hospitable people, we did not (think) proper to proceed on untill after the rain was over, and continued at the house of M[r]. Proulx . . . ." (*Original Journals, op. cit.,* V, 391-92).

[110] That this may have been Pierre-Antoine Tabeau is suggested by the fact that he was, presumably, in the company of Basile Proulx, who was the brother of Françoise-Barbe Proulx, the wife of Jean-Baptiste-Henri Tabeau. Basile Proulx, son of Basile Prou and Geneviève, née Chenier (Chesnier) of Lachine (Tanguay, *op. cit.,* III, 51), is said to have been among the very early settlers of St. Charles (*Original Journals, op. cit.,* V, 392, n. 1). He was certainly there as early as 1799 (American State Papers, *Public Lands,* II, 476) and married, in April of that year, at St. Charles, Therese Chancellier. He must, in later years, have had some connection with Portage des Sioux, founded by François Saucier, 1799 (*House Executive Documents,* Twenty-fourth Congress, first session, No. 59, pp. 75 ff.); for there, in 1827 and 1830 respectively two of his daughters were married, the one, Louise, to François Nouval, the other, Elizabeth, to Louis Clermont. A record has been obtainable of two other children, Joseph and Victoire; but what relation, if any, the Raphael Proulx, who accompanied John C. Frémont to California in 1843 (Roy, Pierre-Georges, *La Famille Frémont,* p. 76), was to him has eluded research.

That St. Charles was the home of Pierre-Antoine Tabeau seems scarcely likely, although a census of Upper Louisiana in 1787, obtained from the Cuban National Archives at Havana (Missouri Historical Society *Collections,* II, 86), shows that there was a "Pedro Tabo" at Florissant then and a "Pedro Tibo" at St. Charles, "las

Antoine — and who can be dubious on that score, since he was so near at hand the previous month? — he disappeared from view completely afterwards, leaving not a trace behind. And here we will leave him for the time being, while we consider at length that which will give him life and long life, let us hope, in history.

The Tableau narrative is one of no ordinary sort. Relating itself to the old Spanish régime in Louisiana through Régis Loisel, who held a commission from Lieutenant-Governor Delassus; to the old French régime in Quebec through the French-Canadians, who figure in its pages; to British North America through the occasional allusions to the Hudson's Bay and North West companies; and, finally, to the infant republic of the United States through its author's contact with the explorers, Meriwether Lewis and William Clark, it combines, in a way, all parts of the continent at the time of one of its most interesting stages, politically. Moreover, its individual history has had its ups and downs. Designed, in the first instance, to supplement Loisel's official report to the Spanish authorities, to be to it a kind of appendix, the shifting scene made it superfluous. Years went by, during which it remained uncalled for and seemingly unknown. Then came another Frenchman into view, Jean N. Nicollet, who, in some mysterious way, most fortunate in the sequel, got hold of it and would have used it to enrich his own topographical report for the United States War Department had not death intervened. Another lapse of time succeeded and only within the last decade and a half or so has Tabeau's narrative of the Loisel expedition again seen the light.[111] Forgotten so long, it is now found competent to

---

pequenas Cuestas;" but neither could have been Pierre-Antoine Tabeau; for the one was sixty-one years of age, the other, thirty-seven, while Pierre-Antoine Tabeau would have been only thirty-two.

[111] An exception to this may, perchance, be found in the fact that two short extracts from what was certainly Tabeau's work appeared, in 1857, in Bibaud, Jeune, *Dictionnaire Historique des Hommes Illustres du Canada et de l'Amerique,* pp. 36-38, 71-72. In fact, his *Relation* is credited to him. See p. 390. The extracts, however, have a closer resemblance to the Montreal version than to the Washington and, if not taken from yet a third version, must have come from it. A discrepancy from both versions appears in the spelling of a word and in a date, the extract, on page 71, giving *Vallée* and *14 Avril 1804,* whereas both the Washington and the Montreal versions have Valé and April 24th as the date of the occurrence described.

serve a greater historical purpose than any previously thought of — to supplement, on the one hand, all the journals emanating from the pioneer work of the Spanish Company of Commerce for the Discovery of the Nations of the Upper Missouri and, on the other, the world renowned of Lewis and Clark.

Though called the Tabeau narrative, the manuscript here translated and edited is anonymous and it was chiefly by means of internal evidence, substantiated by reference to the Lewis and Clark journals that its identity was established to the satisfaction of translator and editor and its authorship ascribed to Pierre-Antoine Tabeau.

Lewis and Clark met several traders on the Upper Missouri, any one of whom, under certain conditions, might conceivably have been the author. All these conditions were met in the person of Tabeau alone. This conclusion was arrived at by the process of elimination. He is the only one of the traders not mentioned by name in the narrative itself. He was the only one adequately equipped by education and experience for the task of collecting and imparting reliable information. Moreover, he was clothed with authority from Régis Loisel. The writer of the narrative had obviously been in Loisel's company. It would be idle to question that the *Sabeau* of Loisel's report was none other than Tabeau. Barring the initial letter, the two names are exactly the same. The substitution of one initial letter for the other can be attributed to the fact that, in transcribing or in translating from the French — assuming that Loisel wrote originally in that language — to Spanish or from Spanish to English, it would be an easy matter to mistake a long-hand *T* for an *S*. Tabeau, then, designated as Loisel's "agent and man of affairs," was in duty bound to keep his eyes and ears open, to be observant, and to make a record of all that might be deemed important.

Between the information of the narrative and that of the various compositions resulting from the Lewis and Clark expedition there is a resemblance so strong as to be positively remarkable. The American explorers acknowledged their debt to Tabeau, a debt of no mean proportions; since, in Captain Lewis' *Statistical Report* alone, the bulk of the information, within the range of Tabeau's sphere of observation, that is, was precisely that of his alleged narrative. Not until that narrative came to light had it been possible to trace the source of the information or to make a comparison that would guage the extent of the explorer's obligation to this particular trader.

The explorers called the trader "Anty," which may have been short for *Anthony,* the English equivalent of *Antoine.* He was living among the Arikaras; but the itinerary map, discovered years since at the Indian Office, if rightly interpreted as their property, would indicate that they expected to meet or did meet a "Mr Peter Tabeau" there.[112] The variation in the Christian name might seem to make identification more difficult, but such is not the case. In fact, the variation serves to make identification easier, inasmuch as Tabeau's full name was Pierre-Antoine. His English-speaking associates would probably resort to the use of one part of it or the other. Moreover, as we have already seen, neither Tabeau nor his brother ever confined himself to a single spelling of his name or a single signature.[113]

These deductions reached independently, it was highly gratifying to have them confirmed and corroborated when a second Tabeau narrative made its appearance. It was one that is preserved among the Roman Catholic archives at Montreal, in the Archbishop's Palace there. It is in French as is the other found in Washington, D.C. Translated, it begins thus:

> The Voyage of Pierre Antoine Tabeaux
> to the Upper Missouri.
> — Extract —
> From his Journal,[114] Commenced at the Mouth of That
> River, June 22, 1803 and ended May 20, 1805.

The question now arises, What relation does the one narrative bear to the other? or What relation did the two bear to each other originally or to a longer literary product, of which they are only parts? A working hypothesis acceptable to the present editor is, that Tabeau, in Loisel's employ but only partially in possession of the ulterior objects of Loisel's mission, kept from the start of their second and last journey together a diary, from which, in his hours of leisure

---

[112] Abel, A. H., *A New Lewis and Clark Map,* The Geographical *Review,* I, 332, 333 n. 11.

[113] See Appendix I.

[114] This was the first intimation I had of such an original source and I have come across no trace of it.

in Kakawita's hut after Loisel's departure and in anticipation of his own, he prepared a synopsis, or summary, which, because of the foremost place that Loisel had been occupying in the whole enterprise and, for all he knew, still occupied, he called, "The Expedition of Régis Loisel . . . ." The coming of Lewis and Clark upon the scene, eager for all sorts of information, may have modified or given a slightly new direction to his thoughts; but it seems certain that he gave to them material that he already had in hand. He did not confine himself to the answering of questions or prepare anything especially for them.

Tabeau went down the river in the spring of 1805 and was unquestionably, up to the time he reached the settlements, in absolute ignorance of Loisel's death, which had occurred the preceding October, unless, indeed, a possible informant had met the barge coming down. In St. Louis were other evidences of change. The Spanish régime had ended, the French likewise, so that, even if Tabeau had been in Loisel's confidence regarding the professed political and scientific purposes of his mission, there was no one to whom he had officially to report or could report. His manuscript was his own to do with as he would.

The question is, What did he do with it? To attempt an answer, we must return to a consideration of what may have been his movements from this time forward. After his appearance in court as an adverse witness against the Loisel claim to the Isle of Cedars, he passed completely from view, so far as any records that I have found available would indicate. There is legal proof, however, that he was back in his native haunts at least by 1819. In poor health, then, and desirous of living quietly, he made over his property — he had considerable real estate in Montreal and Lachine — to his nephew and namesake,[115] who was then the parish priest at Boucherville, with the proviso that he himself should receive a fortnightly allowance for the remainder of his life "and keep his residence in a house built on his farm at Lachine."[116] Thither he retired, but it was not for long, for he died, March 10th, 1820, almost a year to the day after he had

[115] For an account of this younger Pierre-Antoine Tabeau, see Appendix IX.

[116] A certified copy of this "Donation" was obtained from the court records of Montreal and is to be found in Appendix IX.

made his "donation," the date of which is March 4th, 1819. Tabeau was unmarried at the time of his death and, apparently, he had never married.[117]

And now regarding that manuscript which he had prepared,[118] as I believe, for Régis Loisel and which, Loisel being dead, he had never delivered, what more can be said? Did some friend from his far-off student days get word from him about and ask to see it or did Tabeau return almost immediately to Canada and receive the request verbally? Tabeau did not submit the diary itself for reasons stated; but, apparently, he made a greatly improved copy of the synopsis, which had been originally intended for Loisel's perusal and Spanish edification.

To what did Tabeau's revision amount? Thereby hangs a tale. That the manuscript in Montreal is a revision and not the original even a superficial examination reveals. Beside it, the earlier literary effort appears but a rough draft, somewhat less correct in its French, less elegantly composed. In rewriting, Tabeau eliminated most of the errors. He also introduced changes and corrections of dates and facts and he rearranged the whole. This he did by breaking his material up into chapters and, while retaining the topics, apportioning them in a more logical and orderly fashion.

The result was, from the point of view of form alone, a much more nearly perfect composition. Since such was the case, the reader might well inquire, "Why then was it not preferred for publication? Why was it not translated, edited, and substituted for the very obvious rough draft? The answer is not far to seek; for, in the revising process, the narrative had been shorn of all political significance. It had been historically emasculated. It had become a mere fur-trader's account of personal experiences. It still possessed, it is true, the geographical and sociological interest that had distinguished its fore-

[117] For a remark as to possible offspring, see p. 39, n. 101.

[118] I very strongly incline to the opinion that, although the one narrative was a revised version of the other, they were not written for the same person. In arguing thus, I stress the different verb used in phrasing the reasons for writing. Tabeau admits himself that he was *constrained,* or *compelled* to write the first of his two versions; but was complying with a *request* when he wrote the second. In other words, he wrote the rough draft for someone who had a certain amount of authority over him; he wrote the revision for a friend.

runner; but its link with things more strictly historical had gone. In the very title itself appeared the first indication of the great change. The voyage, journey, expedition, call it what one may, that formerly had been regarded as exclusively Loisel's, credited to him by Tabeau himself, had become Tabeau's own.[119] And in the body of the text, through the whole of it, there is the same situation. It is not that Loisel has disappeared. He is there but not in his rightful position of superiority, of seniority. Reduced in rank, he is just such another

[119] Inadequate knowledge or lack of knowledge of the historical background of this expedition, the circumstances surrounding it and giving rise to it, would force this conviction upon any reader. When my view of the case was presented by Major Lanctôt to the gentleman from whom he procured a copy of the Montreal version, it elicited this rejoinder, the natural one, given here in translation:

"I have your letter of the 3rd, relating to that which you call the Tabeau manuscript.

"You believe that your manuscript is the original copy of the journey and that mine is the second copy, revised and corrected. It is possible that you are right, but I am not ready to admit it at once, because I am illy prepared to contradict you as I have at hand for the purpose of comparison only a single page of the Ottawa manuscript.

"In my manuscript, the author, who is undoubtedly P. A. Tabeau, speaks readily of the journey as his journey. It is not always clear, even when he speaks of it, that Loisel is with him, but that appears sufficiently in certain places so that it cannot be doubted. Nevertheless, it does not follow that Tabeau was a subordinate of Loisel's. Nothing indicates that, at least in the text that I possess. The writer speaks as one who has authority over his own affairs as Loisel over his. Why could it not be Loisel who, wishing to leave as his own, a report of the journey he had made with Tabeau, had borrowed the narrative already made by the same Tabeau and had simply changed it in order to adapt it to his own situation? Tabeau who was educated and had studied at the Seminary of Quebec had not the same reasons as Loisel for appropriating the work of another.

"What is strange is that Loisel put at the beginning of his account entire phrases — and word for word — which are in Tabeau's prefatory letter addressed to A. D.

"Is it Tabeau's journal or is it his own current account of which Loisel had had knowledge? We shall know it only if we find the journal of Tabeau, because Tabeau says expressly that he had written a journal.

"It would also be necessary to know — what you can know — up to what point the Loisel text differs from the Tabeau. I believe that the unforeseen advent of my manuscript into the affair will necessitate a much longer preliminary study than you had thought.

"If, after perusal, you think that the Tabeau text is more interesting for publication, I will cheerfully consign it to you.

"I have not yet been able to go to the bishopric to see again the manuscript which I have always believed to be the original one, but I expect to go there tomorrow. Besides, since you have the same text at hand, the only question would be a comparison

trader as Tabeau. At best they are allowed to pose as if engaged in some joint enterprise; but even that is not specifically affirmed. It is all very misleading and very contrary to fact. Loisel was most certainly the head of an expedition, Tabeau his employee, possibly his clerk, since he kept the journal. When Loisel went down to St. Louis to report progress, Tabeau received a promotion. He became, in Loisel's absence, his "agent and man of affairs." It is safe to assume that Tabeau was never Loisel's partner, at all events not on this occasion. If anyone was Loisel's partner in 1803-4, it was Hugh Heney; but, since the trade agreement that they two made, July 6, 1801, was to terminate two years later to the very day and since no record has come to hand of its formal renewal or continuance beyond that date, except for occasional references to it, *La Societé de Loisel & Heney,* as late as August, 1804, in ways that would suggest as I have intimated already, liquidation processes, it seems fair to assume that Loisel was playing a lone hand commercially while fulfilling his engagement with the Spanish authorities. He had his clerks, Tabeau, Vallé, and the rest, but no partner in the strictly legal sense of the term. Standing alone, the narrative of Loisel's expedition is not of great historical consequence; but, taken in connection with his pe-

---

of the handwriting, and I can tell you now that the text of which you gave me a photostat and that which is at the bishopric are not by the same hand.

"As for my notes upon Tabeau, you can rest assured that I will supply you with them. Unhappily, they are not as complete as I would wish them to be. I am still working to augment them and I am not without hope of succeeding. . . . ." (Aegidius Fauteux, Bibliothécaire, to Major Gustave Lanctôt, dated Bibliothèque Saint-Sulpice, Montreal, February 6, 1930).

With reference to one or two matters in the translated letter just given and in elucidation, it may be remarked that there need be no dispute about the authorship. It never occurred to me to consider Loisel as the possible author of either text. He is mentioned in the third person invariably. Furthermore, he was already dead while the writing was yet in progress. The text, referred to as the *Ottawa,* is, of course, the *Washington.* Major Lanctôt had evidently not enlarged upon his theme or told all he could have told. I am inclined to differ about the handwriting, being almost persuaded that it is the same in the two texts; but I have never had for purposes of comparison more than a photographic copy of the prefatory letter and first page of the Montreal version. The notes, so generously offered, were never asked for, this study being already advanced to such a stage that the need for anything except information about Tabeau's boyhood and about a possible wife and children seemed not insistent. I would have liked to find out, however, who Tabeau's correspondent was, the Monsieur A.D., to whom he sent his more polished narrative.

tition and with his memorial, or report, it is. Moreover, it is an incentive to further investigation. Divested of the one feature that constituted a clue to a phase of international affairs, nothing of historical import remains in the revised narrative except the allusions to the Lewis and Clark expedition and they are more casual there than in the rough draft.

We can ponder as we will over Tabeau's strange conduct, over his deliberate suppression of essential facts, yet get little reward for our pains. His motives may have been above reproach, quite innocent, though appearances are against him. It may be that he did not altogether approve of Loisel's political activities, supposing he was privy to them, and took this way of dissociating himself from them. This in itself would have constituted an extenuating circumstance. Then, too, it is entirely possible that he was not in Loisel's confidence, that he knew nothing of the true nature of Loisel's secret mission and, being mystified, thought it wisest to let sleeping dogs lie. After all, the experiences he described were largely his own, the observations he made absolutely his. Why ascribe them to another, who was his superior only for a season and was now dead? The narrative was going to Montreal, to the boyhood home of them both. Why prepare it in such a way that he, the real writer of it in all its forms and the better educated,[120] should figure as the subordinate?

Tabeau's superiority of education is attested throughout and markedly so in a prefatory letter that he attached to the narrative. With a translation of it, this introduction may fittingly close.

To Monsieur A.D.-

Sir & Friend,

You ask me for the diary of the journey which I made on the upper Missouri. I would have sent it to you such as it is, but, in ascending the Missouri and in visiting the nations dwelling there, everything being most monotonous and the same things

---

[120] This assumption may be an erroneous one. I may be arguing from insufficient knowledge. I have seen little, however, to convince me that Loisel's education was above the average. If he drew up the Loisel-Heney trade agreement, I should say it was below. On the other hand, Tabeau's education, whether acquired at the Seminary of Quebec or subsequently by his own efforts, was very much more than ordinary. It included even an acquaintance with classical mythology.

3e

Voiage De P. Ant. Tabeaux Dans le haut Missouri

Extrait

de son journal Commencé A l'Embouchure de Cette Rivierre Le 22 Juin 1803 Terminé le 20 may 1805

Chapitre premier

Des difficultés & des dangers En Montant le Missouri, des différentes Localités, des produits indigènes, tant En fruits qu'en racines Comestibles.

Le Missouri a son Embouchure a Environ 25 arpents de largeur qu'il conserve presque toujours jusqu'aux Villages des ricaras 280 lieües pour Cette raison il devient moins profond a mesure que l'on monte Suivant En suivant les Eaux de la rivierre des osages et 30 lieües, de la rivierre des Kansas a 100 lieües et de la rivierre platte a 200 lieües petite rivierre qui tombent dans [...] ses meandres est a peu pres de droit ouest au sud est. Ses détours Sont longs & souvent peu Sensibles jusqu'à la rivierre platte, mais au dessus les Sinuosités sont Si fréquentes que dans peu d'espace, il fait plusieurs fois le tour du compas. ses eaux sont extrêmement troubles, Surtout dans les Crües, ou elles ressemblent au lait au lait malgré cela elles n'ont sans doute aucunes mauvaises qualités, puisqu'en les [...] ne s'en trouve incommode. il est extrêmement rapide [...] guères qu'au dessus de la rivierre platte & de Celle que l'on que l'on s'apperçoit Successivement de la diminution des courants jusques là ils naissent Surmontables dans les grandes Crües eu égard des Efforts très promptes invincibles. Cette grande rapidité sur un fond de sable mobile, & d'être partout que des passages aussi pénibles que périlleux. C'est par une suite naturelle de Cette mobilité, que les Crües d'eau sont d'après leur nonSaison [...]

FIRST PAGE OF THE TABEAU NARRATIVE

Montreal Version

presenting themselves again and again under the same aspect, the remarks of Saturday often were the same as those of the previous Monday. That is why I decided, in order to avoid tiresome repetitions to combine the similar remarks and events. By this means I send you a product which embodies all that is interesting in the journal and which will be less wearisome for the reader. I have divided the whole into five parts. In the first chapter, I tell of the difficulties and dangers which travellers encounter in ascending the Missouri, the different places, the native products, so for fruits as for edible roots. In the second I give an account of some peculiar animals, of birds, of fish, and of reptiles, of the savage's use of the first, of the way in which they hunt. The third part deals with the tribes which live on the banks of the Missouri, with the wandering nations which periodically roam over its vast prairies, with their numbers, with their different languages, with their work, with their government. Here I take time to relate some very curious facts which show how much we have had to endure from these savages. The fourth gives some observations on trade and on the advantages it offers. Finally, in the fifth part, I speak of manners, customs, religion, superstition, quackery, etc. I have no doubt but that the journals of Captain Lewis and a few others will scarcely agree with mine, in many details of this last chapter, but I flatter myself that, after having associated with the savages in general during thirty years, after having afterwards lived two consecutive years among those in question, I have had more ways and occasions for knowing them, especially as I had business always with them, than one who sees them for a moment, who has only presents to give them and who flatters them by unlimited promises of a most glowing future. He can find them only mild and tractable.

You will notice, if you please, on reading this trash that it was meant only for the Illinois and, as the Missouri is known to almost all those who would have a chance to read it, I did not think myself bound to enter into details of which no one is ignorant, such as the villages established on the two banks, the distances between each trading post, the various rivers which flow into the Missouri. Thus you will find here only a very general idea of this great river and, as for the distance, you will keep as I to the estimation of old travellers who reckon the distance as 450 leagues from the mouth up to the Arikaras and from them 50 to the Mandans.

If the unadorned truth, as is said, could please in itself, I admit that one could read without distaste this account in which I have conjectured nothing and where my remarks have their source in events which happened before my eyes or from deeds which circumstances made indubitable. But as this saying is very dubious, as all that I have said is well known and of little interest, as being perhaps already known, it will not even have the charm of the new, I realize that it ought at least to be presented in a way that will make it readable. But living in an Arikara hut among four families, surrounded by a constant crowd of admiring imbeciles, disturbed every moment in order to dispute over a buffalo robe and to meet while trading all possible disagreements, I have hardly been in the mood to write connectedly and above all with pleasure. Therefore with much ill humor & little talent, I can offer you but a very tiresome narrative and I advise you to read it only on going to bed. I am

respectfully your servant & friend

P. A. TABEAUX.

TABEAU'S NARRATIVE
OF LOISEL'S EXPEDITION TO
THE UPPER MISSOURI

TABEAU'S NARRATIVE
OF LOISEL'S EXPEDITION TO
THE UPPER MISSOURI

THE MISSOURI

IF the truth unadorned could please in itself, as is affirmed, one might read this trash, in which I have attempted nothing purely conjectural, where I have, on the contrary, based all my remarks upon events that occurred before my eyes or upon acts that circumstances rendered indubitable.[1] But, since this principle is not always true and since all I have to say is not only very commonplace and of little interest; but, furthermore, being already known, will not even have the charm of novelty, I know[2] that it ought, at least, to be presented in a way that would make it readable. But, living in a Ricara hut,[3] surrounded by four families and by a continual crowd of ad-

[1] This first paragraph is, with scarcely any change, the concluding one of the covering, or prefatory, letter that accompanied the Montreal version and, in general, the second corresponds to the paragraph before the last of that letter.

[2] In both versions, we find *je scais* for *je sais* and, a few lines farther down, *imbecilles* for *imbeciles* (Tr.).

[3] The hut, as is stated explicitly later on in the narrative, was Kakawita's. There were, at the time, three Arikara villages. The first, in ascending the Missouri, was on an island and of that Kakawita was the chief. Lewis and Clark reached the island, October 8, 1804 (Thwaites, *Original Journals,* I, 183-84) and, two days afterwards, Sergeant Ordway visited it. The following is his account of what he saw:

"Wednesday 10th Oct a pleasant morning. I went down to the village which was built on the Island. found their lodges in this village about 60 in nomber and verry close compact. in a round form large & warm(ly) covered first after the wood is willows and Grass. Then a thick coat of Earth &. C. except the chimney hole which Goes out at center & top. they Raise considerable of Indian corn, beans pumkins Squasshes water millons a kind of Tobacco &. C. & C. they Supply several nations around them in corn as we are told. their is a 2 frenchman who trade here, Mr. Tabbo livees here now. has some Goods & trades with them for their peltry &. C. we left one of our frenchman with Mr Tabbow & took his Soon in his place. all things made ready to hold a counsel with the nation. they have used us in the most friendly manner. Gave us corn & beans dryed pumkins & Squasshes &. C. & C. Some of their women are verry handsome & clean &. C. & C." (Wisconsin Historical Society *Collections,* XXII, 149-50).

miring imbeciles, disturbed every moment in order to dispute over a buffalo robe and to meet, while trading, all possible disagreements, one is hardly capable of writing connectedly and, above all, with any pleasure. Consequently, with much ill-humor and little ability, I can offer only a very wearisome narrative and I advise that it be read only on going to bed. If my remarks can take the place of laudanum there will, at all events, be that advantage to him[4] who compels me to write them.

I shall not undertake to give an exact and geographical account of the Missouri. The way in which I made the voyage did not permit me to observe it with sufficient leisure and precision. Neither shall I take it upon myself to give a new estimate of distances between the different posts and known villages. Although the estimate of the old travelers may not be entirely correct, it cannot make any great difference in counting five hundred leagues from the mouth (of the Missouri) up to the villages of the Mandanes.[5] A description of the rivers which empty into the Missouri will also be wanting, as I have seen only their mouths and have not been able to get definite information concerning either their general course or their

[4] Until the Montreal version made its appearance this was taken naturally to refer to Loisel and I am still of the opinion that it did. It would be in the plural if Lewis and Clark had proposed the writing to him.

[5] In making the revised, or second, copy of the extract from his alleged journal, Tabeau gave the separate distances making up some such total. He began his narrative thus:

"Le Missouri a son embouchure a environ 25 arpents de largeur qu'il conserve presque toujours jusqu'aux villages de ricaras 450 lieuës, par cette raison il devient moins profond a mesure que l'on monte, surtout en perdant les eaux de la rivierre des osages a 40 lieuës, de la rivierre des Kanças a 100 lieuës, de la rivierre platte a 200 lieuës, & de la rivierre qui courre court [sic] a environ 300 lieuës. son cour général depuis chez les mandanes est a peu près du nord-west au sud-est. ..."

A comparison of these estimates with those of Truteau (Mississippi Valley Historical Review, VIII, 157 et seq.) and of Mackay (idem, X, 432 et seq.) presents some interesting differences. Only two of the rivers here mentioned by Tabeau came within the scope of Loisel's memorial (see Appendix VII). They were the Platte, and the Qui Court, or Niobrara. In agreement with Tabeau, Loisel placed the Platte, as had Truteau, two hundred leagues above the mouth of the Missouri; but the Qui Court three hundred and thirty. Mackay, whose computation stopped with the Rivière Blanche, where Perrin du Lac's journey ended, gave one hundred and seventy-one and a fourth leagues as the distance from the mouth of the Missouri to the mouth of the Platte.

sources. Consequently, I shall speak only of the different localities of the Missouri.

As far as I can conjecture the general course of the Missouri from its mouth up to the village of the Ricaras is from north-west to south-east. As far up as the Platte its windings are long and often imperceptible; but, above, its curves are so frequent that in a short distance it often makes the round of the compass. Its waters are always as muddy as those of the Ilinois and its deposits of the same kind.[6] The Savages[7] themselves do not know if this mud comes from one of its branches and, in their war expeditions, they have never gone far enough to find clear water. What is certain is that the water which comes from the large rivers which flow into the Missouri from the west even up to the Ricaras are loaded just as heavily as it is with the same material.

The Missouri preserves its width up to the Ricaras and because of this grows shallower, especially on losing the waters of the Platte and those of the River Qui Court. Moreover, it is not until one gets above these two rivers successively that one notices a diminution of the currents. Up to where they enter it is only by unbelievable efforts and precautions that the Missouri can be navigated. The extreme rapidity of the water over a bottom none too firm makes navigation difficult as well as perilous. It is due to the effect of the mobility of the bottom that the great rises of water not only sweep away high and large sand banks, but also cause good sized islands to disappear, cut

[6] "Les eaux sont extrêmement troubles, surtout dans les crues, ou elles ressemblent au caffé au lait" (Montreal version).

[7] To preserve the spirit of the original text as much as possible *savages,* wild men, as a synonym for Indians has been retained. It was very generally the designation used by early explorers and traders of all nationalities and continued to be that preferred by the French. Remarking upon that fact, Sir Richard Bonnycastle wrote:
"The French Canadian, or *voyageur par excellence,* always treats the Indian and the half-breed, when in the presence of an European, as vastly inferior in the scale of being to himself ; but such is the bond by which custom has united them, that this superciliousness is only shown in one simple word, and is very little evinced in outward bearing. If you ask the *voyageur* what are your *compagnons de voyage* (for the word *crew* is unknown in the polite vocabulary of a canoe), he will answer with the true national shrug, 'Ma foi! monsieur mon capitaine, ce sont des braves gens—des bons enfans—et d'ailleurs, c'est un assez joli canot;—mais, sacré! nous sommes *trois voyageurs,* et trois ne sont vraiment que *des sauvages.*' In short, the Canadian always calls the Indian and the half-breed a *savage*" (*The Canadas in 1841,* II, 14-15).

off wooded points, and create a new bed.[8] In consequence, each great rise, by the changes that it makes, renders useless the directions of operators as to the exact course that should be followed and leaves them only the advantage of judging from afar better than a new traveler could of the variety of the currents, of the formation of the banks, of the depth of the bottom, of the best ways of surmounting obstacles, and, finally, above all, of avoiding dangerous encampments.[9]

[8] A question here arises—did Loisel have personal knowledge and Tabeau also of just such a happening? In July, 1812, John C. Luttig and his party, after having camped at the mouth of the river that the French called *Petite Rivière des Sioux,* continued their journey and "passed Coup Loysele" (Drumm, Stella M., *Journal of a Fur-Trading Expedition on the Upper Missouri, 1812-1813,* pp. 45-46). The year before, Henry M. Brackenridge being in the same neighborhood, likewise "Passed *la coupe a L'Oiselle"* and jotted down the information that "This name originated, in the circumstance of a trader having made a narrow escape, being in the river at the very moment that this cut-off was forming. It had been a bend of fifteen miles round, and perhaps not more than a few hundred yards across; the gorge, which was suddenly cut through by the river, became the main channel" This was effected in a few hours" (Thwaites, R. G., *Early Western Travels,* VI, 81).

[9] Corroborative descriptions of the Missouri River, which was almost universally the subject of extended comment by early travelers, might be given almost *ad infinitum.* Perhaps the most detailed, antedating Tabeau's own, was that of Truteau. See the *Première Partie* already cited and the *Description du haut Missouri,* from which Victor Collot and Perrin du Lac so obviously and so copiously borrowed. A very interesting one by George Champlin Sibley, United States Factor for many years at Fort Osage, where he had opportunity to study the mighty river at his leisure, is to be found among the *Sibley Papers* at the Jefferson Memorial Building in St. Louis and at Lindenwood College, St. Charles, Missouri. Another is that of Gottfried Duden. *See* Bek, William G. (translator), *A report of a journey to the western states of North America, 1824-1827,* Missouri Historical *Review,* Vols. XII and XIII. Catlin's is worthy of remark likewise. See *North American Indians* (edition 1850), I, 17-18. First and last, many travelers have commented upon the superiority of the Missouri to the Mississippi, contending, indeed, that it is, in reality, the main stream, which must have been the thought behind the refrain in the great emigrant song:

To the West! To the West! To the land of the free!
Where the mighty Missouri rolls down to the sea."

One of our greatest travelers wrote that all who journey along it feel that the "Missouri has been ill used in having its name merged, after its junction with the Mississippi; whereas it is the broader, the deeper, the longer, and in every respect, the finer river of the two . . . ." (Murray, Charles Augustus, *Travels in North America, 1834, 1835, 1836,* I, 233). The blame for the transposition rests upon the Indians, so asserts J. P. Dunn (*Indiana: A Redemption from Slavery,* p. 16); but, in the eyes of the Reverend Timothy Flint, it was justifiable credit and not blame at all, although he conceded that the Missouri is "the largest tributary stream in the world" (*Recol-*

For want of this foresight it has often happened that travelers, camped on a bank, have suddenly discovered that it was sinking and, allowing them barely time to jump into their boat, it has disappeared before their eyes. This misfortune happened to me myself the 19th of May, 1804. Happily, having only a few things on land and the sand bank only partly and gradually crumbling away, I had time to embark, although I could not protect all of my powder, fifty pounds of which got wet.

Some *voyageurs* who had camped in a high, wooded cover, not realizing that underneath it was being undermined by the current, believed that they were quite safe at the very moment that the banks crumbled, sweeping away in their fall the trees which engulfed the cargo and the boat. Notwithstanding all the prudence and the foresight possible, these accidents cannot always be prevented; for, even while traveling, one is often obliged to face such risks for lack of other routes. We ourselves owed our safety to extraordinary good fortune, particularly on the ninth of July, about a league above the island of the Little Osages.[10] After repeated efforts made in vain to pass an obstruction (*embarras*), which extended very far out into the water, we were forced to give it up and, as the opposite bank was impracticable, we tried to open up a passage between the shore and the *embarras*. In order to do this it was necessary[11] to cut down many tree-trunks that blocked it, to pull away roots, and to enlarge the channel by digging out the earth. Having spent three hours and a half in this work, we were about to unmoor the barge, fastened at the foot of the *embarras*, in order to guide it to the passage; it had scarcely advanced its length, when a tree, twelve feet in circumference and of a similar length, was uprooted and fell with a horrible noise within ten or twelve feet of the helm. Another similar to it followed at the same instant and their fall, submerging one end of

---

lections of the Last Ten Years, p. 120). For a most appreciative description of the Missouri, "Mother of Floods," see Latrobe, Charles Joseph, *The Rambler in North America,* I, 130-34.

10 " ... particulierement le 9 Juillet 1803,— a quelque milles audessus d l'isle des petits os, près de 80 lieuës des ilinois ..." (Montreal version). Here, it is to be noted, the exact date is given, the year being added.

11 The "il faloit" of the text is corrected in the Montreal version, where appears "il falloit."

the *embarras,* lifted the other end and raised the trunks that we had cut more than twenty feet up into the air. Had the barge remained five minutes longer, where it had been for three and a half hours, I do not believe we should have seen any remains of it.

The 19th of the same month,[12] a tree about thirty feet high and from nine to ten inches in diameter was uprooted directly in front of the barge; but, as we were passing very near to it, it rested gently upon the loaded barge just as it started to lean and we escaped except for a scratch on the shoulder of one of our men. I cite only these two instances out of many, where we just missed being engulfed or harmed by the fall of trees, notwithstanding all our precautions and the foresight of a man named Guenneville, one of the most expert among the pilots of the Missouri.[13]

Great difficulties and frequent cases of shipwreck also occur from what are very appropriately called *embarras.* An *embarras* is an accumulation of trunks, roots, branches and entire trees swept away by the great rises of water, which are caught up first near the banks and are in a short time covered with mud and sand, which finally

12 "quelques jours apres, ..." (Montreal version).

13 " ... malgré les plus grandes précautions & toute la prévoiance d'un patron des plus experts parmi ceux du missouri" (Montreal version). The initial letter of this forehanded patron's name is plainly *G* in the text. In the Montreal version the name is omitted entirely at this place but appears later on and is clearly Quenneville. The person meant was probably the Quenneville of the supplementary instructions to Jean Baptiste Truteau and of the *Première Partie* of his journal. If this was François Quenneville, born 1742 (Tanguay, Mgr. C., *Dictionaire Généalogique des Familles Canadiennes,* VI, 477), he was yet trading on the Missouri, apparently, in 1812 and appears in the journal of John C. Luttig, clerk of the first American Missouri Fur Company, under the name of Queenville, for a biographical sketch of whom, see Drumm, Stella M., *Luttig's Journal of a Fur-Trading Expedition, op. cit.,* p. 60, n. 90. For comment upon Doane Robinson's suggestion identifying Quenneville with Pierre Quenelle, see Nasatir, Abraham P., *Jacques D'Eglise on the Upper Missouri,* Mississippi Valley Historical *Review,* XIV, 53, n. 32. Since Tabeau's spelling of the name here seems to have been Guenneville, it is interesting to recall that George Frederick Ruxton, in the course of his travels in the late forties, met with a trapper, named Gonneville, who "spoke the Sioux language, and was well acquainted with the nation" (*Life in the Far West,* p. 87). Having met an untimely death from a stray shot of hostile Indians, Gonneville was buried on the edge of a creek to which his name was given (*idem,* pp. 89, 91). There were two men of the name of Gonneville in the employ of the North West Company in early years, "Ant." and "Augustin" (Masson, *Les Bourgeois de la Compagnie du Nord-Ouest,* I, 402), and a Palais Gonneville in that of the Missouri Fur Company (*Pierre Chouteau, Jr., Papers* MHS).

stops them altogether. The first ones serve as a stay for others, which serve in turn for those which follow, and all by being entwined and gathered together become a solid mass and form an immovable bridge, all bristling with branches and stumps, which extends far out into the water.[14] The water, incapable of breaking this dyke, escapes from it with extreme rapidity and is often impassable with the oar and impracticable for towing. It is then necessary to cut, to pull away, to tear down. We have often passed entire half days at this slow and difficult work.

The most dangerous *embarras* are those where one may indeed, though with difficulty, overcome the current by rowing. The boat in this case remains some time without motion and the rudder, losing its effect, the boat runs the risk of lurching either upon the *embarras*, under which it can pass by submerging, or out into the open, which offers an equal danger in the stumps which are usually

[14] For a pictorial representation of the Missouri River as Truteau and Tabeau and many another saw it and have seen it from their day to this, full of floating logs, snags, and "sawyers," see *Original Paintings of Charles Bodmer to Illustrate the Travels of Maximilian, Prince of Wied, 1832-'34* (Thwaites, *Early Western Travels*, XXV, Plate 39). What I take to be a similar one is No. 213 of the *Lesueur Collection*, described by Waldo G. Leland, Mississippi Valley Historical *Review*, X, 53-78. Possibly the finest word picture of the stupendous turbid stream is that of Latrobe in his *Rambler, op. cit.,* I, 130-32, 275-80. For a definition of a Missouri River snag, see Palliser, John, *The Solitary Hunter, or Sporting Adventures in the Prairies,* p. 22.

"Sawyer" was a word quite frequently used to designate "a snag or tree so fixed in the river that it oscillates or bobs up and down by the force of the current . . . ." (Drumm, *Luttig Journal, op. cit.,* 39, n. Charles Dickens used and defined the term, when, in his *American Notes,* he described the Mississippi, which might have been the Missouri, so exactly like was the scene, mud and all. It was 1842 and here is what he wrote:

"But what words shall describe the Mississippi, great father of rivers, who (praise be to Heaven) has no young children like him! An enormous ditch, sometimes two or three miles wide, running liquid mud, six miles an hour; its strong and frothy current choked and obstructed everywhere by huge logs and whole forest trees; now twining themselves together in great rafts, from the interstices of which a sedgy lazy foam works up, to float upon the water's top; now rolling past like monstrous bodies, their tangled roots showing like matted hair; now glancing singly by like giant leeches; and now writhing round and round in the vortex of some small whirlpool, like wounded snakes. The banks low, the trees dwarfish, ... mosquitoes penetrating into every crack and crevice of the boat, mud and slime on everything, ... "For two days we toiled up this foul stream, striking constantly against the floating timber, or stopping to avoid those more dangerous obstacles, the snags, or sawyers, which are the hidden trunks of trees that have their roots below the tide . . . ."

to be met with. A well-built barge, which is not overloaded, can without much danger lean sideways against an obstruction, but the ordinary pirogues hardly do this with impunity. Our boat, although large and strong, came within an ace of being lost, on the twenty-second of June, opposite the tavern of Mombrun.[15] The *embarras* was so long that the strength of the rowers imperceptibly decreased and the pilot, seeing that the boat was no longer moving, brought it about a little too suddenly. The stern was not yet clear, the rudder struck and the currents, hitting it crosswise, threw the boat sideways upon the *embarras,* which was fortunately flanked by a great tree long enough for the entire side to rest against. Notwithstanding that, she almost upset in her leaning position and remained hanging there until our crew had rescued and righted her by making a counter-weight on the opposite side. Finally, after many efforts, they succeeded in bringing her to land by sliding her along her flank, still supported by the tree, and she was out of danger and had almost reached the barge, when the rudder caught again, and the boat, lurching out into the open, drifted rapidly upon the same obstruction. This time there remained little hope for us and, as a matter of fact, the shock was so violent that the water came over the side and would undoubtedly have swamped her, if the covers, which jutted far out, being caught between the tree and the pirogue, had not shut out a great deal of the water. With great difficulty the counter-weight of a dozen men put her to rights and so twice in the same place we owed our safety to her strength and height.

Aside from these perilous experiences that I have just described, the boats which ascend in high water have an infinite number of others to avoid to which, generally, they are exposed on every side. The great floods make themselves felt, ordinarily only in May and June; but, contrary to custom, they ceased for us only at the end of

---

[15] The Montreal version is a little more precise as to time and place: " ... le 22 juin 1830, a la taverne a monbrun — 33 lies des ilinois — ..." Mackay placed "Caverne de Mont brun" thirty-two and one-half miles from the mouth of the Missouri (Abel, *Mackay's Table of Distances,* Mississippi Valley Historical Review, X, 433). Lewis and Clark were in the neighborhood of "a *Cave Called Monbrun,*" May 30, 1804 (*Original Journals, op. cit.,* I, 36). On the Lewis and Clark itinerary map, the name appears as *Caverne de Montbrun, Cavern à Montbrun* (Abel, *A New Lewis and Clark Map,* Geographical *Review,* I, opposite p. 344).

August. Furthermore, we encountered all the inconveniences that this river could present to *voyageurs,* whom the currents have impeded. Sometimes our *engagés,* by swimming, carried a long towline to throw over a stump or some solid root and we ascended in this way by means of repeated towing, making sometimes only two or three miles a day. Sometimes they were in the water, tearing up roots or hewing down trees which closed our passage. In coves, where the ground was less firm, it was necessary to cut down trees, the fall of which was to be feared in the channel, and often, moreover, these expedients, being impracticable in the bays and points bordered by young willows, the only way was to seize the branches and to ascend in this manner by passing them from one hand to another, a maneuver less expeditious than fatiguing. These points were almost all inundated. The night having overtaken us many times in such places the rowers, wearied with toil, having lain as best they could upon the boats, refreshed themselves only with difficulty from the labors of the day. Slight elevations were met with at times but scarcely had they been trod upon for an hour or more before the water came through and compelled us to embark. It was hardly possible to spread mosquito-nets over the boats and, of all the inconveniences and sufferings of the voyage, mosquitoes[16] should be put down as the worst, and nowhere can more be seen. During the whole day the boats were enveloped as in a cloud and the *engagés,* who were compelled by the extreme heat to keep the body naked, were covered with blood and swellings. Often our hunters, not being able to endure them, returned at full speed to throw themselves into the boats. What is more they could not aim their weapons when covered with these insects. In short, the mosquitoes, not leaving the crew at liberty to take its food in the evening or its rest at night, exhausted it as much as did all the work of the day and they helped not a little to weaken it to the extent that a part falling ill in succession there was almost never a full force.

[16] *Maringoins,* the word of the French text, Washington version, is, in the Montreal version, changed to the more correct *maringouins.* It was not alone on the Upper Missouri that mosquitoes proved a terrible pest in the early days and many a trader or traveler might be found to dispute with Tabeau the statement he made on revision, " ... & il y en a certainement plus dans le haut missouri, que dans aucune partie du monde."

63

The dearth of hunting is another necessary result of high water. The animals, not being able to approach the Missouri, remain far away on the prairies and upon the high land along the little rivers. Thus this resource, always precarious, was infinitely so for us, to whom it was becoming every day more needful. As a voyage, retarded by so many mishaps, did not allow us to reach, as early as planned, the places where we had thought to find Savages, the provisions of the crew were short from the twenty-second of August until the village of the Mahas[17] Happily, Mr. Loisel had in his cargo some hundreds of pounds of flour; but this amount could furnish subsistence to thirty men for a few days only.[18] Besides, boiled flour without fat is a very mean nourishment for men who work without intermission. However it might be, this resource, joined to the activity of our hunters, sustained us almost a month, sometimes in abundance, but very often in want. We had frequently the luck to meet old bulls that are called here, coast-guards, because, not having the strength to go far, they were found in this locality constantly. It is to be presumed that many that we killed paid but a few hours

[17] For almost contemporary accounts of the location of the Maha, or Omaha, villages and the condition of the tribe, see Truteau, American Historical *Review*, XIX, 307; Mississippi Valley Historical *Review*, VIII, 161; and Perrin du Lac, *op. cit.*, p. 208. The authoritative work on the sociology of the tribe is La Flesche, Francis, *The Omaha Tribe*, Bureau of American Ethnology *Report*, 1914-15.

[18] A comparison of the two texts here will illustrate rather well Tabeau's method of revision and his disposition to ignore Loisel.

" ... car une marche rallentie par tant d'obstacles, ne nous ayant pas permi de nous rendre aussitot que nous l'avions présumé aux lieux ou nous pensions trouver des Sauvages, les provisions de l'équipage ont manque dès le vingt deux d'aoust au village des mahas. heureusement que mm. loisel avec dans sa cargaison quelques cents livres de farine, mais dont le quantité ne pouvoit fournir que quelques jours a la subsistance de trente hommes. ..." (Washington version).

" ... car une marche relentie par tant d'obstacles, ne nous ayant par permis de nous rendre aussitot que nous l'avions présumé aux lieux ou nous esperions trouver des sauvages, les provisions manquerent a l'équipage dès le 22 d'aoust, deux mois après notre départ, a peu près a 300 lieuës des ilinois. heureusement que nous avions en réserve quelques sacs de fleur pour nôtre provision particuliére, qu'il a fallu sacrifier; encore la quantité n'a-t-elle pu fournir que quelques jours a la subsistance de trente hommes, en bien oeconomisant ..." (Montreal version).

The "avec" in the Washington version was obviously a slip of the pen for *avait*. The plural form of the verb being required in the Montreal version, Tabeau put it there.

earlier the debt to nature.[19] The Savages even claim that they thus expose themselves to view on the hills in order to invite the hunter to free them from a life that they have come to find burdensome. We rendered them this service cheerfully; but their flesh, although hard and glutinous, seemed to us quite tasty and it was too necessary to us not to deprive us of all the merit of doing a kindness.

Those who travel at low water on ascending the Missouri escape the greater part of the dangers that I have just described. The currents are infinitely less rapid; and, as the sand-banks follow one another and are everywhere uncovered, the *voyageurs* ascend almost always by means of the pole and avoid all the *embarras,* the landslides and other obstacles. For the same reason the Missouri is then very dangerous to descend, especially above the River Platte, where there being but a single channel sufficiently deep, but very difficult to distinguish, one may often miss it and run aground on the banks where the rapidity of the current may upset a boat or force it ashore. Below, the channel is often very narrow and, being filled with trunks of trees and with logs firmly fixed in the earth, it is only by winding in and out that one avoids their encounter and this maneuver, not always possible of being executed with the requisite speed, the boats are broken or swamped. Three-fourths of the ship-wrecks in descending the Missouri have occurred in this way.

Game is very abundant at low water. From the River of the Osages to the River Platte the roebuck is seen everywhere, bounding over the flats; turkey hens abound on the points; wild cats are common; and bears are met with quite often. Above this river, particularly on the points and on the islands, herds of does and some roebucks are found, but neither the one nor the other is sufficiently common for us to advise anyone's venturing to hunt with a small-sized party.

[19] This is an expression that was much in vogue in the first half of the nineteenth century, a lingering influence, perhaps, of the emphasis that had been put upon Nature and her laws in the eighteenth. It is found, not alone in travel narratives, but in official communications likewise. President Monroe used it, for example, when referring to the men of American Revolutionary War times, "Most of those very meritorious citizens," wrote he, "have paid the debt of nature and gone to repose" (*First Annual Message,* December 2, 1817, Richardson, James, *Messages and Papers of the Presidents,* II, 19).

The two banks of the Missouri are well wooded as far as the approaches to the River Platte. With the exception of the cottonwood, the papaw, and the persimmon, which rarely grow above the River of the Kancas, almost the same kinds of trees are seen there as on the Ilinois.[20] Then vast and high prairies, separated from the river by low and humid plains, present to the eye a monotonous expanse. These low plains are ordinarily inundated by the waters of the Missouri and, as they are bounded by a strip of land a little higher, which borders the river, they are without an outlet and the water stays there a very long time. The streams and little rivers become more and more rare in ascending and, above the River Qui Court, they are seldom seen.

Then the hills again approach the Missouri and offer a different and an uglier perspective.[21] The wooded points, at a great distance from each other, are rarely half a league in length by three or four arpents[22] in breadth; the greater part of them offer only a narrow border of cottonwoods, willows, squat ash, and stunted oaks. The little islands, subject to inundation and to being washed away by the high waters, become gradually still more rare and are seldom seen above the Ricaras. From the River Qui Court up to the Fork,[23] a

20 The thought of this passage is somewhat better and more fully expressed in the following:

"les deux rives du missouri sont assez bien boisées, jusqu'aux approches de la rivierre platte, & c'est là ou commence ce qu'on nomme ordinairement le haut missouri, par ce qu'audessus tout devient different. jusques là, si l'on excepte l'asseminier, le piaqueminier, & le cotonier, qui ne croissent gueres audessus de la rivierre des kanças, on voit presque toutes les especes de bois de haute futaie & les mêmes arbrisseaux qu'aux ilinois. ..." (Montreal version).

21 Tabeau saw fit to modify this, writing, in his Montreal version, "& offrent une perspective encore differente, mais beaucoup plus désagréable."

22 The arpent was the "French acre, a square the side of which is 193 feet, 3 inches ..." (*Pond Papers*, Michigan Pioneer and Historical *Collections*, XXXVII, 437, n. 64, 437-38; Scharf, *History of St. Louis City and County*, I, 135, n.; Quaife, *Askin Papers*, I, 28, n. 4). According to Bradbury (Edition of 1817, p. 189): "The arpent is to the statute acre nearly in the proportion of 83 to 100." For the estimate put upon it by the United States Commissioners on Land Claims in 1806, see American State Papers, *Public Lands*, I, 264.

23 In Missouri River parlance, by the "Fork" was invariably meant the River Cheyenne and, according to Truteau, it was some hunters who first applied the name (Mississippi Valley Historical *Review*, VIII, 165). The "Courche" of Loisel's memorial (Appendix VII), being, as he himself said, the River Cheyenne, is obviously the

distance of about a hundred and twenty leagues, I noticed six in a radius of probably one league. They are the two islands of the Poncas, the island of Bonhomme, the island of Basque, and the two Cedar islands.[24] These last two are covered with the most beautiful red cedars that one could desire.

Behind and between all the low points are small arid hills, the greater part bare or covered with short grasses, which show only a hard, black surface, as if burnt. On following the shore many layers

---

result of a misreading of the text, French or Spanish. At their junction, the Upper and Lower Red rivers were called, similarly, "The Forks" (Harmon, Daniel, *Journal of Voyages*, edition of 1820, p. 141), sometimes, also, the Qu'Appelle and the Assiniboine. For the use of the term by Simon Fraser, see Letter to James McDougall, dated Natleh, 30 September 1806, Canadian Archives *Report* 1929, p. 153, and for "Fort Fork" at the junction of the Smoky with the Peace River, Howay, F. W., *An Identification of Sir Alexander Mackenzie's Fort Fork*, Royal Society of Canada, *Transactions*, 1928, XXII, 165-73. Thwaites calls attention to the fact that the Cheyenne River of North Dakota must not be confounded "with the Missouri affluent in South Dakota." The former "is the largest western tributary of Red River of the North" (*Early Western Travels*, XXII, 342 n.).

[24] In the matter of these geographical details, Tabeau is not altogether in agreement with his contemporaries. If by the "Fork," he really did mean the Cheyenne, he might have added to the number of his islands very considerably. By Mackay, by Truteau, and by the maker or makers of the Lewis and Clark itinerary map, the island of *Bonhomme* was placed below instead of above the River *Qui Court*. It retains the name today, a name that has also been given to a South Dakota county and town. Tabeau's "l'isle au Basque" was Truteau's "l'isle abasque" and situated in the vicinity of the present Wheeler, South Dakota. Mackay called it "Ile du Basque" and the legend of the itinerary map is, "I au Basques," of the Perrin du Lac, "J. des Basques." A post of the Company of the Missouri was near the cedar island next beyond; and, if by the second cedar island, Tabeau meant the one on which Loisel's fort was, then he must have meant the Cheyenne when he spoke of the "Fork." That he did mean the site of Loisel's building is quite evident from the additional details of the Montreal version:

" ... depuis la rivierre qui courre jusqu'aux villages des ricaras, espace d'environ 120 lieuës, on en trouve six remarquables en ce qu'elles ont environ une lieuë de circuit, ce sont les deux isles des poncas l'isle a bonhomme, l'isle aux basques, & les deux isles aux cédres, ces deux derniéres dont l'une est a 15 lieuës audessus de la rivierre qui courre & l'autre a 50 lieuës audessus des ricaras, sont couvertes des plus beaux cédres rouges qu'on puisse désirer. nous avons construit un fort de pieux dans la derniere ou nous avons hyverné avec les titons, de 83 a 84.-"

With reference to the passage just quoted it will be observed that Loisel's name is not mentioned and that a joint enterprise is hinted at. The dates, as given, are decidedly wrong. Quite likely the transcriber mistook in each instance *0* for *8*.

In between the two cedar islands were many others that Tabeau failed to mention.

of earth of diverse colors are to be seen on the bluffs. I noticed stratas of yellow, red, sulphur, and verdigris[25] which could perhaps be used by daubers. The Savages use them for paste, especially that from a black earth. They color their buffalo-robes and other skins with it and neither the rain nor the longest use effaces the imprint. Among these stratas of earth there is also found some plaster, which is also very common upon the small hills. A quantity of pumice stones which were found upon the bank indicates volcanoes, and the Savages know them in the Black Hills; but they could not tell me anything about the nature of the lavas nor about the time and the force of the eruptions.

I say nothing about the minerals, having seen no sign of them and not having been able upon this subject to draw any information from the Savages to whom all the glittering pebble-work is mineral.[26] Nevertheless, the Chayennes let me see a bit of lead mineral which they had brought from the Black Hills. Brackish springs are more common and, a little above the island of the Poncas, on the west bank, a brook supplies them very strong and abundant and in sufficient quantities to lead us to believe that their sources are not far distant. The Ricaras assert that they are common on the prairies which separate them from the Black Hills[27] and our hunters upon the Fork, having barely tasted some spring-water, were purged as by a strong dose of Glauber's salts.[28]

[25] The "verd degris" of both versions might more correctly be *vert-de-gris*.

[26] Loisel, following out his own instructions had probably asked Tabeau to be on the watch for signs or news of mineral wealth; for, as John Meares once remarked (*Voyages, 1788 and 1799*, p. 248): "The Spanish .... have the keenest scent of any people for those riches which are contained in the bowels of the earth ...." and Loisel's *Memorial* would support the supposition that minerals came within the purview of his investigation.

[27] In the Montreal version, the paragraph ends with the reference to the Black Hills, *des côtes noires,* and, from this point, the arrangement of material as between the two versions begins to differ, the equivalent of the succeeding paragraph coming in, in the Montreal version, after a consideration of the fruits and roots, *Des Fruits et Des Racines,*" which precedes that of the animals, the latter constituting "*Chapitre 2ème.*"

[28] For almost precisely the same account of the purgative property of the Missouri River water, it being pronounced as effective as a dose of Glauber's Salts, see Lewis's *Statistical View* (1807), p. 180. See also the journal entry for April 11, 1805 (*Original Journals*, I, 295; Coues, *History of the Lewis and Clark Expedition,* I, 266, and

I believe that a fuller description is not necessary to show that the Missouri, at least from the River Platte almost up to the Ricaras, cannot be suitable for a large settlement and that the lack of wood alone would be more and more an insuperable obstacle. The soil would not be quite as unproductive on the wooded points as on some of the islands and the Ricaras, who cultivate both, reap there a considerable amount of maize and other crops as a result of their planting. It is true that they cultivate only new lands, being forced to change their habitation often for want of wood which they exhaust in five or six years.[29] The Mandanes, also tillers of the soil, are more con-

---

n. 22). Alexander Henry, on his way to the Missouri, remarked of some lakes about six leagues distant, "The beach is often covered with salt which has the same taste as Glauber Salts and produces the same effect" (*Coventry Copy*, I, 434, with which compare Coues, *New Light on the History of the Greater Northwest*, I, 316, n. 33), an observation that Lewis similarly made (*Original Journals*, VI, 51). From the Montreal version the allusion to Glauber's Salts is omitted, although not that to the mineral character of the waters:

"je ne dis rien des minereaux n'en ayant vu nulle appearance, & n'ayant pu tirer des sauvages aucune lumiere a ce sujet, les chasseurs françois ont rencontré quelquefois des fontaines dont les eaux sulphureuses & saumâtres sont très purgatives, & quelques uns des nôtres l'ont éprouvé a leurs dépends. A quelques arpents audessus de l'isle des poncas, a gauche en montant, un petit ruisseau fournit des eaux salines très fortes & assez abondantes a l'embouchure, pour faire croire que ses sources ne sont pas éloignées, les ricaras disent qu'elles sont très fréquentes dand l'espace qui les sépare des côtes noires.-"

29 While Truteau was dwelling with the Arikara Indians, 1795, they abandoned the villages they were then occupying, "pour ce retirer au près des mandannes" (Mississippi Valley Historical *Review*, VIII, 164-65). They were "at a distance of nearly four hundred and thirty leagues from the Illinois" (Missouri Historical Society *Collections*, IV, 31). For Charles La Raye's description of them as they appeared in 1802, see David I. Bushnell's *Villages of the Algonquian, Siouan, and Caddoan Tribes West of the Mississippi*, Bureau of American Ethnology, *Bulletin*, No. 77, p. 168. As Lewis and Clark ascended the Missouri, in 1804, they noted the remains of several abandoned Arikara villages (*Original Journals*, I, 172, 175, 179, 181; *Ordway Journal*, pp. 143, 144, 147, 158), one of which appeared to have been occupied as recently as the preceding winter (*Original Journals*, I, 182). Some of these abandoned Arikara villages are indicated on the Lewis and Clark itinerary map (The Geographical *Review*, I). Since Grand River in South Dakota is known to the Sioux generally as Arikara River, it is "probable that the Arikara formerly had their residence there for a long period" (Mooney, James, *Calendar History of the Kiowa*, Bureau of American Ethnology *Report*, 1895-6, p. 158). W. P. Clark thinks that the common home of the Arikara and the Pawnee must have been the Platte (*The Indian Sign Language*, p. 282) and that to that ancestral home the former returned in a body in 1833, continu-

stant in their homes; because the timber begins to increase in their territory and the larger points are far better supplied with trees. Nevertheless, from the River Qui Court up to their place inclusively there are to be found only very inferior cottonwoods, suitable for making ordinary pirogues.[30]

ANIMALS

THE buffalo is the most common animal of the Upper Missouri[1] and it is of the greatest usefulness to the large number of wandering nations that dwell there.[2] The twenty-fifth of January some Ricaras coming from the Fork, some others from near

---

ing there with the Ski-di band of the latter two years (*idem,* p. 283). The fact of their going is not disputed; but the dates given are not those of contemporary evidence, the one is a little too late, the other, a little too early. For references to the *Fort Tecumseh Letter* Book and other contemporary sources on this matter, see Abel, *Chardon's Journal at Fort Clark,* n. 30 and n. 494.

[30] Because of the inclusion of the Gros Ventres as agriculturists, the enumeration of the vegetable products cultivated, and the misfortune overtaking the Arikaras in 1830, it seems wise to quote from the Montreal version the closing paragraph of *Chapitre Premier*:

"Je pense que sur la description que je viens de faire du haut missouri, on ne croit guères susceptible d'établissement, au moins depuis la rivierre platte jusques chez les mandanes, & que le deffaut de bois y mettra toujours un obstacle invincible. la nature du sol an général se refuseroit a toute production, il est vrai que la terre ne seroit pas mauvaise dans quelques pointes basses & quelques isles dont j'ai parlé, & les ricaras qui cultivent les unes & les autres, récoltent assez de mahy, de feves, de citrouilles &c. en rason de leurs semences. mais il faut remarquer qu'ils n'ensemencent que les terres neuves, étants forcés de changer souvent d'habitation, faute de bois qu'ils ruinent en cinq a six ans, d'ailleurs ces pointes & ces isles sont petites, très éloignées les unes des autres & la plupart sujettes a l'innondation, comme l'ont éprouvé les ricaras qui ont perdu toute leur récolte en 1803. les mandanes & les gros ventres qui sont aussi cultivateurs, sont plus constants que ceux-ci sur les mêmes éstablissements, parce que là les pointes sont plus grandes & que les bords du missouri commencent a être boisés de plus en plus en montant. ce qui est certain c'est que de bien audessous de l'isle aux cédres, jusques chez les mandanes inclusivement, on ne trouve (encore que très rarement) de mauvais liards propres a construire de médiocres pirogues."

[1] This note appears in the margin of the original text: "which I call thus above the River Platte."

[2] Had Tabeau's highly instructive and interesting narrative been published at the time it was written, H. A. Trexler's statement would not be true that "The first trav-

the Mandanes reported that, in this space of ninety leagues, they saw — if I may say so — only a single herd that overran the prairie. Two days after, some Chayennes coming from the Black Hills, found so many in their journey of seventy leagues that they reckoned them as countless upon this area of 6,300 leagues.[3]

Every autumn these animals periodically pass from the north to the south, from whence they return in the springtime at the first good weather. The winter obliges them to abate their march and to approach the great rivers, as much to be in the shelter in the ravines as to find pasture there on the low points and in the brush of the little streams. The small rare herds of bulls are always separated from the cows in this season and the only bulls to be found there are the young ones that follow their mothers. They do not approach each other and mingle until towards the fifteenth of July and this reassembling that nature has ordered for the increase of the species lasts hardly more than a month. The great disproportion of males and females makes it so that a large number of cows do not produce at all and that the bull is so weakened that he cannot recover soon enough to endure the rigor of the winter and that even those that vigor and youth have sustained do not regain their weight until the middle of May. Therefore, the buffalo (bull) is never fat except for two months in the year while the cow, on the contrary, is almost always so. I know that upon the banks of the Belle Riviere[4] (Ohio) and of

---

clers to describe the buffalo country of the upper Missouri were Lewis and Clark. They wrote in minute detail of all the natural resources, but especially of the game" (*The Buffalo Range of the Northwest,* Mississippi Valley Historical *Review,* VII, 349).

[3] In his revision, at the beginning of his second chapter, Tabeau was able to add to his witnesses:

"Le buffle ou boeuf ilinois est l'animal de plus grande nécessité pour le grand nombre des nations ambulantes qui l'habitent. aussi y est-il le plus commun & dans une abondance incroyable. Le 18 de janvier, des ricaras arriverent chez moy de chez les mandanes, le même jour que l'autres revenants de la fourche, ce qui fesoit 90 lieuës le long du missouri. les uns & les autres me rapporterent qu'ils n'avoient vu, pour ainsi dire, qu'un même troupeau qui couvroit tout cet espace. Deux jours après des chayennes venants de soixante dix lieuës dans la profondeur *sud-west,* & quelques Sioux venant de 40 lieuës *est* du coté de la rivierre des mohens, m'ont fait le même rapport que les premiers. quel nombre innombrable d'animeaux, sur une superficie de près de dix mille lieuës!"

[4] The Ohio River, notwithstanding the assertion of George Catlin (*North American Indians,* II, 185) that the French called the Wisconsin, *La belle rivière.*

the Mississippi the buffalo recovers speedily among the canes and other rich pasturage; but here where he travels only over vast arid prairies, where, in the fall, he finds in some valleys only pasture that is dry and without substance, where the earth covered with snow in November reappears only at the end of March, he cannot regain strength until the grass of springtime becomes sufficiently nourishing.

The cow [buffalo] leaving the banks of the Missouri at the first good weather, the wandering tribes leave also in order to follow her by wandering as she does. From then on up to August, only the people who till the soil are seen there;[5] for the others are not able to subsist as the cow is their only resource. In truth, she furnishes them not only everything of absolute necessity but also much that is useful and even superfluous. The flesh is a substantial food and one to their liking; the skin serves for lodging them well and for clothing them in every season; the horns and the bones give them implements and necessary tools; the sinews give them thread; the paunches make their vessels; and the spun wool yields the women ornaments and other superfluities. Finally, there is the head which serves them for household gods. It is evident that with the bow and arrow the Savages of the Upper Missouri can easily do without our trade, which becomes necessary to them only after it has created the needs.

But, if the hunt is a resource so general for the wandering nations, it is no less precarious and there are frequent instances of families and of entire tribes, which, notwithstanding their precaution of drying their meat against a shortage, have experienced horrible famine and have sometimes died of hunger. During the months of November and December, 1804,[6] the Bois Brulés, the Okondanes, and

5 " ... qui sont les mahas, les poncas, les ricaras, & les mandanes," inserts the Montreal version, omitting the Gros Ventres added earlier.

6 In re-narrating this incident, Tabeau made a correction or a mistake in the year, substituting intentionally or inadvertently 1803 for 1804. He likewise omitted the name of Hugh Heney:

"pendant les mois d 9bre & 10bre 1803 = les bois brulés, les okondanes & les saones, trois tribus *sioux titons,* dont les premiers étoient avec nous a l'isle aux cédres & les autres quinze lieües plus haut, ont été réduits a la derniere extremité. ..."

In neither version does Tabeau give a clue as to what month he meant by "9bre." Did he mean the one with the numeral *nine* or did he mean the ninth in the Gregorian calendar, September? A similar question applies to "10bre."

the Saones, Siouses tribes, the first of which was with us[7] at the Isle of Cedar and the others with Mr. Henney[8] at the Fork, were reduced to the last extremity. It is true that the Bois Brulés, on our arrival among them, deprived themselves in our favor of more than a thousand pieces of dried meat;[9] but this quantity would have supplied food for only a few days longer for eight or nine hundred mouths. Besides, the situation of many families, almost dying, often compelled us to supply them in our turn and their own provisions, better economized in our hands, have certainly been of more prolonged help to them. The begging dancers, the lodge of the soldiers, that of the chiefs and principal men carried away from us many pieces daily; not that their manner of demanding was positively menacing, but prudence did not permit us to refuse them in this critical circumstance, where it was even astonishing that hunger did did not drive them to some act of violence in order to carry away our provisions which they always believed more plentiful than they were. The women came in a crowd to trade certain trifles, sure of obtaining a few pieces of dried meat into the bargain. When our *engagés* took their meals they surrounded them, holding their babies to the breast, the innocent cries of whom and the expressive signs would have excited compassion in the most unsympathetic man. I say nothing of their favors which they offered for a few mouthfuls. The husbands, who seemed to pardon the union, paid no attention, being sufficiently occupied in disputing over the soup and in quarreling, even to overturning the kettle sometimes to their great regret. Finally, at the beginning of January, the cold weather brought back the cow and the abundance lasted until the departure of the Savages at the end of February. Their quick forgetfulness of the past and their indifference in this respect proved conclusively that they were accustomed to these long privations.

[7] Loisel and Tabeau.

[8] Hugh Heney. By reference to n. 6, it will be seen that the name of Heney was also left out in the revision, although he must have been one of "les autres quinze lieüs plus haut." Mentioned as Heney is in the Washington text, the question might well be asked, Was the Loisel-Heney trade agreement of July, 1801 (See Appendix VI), slated to expire one year hence, yet in force in the winter of 1803-4, when Loisel and Tabeau were at the Isle of Cedars?

[9] "ces piéces peuvent être évaluées 15 lbs chaque" (Montreal version).

When the Ricaras lack maize, which happens very often, they find that the buffalo cow is also a very uncertain resource. On my arrival at their village,[10] I found there only some old people exposed to every danger and hardly keeping up the remnant of their vitality with flowers of the summer pear, with young branches of willow, with sweet grass, and other herbage. Even after the return of the hunters, who for two months scoured the prairies, and until the young pumpkins were eatable, the three villages lived in a state of destitution, which would pass among us for dreadful famine. I myself paid almost the price of a buffalo-robe for a piece of dried meat weighing four or five pounds, of which the owner divested himself only out of respect.

The 14th of July[11] a dead buffalo passed in the drift in front of the island.[12] The old men, the women, the children, all swimmers, threw themselves before it and tried to stop it. The odor spread itself over two or three acres and I found it impossible to draw near. Nevertheless, as hungry wolves, they disputed among themselves and fought, while tearing and rending this disgusting prey.[13] A part was

---

[10] The Montreal version supplies us with the exact time of this arrival:

" ... a mon arrivée a leurs villages le 24 de may 1804, je n'y ai trouvé que quelques vieilles personnes abandonées a tout hasard & quelques enfants ..."

[11] Another instance of correction or change in time:

"Le 14 de juin, avant le retour des chasseurs, un boeuf mort probablement depuis longtemps, passe a la dérive, devant le village ou j'étois fixé ..." (Montreal version).

[12] The island, not mentioned in the revision, must have been the one on which the Arikara village was and the year, 1804.

[13] For this, to us, disgusting practice Chardon's *Fort Clark Journal* affords instances. Alexander Henry noted that the dried meat of the Big Bellies (Gros Ventres) was "nearly in a putrid state, the pieces would scarcely adhere together. This however is entirely to their taste and they very seldom make use of meat until it is rotten" (*Coventry Copy*, I, 505-6; Coues, I, 356-57). The Mandanes, he also affirmed, seldom eat their meat until it smells (*Coventry Copy*, I, 448-49) and much preferred the drowned buffalo to the hunted and killed (*idem*, p. 479). From Charles Mackenzie comes similar testimony:

"Buffaloes and other animals are in immense numbers destroyed every winter by the Missouri Indians. In stormy weather whole droves run from the Mountains and plains to seek shelter in the woods which form the margin of the Missouri — many of them attempting to cross when the weak sink and are drowned — and in the Spring both sides of the River are in several places covered with rotten carcasses and skeletons of Buffaloes, Elks &c.— these dead animals, which often float down the current among the ice for hundreds of miles, are preferred by the natives to any other kind of food: — When the skin is raised you will see the flesh of a greenish hue, and

eaten raw on the spot and the remainder brought to the village, chasing us away by its odor.[14] Some days before, three families had arrived, weakened by the long fasts and hardly able to stand after three months' journey across the prairies. The Sioux, the Chayennes, and other wandering nations reckon everything from the periods in which famine has made terrible ravages among them, the details of which would take too much time to narrate and I return to the animals.

After the cow, the deer is the most useful animal to the Savages who live on the Upper Missouri. But, although very common, es-

---

ready to become alive at the least exposure to the sun; and is so ripe, so tender, that very little boiling is required — the stench is absolutely intolerable — yet the soup made from it which is bottle green is reckoned delicious: — So fond are the Mandanes of putrid meat that they bury animals whole in the winter for the consumption of the Spring.

"The water of the Missouri this Spring [1805] was uncommonly low, and in consequence drowned animals were not so very abundant as usual at the breaking up of the navigation. However there were still plenty, and I had the opportunity of observing the courage and dexterity of the young Mandanes among the floating ice, hauling ashore some scores of these nauseous carcasses, while the women, as active as they, were securing for fire all the drift wood within their capacity" (Mackenzie, Charles, *Some Account of the Missouri Indians in the years 1804, 5, 6 & 7*, pp. 36-38, *Masson MSS*, Photostat, Dominion Archives, Ottawa).

An idea of the number of drowned buffalo that might be available for the needs of the Missouri Indians can be obtained from the number counted by John Mac-Donell farther north:

18 May 1795 — "The Brigade & I left the Forks of the River qui appelle about Sunrise say 9 Canoes & 3 Boats, well loaded — My canoe having an extra man I took the lead, intending to have spare time to Hunt, and prepare for the arrival of the other craft at Mountain a la Basse — Observing a good many carcases of Buffaloes in the River & along its banks, I was taken up the whole day with counting of them & to my surprise found I had numbered when we put up at night 7360 Drownd & Mired along the River and in it — It is true in one or two places I went on shore & walkd from one Carcase to the other where they lay from three to five files deep . . . ." (*Journal of "John MacDonell,"* 1793-1795, *Masson MSS*, Photostat, Dominion Archives, Ottawa).

[14] A first reading of the original of the Washington version, blurred here almost to the point of obliteration, would warrant, "& le reste apporté au village nomme en chasse par son odeur" (and the remainder carried to the village, called from the hunt by its odor); but a reference to the typewritten copy of the Montreal version, where the corresponding passage reads, "& les restes apportés au village, nous en chassent par l'odeur insupportable," justifies the sentence as given, although it appear, syntactically, incomplete.

pecially in the springtime[15] on the low points and on the islands, they are not sufficiently so to feed and to clothe these ever numerous hordes. Besides, no special hunt is made of them there but only an incidental. The fat roe, very inferior to the cow, is, nevertheless, very good meat and the deer is of all the animals the one that yields the most beautiful tallow in very great quantity. The skins furnish the women with garments, finer and better for wearing than does the hide of the cow, and the antlers supply many tools that are a necessity to them. The men make of them bows strengthened with sinew, which are highly prized as uniting elegance with strength and elasticity. The deer pursues the female in August and, as the females are also in a disproportionate number, this sultan is exhausted with his seraglio and would perish as the buffalo if he took as much pleasure in the prairies; but, contrariwise, he, immediately after his amorous labors, confines himself to the low points and the islands where the pasturage suffices to recuperate him before the winter. The doe, like the female of the roebuck, bears one, often two, and sometimes three fawns.

Roebucks are found on all the wooded points, especially as far up as the River Qui Court. But above these points they are so few and so small that the species would be exterminated in a short time were the Savages to hunt there. The flesh, so delicate everywhere else, is there only very passable and, however fat it may be, is always without savor. That of the black-tailed roebuck is still more unsavory.

The black-tailed roebuck,[16] although of another species, differs little from the common roebuck. Nevertheless, it is generally larger with a black tail as well as a long black stripe upon the back. Its ears are longer; but that which the more distinguishes it, is its singular run. It jumps like the rabbit and its haunches are bent in such a way that at each leap it seems as if about to squat. More timid or more cunning than the common roebuck it is more difficult to surprise and is rarely deceived by the hunter whom it has seen or heard. It does

15 Here also Tabeau corrected himself:

" ... mais quoiqu'assez commun surtout en automne dans les pointes basses et dans les isles, ..." (Montreal version).

16 For an account of the black-tailed deer, see Grinnell, *op. cit.*, II, 267; Palliser, John, *Solitary Rambles and Adventures of a Hunter in the Prairies*, p. 176; Thwaites, *Early Western Travels*, XXII, 340, n. 309.

not stay long anywhere except upon the hills, from whence it may discern from afar everything around it. Although the two species copulate with the female in the same season, the Savages assert that they do not pair and that even then they always feed apart. Moreover, both are too rare for their hides to enter into the speculations of commerce.

The skin of the antelope,[17] however, would be a very important article, if it should acquire some value.[18] The antelope is found on the prairies in numerous herds that leave the Black Hills in the spring and return in the autumn.[19] Thus they cross the Missouri twice. It is at these crossings that the Savages and particularly the Ricaras kill as many as they wish. They choose for this hunt the least rapid and deepest passages and, dividing into two parties that occupy the two banks, the one shoots the herd in the water and the other, hidden on the opposite bank, shows itself only when the herd is leaving the water and, terrifying it by cries, compels it to go back. This maneuver is repeated from each side until these animals,

[17] The word in the French original is *cabril* and, by that name, the animal was quite generally known. On his way to the Mandans, Alexander Henry wrote, "Herds of Cabriee or Jumping Deer were always in sight in every direction" (*Coventry Copy*, I, 416; Coues, I, 305) and again, "We generally had Cabriee in sight every moment, but they were so shy we could not get a shot at them" (*Coventry Copy*, I, 416; Coues, I, 306). Lewis and Clark, who are credited with introducing the "cabril," or American antelope, *antilocapra americana* to the scientific world (*Original Journals*, I, 141; n. 1; *Early Western Travels*, VI, 103, n. 40; Coues, *Lewis and Clark*, I, 109), called it a goat, for which the Spanish equivalent is *cabra*, and the creoles of Louisiana use the word, *cabril*, to signify the goat. The mountaineers in Ruxton's time called the antelopes goats (*Life in the Far West*, p. 10 n.), yet some fifteen years earlier, on the Upper Missouri, the word, *cabrie*, was still in use. See *Fort Tecumseh Journal, 1830*, MHS.

For a survival of the word in a derivative form along the Mexican border, see Ingersoll, Ernest, "An Adventure in Etymology: Origin and Meaning of Some Animal Names," *The Scientific Monthly*, February, 1937, p. 158.

[18] Tabeau inserted later:

"la peau de cabril au contraire pourroit en devenir un considérable, si cette peleterie acquerroit quelque valeur, mais un marchant de mont-real en ayant envoyé a londres un couple de cents, la vente n'a pas répondu a l'espérance du traiteur. ..." (Montreal version).

[19] "The *Antilope* or Cabra are found in great abundance as low as the Cheyenne River, and are seen scattering as low down as the neighbourhood of the Mahar village. (or 800 Ms.ᵘᵖ)" (*Original Journals*, VI, 122). For the antelope and its habitat, see Cox, Ross, *Adventures on the Columbia River*, p. 190.

wearied and discouraged, lose their strength (and) injure each other by seeking, panic-stricken, to lean against one another. Then the two parties, all excellent swimmers, armed with sticks, fall upon the herd and, increasing the confusion by their horrible cries, kill as many of them as can be dragged to land. And, in one single crossing, the Ricaras have killed as many as four hundred.[20]

In the ordinary hunt, the antelope is at least as difficult to surprise as the roebuck; but, as it is much more curious, the hunter hides himself so as to show only the movement of some branches or even of an arm, uplifted from time to time. The worried animal, although cautiously and with many starts, finally approaches within range of the gun. By its actions, especially when it is only slightly wounded, it is evident that it is extremely sensitive to pain. Like the roebuck it sheds tears and seems to implore the pity of its slayer. The female, a little smaller than the female of the roebuck but larger than our nanny-goat, bears as many as three little ones and rarely four. Its flesh is, according to my taste, more delicious and much resembles mutton when it is fat, but that is very seldom, as it feeds ordinarily only upon small hills where it finds neither rich nor succulent herbage. Its liver is a delicious food roasted. The Ricara women have a superior way of dressing the skins of the antelope and make of them a pliable leather which they use for fine garments for the two sexes.

Wolves of the woods, gray and white, are very common and follow the buffalo cow in hordes. In March and April, they are often met with, mad, and they attack and kill anything they meet. The Ricaras frequently lose their horses in these encounters and some people, notwithstanding their resistance, have themselves been victims. These wolves are always alone and are easy to distinguish by their walk and the symptoms of madness. But, like the savage warriors, they often attack one in bed at day-break and a Mr. Valé,[21]

[20] For the method of hunting antelope described by Brackenridge, see *Early Western Travels*, VI, 103.

[21] This was, undoubtedly, the "Jon Vallie," of the itinerary Map (The Geographical *Review*, I, 336, n. 29) and of the following journal entries:

2 October 1804 — " . . . . a frenchman came over to us this morning, we found him to be M^rValley, the Trador among The Souix nation he could talk English . . . . he came with us a Short distance & returned" (*Ordway Journal*, Wisconsin Historical Society *Collections*, XXII, 145).

1 October 1804 — ". . . . we Saw a man opposit to our Camp on the L. S.

clerk of Mr. Loisel,[22] unfortunately experienced such an attack in company with an *engagé,* the twenty-fourth of April, 1804. The two men were sleeping peacefully at break of day when the *engagé,* Calvé,[23] wrapped in his blanket felt something walking upon him.

---

which we discov^d. to be a Frenchman, a little of[f] (*from Shore among*) the Willows we observed a house, we Call to them to come over, a boy came in a canoe & informed that 2 frenchmen were at the house with good[s] to trade with the Seaeux which he expected down from the rickerrees everry day, Sever'l large parties of Seaeux Set out from the *rees* for this place to trade with those men.

"This M^r. *Jon Vallie* informs us that he wintered last winter 300 Leagues up the Chien River under the Black mountains . . . . This frenchman gives an account of a white booted turkey . . . ."

2 October 1804 — " ... M^r. *Jon Vallie Came* on board and proceeded on 2 Miles with us . . . ." (*Original Journals,* I, 175-76, 177). See also Coues, *Lewis and Clark,* I, 150).

There were a number of men of the name, Valé, or Vallée, in the Indian trade, several to whom trade licenses had been issued (Dominion Archives, Ottawa). There was a Jean-Baptiste Lavallée, interpreter, for the North West Company, in 1804, on the *rivière aux Anglais* (Morice, *op. cit.,* p. 172) and a Louis Vallée, a guide, who, at that same time, had his residence on Red River (*idem,* p. 309). For other references to a Vallé in the North West Company service in 1804, see *Charles Chaboillez Journal,* Masson MSS; an anonymous *Journal, 1804-5, idem;* and the Coventry Copy of the *Alexander Henry Journal,* Dominion Archives, Ottawa.

From the constant allusion in the "Missouri Land Cases" (House Executive Document, Twenty-fourth Congress, first session, No. 59) to Jean Baptiste Valé, aged seventy-two, as "senior," it would seem he must have had a son or grandson of his own name, who may have been, in 1803-4, clerk to Mr. Loisel; but no trace of him has been found. For a François Vallé, who, in 1810, when he returned to civilization just in time to attend his mother's deathbed, had been about six years in the Upper Missouri country, having gone there originally with Pierre Ménard, who was, apparently, from the salutation of letters in the *Vallé Collection* (Missouri Historical Society), his father's cousin, see Douglas, Walter Bond (editor), *Three Years among the Indians and Mexicans,* p. 38, n. 27.

[22] The incident of Valé's encounter with the mad wolf afforded to Tabeau, in the writing of his Montreal narrative, another opportunity for the suppression of Loisel's name, also of Heney's:

" ... mons^r valé chasseur l'a malheureusement expérimenté avec un de nos engagés le 24 avril 1804 == tous deux dormoient paisiblement a l'aube du jour, lorsque l'engage nome calve, bien enveloppé dans sa couverture sentit qu'on marchoit sur luy; ... le jour même on a pansé la plaie en mâchant une racine connuë sous le nom de dois blanc de prairie, & fort commune aux ilinois ..." (Montreal version).

[23] At least three French-Canadians of this name were recipients of trade licenses from Quebec, Paschal from Point Clair, Joseph from Lachine, and Jean Marie. The first and the third were definitely for the Michilimackinac trade. A Joseph Calvé, who became a trader among the Sacs and Foxes, figures repeatedly in the Haldimand cor-

He had barely seen the wolf, which had slightly scratched the arm that he had used to cover himself up again; but the cry and the movement resulted in causing both Mr. Valé and the infuriated animal to make a leap which brought them face to face. The maddened wolf, presenting his mouth open, Mr. Valé, naked and unarmed, bravely seized its lower jaw and had the courage to drag the wolf up to a gun which, with the use of but one hand, he succeeded in breaking upon the animal's head. During this singular combat, Calvé rushed to a canoe from which he brought an ax with which he finally freed Mr. Valé. For more than six months the latter could not use his hand, the thumb of which, in particular, was badly lacerated. The same day Mr. Henney, a trader among the Sioux, meeting him (Mr. Valé), dressed it by chewing a root[24] known by the name of white

---

respondence and, in the words of Thwaites, "He was accused by Sinclair of treachery, but succeeded in justifying his conduct . . . . , being sent in 1783 to notify the tribesmen of the Anglo-American treaty of peace" (*British Régime in Wisconsin*, Wisconsin Historical Society *Collections*, XVIII, 405, n. 5). That the Joseph Calvé of Cahokia, who married Eulalie Dubreil, August 29, 1798, at St. Louis (Collet, *Index to Marriages*) was his nephew seems scarcely possible, since his father was another Joseph, his mother being Marie Marechal, who died, 1791. From *Hunt's Minutes* (Missouri Historical Society), it is discoverable that as early as 1790 the younger Joseph had property in St. Charles, Missouri (I, 30) and as late as 1802 in Portage des Sioux (*idem*, p. 236) and in *Village à Robert*, now Bridgelin (*idem*, II, 33). It seems conceivable, therefore, that he may have been the engagé of the incident narrated by Tabeau. For French-Canadians of the name resident at Ste. Geneviève, Missouri, see Tanguay, II, 527.

24 Of this plant, which Coues, somewhat contemptuously says, "everybody knows," "except the botanists" (*History of the Lewis and Clark Expedition*, I, 238, n. 21), Lewis sent a specimen to President Jefferson, acknowledging in an accompanying letter his indebtedness to "Mr. Hugh heney a gentleman of rispectability and information who has resided many years among the natives of this country from whom he obtained the knowledge of its virtues. Mr Haney informed me that he had used the root of this plant frequently with the most happy effect in cases of the bite of the mad wolf or dog and also for the bite of the rattle snake . . . . (Meriwether Lewis to Thomas Jefferson, dated Fort Manden, March 5, 1805, *Original Journals, op. cit.*, VI, 157-58). It was only a few days before that Haney's messengers, "two men of the NW Comp^y" had arrived at Fort Manden, bringing the "Root and top of a plant" with instructions how the cure might be effected (*idem*, I, 266-67). Major Long heard that the Indians considered the *Gerardia* "to be a specific against the bite of the rattlesnake" (Keating, *op. cit.*, I, 347-48), a simpler remedy by far, apparently, than even the Brunton Poison Lancet, the great recourse of British officials in India.

This was not the first visit that Hugh Heney had made to Fort Manden. On the occasion of the first visit in December, he had given various kinds of information.

wood of the prairie and very common in the Ilinois. Whether the wolf was not mad or whether the root was truly efficacious against the madness, as it certainly is against the venom of the rattlesnake, the only result was the effects of an ordinary bite. Mr. Henney and many Ricaras assured me that they have often used it with success, particularly upon horses.

A kind of little gray fox, the hare, and the skunk[25] are very common in the Upper Missouri[26] and a quantity of these skins could be used in trade if the price should encourage the Savages to hunt for them. The English companies of the North-West and Hudson's Bay get a great many of them from the Mandanes by giving indifferently for each skin the price of a half beaver. The hare is much larger here

---

"We found Mr. Henny," records Clark, December 17, 1804, "a Verry intelligent Man from whome we obtained Some Scetches of the Countrey between the Mississippi & Missouri, and Some Sketches from him, which he had obtained from the Indin[s]. to the *West* of this place also the names and charecktors of the Seeaux &c." (*Original Journals*, I, 237, 238). Larocque noted the curiosity of the American explorers the same day, entering the following into his journal:

17 *December 1804* — "We remained here all day (Fort Mandan), The Captains Enquired a great deal of M[r] Heney, Concerning the Sioux Nation, & Local Circumstances of that Country & Lower Part of the Missouri — of which they took Notes — . . . ." (*Masson MSS*, Dominion Archives, Ottawa).

Of Heney's return visit in February, the following Journal entry of Larocque's may be an intimation:

14 *February 1805* — "Mr Heney got 3 dress'd Skins Smoked for the Purpose of making Shoes for the People that are to Come with me" (*idem*) back to the Missouri.

[25] There are several *bêtes puantes*, the fox, the martin, the badger, the polecat, or skunk, and also one variety of weasel; but "la Bête puante" of the Tabeau narrative was, presumably, none other than the skunk, the stinking beast *par excellence*, concerning the most awful odor of which, see Le Jeune's *Relation*, 1634 (Thwaites, *Jesuit Relations*, VI, 315) and also John Bradbury's account (*Travels in America*, pp. 27-28 n.). By the early traders the polecat was regarded as of "three species . . . . the first is the common polecat; the second is called the mink; and the third, the stinking polecat" (*Canadian Magazine*, I, 399 (1823). The French word, *blaireau*, was applied to the badger (Coues, *Lewis and Clark*, op. cit., I, 226), corrupted by Clark into 'brarow" (*Original Journals, op. cit.*, I, 95, n. 1).

[26] To the animals listed here, Tabeau added the common polecat, "*pichoux*," rightly distinguishing it from the "bêtes puantes," which he described as "en abondance & d'une grosseur surprenantes." He had probably in mind the skunk, or *putois*, when he said, "J'en ai pesé une du poids de douze livres & les sauvages m'ont assuré en avoir tué de beaucoup plus grosses" (Montreal version).

than in Canada[27] and I have seen a skunk weighing a dozen pounds, although, according to the Savages, it was not one of the largest. Red foxes are met with now and again, as also lynxes and, if I trade a few musk-rats, I get them from the Sioux who take them from little lakes in the heart of the prairies. The porcupine abounds on the banks of all the little wooded rivers; but this little animal, so delicious elsewhere, is not eatable here, so thin is it in every season.

On the level lands, sometimes near the river but more often in the depths of the prairie, there are swarms of small animals that are here called prairie dogs.[28] This animal very much resembles the gray squirrel of the Ilinois. It is a trifle larger, carries, as does the squirrel, its tail up, is as broad, but shorter. Its incisors, which are its only teeth, are larger (than the squirrel's) and quite as sharp. It has also a larger stomach, rough hair of a grayish color, the head exactly like that of the squirrel. It has the same gentleness and the same vivacity in all its movements. Many of them (the prairie dogs) are always stationed as guards and as sentinels upon their little knolls at the edge of their holes into which they plunge, all at the same moment, at the cry of the one that sounds the alarm. These knolls are placed near to one another in the form of a savage village and a single opening at the top leads to many holes. At the bottom of these holes, at an astonishing depth, are the lodgings. These little republics are al-

[27] " ... Le liévre est aussi très commun & beaucoup plus gros qu'en Canada. Les sioux me traitent quelques rats musqués, mais ils les tirent des petits lacs qui se trouvent dans la profondeur des prairies. On traiterait une bonne quantité de toutes ces menuës peleteries, chez les ricaras, si le prix les encouragoit a y faire la chasse, mais elles valent trop peu aux ilinois. Les compagnies angloises du nord-west & de la baie d'udson, en tirent beaucoup des mandanes, aux quels elles les paient raisonnablement. On trouve le porce-épi ..." (Montreal version).

[28] Of the many parallelisms between the Tabeau narrative and the various journals commemorative of the Lewis and Clark expedition, there is scarcely one of greater interest and significance than that having to do with prairie dogs. The prairie dog, *cynomys ludovicianus,* was another of the animals introduced to the scientific world through the medium of the American explorers. From that time forward, it has never ceased to arouse the curiosity of the chance traveler. Note, for instance, among the records of the first half-century, Bradbury, *op. cit.,* p. 73; *Early Western Travels,* V, 94-95, 119; Brackenridge, *idem,* VI, 103; Catlin, *op. cit.,* I, 76-78; Murray, *op. cit.,* I, 295-96. Lewis and Clark were not far from Loisel's cedar island when they first found occasion to mention the quaint little animal that they and others after them frequently called "the barking squirrel," their "burrowing squirrel" being most likely the gopher (Coues, *op. cit.,* I, 271, n. 30).

ways situated on the vast, level prairie and, as they are a great distance from water, there is reason to believe that these animals do not use it.[29]

From the description that I have given of the banks of the Missouri, destitute of wood, noticeably above the River Qui Court, it must be judged scarcely suitable as a home for the beaver. It is even less suitable for the otter which delights only in the marshes or in the rivers abounding in fish. Therefore, one hardly ever sees any of the former and only a very few of the latter; and, if certain Frenchmen have made two or three successful hunts, it is not upon the Missouri itself but in voyaging upon rivers where nature has provided for the support of these amphibians.[30] Yet these successes not having been often repeated makes us question if the beaver, constantly

[29] This marginal note in the Washington version was made a part of the text and added to the Montreal version, strong evidence of revision: "Capt Lewis sent to the President one of these animals and it, in truth, never drinks." The first contact of the American explorers with the prairie dog was in the first week of September (*Original Journals,* I, 141) and, on the twenty-second of the same month, they reached the place where Loisel wintered, as someone informed them, in 1803-4 (*idem,* p. 160). Tabeau's note respecting the prairie dog sent to Washington must have been inserted after he had had time to hear of its ability to get along without water. The additional information in his Montreal narrative is not without interest:

" ... j'en ai amené un de chez les ricaras, que le captne lewis envoyoit au président des états-unis, & j'ai éprouvé que ce singulier animal ne boit jamais. le captne lewis l'avoit déja gardé trois mois luy même, sans pouvoir luy faire avaler une goute d'eau quoi-qu'il acceptat bien familierement du biscuit, du mahy, des noix &c.═" (Montreal version).

[30] Jean Baptiste Truteau, ten years before, had been only slightly more encouraging as to the chances for successful beaver-hunting:

" ... jay campé ce jour la a deux lieux plus bas que la rivierre qui court. cette rivierre a la gauche De missouris est estimé a soixante et dix lieux du grand village des mahas, et ainsy éloignée de trois cent cinquante lieux de l'embouchure du missouri, selon le rapport des sauvages. elle est la plus abondante en castor et loutres de tout ce continant, mais elle roule ses eaux avec tant de force et de rapiditée, que l'on ne peut, soit disant, y navigué, ni en montant ne en descendant. le villages des poncas est situé a une lieux plus haut, prés du missourie. le commerce des pelteries avec cette nations seroit avantageux, s'il [si] les mahas, quoique leurs alliers, ni [n'y] portoient obstacle, empechant les traiteurs d'y parvenir l'automme, ne les soufrant que tres rarement y aller le primtems faire la trocque des marchandises qui leur restent aprés en avoirre tirés aux même la milleure partie." (American Historical *Review,* XIX, 308).

preyed upon as in the River of the Osages, of the Kancas, and in all the Lower Missouri, would not soon be exterminated.

A man named Noreau[31] made, some years ago, a fairly successful hunt in the river which bears his name, the mouth of which is ten leagues below the Ricaras. But it would have had to be well stripped not to supply, on a first hunt, three or four hundred pounds and I know that there are no more there today. The Ricaras, to whom mice are mountains, say, of course, that in all the little rivers and on the land, which separates them from the Black Hills, the beaver is plentiful; but it is evident that, when asked to enter into details, they regard as an immense number dwellings which they meet with, scattered here and there, and that if they knew and wished to hunt there they would destroy in a year all those that exist in a circle of two hundred leagues.[32]

Some Yincton hunters whom I see every day and who, knowing some French, traded more than a hundred beaver skins each when

31 A mistake for Moreau. The river is now known as the Owl. The old Arikara name for it was *"Sur-war-car-na, or Park"* (*Original Journals*, I, 182), given in the Biddle edition as the "Sawawkawna, or Pork river" (I, 99) and, in Bradbury (Edition of 1817, p. 109), as the *"Cer-wer-cer-na."* By Tabeau's contemporaries, this quite considerable stream, "draining," as Mr. Quaife says, "several counties of western South Dakota" (Wisconsin Historical Society *Collections*, XXII, 148, n. 3) was very generally known as the Moreau; but after whom named seems not to be remembered. The trade licenses for 1769 and 1770 furnished four names, Antoine Moreau, Joseph Moreau, Louis Morau, and Pierre Moreau, only one of which re-appears, so far as noted, in Missouri annals. There was a Joseph Moreau in Florissant in 1799 (Houck, Louis, *History of Missouri*, II, 69). A François Moreau had property there also, likewise in Ste. Geneviève and St. Louis. He died about 1800 ("Hunt's Minutes," II, 16, Missouri Historical Society). A Baptiste Moreau had a lot in New Bourbon in 1803. Clark referred to the stream as Murow Creek on at least one occasion (*Original Journals*, I, 38).

32 The corresponding paragraph in the Montreal version has some additional sentences, the first of which contains the mention of Quenneville, previously alluded to and here, presumably, correctly spelt. These sentences form a separate paragraph a little farther on in the Washington:

"... le nomé quenneville bon pêcheur au castor ayant plus de confiance que moy dans leur rapport, se determina le 11 a'aoust 1804 a suivre les chayennes dans toutes leurs courses aux environs des côtes noires, & m'a assuré a son etour le 11 d'avril suivant, qu'il n'en avoit presque point vu dans tout son voïage. ce qui prouve encore plus clairement qu'il n'y en a point, c'est qu'ayant emporté avec luy quelques marchandises, il ne m'a apporté en retour que 84 lbs de castor, quoique ces sauvages se soient surpassé cette année, ayant eu un traiteur pour la premiere fois — " (Montreal version).

they hunted in the territory of the St. Peter's River,[33] brought me fifteen skins this year after having scoured all the fall the east bank of the Missouri and having visited the sources of all the little rivers and streams emptying into it in a space of more than a hundred leagues. The chief of the tribe tells me that the beaver begins to be common only beyond the great prairies and at the approach of the branches of the St. Peter's River. And he declared to me that because of it he abandoned the Missouri, although the buffalo cow was far more abundant there.

Another tribe of Yinctons now located on the River James,[34] accustomed to the beaver hunt, who hunted them extensively on the branches of the River of the Mohens,[35] also scoured the east bank of the Missouri and made only a very ordinary catch in 1803. This year they wintered with Mr. McLancll[36] on the same river and have

[33] *rivierre S^nt pierre* in original. This name or its English equivalent was used by all the early fur traders; but, in 1852, the present appellation, Minnesota, was substituted by direct action of the United States congress. See Joint Resolution, June 19, 1852, *United States Statutes at Large*, X, 147. There is no known origin of the earlier name; but it appears "not unlikely that the name may have been given by le Sueur, in 1795, in honor of M. St. Pierre de Repautigni, to whom Lahontan incidentally alludes, as being in Canada in the year 1789" (Keating, William H., *Narrative of the Long Expedition*, I, 322). For other theories, see Coues, *Expeditions of Zebulon Montgomery Pike*, p. 76, n. 74. "The Souris River was called the River St. Pierre by Verendrye in 1738, and his men ascended it to cross over to the Missouri" (Bell, C. N., *Historical Names and Places of the Canadian North-West*, Manitoba Historical and Scientific Society *Transactions*, No. 15, p. 5).

[34] *rivierre a jacques* in original. See also Truteau, American Historical *Review*, XIX, 307. By inadvertence, perhaps, the name appears in the *Description du Haut Missouri* as la *riviere St. Jacque*, a plausible instance of the association of ideas. See Mississippi Valley Historical *Review*, VIII, 161. It has, in more recent times, been variously called, the James, the Yankton, the Dakota. See *Original Journals*, I, 126, n. 1, and 190. For more about the river itself, see Douglas, Walter B., *James's Journal*, p. 25, n. 19; Drumm, Stella M., *Luttig Journal*, p. 48, n. 60.

[35] *rivierre des mohens* in original. Probably the Des Moines, of which a variant was *Rivière de Moyen*. For the etymology of "Des Moines," see *Original Journals*, I, 45 n., 103; VI, 96.

[36] Although the name of the hunter on the *rivierre des mohens* is clearly *mm. McLanell* in the text of the Washington version, it is not inconceivable that McDonell may have been meant or McClellan. Robert McClellan was, at one period of his career, a trader among the Omaha (*Original Journals*, VII, 379). For his association with Ramsay Crooks, whose partner he was "in trading expeditions on the Missouri," see Fuller, George W., *The Inland Empire* . . . . , *op. cit.*, I, 189, and for allusions

had no better success, while the Mahas and the Poncas, who hunted lower down, brought in a very good number.[37]

Finally, ten French hunters, equipped by Mr. Loisel,[38] armed with more than fifty traps, all active men, vying with each other all the spring and some days of autumn as to which one shall work most, believe they have taken almost all the beaver to be found upon the two banks of the Missouri, between the Isle of Cedars and the Ricaras, a space of about seventy leagues, and all their hunt did not yield two hundred pounds. Some of these same hunters entered upon the river named the Fork[39] at the beginning of October, 1803, which they ascended, continuing their hunt until the ice stopped them. In all their journey they found only a few beaver dams two or three leagues apart and they were compelled to retrace their steps after spring, having lost their time and money. These hunters, having imparted to me some information about this great river, I am going to say two words about it in passing.

The Fork has its sources in the Black Hills and appears to flow from west to east. To give a description of its two banks would be to repeat that of the Upper Missouri, even to the woods and islands.

---

to his having entered the service of the North West Company after having been with the Pacific Fur Company, see *idem,* pp. 191, 199.

37 The corresponding paragraph in the Montreal version is much abbreviated and all three of the proper nouns just commented upon omitted.

38 Here again Tabeau, in his revision, omits the name of Loisel and arrogates to himself equal credit with someone with whom he tacitly admits he was associated:

" ... enfin dix chasseurs françois équipés par nous, ayants plus de cinquante piéges, dans tout le printemps & plusieurs jours de l'automne, croient avoir prix a bien peu près tout le castor qui s'est touvé entre l'isle aux cédres & les ricaras, espace d'environ soixante dix lieuës, & toute leurs chasses n'en ont pas fourni deux cents livres, ces mêmes chasseurs sont entré en 8bre 1803 — dans une grande rivierre nomée la fourche, dans le haut de la qu'elle ils ont hyverné; & n'ayant trouvé que quelques loges de castor distantes les unes des autres de deux & trois lieuës, ils ont été contraints de retrograder dès le printemps, ayants perdu leur temps & leurs dépenses. ⸗ " (Montreal version).

39 "a deux lieux au dessus des habitations des ris sort la riviere des chaguienne, que des chasseur ont nommé la fourche: Cette riviere est assé large mais peu profonde de sorte qu'on ne peut y naviguer quavec beaucoup de peine, elle prende ses sources fort loin son embouchure, dans des Côtes de roches Escarpées, du côté du Soleil couchant elle se Separent en plusieurs fourches sur le haut, bien fournies en bois & tres abondantes en Castor" (*Description du haut Missouri* par Jean Bap*te* Trudeau, voyageur, Mississippi Valley Historical *Review,* VIII, 165).

Both, almost similar, are there, only still more rare. The rapidity of the river is great and the bottom of moving sand causes the water to roll by in waterfalls and a boat, run aground, to be engulfed in an instant. At high water the currents are not navigable and the waters, disturbed by their own fall, are so choppy that loaded pirogues cannot descend on them. The animals are scarcer here than upon the Missouri, the environs furnishing no pasturage and resembling the deserts of Arabia. Nevertheless, hunters met there for some days herds of buffalo cows and the two specie of deer. The porcupine is very common but is always thin. On the upland on nearing the Black Hills, some pines, thick-set and dwarfish, are seen.

A man named Guenneville, having left the village of the Ricaras the 11th of August, 1804, followed the Chayennes in all their ramblings in the neighborhood of the Black Hills and elsewhere and assured me on his arrival the 11th of April[40] that on going and returning he did not see beaver three times. His trading has brought him only eighty-four pounds and he did not leave one in the hands of the Savages, who, meeting a trader for the first time, surpassed themselves in the hunt.

I believe that it is not necessary to add that the beaver and the otter cannot become objects of trade with the hunters, the Sioux and the Ricaras, at least from the River Qui Court up to the Mandanes inclusively; for I understand that these could scarcely furnish them for the English companies. Let no one believe that it is for this object that they (the British companies) maintain near to them such costly establishments. Their chief aim is always to be provided for intercourse with the different posts and to trade with the roaming nations above the Mandanes.[41]

[40] This way of referring to a very definite time as of the recent past helps to determine the date of the writing of the Tableau narrative and justifies the view that neither the Washington version nor the Montreal was the original draft. The date here meant must have been, April 11, 1805. On April 7th, the barge from Fort Manden started upon its journey down the river and Tabeau joined it at the Arikara village, his request to be allowed to do so having been readily granted by Lewis and Clark (*Original Journals,* I, 283-87; *Ordway Journal,* Wisconsin Historical Society *Collections,* XXII, 190-91). Either Tabeau did not do much of his writing in Kakawita's hut, after all, or the two copies that have come down to us of his narrative are both revisions.

[41] This observation as to the ulterior purposes of the British fur companies was

BIRDS

AQUATIC birds, not finding food upon the banks of the Missouri, never linger there and, except the bustards and ducks which rest on the marshes, they very rarely fly along them. Small birds cannot be numerous in the desert places so little adapted to attract the nightingale,[1] the goldfinch,[2] and the many kinds that throng the groves of the Ilinois. The plovers in the autumn and the spring and the pheasants in every season are abundant. Turkey-hens are seldom seen above the River Qui Court. The hawk, the merlin, the crow, the owl, and others similar are very common.

The magpie, the most beautiful bird of the country, is here the plague of the savages' horses. These barbarians are so clumsy and so careless with their wooden saddles that often the horse's skin and

---

probably made for the benefit, not so much of the Spaniards, as of the Americans; for, though there may have been some doubt in Loisel's mind as to who would eventually be the possessors of the country, there was certainly none in Tabeau's. Moreover, although the British traders, notably François Antoine Larocque and Charles Mackenzie, who were on the Upper Missouri in the winter of 1804-5, do not betray in their writings any acquaintance with Tabeau or knowledge of his existence, they very likely did hear of him and he of them; and, in his intercourse with the American explorers at Fort Mandan, no doubt Tabeau discussed pro and con the merits of the British position and realized how intense were the prejudices of Meriwether Lewis. These their owner revealed in the way remarked upon by Charles Mackenzie:

"Mr. LaRoque and I having nothing very particular claiming attention, we lived contentedly and became intimate with the Gentlemen of the American expedition; who on all occasions seemed happy to see us, and always treated us with civility and Kindness. It is true Captain Lewis could not make himself agreeable to us — he could speak fluently and learnedly on all subjects, but his inveterate disposition against the British stained, at least in our eyes, all his eloquence. Captain Clark was equally well informed, but his conversation was always pleasant, for he seemed to dislike giving offense unnecessarily" (*Some Account of the Missouri Indians in the years 1804, 5, 6 &7*, Masson MSS, Photostat, Dominion Archives, Ottawa).

Lewis's prejudices deepened with the years and manifested themselves, during his governorship of Upper Louisiana, in the ready credence he gave to all sorts of rumors about British machinations among the Indians (*Frederick Bates Papers*, MHS). His greater cordiality towards Hugh Heney arose, perchance, from the somewhat equivocal position in which that individual of fluctuating allegiance must have found himself. It was, however, Clark who finally made advances to Heney with the idea of profiting from his acquaintance with and influence over the Sioux. See Letter, July 20, 1806, *Original Journals*, V, 282-86.

flesh from the neck to the rump are torn away.[3] The voracious bird at the sight of this raw and living flesh buries its claws in it and tears the poor sentient animal.[4] The horse kicks, prances, runs about with all its might, but in vain. The bird, fixed on the sores, loosens its hold[5] only when the horse throws himself upon his back to roll. Yet scarcely does he rise up once more than the enemy seizes again its opportunity. It is observable that among a large number of galled horses, the magpie always chooses that one that it has once tasted, so

[1] Since, as Mr. Elliott Coues says, there is in North America "No species of nightingale (*Daulias luscinia*) in any proper sense of the word" (*History of the Lewis and Clark Expedition*, I, 14, n. 27), it behoves us to conjecture what bird Tabeau could have meant by his "rossignol." That he did not mean the song sparrow, which is called the "nightingale" by the French-Canadians of today, who interpret its early morning song to be,

> Sem, sem ton blé
> Le printemps est arrivé,

seems more than likely; inasmuch as in Bonnycastle's time (*The Canadas in 1841*, II, 50) and probably in his also the cardinal bird, *Cardinalis Virginianus*, was known in Canada as the *rossignol*. This opinion is supported by the fact that Lewis and Clark met with a bird, which, as Clark records (*Original Journals*, I, 38), "Sang for us all last night," which they called a nightingale, and which has been generally identified with the cardinal, or red-bird. The weak point in the argument is that this bird is popularly called, the "Virginia nightingale," and, since both Lewis and Clark were Virginians born and bred, it would seem strange that they were unacquainted with it, yet such they must have been; for Clark writes, that it 'is the first of the Kind I ever heard" (*idem*, pp. 38-39). On the authority of James N. Baskett, it might be further remarked that "The ordinary mocking-bird sings in the night; so also, occasionally do the catbird and the brown thrasher."

[2] "chardoneret" (chardonneret?) — (Tr.).

[3] The Indian lack of consideration for their horses was often criticized by travelers. Bradbury wrote, "The Aricaras do not provide any better for their horses than the other nations of the Missouri. They cut down the cotton wood (*Populus angulosa*) and the horses feed on the bark and smaller branches. I have seen instances exhibiting proofs that these poor animals have eaten branches two inches in diameter" (*Travels in America*, p. 165) and Captain Thomas Blakiston, who was with Palliser, when he made his famous reconnaisance, but prepared a separate report, differentiated, in this respect, between the Crees and the Assiniboines on the one hand and the Blackfeet and Kootenays on the other, the former being culpable as were the tribes of the Missouri (*Further Papers Relative to the Exploration by the Expedition under Captain Palliser*, p. 46).

[4] For the Corvus and its delight in flesh, see *Original Journals*, VI, 135. It was remarked upon as being very common in the neighborhood of the Arikara villages (*idem*, vol. i, p. 181) and of beautifully variegated plumage (*idem*, VI, 130-31). The creek that Lewis and Clark named "Corvus Creek" is now the "American Crow" (Wisconsin Historical Society *Collections*, XXII, 131, n. 6).

that the beast finally succumbs, if it be not rescued. Some owners, more through interest than through pity, cover the sores with a piece of leather or with a buffalo paunch sprinkled with ashes.

The kiliou,[6] or calumet bird, is not rare. This eagle, prized by all the savage nations, is prized most by those of the Upper Missouri, who for the tail alone give a large price. Among the Mandanes the entire plumage is worth a horse. This fictitious value is from pure caprice, the shape and colors being very ordinary. The feathers of the tail, of a dull white, are ornamented at the tip with some black lines, the remainder of the plumage being a grey-brown. The wing-feathers are mottled.[7] Perhaps this great value is given because of the strength and courage of the bird; for, although the smallest species of eagle, it shows itself really a king of birds and no other tries to dispute with it its prey. I myself watched one a long time on the River of the Osages,[8] upon the carcase of a deer, surrounded by grey eagles, buz-

---

5 "ne tâche prise," omitted from the body of the text, appears in the margin of the Washington version. It is transferred to its proper place in the Montreal version.

6 *Le Kiliou*, the golden eagle, *Aquila chrysaetos* (*Original Journals*, I, 199, n. 1). For an account of the Golden Eagle, its habits and habitat, see McArthur, Alexander, *Our Winter Birds*, Manitoba Historical and Scientific Society *Transactions*, 1887, pp. 2-4. The Montreal version limited the place of non-rarity but added some interesting facts:

"le kiliou ou oiseau a calumet n'est pas ici fort rare ... les plumes de kiliou sont employées a orner les calumets de cérémonie & surtout a distinguer les exploits des guerriers. il n'est pas permi[s] a tout homme de porter la plume de kiliou, & la maniere dont elle est posée sur la tête, indique le genre de prouesse qui distingue le heros. ce sont les croix d'ordres. ═ peut-être que la grande considération qu'on a pour cet oiseau est donée a sa force & a son courrage, car quoiqu'il soit le plus petit parmi les differentes espéces d'aigle, il se montre vraiment en roy des oiseaux. aucun autre ne se hasarde a partager sa proie. j'en ai admir un moy même fort longtemps dans la rivierre des osages ..." (Montreal version).

7 *matachées*, intended, no doubt, for matachier, meaning of different colors, or possibly, for tachées (Tr.). The passage where it occurs is not in the Montreal version.

8 This statement, seeming to imply a stay of some duration on the lower Missouri, would incline one to think that Pierre-Antoine Tabeau was the "Canadian hunter" (*Account of an Expedition from Pittsburgh to the Rocky Mountains* by Major S. H. Long, 1819-20; *Early Western Travels*, XIV, 165), after whom Tabeau Creek in Lafayette County, Missouri was named. In the time of Lewis and Clark, it was only fifteen yards wide (*Original Journals*, I, 52; Biddle edition, I, 16). "It joins the Missouri near Berlin, Lafayette County" (Quaife, Wisconsin Historical Society *Collections*, XXII, 87, n. 1). In Major Long's day, "Tabeau settlement," on its banks, had two houses. Coues, in his *Expeditions of Zebulon Montgomery Pike*, p. 379, n. 34,

zards,[9] crows, and many other birds of prey, all perched respectfully quite a distance off and that approached the meat only when his majesty, flying away, tacitly gave them permission. In general, all the feathers of the bird, suitable for ornamenting arrows, have some value and the Ricaras in autumn make a special hunt in order to obtain them. This is how they get them:

The hunter digs a ditch on a broad, flat prairie, wide and deep enough for him to lie at his ease. He covers it with straw or with interlaced branches in such a way that, invisible himself, he can see the bird when it pounces upon a rabbit or other bait fixed on the surface. The bird, seizing the prey, finds itself caught by the feet and dragged to the bottom of the ditch. The same bait sometimes deceives many of them in a day. But it also often happens that the hunter passes many days in the ditch without seeing a single bird and, if his industry is wonderful, his patience is no less so.

FISH

THE Upper Missouri does not abound in fish to the extent to which the Lower does. The catfish,[1] small but very delicate, is the only fish sought and it is so rare that the old Ricaras, great fishermen, patiently pass days and nights in an endeavor to catch a couple of them and oftentimes they get none at all. From

---

asserts that, though the Vermillion was called "Little Tabeau Creek," the name was not supposed to have a personal significance. "Big Tabeau Creek" is one of the affluents of the Osage.

[9] *Carancros*, a *caracara*, variants are *carancha, carancho* (Tr.).

[1] *la Barbuë*, the cat-fish. "The cat-fish," wrote Palliser, in his *Solitary Rambles and Adventures of a Hunter in the Prairies*, p. 229 — and he was then in this very same region — "is one of the finest flavored I ever ate; firm, white, and very rich; the men (Boucharville, Paquenode, and Peekay) called it 'barbue.' It is a quaint little fish, like a miniature dolphin; has double fins, besides those on its back, and a preposterously long beard-like excresence from each side of its mouth." The fish that passes under the name on the Eastern Shore of Maryland must be a different thing altogether, since the white people profess to despise it. In revising his narrative, Tabeau improved the literary style at this place and modified some of his statements. He did not confine Arikara fishing for *la barbuë* to the aged and, said he, *"nous mêmes avons pêchés constament, & toujours avec très peu de succès."*

the village of the Mahas up to the Isle of Cedar, want did not permit us to neglect this means of obtaining food but it was constantly resorted to without success. Throughout our voyage our fishermen did not catch a dozen. From the Isle of Cedar up to the Ricaras three experienced fishermen caught, from the 18th of April to the 24th of May, three little catfish, each weighing two pounds. The Missouri has, undoubtedly, other fish; but, as the only way of fishing is with a line and as the catfish alone nibbles at the bait, no other fish is caught. Still I saw some sword fish there and Mr. Loisel found upon the shore, in 1801, a bone the size of which made him surmise that the fish to which it belonged was larger than a buffalo. He had the misfortune to lose it in the course of his voyage.[2] The mooneye,[3] a very large fish, ascends, in schools, a little river, named *La Rappa,*[4] which is a league from the isle of the Ricaras. At the beginning of July, a fisherman can catch as many of them as he cares for during

[2] Tabeau further said, changing his details somewhat:

" ... j'ai vu de très gros poissons armés & je tiens de m^r loisel & de tout son équipage, qu'en 1801 — il a trouvé sur la grévé, près des ricaras, un os de poisson dont la grosseur devoit excéder celle d'un boeuf. il a eu le malheur de la perdre dans le cour de son voïage. les sauvages font bien des contes au sujet d'un poisson énorme, qui saisit par le nez les animeaux qui boivent & les entraine avec luy. une espece de sardine, mais plus grosse monte en foule dans quelques petites rivierres. on en prend alors autant qu'il plait, mais il faut pour cela que les eaux soient hautes dans la saison, autrement les embouchures sont a sec.

"on voit ici peu d'espéces de serpents & de couloeuvres qui se rencontrent aux ilinois. mais en récompense le serpent a sonétes y est beaucoup plus commun. heureusement que les plantes qui attirent le venin ne sont pas rares, & que tous les sauvages connoissent le bois blanc de prairie dont j'ai déja parlé. =

"un sorte d'arraignée noire, de la grosseur d'un oeuf de pigeon, dont les pattes sont courtes, se tient ordinairement dans les pailles & s'attache quelquefois aux vêtements des passants. il faut que cet insecte porte un terrible venin, puisqu'un de mes hommes, n'en ayant été que légerement touché sur la main, il a souffert une douleur insupportable, & qu'a moins d'un quart d'heur tout le bras s'est enflé étonament. le bois blanc de prairie a encore dans cette occasion produit son effet ordinaire. les sauvages craignent cette araignée plus que le serpent & raccontent mille histoires a ce sujet. je ne dis rien des autres insects n'ayant conu que celuici de particulier. =

[3] *"La Laqueche"* intended for *La quesche* (Tr.).

[4] In the paragraphs quoted in the preceding note, where normally it should appear, there is no mention of this stream. In the Washington version, we have *une petite rivierre nomee La rappa* in the body of the text and *Les Barrieres* in the margin. Since, as Tabeau goes on to say, this small river was *une lieue de l'isle des ricaras,* he, unquestionably, had in mind what came to be known more generally as the *Maropa,* the Owl, or Rampart Creek of today. Maropa was a name not unknown

the fifteen days that they remain there; but, in order that he may do
this, the water must be high in the Missouri, otherwise, the dried-up
mouth of *La Rappa* would bar the fish.[5]

FRUITS

THE banks of the Upper Missouri and the nature of their soil
indicate that few fruits will be found; but, although the
kinds be few, each kind yields abundantly. The choke cherry,[1] the currant,[2] and the plum tree fill the valleys and border the
streams.[3] The name of wild pear[4] has been given to an excellent

---

to Captain Clark yet, in his journal entry for October 8, 1804, it would seem as if he
did his best to adhere to Tabeau's rendering:

" ... passed a Small river of 25 yards wide Called Rear par or Beaver Dam R. ..."
(*Original Journals*, I, 183). A little higher up he and his companions reached the
island on which stood one of the Arikara villages (*idem*). Les Barrieres would indicate the alternative name of the stream. The expression, barrier, as indicative of a
contrivance for catching fish or beaver, a sort of weir, occurs in several of the fur-
trader journals examined with a view to the editing of this narrative. Charles Chaboillez, under date of September 1, 1797, wrote, ". . . . camped at the Grand Gal-
lais near the Barrier . . . ." (*Masson Papers, op. cit.,*) and, similarly, Alexander
Henry, in July, 1806, recorded the fact that he crossed *Riviere la Souris* at the "passage near the Sturgeon Barrier upon a shoal of gravel and sand" (*Coventry* edition,
I, 623). For Thompson's use of the name, "Fishing Weir," for "Barrier River," see
Coues, *New Light on the Early History of the Greater Northwest,* II, 471, n. 34.

[5] Following this, Tabeau, in his Montreal version, introduces a section, *Le Cerne,
ou chasse en commun,* for which see Appendix VIII.

[1] *le cerisier a grappe,* cerise de Virginie, ". . . . the fruit of the *Prunus padus
Virginiana,* which is considered to be very indigestible . . . ." (Maximilian, *Travels
in the Interior of North America, Early Western Travels,* XXIII, 83). For a further
description of the choke-cherry, see *Townsend's Narrative, idem,* XXI, 249 and, for
the use made of it, *idem,* p. 268.

[2] *le gadelier Sauvage,* the Golden Buffalo, Missouri, or Crandall currant, *ribes
aureum.* The currant, *ribes aureum,* was found by Bradbury growing in profusion on
one of the cedar islands of the Missouri, the "Little Cedar Island," as he called it,
above the River *Qui Court,* or Niobrara. It was a "Beautiful spot" (*Early Western
Travels,* V, 99-100). In his chapter on "Useful Plants" (*Cheyenne Indians,* II, 175),
Grinnell mentions several varieties of currants, the red, the yellow, the black, known
to the Cheyennes and their neighbors.

[3] The passage corresponding to this, in the Montreal version, is, "le cerisier a
grappe, le grosseillier & gadelier sauvages, le prunier remplissent les coulees & bordent
tous les ruisseaux." Did he wish to add the gooseberry or is *gadelier* the Canadian
French term for groseille?

[4] *poire* in both versions. A different fruit, presumably, from the summer pear,

fruit which has the shape of a pear. It is purple in color, as large as a medium-sized strawberry, and grows upon a shrub seven or eight feet high. It is very luscious and the savages value it more than they do the choke cherry. The women pile up the fruit and dry it in the sun. Then they add to it some fat and dried meat, almost pulverized, and make a paste or rather a kind of ointment which they roll into balls[5] of an oval shape and of the size of an egg. The saliva and the dirt of the hands give consistency to them. This dish[6] is much sought after and is highly esteemed.[7]

---

alluded to on page 12, *fleurs d'oignonet*. The "Summer pear" was the cactus fruit, the prickly pear so-called, the *Opuntia*, for the preparation and use of which, see Grinnell, *op. cit.*, II, 180-81; Henry, *Coventry Copy*, I, 443; Coues, *New Light on the Early History of the Greater Northwest*, I, 321, n.42.

[5] "Boulelettes," corrected to *boulettes* in the Montreal version.

[6] "mest" in both versions, a slip of the pen for *mets*.

[7] As one of the very early descriptions of this Indian food preparation, pemmican, that of Alexander Mackenzie might well be quoted. "The provision called Pemican, on which the Chepewyans, as well as the other savages of this country, chiefly subsist in their journies, is prepared in the following manner. The lean parts of the flesh of the larger animals are cut in thin slices, and are placed on a wooden grate over a slow fire, or exposed to the sun, and sometimes to the frost. These operations dry it, and in that state it is pounded between two stones: it will then keep with care for several years. If, however, it is kept in large quantities, it is disposed to ferment in the spring of the year, when it must be exposed to the air, or it will soon decay. The inside fat, and that of the rump, which is much thicker in these wild than our domestic animals, is melted down and mixed, in a boiling state, with the pounded meat, in equal proportions: it is then put in baskets or bags, for the convenience of carrying it. Thus it becomes a nutritious food, and is eaten, without any further preparation, or the addition of spice, salt, or any vegetable or farinaceous substance. A little time reconciles it to the palate. There is another sort made with the addition of marrow and dried berries, which is of a superior quality" (*Voyages from Montreal, ... through the Continent of North America . . . . ,* pp. cxxi-cxxii, n.). For the same or additional information, see Franchère, Gabriel, *Personal Narrative,* p. 332 and n.; Thwaites, *Early Western Travels,* VI, 380, n. 197; Wisconsin Historical Society *Collections,* XIX, 226, n. 37; Keating, William H., *Narrative of an Expedition . . . . under the Command of Stephen H. Long,* I, 428-29, n.; Neill, Edward, *History of Minnesota,* p. 451, n. 1; Larpenteur, Charles, *Forty Years a Fur Trader on the Upper Missouri,* I, 60; Frémont, John C., *Memoirs,* p. 51. In a recent article on Peter Pond, Harold A. Innis makes the following interesting comment, "The source of pemmican, contrary to general belief, has not been definitely located. There is some reason to believe that it was a cultural trait of the Chipewyans or of the northern Indians of Athabasca, and that the Plains Indians prior to the coming of the White men had subsisted on dried meat. It is possible that Pond made a valuable contribution in adapting the pemmican which he found in use among the Athabascan Indians to the

FRUITS

The wild grape[8] is very common on all the wooded points, the islands, and the banks of the streams. It is generally superior in quality to the grape of the Ilinois.[9] The women, after they have taken the grapes from the bunch, press out the juice. This they boil until it thickens. It is then a sauce which is used with the balls of wild pear, maize flour, and flour of the prairie turnip.[10] Of the last-named I shall say more presently.

---

development of the trade from the Saskatchewan. The production of ample supplies of pemmican in Athabasca and the Saskatchewan was basic to the conduct of the trade in Athabasca and to the organization of the Northwest Company" (Royal Society of Canada, *Transactions,* 1928, Third Series, XXII, 136-37). Alexander Henry took great pride in his way of making pemmican for the trade and thought it most superior. See *Coventry edition, op. cit.,* I, 319.

[8] Tabeau's *le raisin sauvage* is the *vitis vulpina.*

[9] "il est généralement d'une qualité superieure a celui des ilinois. This has become, in the Montreal version, "il est le méme qu'aux ilinois."

[10] Anticipating to some extent Tabeau's remarks about the prairie apple, or prairie turnip, known to different travelers under different names; e.g., the Dakota, *Tipsinna* (Neill, *History of Minnesota, op. cit.,* p. 506, n. 1), the *pomme des prairies* (Frémont, *Memoirs,* I, 45); but, usually, as *pomme blanche,* the *psoralea esculenta* (*Original Journals, op. cit.,* I, 73, n. 1), or *psoralea lanceolata* (Grinnell, *op. cit.,* II, 178) of the botanists, it may be noted that Murray found it an equally popular article of diet among the Pawnees.

"The Indians," he wrote, "had little or no food, except such as they could pick up. Of these, the principal was an esculent root, something between a potato and a radish, most greedily sought by the Indians when going to the Buffalo country; they are then often reduced to a state approaching to starvation; and I have seen these roots dug out two, three, or even four miles from the regular trail. I ate them, and they appear somewhat nutritious and not unpalatable, but under any other circumstances would be thought tasteless and difficult of digestion. They are eaten raw, and I have never seen any attempt to cook them among the Pawnees; but they are said to be tolerably wholesome, as well as palatable, when boiled or roasted. The Canadian French call them *Pomme blanche* . . . . Some of the Missouri tribes call them Nu-ga-re" (*Travels in North America,* I, 265-66). Murray further wrote, when his experience had grown somewhat (*Prairie-Bird,* p. 94, n.), "Pommes de prairie are small roots, somewhat resembling white radishes, that are found in great abundance in the Western Wilderness, being in some places the only esculent vegetable within a range of several hundred miles; when eaten raw they are tough, tasteless, and hard of digestion, but if boiled or stewed, are tolerably palatable and wholesome." Captain Thomas Blakiston of the Royal Artillery thought the tuber mis-named. "It is called," he wrote, "the 'prairie turnip,' but assimilates to that root only, I think, in growing under ground, being more the shape of a carrot or rather Jerusalem artichoke, and by no means of the most tender nature" (*Further Papers Relative to the Exploration by the Expedition under Captain Palliser,* p. 39). Palliser himself, on the

A little above the village[11] of the Mahas a fruit is found which is peculiar to the Upper Missouri. Travelers call it "fat of the buffalo,"[12] probably in derision and for, or in recognition of, those who discovered it and for whom it served as a food in time of famine. It has the size, the color, and almost the shape of our currant, yet has

occasion of an earlier adventure, found a bear, "a lean hungry-looking monster, prowling about searching for *pommes blanches* . . . ." (*Solitary Rambles* . . . . *op. cit.,* p. 277) and John Pritchard is said to have subsisted for about forty days on the "bulbs of pommeblanche" (Bryce, George, *Remarkable History of the Hudson's Bay Company,* p. 173). For Catlin's description of the curved stick used by the squaws in digging this tuber, see *North American Indians* (1850), I, 56.

11 "On commence au village des mahas, à 300 lieuës de l'embouchure du Missouri, à trouver un fruit ..." (Montreal version).

"le vilage des mahas, est situé dans une belle prairie a environ une lieux de distance du missouris et a deux cent quatre vingt lieux des illinois ..." (Journal of Jean Baptiste Truteau, *Premiére Partie,* American Historical *Review,* XIX, 307).

"La grande riviere platte ce decharge dans le missouri a la Gauche en montant a deux cent lieux au dessus de lambouchure de ce dernier, a Cinquente lieu plus haut a la droite on trouve la petite riviere des Sioux qui n'est navigable quavec des Canot de chasse. Sa source est peu eloigne de sa sortie. trente lieu plus haut à la Gauche habite la nation mahas leur Cabanne sont batis à deux lieux de distance des bords du missouri ..." (*Description du haut Missouri* par Jean Bapte Trudeau, voyageur, Mississippi Valley Historical *Review,* VIII, 160-61).

"A quatre-vingt-dix milles de la première rivière des Sioux, (735 milles au-dessus de l'embouchure du Missouri) est la rivière et le village des Mahas ... Leur village est situé dans une belle plaine, aux pieds d'un agréable coteau, à une lieue du Missouri ..." (*Voyage dans les Deux Louisianes* par M. Perrin du Lac, p. 208).

12 Under date of August 24, 1804, Clark recorded in his journal:

"Great quantities of a kind of berry resembling a current except double the Size and Grows on a bush like a Privey, and the Size of a Damsen deliciously flavoured and makes delitefull Tarts, this froot is now ripe" (*Original Journals,* I, 119). Thwaites adds, "Buffalo-berry, or beef-suet tree (Fr. *Graisse du boeuf*), *Shepherdia argentea"* (*idem,* n. 1). To the Mandans this fruit was known as *as - sáy* and to the Arikaras as, *nar-nis* (*idem,* p. 161, n.), the Indian name or names seeming to signify, rabbit-berry (Coues, *Lewis and Clark,* I, 176). For Catlin's account of these same berries, buffalo-berries to him as to many others, see his work, previously cited, pp. 72-74. Grinnell, on his own experience and on information derived from Father De Smet's *Western Missions* and from Gilmore, *Uses of Plants by the Indians of the Missouri River Region* (Bureau of American Ethnology, *Report,* Washington, 1919), enlarges on the earlier accounts of this berry and it is interesting to observe that both he and Olin D. Wheeler seem to think that the present name, *bull-berry,* is of very recent origin, whereas that was the one that Francis A. Chardon, trader among the Mandans, 1834-39 and, later, among the Gros Ventres, and his contemporaries, for the most part, were accustomed to use. A yellow variety of the berry was noticed by Wheeler on the banks of the Yellowstone (*The Trail of Lewis and Clark,* II, 360).

upon its skin some gray spots which are removed by rubbing. It is an acid which, when fully ripe, loses enough of its sourness to become very agreeable to the taste. It does not grow in clusters but hangs in bunches upon the bark and thorns of each branch. As all the berries touch and as the leaves are few and small, only the fruit, so to speak, is seen and it offers a small tree and branches of a beautiful red. The tree is extremely bushy, its interlacing and spiney branches springing out almost at the foot. Its height is from three to seven or eight feet. The wood is very tough and is used by the Savages for their best arrows. The bush always grows near the water and yet I have observed that the bushes of which the roots had been a long time in water had no fruit. Both banks of the Missouri and all the islands from the village of the Poncas up to the Mandanes are lined with this bush.[13]

The Indian fig[14] takes its name from its shape. It is a root that shows neither trunk nor leaf. A sort of cake, green in color, two or three inches wide and about five or six lines[15] thick, almost oval in shape, springs from the earth and forms, with others like it, a circle having a diameter of about two feet. This plant, being covered with strong, sharp thorns and being very common on the prairies, compels the Savages and travelers to reinforce their shoes with a heavy raw hide. The fruit of this plant is large as an olive and pale red and is set between two thorns which form a pretty border all about it. It is an acid fruit, pleasant to taste, and, like the fat of the buffalo, makes excellent jellies. This plant can be grown in boxes and I have seen some of them in Montreal at the home of a person interested in curious things.[16]

Necessity has disclosed to the wandering Savages many nourish-

[13] The concluding sentence in the Montreal version, "les deux rives du missouri en sont bordees depuis la rivierre qui courre justqu'aux villages des mandanes. =", offers a slight modification.

[14] *la raquête*, corrected to *la raquette* in the margin and in the Montreal version, where appears the following: "La raquette a toute la forme & la couleur d'un aloé."

[15] The French line, as a measure, was equal to .0888 of an English inch.

[16] The closing sentences of the Montreal version present some changes:

" ... le fruit l'on appelle pomme de raquette, de la grosseur d'une olive, oval, & d'un rouge pale est toujours place entre deux epines & forme une tres jolie bordure tout autour de la raquette. c'est un acide de fort bon gout & qui comme la graisse de boeuf feroit des gelees delicieuses.="

ing roots, which often preserve them from death during the frequent famines to which they are exposed. They know many that I had no opportunity of seeing and that they speak of as a great resource in distress. But the prairie turnip is the most common and is not only reserved for these occasions but is used much even in times of plenty. This root has almost the shape of a turnip. It is covered with a hard and very thick black skin which is easily detached and always removed whether the turnip be eaten raw or boiled. The women cut it in pieces, which they dry in the sun and afterwards pound and reduce to flour. They make of this flour a rich, nourishing, and palatable soup.[17] All the wandering nations leave regretfully the districts where the prairie turnip grows abundantly and leave it, too, only after having dried great quantities of it. The Caninanbiches,[18] Chayennes and others, who, independently of their chargers, have many horses not laden, are rarely without this flour and, during the visit that they paid to the Ricaras, they bartered it for maize at a profit of three or four measures for one.[19]

[17] This was the experience of Brackenridge who found it "pounded and made into a gruel" (*Early Western Travels,* VI, 116).

[18] The Caninanbiches were the modern Arapaho. In the *Description de Haut Missouri,* they appeared as Tocaninanbiche (Mississippi Valley Historical *Review,* VIII, 167). Elsewhere, Truteau referred to them as Caminabiches (Missouri Historical Society *Collections,* IV, 31). In yet other contemporary narratives, occur the variants, Canenaviech, Kaninavisch, Kunnanarwesh, Kunnawarwish, and, in Alexander Henry's journal (*Coventry Copy,* I, 558), Caveninavish. For two of the best accounts of the Arapahoes, see Mooney, James, *The Ghost-Dance Religion,* U.S. Bureau of Ethnology *Report,* 1892-93, pp. 953 *et seq.,* and Dorsey, George Amos and Kroeber, Alfred L., *Traditions of the Arapaho,* Field Columbian Museum *Publications,* No. 81.

[19] It is at this point in the Montreal version that the material referred to comes in. It is sufficiently different in its concluding sentences to be worth quoting; for, in the light of the disasters of the last few years, Tabeau will be envisaged as not a bad prophet:

" ... il est vrai que la terre ne seroit pas mauvaise dans quelques pointes basses & quelques isles dont j'ai parlé, & les ricaras qui cultivent les unes & les autres, récoltent assez de mahy, de feves, de citrouilles &c. en rason de leurs semences. mais il faut remarquer qu'ils n'ensemencent que les terres neuves, étants forcés de changer souvent d'habitation, faute de bois qu'ils ruinent en cinq a six ans. d'ailleurs ces pointes & ces isles sont petites, trés eloignées les unes des autres & la plupart sujettes a l'innondation, comme l'ont éprouvé les ricaras qui ont perdu toute leur récolte en 1803. les mandanes & les gros ventres qui sont aussi cultivateurs, sont plus constants que ceuxci sur les mêmes établissements, parce que là les pointes sont plus grandes & que les bords du missouri commencent a être boisés de plus en plus en montant, ce qui est

NATIONS WHICH ROAM OVER OR INHABIT THE UPPER MISSOURI[1]

THE Missouri from its mouth up to the Mandanes is inhabited or frequented by fifteen or sixteen different nations, several of which are very numerous. Farther up, according to the report of the Savages, they are innumerable, the Chayennes alone counting thirty-two of them for enemies, although I think they consider some tribes as nations. However it may be, I shall speak only in a general way of them, in their place, as I know little about them. As for the Saakis,[2] Osages, Kancas, Panis, Otoctatas, Mahas, and others, the trading, which is carried on annually with them, has given more information to those who will read this scribble in the Ilinois than I can give and, as I am sure that it will not go beyond,[3] I shall speak only of those who have been very little visited. I shall begin with the Poncas.

The Poncas,[4] formerly very numerous, are those among whom

---

certain c'est que de bien audessous de l'isle aux cédres, jusques chez les mandanes inclusivement, on ne trouve (encore que très rarement) de mauvais liards propres a construire de médiocres pirogues."

[1] This is Chapter III in the Montreal version, following immediately after that section of Chapter II that is entitled "Le cerne — ou chasse en commun."

[2] In his revised version, Tabeau eliminated the Sacs (*Saakis*), who, properly-speaking, did not, in his time, belong to the Missouri. To illustrate how Tabeau's spelling of Indian names is intermediate between that of Du Pratz's day and the present, reference should be had to the latter writer's notable work, particularly pages 251-52 and others very like.

[3] " ... quand aux Saakis, osages, Kanças, panis, otoctatas, mahas et autres, le commerce qui se fait annuelement avec eux, a informé mieux que moy ceux qui liront ce griffonage aux ilinois, & comme je suis persuadé qu'il ne passera pas, outre, je ne parlerai, que de celles qui ont été moins frequentées en commençant par les poncas. —" (Washington version).

" ... je ne parlerai point ici des osages, kanças, panis, mahas, otoctatas & autres, que le commerce qui se fait continuelement avec eux des ilinois, a fait parfaitement connoitre, ainsi je ne parlerai que de celles qui n'ont été que peu ou point du tout fréquentes, en commençant par les poncas" (Montreal version).

[4] " ... je n'ai pus partir de mon hyvernement que le vingt cinq de mars, et je suis arrivee le meme jour aupres du village des poncas; le lendemain jay entre cher (chez) eux. leurs cabanes sont baties a environ une demy lieux du missouris" (Truteau,

small-pox has made the greatest ravages. Less sociable or more belligerent than their neighbors, they have had many enemies whom they resisted longer than one would expect, considering their respective forces. They still had in 1804 eighty men bearing arms; but an invasion of Sioux Bois Brulés has since destroyed more than half of them. Sixty men and some women and children were carried off into slavery, the greater part of whom were freed last winter at the solicitation of the Mahas, with whom the rest of the nation has at present taken refuge in order to escape entire destruction.[5]

The Poncas, the Mahas, the Kancas, the Osages, the Arkancas, speak the same language, although with slight differences. The Otoctatas, the Missouris, the Ayowois, Woinebigos,[6] or Puants, are, moreover, similar enough to them in their language to make one think that without a doubt they are all descended from one and the same primitive nation and that the common language has undergone more or less change because of the period of separation. But this epoch is so far back and they (the tribes) now live in places so remote from each other that today they do not recognize each other as kin and often make war mutually.

The Poncas are tillers of the soil and, to some extent, hunt the deer and the beaver; but, although they should have up to the present been able to furnish many peltries, their trade would never have made up for their exactions.[7] Of all the nations the Poncas are the most addicted to brigandage and few traders have come into con-

---

Première Partie, American Historical *Review,* XIX, 332. For a slight discrepancy, see *idem,* p. 308).

"La nation poncas a ses habitations, situé a deux lieux plus haut que son embouchure leur Cabanne sont batie sur une eminence au bord dune Grande pleine eloigné d'environ une lieu du missouri, ..." (*Description du haut Missouri,* Mississippi Valley Historical *Review,* VIII, 162-63).

[5] "... mais au printemps 1805 — une incursion des titons en a détruit plus de la moitié. soixante femmes & enfants ont été trainés en esclavage chez les bois brulés seuls, qui cependant en ont rendu la plus grande partie, a la sollicitation des mahas, chez les qu'els la reste de la nation est obligée de se refugier pour éviter son entierre destruction.—" (Montreal version).

[6] *Woinebigos ou puants"* (Washington version); *"woinebigaux"* (Montreal version).

[7] "... mais on n'a jamais fait avec eux de traite avantageuse, ..." (Montreal version).

tact with them, even in their village, without suffering from the meeting. The Sioux rendered a service to commerce by compelling this fierce horde to unite with the Mahas and they have removed thereby the strongest barrier to intercourse.[8] They spent last winter with Mr. McLanell, who found them, since their union with the Mahas and the chastisement of the Sioux, very mild and honorable. The latter (the Sioux) would become more tractable themselves, perhaps, if they were to receive the correction which they rightly deserve.

THE SIOUX[9]

The assembled Sioux number at least four thousand men bearing

[8] The two concluding sentences are omitted from the Montreal version:

" ... ils ont passé l'hyver dernier avec m. McLanell, qui les a trouvé fort doux & fort honêtes depuis leur jonction avec les mahas, & la correction des Sioux, qui deviendroient peutêtre eux-mêmes plus traitables, s'ils en recevoient une qu'ils méritent a justes titres.==" (Washington version).

[9] Several classifications of the Sioux have been attempted since Tabeau ventured upon his and his was, by no manner of means, the earliest. For some of the more important, coming subsequent to his, see Powell, *Indian Linguistic Families,* U.S. Bureau of American Ethnology *Report,* 1885-86, pp. 111-18; Dorsey, J. O., *Siouan Sociology, idem,* 1893-94, pp. 205-44; McGee, W. J., *The Siouan Indians, idem,* pp. 153-204. Tabeau's bears so close a resemblance to those gathered together by Lewis and Clark and published in the journals and in the *Statistical View* respectively that there is little danger of going far astray in asserting that his and theirs had all a common source. In fact, such discrepancies as exist between the two principal classifications that the American explorers prepared are easily traceable to Tabeau. Dorion and Heney and Tabeau were all qualified, in a measure, to speak authoritatively of the Sioux from having had commercial dealings with them; but the Sioux bands were many and widely spread so that a classification of them was bound to be an exceedingly difficult undertaking. For the "Naywatame Poets" as a possible lost band of the Sioux, see Kenney, James F., *The Career of Henry Kelsey,* Royal Society of Canada *Transactions, 3rd series,* XXIII, 47, n. 49 and, on the subject of classification, see Wisconsin Historical Society *Collections,* XVI, 193, 194, also Maximilian, in Thwaites, *Early Western Travels,* XXII, 305. Tabeau's recourse was to the old French method of grouping the various bands according to habitat by the aid of their own patronymics; e.g., People of the Lakes, People of the Leaves, etc. For something similar to this, see *French Régime in Wisconsin,* Wisconsin Historical Society *Collections,* XVIII, 133, n. 69. For a presumable Dorion contribution to the knowledge of Lewis and Clark, see *Original Journals,* I, 132-33; but of all they received from their various sources, the part that most nearly resembles, in outline, Tabeau's is that given under date, December 27, 1804, which Coues calls "but a slight sketch" (*Lewis and Clark,* I, 216, n. 42) and which, considering the time of its insertion in the journal, may well have been contributed by Hugh Heney, whose knowledge was probably much the same as Tabeau's. Heney had recently been to

arms and, with the exception of two weak tribes,[10] who are tillers of the soil near the St. Peter's River, are all migratory. Spring and summer they follow the cow over the vast prairies that separate the St. Peter's River from the Missouri and, in the autumn, they follow her still by approaching again with her the great rivers where each tribe fixes its winter encampment. The entire Sioux nation is divided first into five principal tribes, which are subdivided then under different chiefs and diverse denominations. There could be added here the Asseniboanes, their enemies, who speak the same language and have, without a doubt, the same origin. This language, by lapse of time, has undergone changes, so varied in pronunciation and in nomenclature, that a Sioux of the lakes who should visit those of the Missouri would not understand the different tribes any more than a Parisian who should visit the provinces of France would understand or be understood.

General Division of the Sioux[11]

1st—— people of the lakes		The first three dwell near the St. Peter's River. A part of the fourth visits it as well as the River of the Mohens.[13] Another part occasionally the Missouri, territory proper to the Titons alone.
2nd—— people of the leaves		
3rd—— Seissitons		
4th—— Hyinctons[12]		
5th—— Titons		

Fort Mandan and had been questioned closely by Lewis and Clark. Larocque's journal entry for December 17, 1804 is as follows:

"Monday 17th We Remain'd here all day, The Captains Enquired a great deal of Mr- Heney, Concerning the Sioux Nation, & Local Circumstances of that Country & Lower Part of the Missouri — of which they took Notes— ..." (*Masson MSS*, Dominion Archives, Ottawa).

[10] Tabeau's *tribus* has been literally translated to avoid confusion, notwithstanding that the usage of today would employ *band* to express the same idea.

[11] In copying Tabeau's classification of the Sioux, his spelling of Indian names has been retained even though in many cases a modern could have been substituted to advantage. It will be found very profitable to compare the classification given here with that of Meriwether Lewis's *Statistical View* (American State Papers, Indian Affairs, I, 715).

[12] "Yinctons" (Montreal version).

[13] "rivierre des Mokins" (Montreal version). Evidently a slip of the pen since, later on, mention is made of "la rivierre des mohins."

PARTICULAR DIVISIONS OF EACH OF THE FIVE TRIBES

PEOPLE OF THE LAKES	PEOPLE OF THE LEAVES

Kiouxas ⎫
Tintatons ⎬ Tillers of the soil
Mindewacantons ⎭
Matatons

Warhpetons
Otherhatons[14]

SEISSITONS

Karhes
Warpecoutais
Mayakidjaxes

These three tribes form the base of all the trade of the St. Peter's River.[15]

	HYINCTONS	TITONS

These are Yinctons[16] of the North, 260 lodges. There are about five hundred men under a great chief named Matowinkay.

Saones-Yinctons
Kiouxas-Yinctons

Raharhatons

Hont-patines
Passandoucas
Wasicoutais

Sitchanrhou-Titons
Okondanas
MineKanhini-yojou
Saones-Titons

These are subdivided into a dozen different bands as follows:

Sitchanrhou-Yinctons
Tacohimboto[17]
Seascapé

These are Yinctons of the South, now at the James River.

---

14 "Othéhatons" (Montreal version).

15 At this point, according to the copy of the Montreal version that is at my disposal, there is inserted the following remark:

"il faut observer que je me sers de la lettre h après une r pour indiquer que la prononciation de la syllabe se fait de la gorge, & en effet on ne peut aspirer l'h après cette liquide, sans un coup de gosier."

16 Lewis assigned to the Yanktons of the North, or Plains, 500 warriors and 200 lodges and gave 1,600 as the entire population. They have been identified since his time with the better known Yanctonnais. See Coues, *Lewis and Clark*, I, 95, n. 2.

17 "Tocohim-cotaux" (Montreal version).

103

SUBDIVISION OF THE FOUR TITON TRIBES

THE SITCHANRHOU

Issanhati

Watchihoutairhe

Tchocatonhan[18]

Woisage

THE SAONES-TITONS

Tatchindi-chidja

Hitasiptchone[19]

Hont-papas

THE MINICAN-HINIYOJOU

Minican-hojou

Tacohiropapais

Waniwacteonilla[20]

THE OKONDANAS

Okondanas

Chihaut

The Okondanas and the Chihauts formerly connected a n d living with the Ris,[21] were agriculturists, but a war having come between the Ricaras and some Sioux bands, these two bands sided each one with one of the opposing parties. Although they were re-united afterwards, there was no longer any question of cultivation.[22]

All these thirty tribes, particularly those of the Titons, yield still other divisions which are under the leadership of subordinate chiefs. These chiefs return to the rank of companions when the tribe is all reunited. If this nation had more insight and policy, it could form a chain that would render it yet more formidable to all of its neighbors than it is. But their separation and mutual remoteness, necessitated by their form of hunting which does not permit of their living together in too great numbers, divides interests and causes those of the St. Peter's River, those of the River of the Mohens, and those of the Missouri to regard each other as strangers. Then, too, the spirit of unsociability and of discord which exists among the particular tribes; the ambition and the jealousy of the too numerous chiefs; and most of all the national character, naturally brutal and fierce,

18 "Tehokatehon" (Montreal version).

19 "Hitachiptchone" (Montreal version).

20 "Waniwactaionila" or "Waniwactaionita" (Montreal version).

21 This is one of the several abbreviations of Arikara. "Les aricaras, appeles par abrige les ris," wrote the author of *Description du haut Missouri*. See Mississippi Valley Historical *Review*, VIII, 164. The abbreviation is not used in the corresponding place in the Montreal version.

22 " ... & quoiqu'elles se soient réunies depuis entre elles & reliées de nouveau avec les ricaras elles n'ont pas reprise l'agriculture, tant la vie vagabonde plait aux sioux en général." =

cause particular enmities to arise, which not only destroy the general harmony but especially that of the various units. Individual quarrels arise which perpetuate, in families, hatred and revenge. Thus by a just defiance, which experience sanctions, a Titon is always armed even in his lodge.

Insubordination and the misuse of authority are a necessary result of this multiplicity of chiefs, who dispute with envy the shadow of power. I have known only one of them whose ascendency over the spirit of the Yinctons of the North, whom one can say that he commands, is remarkable enough to be commented upon. This savage, named Matowinkay, possesses advantages of the body, of the mind, and of the soul. At the head of two hundred and sixty lodges, which make about five hundred men,[23] he is loved and respected by them so that they obey him blindly. His reputation and this authority so rare in the Upper Missouri gave him an extraordinary influence over strangers and especially among the Ricaras where he enjoys much more consideration than their own chiefs. A trader under his protection is safe from every insult; but, as Matowinkay never possesses anything and as his rank demands gifts, his favors are costly and some traders have paid very dear for them. I should have liked Capt^u Lewis to have met him on the Missouri; for I believe that, honoring him as he deserves, he would have made a very trustworthy ally.[24]

Among the Titons[25] the chiefs have authority only when it is a question of pillage; but, if it is a question of calming a riot, of stop-

[23] The size of a Sioux lodge is indicated in a parenthetical clause introduced into the Montreal version: "(ce qui fait environ 650 hommes les sioux comptants 100 hommes par 40 loges, & ce calcul & assez juste)."

[24] No better evidence of Tabeau's friendly attitude towards the American explorers, as revealed in his desire to co-operate with them and to serve them to the best of his ability by putting his superior knowledge at their disposal, need be desired than in his obviously sincere regret at Lewis's failure to meet this chief, whom Lewis called, *Mah-to-wy-ank-ka*, a regret that Tabeau did not embody in his Montreal revision. The comment of the *Statistical* View upon Mah-to-wy-ank-ka is, "Said individually to be very friendly to the whites. He possesses great influence in his band and nation" (*op. cit.*). For the council held by Lewis and Clark with several of the Sioux chiefs, see Ordway's journal (Wisconsin Historical Society *Collections*, XXII, 119-23).

[25] "Parmi les titons, (qui sont ceux avec les qu'els nous avons eu plus d'affaires) ..." (Montreal version).

ping pillage, of aiding a trader in his expeditions, all authority is as nought before the opposition of a single individual.[26]

Mr. Loisel, planning to send a party from the Isle of Cedar for the Saones and Okondanes at the Fork, under the conduct of Mr. Henney, learns that an old soldier, named Mato-kokipabi, murmured and proposed to stop the vessel. Mr. Loisel, prudently foreseeing that the stopping of the loaded pirogue would be considered as making her a lawful prize, calls an assembly of chiefs and of counsellors, in which was also the old soldier.[27] Black Buffalo,[28] the Partisan,[29] Medicine Bull,[30] and Manzomani, four principal chiefs, represent

[26] " ... contre l'opposition d'un simple soldat, comme on le va voir" (Montreal version).

[27] "comme nous projettions de faire partir de l'isle au cédres ou nous étions avec les bois brulés, quelques marchandises que je devois conduire moy même chez les saones & les okondanes, hyvernants a 15 lieuës plus haut que nous, nous apprenons qu'un vieu soldat nomé mato-co-ki -pa-bi (celui qui effraye l'ours) se proposoit de nous arrêter. prévoiants que la voiture chargée, une fois arrêtée, pourroit subir le sort d'une prise légalle, nous fesons une assemblée de chefs & considérés, ou se trouvoit aussi le vieu soldat ..." (Montreal version).

[28] Literally *Black Buffalo Bull*. When Gravelines arrived at Fort Mandan, February 28, 1805, as a messenger from Tabeau to Lewis and Clark, he spoke particularly of this Teton chief, whom he called, "Black Buffalo" and of the friendliness of his disposition towards the Americans (Coues, *Lewis and Clark,* I, 239. Black Buffalo attended the treaty-making at Portage des Sioux at the close of the War of 1812 (*Niles' Register,* IX, 112) and died at St. Charles, Missouri, July, 1815. For the oration delivered over his grave by the Omaha chief, Big Elk, July 14, 1815, see Bradbury, *Travels in the Interior of America,* pp. 220-21, and for a sketch of his life subsequent to 1804, see Drumm, *Luttig Journal,* p. 56, n. 82.

[29] This second chief of the Teton Sioux had a generally bad reputation on the Upper Missouri, a reputation that lived long after him. The Lewis and Clark narratives substantiate, though meagerly, what Tabeau relates concerning him. His importunity was quite habitual (Coues, *op. cit.,* I, 142). Of his hostile demeanor on one occasion Patrick Gass saw fit to make special mention. A fellow chief stigmatized him as double-faced and, because of his conduct, Clark called the island on which he was encountered, "Bad-humored Island." He was another one of the peace deputation taken down by Manuel Lisa to Portage des Sioux in 1815 (Drumm, *Luttig's Journal, 1812-1813,* p. 90, n. 137) and may have been identical with *Le Grand Partizan,* who attended the council that Captain Pike held on the St. Peter's in 1805 (Pike, Zebulon Montgomery, *Exploratory Travels through the Western Territories of North America,* p. 36).

[30] The *Tartongawaka,* Buffalo Medicine, of the Lewis and Clark journals. Only three principal chiefs are mentioned by name in the Montreal version: "le boeuf noir premier chef, le partisant second, manzomani troisiéme & plusieurs autres approuvants nôtre projet, représentent fortement ..."

strongly that they have already only too many foreign enemies without alienating their own nation by a procedure so unjust; that the Titons of the Fork, the Chayennes, and others, who are on the point of going there, would not fail to avenge the insult and the wrong which would be done them by stopping the merchandise which is destined for them; and that, furthermore, their tribe alone being incapable of furnishing enough peltries for all the merchandise of the trader, the French would withdraw discontented. Eventually, after many other reasons, the old soldier, without taking the trouble to refute them or to explain his own reasons, declares laconically that he does not wish the merchandise to leave and that he establishes himself as guardian of the stores. At this conclusion, the chiefs depart in silence and no one dares to oppose the will of a simple soldier.[31]

Presents offered, supplications, mediation of friends could not overcome his obstinacy, founded upon a particular revenge against the Saones, who had lately stolen some of his horses, and against Mr. Loisel, whom reason, prudence, and economy had compelled to decline his daughter in marriage.[32] Not that delicacy was offended by this refusal, made besides under fair[33] pretenses, but the hope of rolling in the wealth of the son-in-law was frustrated. It is true that secretly all were delighted that his opposition succeeded as they hoped themselves to trade the peltries of the strangers by an intermediary commerce to which they are accustomed and to sell to us then with profit—what actually took place.[34]

The prejudice that the obstinacy of this Savage brought to Mr. Loisel could not be estimated.[35] 1st. The excess of merchandise

[31] This incident has, interestingly enough, the flavor of the famous story of the vase of Soissons in old Frankish annals.

[32] This is the first instance, in connection with this affair, that the name of Loisel is brought into the Montreal version. The Indian custom hinted at is too well known to need discussion. Travelers frequently found themselves compelled to decline proffers of the sort; but traders, more often than not, took advantage of the opportunity that a union within the family of a chief afforded to increase their prestige and influence.

[33] "sous des pretextes honêtes" in the original, a slip of the pen, no doubt, for *honnêtes* (Tr.).

[34] This last sentence in the paragraph is altogether lacking in the Montreal version. It is, therefore, not possible to check on such words as *peleteries*, by which it is assumed, pelleteries was meant.

[35] Again Loisel is ignored in the Montreal version.

among the Savages always lessens the estimate of its value and the
Bois Brulés, finding themselves overloaded, demanded it at a very
low price, to the end, that there is nothing left of it. 2nd. The fear
of an expedition in their absence fixed them, as it were, about us so
that they did little hunting and, consequently, there remained more
of unsold merchandise. 3rd. It would all have been traded even the
first year with the Saones, Okondanes, Ricaras, and Yinctons and, by
this means, the delay and the large expense of a second winter encampment had been spared. 4th. The price of each article, fixed by
the Bois Brulés, made a rate to which it was very difficult not to conform this year and which made the risks of pillage great, as well to
Mr. Valé, as to me.[36] 5th. Having succeeded among the Ricaras in
1803, it was possible to succeed among the Mandanes the following
year, should it be only with some baubles, by taking there the necessary knowledge and by preparing for commerce the nations above,
who alone could render it important and lucrative. 6th. This example of the Bois Brulés would not fail to be imitated, even by those
who then blamed their conduct only because they suffered from it.

It is true that, under our new[37] government, which, without being the tyrant of the Savages, knows also not to be their slave, things
may change completely so that these happenings will probably no
longer have to be feared and that we can even hope for some kind of
order among the Bois Brulés, since Black Bull,[38] distinguished and

[36] Only three results are enumerated in the Montreal version and the fourth being one of those omitted, the reference to Mr. Valé is necessarily omitted likewise.

[37] So easy and natural a reference to the American authority recently installed
points to no great attachment on the part of Tabeau to either of its predecessors.
This thought is further strengthened by such differences in phrasing as appear in the
Montreal version:

"on pourroit peut-être esperer quelqu'espéce d'ordre parmi les bois brulés depuis que ta-tanga-saba (le boeuf noir), élevé un premier rang par le gouvernement
amériquain, sent qu'il est autorisé a commender a toutes les tribus, sans s'inquiéter
des autres chefs, qui sont devenus ses subalternes. mais je crois qu'il faudra quelques années pour que l'autorité du congré influë sur le gouvernement des sioux. ..."

Several things mentioned here and there in his narrative indicate that Tabeau
expected better trade conditions under the United States government than had obtained under the Spanish. For Larocque's understanding of what the American
methods were likely to be, see his journal entry for November 29, 1804 (Dominion
Archives, Ottawa).

[38] Tatanga Saba [marginal note]. The equivalent of this name in the Lewis
and Clark journals is *Untongasabaw*. See Coues, *Lewis and Clark,* I, 132. For his

elevated to the first rank, will feel that he has the right to command all the bands indifferently without having to use so much precaution with the other chiefs, who will have become his subalterns. This Savage is of a good character, although angry and fierce in his fits of passion. He is a friend of the whites, intelligent enough to know that it is to the interest of his nation to treat them kindly. He is frank and above-board with them in private, but shrewd and politic in public, particularly in the presence of people who are not dependent upon him. His bravery, his spirit, and his generosity have already given him great preeminence over all the other chiefs; but this deference, as of etiquette, had no influence upon their deliberations or else his opinions, approved in his presence, were of no consequnce and of no effect outside the council. His tribe,[39] the bravest and the most numerous, conforms cheerfully to all his wishes and it is really due to his ascendency over it that we have no cause to complain of it and that all his people are easily distinguished in the trading. But, on the whole, his authority does not extend very far and, either through caution or necessity, he is always satisfied with pitying us in the pillage of the Partisan[40] and his followers. It is true that this rogue had the advantage of him in having first discovered Mr. Loisel on his first[41] voyage and that, because of a custom established among

---

attempt to detain the American expedition by force after presents had been bestowed upon him and others and he himself recognized as principal chief, see *Ordway Journal,* Wisconsin Historical Society *Collections,* XXII, 138-39.

[39] The Issanhati [marginal note]. Les Issanhati, or Santee, one of the subdivisions of the four main divisions of the Teton Sioux.

[40] Mandotahang [marginal note]. The Mando-tahang of Tabeau's rendering is the Tortohonga of Lewis and Clark's (Coues, *Lewis and Clark,* I, 132) and the difference between the two names is great enough to suggest that here, at all events, Tabeau was not their informant. Ordway's "Medethunka pertizon" (Wisconsin Historical Society *Collections,* XXII, 122) was evidently an endeavor to combine the name and its meaning.

[41] Whether by this *"premier voïage"* of Loisel's is meant the one of 1802, on which Tabeau, according to his own deposition (see Appendix V) accompanied Loisel, or some yet earlier one it is impossible to determine. Loisel, in his Memorial (see Appendix VII) refers to the voyage of 1803 as his "last;" but, so far as is known with certainty, he never made but two, possibly three, to the Upper Missouri. If Tabeau means the voyage of 1802, he concedes to Loisel, in this instance at least, a measure of superiority.

the Sioux, the trader is always under the protection and care of him who finds him.

I have already said that the Titon chiefs are only too powerful, when it is a question of doing evil; but it is not necessary to attribute this obedience to respect for authority. This obedience springs really from the disposition of individuals, to whom the orders, in such a case, are never repugnant, who are, indeed, very glad to use it for a pretext. For this reason, all the schemes of the Partisan against the public peace and against our interests have always had all the success that he could desire. This man, true disturber of public quiet, has invariably found means to thwart the intentions of Black Bull and to make his pacific plans miscarry.

The 5th of September, 1803, Black Bull, urgently entreated by the Mahas and the Poncas near the James River, accepts their invitation and arranges to speak to them of peace;[42] but, in order not to leave any pretext for the machinations of the Partisan after his own departure, he announces publicly his intentions and consults him himself. Opinions are unanimous; but the traitor, envious of the honor and the presents which his rival would receive, too detested to dare to venture far from the village in order to accompany him, foreseeing also that peace would bring these strangers into treaty with us, plots during the night and sends off six warriors before dawn. Black Bull, informed in the morning of the treachery, contents himself by dissimulating as usual. These warriors steal six horses from the Poncas, who by just reprisals some days after take away nine from the Bois Brulés, seven of which composed the entire drove of innocent Black Bull. The Partisan congratulates himself on the double success of his wickedness; but Black Bull himself, reduced all the winter to serve as a beast of burden, breathed only vengeance against the Pon-

---

[42] "Le 5 de 9bre 1803 ═══ le boeuf noir reçoit une députation des mahas, campés a environ 70 lieuës de nous, qui le prioient de leur rendre visite il accepte l'invitation & se dispose a leur porter des paroles de paix. ..." (Montreal version). Again there arises some perplexity about the date; but, since winter is specifically mentioned farther on, as if that were the season about to be entered upon, "9bre," occurring in both versions, must refer to November, it would seem, and this view could be accepted were it not for the fact that, as shown on p. 127, n.84, Tabeau apparently counted the months from January without reference to their Latin names. For a contrary view, see p. 117, n.59.

cas and very effectively satisfied it, as was seen on the twenty-fourth Floréal.[43]

This man called the Partisan, the chief of a band[44] of the Bois Brulés, the largest after that of Black Bull, is a true Proteus,[45] who is seen in the selfsame day faint-hearted and bold, audacious and fearful, proud and servile, conciliator and firebrand. At the same instant in which, in favor of the trader, he fixes advantageous prices, he excites his agents to force their reduction. His is a character, hard, discontented with all and with himself, fidgetty, ambitious in the extreme. Having neither the prudence nor the courage necessary to elevate himself, he is without perseverance in the use of the methods he employs so unskillfully. Indeed, the only one in which he is interested is liberality and that he exercises at the expense largely of the trader. But, as conduct is mostly the expression of habits, an account of some of his unworthy proceedings will make him better known.

The envious Partisan is hostile to all those who lay claim to the least consideration and, consequently, he is hostile to Manzomani,[46] chief of the weakest of the Bois Brulés bands. This personal hatred, propagated by party spirit, was diffused throughout the two hordes. The thirty-first of August, this monster of iniquity, dissatisfied with Mr. Loiscl, who concerned himself little with their dissensions, did

---

[43] "comme on l'a vu au flo 24 = " (Washington text); "comme on l'a vu au flo 18 = " (Montreal text). Two theories suggest themselves as to what "flo" stands for. If it stands for folio, it may, in the case of the Washington text, refer to the paragraph beginning:

"Les poncas autrefois fort nombreux sont ceux ou il paroit que la petite vérole a fait de plus grands ravages ...", the corresponding paragraph of which is, as it happens, on page 18 of the Montreal text. The other theory is, that "flo" is an abbreviation for *Florial*, the eighth month in the calendar of the first French republic, which extended from April 20th to May 19th. If the latter theory be tenable, then, in writing his revised narrative, Tabeau had occasion again to correct a date.

[44] The Wat-chioutairhe [marginal note]. Les Wat-chiotairhe, another band, the second, of the first division of the Teton Sioux.

[45] "Ce monstre que les François noment le *partisant* est un veritable prothee ..." (Montreal version). Proteus was the Old Man of the Sea in Greek mythology. In his *History of Louisiana under Spanish Domination,* p. 324, Gayarré quotes from Pickett's *History of Alabama,* I, 142, a characterization of the Creek chief, McGillivray, that bears a most astonishing resemblance to this of the Partisan by Tabeau.

[46] *Celui qui marche sur la marchandise* [he who marched upon the merchandise] in the margin of the Washington text.

not ally himself with his party, gave back to him, in one of his jealous rages, a flag that Mr. Loisel had bestowed upon him.[47] His vanity and his ambition were too well known, however, for this sort of abdication to appear sincere and not to betoken some meditated perfidy. In truth, an hour later, we learnt that one of his agents had cocked his gun, which, missing fire, just avoided hitting one of our workmen, and that, but for the intervention of others, he would have accomplished his assassination. Perhaps the man had orders to frighten only; for a Savage, who plans murder, keeps his gun well in order.

The 6th of September Mr. Loisel, wishing to have some trinkets reach the Fork, wrapped them in the beds of the *engagés,* without other cargo, and engaged a canoe at daybreak.[48] At the moment of departure, some soldiers, sufficiently good-humored, opposed the going and all returned to the fort quietly. But the Partisan, who let no occasion escape for doing mischief and for extorting presents, stirred up the men and, in a trice, more than fifty armed men appeared at the door. The capote[49] of one of our men was cut off him and the

---

[47] " ... Le 31 d' 8bre. ce monstre d'injustice mécontent de ceque mm. loisel, qui s'inquietoit peu de leur dissention, ne se rangeoit pas de son parti, luy remet dans une de ses fureurs jalouses le pavillon qu'il en a reçu. ..." (Washington text).

" ... cet envieux aurroit voulu que nous n'eussions aucune considération pour ce dernier, & dans une de ses fureurs jalouses, il nous rapporte le 31 8 bre le pavillon qu'il avoit reçu du gouverneur espagnol. ..." (Montreal text).

Taken together the two passages just quoted reveal a political connection that neither alone can, a connection that, from information derived elsewhere, is known to have existed.

[48] The corresponding passage in the Montreal version is important as a clue to the existing business relationship between Loisel and Heney. This was about a year before Lewis and Clark encountered Heney, then an employee of the North West Company.

"le 6 de 9bre mr loisel voulant envoyer quelques couteaux & autres minuties a mr heney résident a la fourche. ..."

[49] No translation of "Le capot" (la capote?) into the terminology of today can possibly be adequate to convey the idea required. The garment, called a capote, was a part of the regular stock in trade during the best days of the peltry traffic. John Thomson has an entry in his journal (1798): "Saturday the 6th very cold . . . . Sold him a Illinois capot, a pr. corduroy trousers & a ps gartering . . . ." (*Masson MSS,* Dominion Archives, Ottawa); Porter, in his, kept at Slave Lake, 1800, says, (July 30th) ". . . . I was always obliged to Keep my Pistols in my Capot whenever I went to them (the Indians) . . . ." (*idem*); Henry, in his, November 28, 1804, confessed, "We had nothing but our Capots to cover ourselves with" (*Cov-*

others thrown into the house received two shots. The rogue in the crowd incited anger everywhere and cried in a loud voice, "How then do your arms serve you? Why not hunt the French as you do the wild cow?" Neither Black Bull nor anyone else trusted enough to his ascendency to dare to appear or to stem this oratory and Mr. Loisel was constrained to have recourse to the universal remedy. A very considerable present brought calm after the storm; but, an hour afterwards, a quarrel having arisen between two individuals, the Partisan claimed his flag again and exacted a second present so as to allay this new difference.

The 12th of the same month he entered the store followed by our pretended soldier; but really his own, as he was his creature. They jumped over the counter and ventured as far as a separate apartment which contained the packed merchandise and that destined for the Fork. Notwithstanding all prudent opposition, he pretended to be a clerk of the custom-house, searched sufficiently well to discover a certain quantity of hidden blankets belonging to the equipment for the Fork.[50] To recommend discretion to him or even to buy it would have been wild, so the blankets were forcibly dedicated to the present trade and the clerk left but without anyone perceiving that he had deducted his fees by pilfering a blanket ornamented with spots. This success emboldened him to repeat his visit the next day and with much more insolence. He removed the cases; he threw down the pieces; he rummaged everywhere; and he examined with all the air of an owner. At last, unknown to him, Black Bull, the other chiefs and companions are sent for, as it is hoped that, at least through shame or through policy, he will restrain himself in their presence. Besides, it is necessary to put an end to his interference and to know at all events on whom to rely. He slips away at their arrival and only after many invitations does he return to assist at the council. Black Bull makes it understood that the French, not being under his care, he has nothing to say. Manzomani draws a comparison be-

---

entry Copy, I, 353); and Palliser, similarly, "My large winter grey woollen shooting-coat (or capote) was completely worn out" (*Solitary Rambles* . . . . , p. 334) and "clothed as we were in white blanket capotes" (*idem*, p. 128). For an attempt at a definition, see Schlarman, *From Quebec to New Orleans*, p. 302).

[50] The Fork is not mentioned in the parallel paragraph of the Montreal version.

tween us and the traders of the River St. Peter's that is not in our favor. Who would believe that the Partisan alone is interested in us? Has he not in a long speech endeavored to comport himself well with us and to watch over our peace? Why has he himself fixed the trade, by taxing each article at an advantageous price, and has promised that no one in the future should hesitate to conform to it? The perfidious one attained his ends. He saw a present which Mr. Loisel was obliged to increase at the application of the aide-de-camp.[51]

The 17th, some Savages, having arrived from the River St. Peter's, report that merchandise is plentiful there and that the English squander it upon the Savages. They put also into the mouth of the traders most pernicious talk, very disparaging and very debasing to us.[52] It is necessary no longer to reawaken the insatiable greed of the Partisan. He intrigues, he agitates, he incites, he inveighs against our meanness, forbids dealing with us, and encourages reserving the pelts for the River St. Peter's. He schemes secretly and prepares the storm which bursts at last, the twentieth of the month. At daybreak, the Partisan, the old soldier, and Manzomani being in the house, our two soldiers enter, their bodies blacker than the crows they carry at the croup, indicating that the affair is important. They at once close and lock on the inside doors and windows and take up their position as sentinels. Not one of us is free to leave, unless some need urges him; no Savage can enter; and Black Bull, phantom of first chief, demanding to be let in, goes quietly away at a word that the Partisan says in his ear. We are kept thus in great silence until three o'clock, when, after the most offensive reproaches and the most hu-

[51] " ... le perfide étoit parvenu a ses fins; il voioit un présent (car sans cela point de conseil) que m^r loisel a encore été obligé d'augmenter a la réquisition d'un aide de camp, qui dans toutes les assemblées fesoit toujours cette motion. = " (Montreal version).

" ... le perfide étoit parvenu a ses fins. il voioit un présent, que mm. loisel a encore été obligé d'augmenter a la réquisition de l'aide de camp. = " (Washington version).

[52] "Le 17. — quelques Sauvages arrivés de la rivierre S^t. Pierre, rapportent que les marchandises y sont a foison, & que les anglois les prodiguent aux Sauvages. ils mettent en outre dans la Bouche des traiteurs les discours les plus pernicieux, les plus dénigrants & les plus avilissants pour nous. ..." (Washington version).

"cinq jours après quelques sauvages rapportent que les marchandises sont a foison sur la rivierre s^t pierre, & que les traiteurs les prodiguent pour ainsi dire. ..." (Montreal version).

miliating comparisons with our competitors, we are told that the doors are closed in order to prevent trade as it is necessary to lower prices and to give up a barrel of brandy. It is thus that this detestable chief, in order not to take anything under the name of pillage has recourse to violence so as to obtain under that some voluntary gift. Finally, the barrel is delivered with many other presents and it is agreed that trade will remain on the same footing. The soldiers, being dismissed and paid, we are released.

As the Partisan is walking one day along the shore with Black Bull, a kinswoman of the former comes to fetch water. Not having been able some days before to obtain her favors, he would have avenged himself by killing her, if his gun had not missed fire two or three times. Black Bull, although of a strong and fiery temperament, who certainly does not fear him, has the tact to contain himself by saying to him merely:

"This is enough; you see that the gun does not wish to kill." I should never end if I wished to recount all the traits of the Partisan revealed in his relations with us.[53] I have cited those that have just

[53] From this point, Tabeau's revised version is so markedly different as to warrant the quoting of the remainder of the paragraph:

"Je ne finirois pas si je voulois rapporter tout ce que nous avons eu a souffrir de ce détestable chef & ses adhérents; on trouvera sans doute que nous avons montré plus de patience que de courage & qu'avec quinze hommes dans un bon fort inaccessible a des sauvages, nous pouvions nous faire respecter, répousser l'insulte & même châtier l'insolence. Ce reproche seroit juste en nous supposant parmi les outawas, les saakis, les chawoinons & bien d'autres que les traiteurs rossent sans conséquence; encore cela ne peut-il guères avoir lieu que dans une querelle particulière, ou la nation ne prend aucun intêret. Mais ici nous étions informés, à n'en pas douter, que plus de 400 hommes n'attendoient qu'en prétexte plausible ou spécieux pour déclarer une guerre ouverte. = en ce cas, dénués de toutes provisions, que nous ne pouvions tirer que d'eux mêmes, que serions nous devenus dans nôtre fort imprénable? en supposant même que nous eussions eu tous les moyens de tenir tout l'hyver, avec qui aurrions nous traité? que faire d'une pacotille de trois mille louis Comment se tirer d'embarras le printemps? il aurroit été absurde de penser a une réconciliation; la moitié des marchandises n'aurroit pas suffit pour satisfaire chaque mécontent, & certainement qu'en permettant l'entrée du fort, tout aurroit été comme de bonne prise. après cette petite apologie, j'assure que si ceux qui nous désapprouveront connoissoient la férocité des titons, qui n'ont rien a perdre, habitués a se passer de traiteurs & s'inquiétants peu d'en être privés a l'avenir, uniquement occupés des profits présents qu'offroit un pillage dont nous étions tous les jours menacés, j'assure, dis-je, que loin de blâmer nôtre peu de résolution, ils nous plaindroient d'avoir été dans la dure nécessité de souffrir des traitements si rudes & si

been read as sufficient to make him known and to prove at the same time that the willing are always ready to follow the evil impulses of a wicked chief, and to prove the absolute lack of all authority when it is a question of being opposed to the committing of crimes. I repeat, nevertheless, that Black Bull, distinguished and renowned by the government[54] as chief of the Bois Brulés in general, will be so in the nation and that, if he is once determined to make his rights respected, he will easily succeed.

THE SOLDIERS[55]

The authority of the soldiers, especially when they are elected[56] by an assembly, whether it be to watch over the carrying out of the laws of the *cerne*[57] or over that of some public decision, whether relative to the store of the trader, etc. gives them the right, in the exercise of their duties, to be severe arbitrarily towards every delinquent, to kill his dogs, his horses, to break his weapons, to tear the lodges into tatters, and to seize indifferently[58] upon all that which belongs

---

humiliants. nous pouvions certainement pousser dehors a grands coups de bâton chefs & soldats, mais il est difficile de se déterminer a tout risquer & probablement a tout perdre; de façon qu'ayants été tentés plus d'une fois d'en venir là, toutes nos délibérations ont toujours été terminées par ce triste adage: plutot plier que rompre." The old adage, with which the paragraph closes, *Better bend than break,* is from La Fontaine.

[54] The American, because of the recognition accorded by Lewis and Clark, September 25, 1804 (*Original Journals,* I, 164; *Ordway Journal, op. cit.,* p. 138).

[55] In other words, Indian Police.

[56] "només" (nommes?) (Washington version); élevés" (Montreal version).

[57] The "cerne," the French word for circle, of the original text might well be retained here; for it was used interchangeably with its assumed English equivalent, "surround," which, though a verb, came to be used technically as a noun by buffalo hunters. Travelers like Charles Augustus Murray (*Travels in North America,* I, 336-37) and traders like Francis A. Chardon (*Journal at Fort Clark among the Mandans,* pp. 15, 26 and n. 331, n. 355) used *cerne* and *surround* synonymously. For a very early and yet very concise description of what came to constitute the surround, consult the account of Henry Kelsey, an employee of the Hudson's Bay Company, writing in the seventeenth century (*Kelsey Papers,* p. 13). For the Mandan "surround" in the time of Alexander Henry, see his *Journal* (*Coventry Copy,* I, 471; Coues, *New Light on the Early History of the Greater Northwest,* I, 336-37). For Tabeau's special treatment of *Le Cerne ou Chasse en Commun,* appearing as a separate and distinct whole in the Montreal version only, see Appendix VIII.

[58] "indifferamant" (indifferemment?) in both versions.

to him. But as their right is only temporary, as they will in their turn be subject to the same sort of power and, besides, as nothing can shelter them from secret vengeance, they fear as much as they are feared and become officers of show. Nevertheless, they rise sometimes above these considerations and one of ours gave us proof of it, October 7, 1803; but, in accordance with custom, vengeance followed close.[59]

A young man, curious to know what passed in the store, mounts upon the roof and in defiance of the order of the soldier, insists on looking, putting his face to an opening between two planks. The soldier, wasting no time in threats, draws out the ball from his pistol and fires close to the young man's face. The Savage, burnt and blinded, falls all over blood and goes back to his lodge. No one murmurs; it is the soldier's right; but there remains that of the avenger. The next day at evening, the night being very dark, Mr. Loisel's dog is wounded ten steps from the tent by an arrow which pierced him through. The soldier learns of the deed towards midnight and comes to us, armed with his pistol. He asks us to tell him the author, whose flight and the darkness had not allowed us to recognize. He departs furious, kills the first dog he meets and loads again, not wishing to end his vengeance at that. A second soldier arrives and does as much. We listen to an haranguer who cries to lay violent hands without distinction upon all the dogs of which there are perhaps a thousand in the camp. Instantly, a number of armed men leave the bushes and all the proscribed innocents would have been killed if Mr. Loisel, to avoid evil results, had not stopped the executioners by praying them to have compassion on the women, who alone would pay the penalty for an offense of which they were innocent.[60] A roll of tobacco and the pipe calm the men.

[59] The variation between the two texts determines, in at least this one instance, Tabeau's way of reckoning time:

"... cependant ils passent quelquefois pardessus ces considérations & un des notres nous en a doné une preuve le sept d'8bre. 1803, mais suivant l'usage la vengeance a suivi de près" (Washington version).

"... cependant un des nôtres le 7 d'october 1803 nous dona une preuve de son zéle, mais il faut remarquer qu'il avoit a satisfaire un ressentiment particulier, le sujet qu'il a chatié étant d'une tribu presque énemie — *voici le fait*" (Montreal version).

It is necessary to remark that the soldiers belong to the tribe of the Partisan and that all the blows fell upon the dogs of Manzomani. This proves that there was less thought of avenging Mr. Loisel than of satisfying particular hatred.[61] A poor old woman in the tumult ventured to say a word in order to save the life of her favorite dog, but a pistol having missed fire in his stomach the old woman has not harangued.

If the soldiers to whom the guard of the store is committed were honestly charged, if they really sought the interest and the safety of the trader, they would not give up even to avoid a great many difficulties. But, established under these fine appearances, they have really in view only the interest of the Savages, whom they wish to gain over by favoring them, and the gratuities of the trader, to whom they make their protection count yet more shamelessly. Such was at least the conduct of two of ours at the Isle of Cedars; for they every day exacted new pay. True they had not been elected by the French or by the nation and, as creatures of the Partisan alone, it was hardly meet for them to go contrary to his designs and his secret plans. But then they believed it made a great difference to observe neutrality and not to encourage those who complained of the trade. If they have been sometimes ranged on the side of Mr. Dorion,[62] who is in

60 "les chiens sont les cheveaux des femmes" [the dogs are the horses of the women] in the margin of the Washington version. "les chiens sont le bêtes de charge des femmes" (Montreal version).

61 This sentence omitted from the Montreal version.

62 The same Dorion, no doubt, who served Lewis and Clark as Sioux interpreter, whom they permitted to linger behind, for a while, with the Yanktons (Coues, *Lewis and Clark,* I, 132), and from whom they must have obtained some of their information regarding the Sioux. From Clark's entry of August 29, 1804, it will be seen that two of the name, a father and son, were then with the expedition (*Original Journals,* I, 128) and Clark's "old Durioun" (*idem,* p. 46) was the former and most likely the interpreter (*idem,* pp. 103, 110). It was of these people that Honoré Taisont complained to Delassus in 1799 because of their conduct on the Des Moines, referring Delassus to Régis Loisel for specific information in the premises (*Pierre Chouteau Collection,* Missouri Historical Society). Thwaites, quoting J. N. Baskett, identified the younger Dorion as the same who was afterwards slain on the headwaters of the Columbia while trapping for the Astorians (*Original Journals,* I, 128 n.). For the serious trouble that developed between Dorion and Manuel Lisa, see Bradbury, *Early Western Travels,* V, 121-22. Bradbury was with Hunt's party and Brackenridge with Lisa's and the feud between Lisa and Dorion proved so serious that the two parties were completely estranged except for the in-

charge of this district, it is only when their particular resentment found satisfaction and, if they have been of some use, it is because their presence impressed somewhat those who were not their friends. Apart from these circumstances, they were indifferent to everything else. Mr. Dorion escapes the tomahawk of a rogue by drawing a pistol; he is threatened with assassination by another and obliged to spend three days without going out; a man named La Rivierre[63] escapes a gun-shot; there is a plan to kill us on leaving a feast;[64] Mr.

---

tercourse that Bradbury and Brackenridge, entirely disinterested, were able to carry on. For Louis Dorion who was, in 1804, in the employ of the North West Company, see Morice, *op. cit.*, p. 91.

[63] Although *Riviere*, or *La Riviere*, and *Rivet* are two totally distinct French names, it none the less seems possible that the man here referred to by Tabeau was no other than the *Rivet* of the Lewis and Clark narratives, the person who distinguished himself with the Indians by performing the marvelous feat of dancing on his head (*Ordway Journal, op. cit.*, pp. 167, 175). Rivet was one of the two men of Gravelines' party that, having been plundered by the Mandans, were met with by the Americans not far from the mouth of the Cannon Ball River, October 18, 1804 (*idem*, pp. 155, 167, n. 3, 181). He and a companion, "Greinyea," (Grenier?) wintered at Fort Mandan (*Original Journals,* V, 350), went down with the barge to St. Louis in April, 1805 (*idem,* I, 283, n.2), and returned to the Upper Missouri in the summer of 1806, Lewis and Clark meeting with them again in August (*idem,* V, 349-50). Mrs. Eva E. Dye appears to have convinced herself and Mr. Thwaites that this trader among the Arikaras was a certain François Rivet, who became one of the early settlers of Oregon (*idem,* I, 283, n. 2).

Since Tabeau nowhere furnishes the Christian name of La Rivierre, it is useless to try to select him from the many possibilities, if the theory as to his identity with Rivet be untenable. The trade licenses of the seventies show Augt. La Riviere of Vaudreuil, Beaulache Larivière of St. Ours, Clement Larrivierre, Jacques Lariviere, Joseph Rivard, Pierre Rivet, Joseph Des Rivieres, etc. A François La Riviere was licensed for the Michilimackinac trade in 1775 and, according to Morice, *op. cit.,* p. 164, one François Lariviere was an interpreter for the North West Company on *la riviere aux Anglais* in 1804. Antoine Riviere and his son Baptiste, who were among the first emigrants from Illinois to Laclede's settlement (Scharf, *op. cit.,* I, 67, n., 167-68) were probably of the same family as the Antoine Lariviere and B[te] Larivierre of the trade licenses, 1774, 1775. There was still a La Riviere on the Missouri in 1829. See Letter from Daniel Lamont of the *Upper Missouri Outfit* to Pierre Chouteau Jr., dated Otoe Establishment, August 29, 1829, *Pierre Chouteau Collection,* Missouri Historical Society. He was probably the "Ant[ne] Riviere" of a *List of Employees* of the *Otoe Outfit,* American Fur Company, Western Department, 1827 (*Pierre Chouteau-Maffitt Collection, idem*). For "Francis La Riviere," see American State Papers, *Public Lands,* II, 556 and, for "Reeveys Prarie," *Original Journals,* I, 68.

[64] " ... on projete de nous assassiner en sortant d'un festin." (Washington ver-

Dorion is insulted by the young people who often blow out his candle and throw it on the ground; the kettles, the tools, the clothes, the cash-boxes of the *engagés* are carried off every day; the pipes, the tobacco, always kept in the house by Mr. Dorion for the annoying use of the public, disappears frequently. But, in all these troubles, the soldiers are tranquil and tolerant, indicating that, if they were not accomplices, they either did not disapprove of the conduct of the offenders or dared not bring them to order.

It is seen that if things have not been actually instigated by the Bois Brulés, even to the complete pillaging of the merchandise of Mr. Loisel,[65] it is not to the soldiers that this moderation is due and still less to the power of the chiefs. I shall not make a mistake, perhaps, in saying that we owe our safety to vanity, to politics, and to ambition.

1st. Each tribe was afraid of furnishing to the others an occasion for reproach upon its conduct in regard to the French and of being blamed for public sufferings, if they did not come after us.

2nd. A general pillage would have caused talk among all the neighbors, especially among the Yinctons whom the Bois Brulés see every spring at the rendezvous of all the Sioux, of which I shall speak later. The fear of appearing, as they say, ashamed in this general assembly was very influential in leading them to save appearances at least.

3rd. Some understood that the surest way of gaining glory and especially marks of distinction was to declare themselves in our favor.[66] This motive awakened, a little late it is true, the ambition of one called Le coeur sans pareil (The Heart without Compare), a sub-

---

sion); "on projette de tuer m^r. loisel, m^r. dorion & moy en sortants d'un festin la nuit" (Montreal version).

65 "on voit que si les choses n'ont pas été pousses par les Bois brules, jusqu'au pillage complet des marchandises de mm. loisel, ce n'est pas aux soldats qu'on doit cette moderation & encore moins au pouvoir des chefs .." (Washington version).

"on voit que si les véxations des titons n'ont pas été poussées jusqu'au pillage des marchandises, ce n'est pas aux soldats que nous devons cette modération, encore moins a l'autorité des chefs. ..." (Montreal version).

66 " ... Troisièmement, quelques-uns ont compris que le plus sûr moyen d'acquérir de la gloire & des marques de distinction de la part du gouverneur espagnol, etoit de se declarer en notre faveur; ..." (Montreal version).

ordinate chief, but one of the bravest and most intelligent of the nation. This redoubtable man stations himself one day of his own accord at the door of the store and boldly declares that he is determined to die there. His known bravery causes the agitators to believe his word and everything is very quiet after that. After the camp moved, he with his family remains with us almost a month, accompanied for some time by the obstinate old soldier of whom I have spoken. They feared that some horde, evilly intentioned, would retrace its steps in order to find us at its mercy. In reality, Manzomani and one of his pretended soldiers, followed by about thirty men, had remained behind and comes with the intention of obtaining on credit twenty-four guns which we had and probably of seizing them if we refused to let them have them. But, finding us better protected than they had supposed, they tried to procure them from us voluntarily and, not succeeding, contented themselves with some packages of tobacco.[67]

This Manzomani, with all his own band and some individuals from other bands, departed to seek the Chayennes upon the branches of the Fork, so that he might trade with them for the beaver, which he supposed they had and which they had not, and to bring it to the Isle of Cedars, where Mr. Loisel prudently said the merchandise was intended for them the following winter.[68] All the other Titons, by different routes upon the east bank go into the heart of the prairies to a kind of market,[69] where are found also every spring the Yinc-

[67] Following something that closely corresponds to this, the Montreal version enters upon an account of the Sioux rendezvous, meeting-place, or fair, introducing the subject thus:

"je vais terminer cet article en parlant d'un *rendez vous* qui a lieu tous les printemps dans la profondeur des prairies. c'est une espéce de foire où se rendent tous les titons par des routes differentes, & où se trouvent aussi les yinctons, les seissitons, les gens de la feuille & souvent même des gens des lacs ..."

[68] This sentence is omitted from the Montreal version.

[69] It is interesting to compare with Tabeau's account of the Sioux annual gathering other accounts that have come down to us. They all agree in essentials:

(a) " ... Les nations Siouse sont celles qui font le plus de chasse aux Castors et autre bonne pelleteries du haut missouri, il parcourent toutes les rivierres et les Ruisseaux sans craindre personne. Ils en elêvent tous les printems une Grande quantité de notre territoire qu'il vont echanger pour des marchandises avec les autres peuplades Siouse situé sur la Rivierre St. Pierre et des moins frequanté par les march de Canada, il seroit facile d'établir sur le missouri des magazin de marchandises pour

tons of the North and of the South, the Scissitons, some people of the *Leaves* and often even some of the *Lakes*. This concourse is sometimes composed of a thousand to twelve hundred lodges, about three thousand men bearing arms.[70] Much trading is done there. Each man brings different articles, according to the places over which he has wandered. Those who have frequented the St. Peter's River and that of the Mohens[71] furnish guns, kettles, red pipes, and

---

leur fournire leur besoin et avoir le Commerce de leur pelleteries" (*Description du haut Missouri,* Mississippi Valley Historical *Review,* VIII, 176-77).

"Les Sioux qui s'y rendent chaque année après leur chasse, y apportent non-seulement leurs pelleteries, mais encore celles des peuples septentrionaux, auxquels ils donnent en échange de la poudre à tirer, du plomb en lingot ou en balles, quelques fusils, du vermillon, et autres bagatelles dont ils font grand cas." (Perrin du Lac, p. 196).

The following account of the annual Sioux fair is quoted because reasonably detailed, notwithstanding that it comes from one of the fairly contemporary narratives of the Lewis and Clark expedition, designated by Mr. Victor Hugo Paltsits as "counterfeit" (*Original Journals, op. cit.,* I, XLVI *et seq.*).

"They (the Sissatone) claim the country in which they rove, embracing the upper portions of the Red river, of lake Winnipie, and St. Peters: it is level country, intersected with many small lakes; the land is fertile and free of stone; the majority of it open plains. This country abounds more in the valuable fur animals, the beaver, otter, and martin, than any portion of Louisiana yet known. This circomstance furnishes the Sissatones with the means of purchasing more merchandise, in proportion to their number, than any nation in this quarter. A great proportion of this merchandise is reserved by them for their trade with the Tetons, whom they annually meet at some point previously agreed on, upon the waters of James river, in the month of May. This Indian fair is frequently attended by the Yanktons of the north and Ahnah. The Sissatones and Yanktons of the north here supply the others with considerable quantities of arms, ammunition, axes, knives, kettles, cloth, and a variety of other articles; and receive in return principally horses, which the others have stolen or purchased from the nations on the Missouri, and west of it. They are devoted to the interests of their traders" (Fisher [1813], pp. 148, 151). For Meriwether Lewis's reference to the periodical Sioux gathering, see *Original Journals,* VI, 45. The fair, or market, was still being held in Catlin's time. On the occasion of his second visit to the Upper Missouri, 1835, the traders from Fort Pierre were about to attend it on the James River, William Dickson, son of Colonel Robert Dickson and of the sister of the Yanktonais chief, Red Thunder, being in charge (Robinson, Doane, *History of the Dakota, or Sioux, Indians,* South Dakota Department of History *Collections,* II, 171).

[70] "# Les Sioux comptent 100 hommes par 40 loges & ce calcul est assez juste." [The Sioux count one hundred men to forty lodges and this count is very correct]. In the margin of the Washington version.

[71] "... la riviere St. Pierre & cette des Mohens ..." (Washington version). "... les rivierres st pierre & des mohins ..." (Montreal version).

bows of walnut. The Titons give in exchange horses, lodges of leather, buffalo robes, shirts and leggings[72] of antelope-skin.

Although very often this general meeting produces disturbances among tribes already unfriendly, it serves more commonly for their reconciliation and for peace. The tribes of the St. Peter's River, more powerful although less numerous, but far more enlightened through their association with the whites, become mediators among our fierce hordes and make them see the necessity of unity among them. It is certain that these Savages urge them above all to treat the French kindly as they are the only people from whom the redskins can derive real advantages. But, on the other hand, they strike a terrible blow at the peace of the traders of the Missouri by informing the Titons of the value of the merchandise upon the St. Peter's River and by exaggerating through vanity all the kind and generous hospitality that they receive there, so that some Bois Brulés reproach Mr. Loisel for having brought to them neither onions nor mustard.[73]

THE RICARAS[74]

Of the eighteen fairly large villages,[75] situated upon the Missouri at some distance from each other, the Ricaras are reduced to three

[72] " ... & des mitasses de peau de cabril. = " (Both versions). The word, *mitasse* seems to have been derived from a word in the Cree language, *métass*, legging. See Harmon, D. W., *Journal of Voyages and Travels*, p. 387. Because the garment was made to extend much above the knees in front, the name, *pantalons*, as applied by Perrin du Lac [*Voyage dans deux Louisianes*, p. 327 n.] was not inappropriate.

[73] The last two sentences of this paragraph are not to be found in the Montreal version.

[74] In no other place I know of will be found so full a description as here of the Arikara tribal formation except possibly in that part of Truteau's journal translated by Mrs. Beauregard. The two accounts are in substantial accord despite some differences of detail, the most serious being in the matter of the tradition respecting the original size of the tribe. The eighteen villages that Tabeau heard of were reported as thirty-two to Truteau. Perrin du Lac echoed Truteau and the following is his story:

"Les Ricaras, autrefois une des nations les plus nombreuses de l'Amérique septentrionale, ont eu jusqu'à trente-deux villages, détruits pour la plupart par les Sioux ou dépeuplés par la petite vérole. Le petit nombre qui a échappé à cette maladie, (laquelle a chez ces peuples des suites bien plus fâcheuses encore que chez nous), s'est réuni depuis quelques années en une seule peuplade, qui compte mille à douze cents guerriers. Ainsi que ceux qui se trouvent plus au nord et au nord-ouest, ils n'ont eu jusqu'à présent que très-peu de communication avec les Blancs, et ont con-

very mediocre ones, the smallest of which is a league from the other two. They comprise in all about five hundred men bearing arms. Some hostile inroads but, in particular, the smallpox unexpectedly made this terrible ravage among them. These three villages are to-day composed of ten different tribes and of as many chiefs without counting an infinity of others who have remained, after the disaster, captains without companies. The 26th. of August circumstances determined me to call an assembly of chiefs and counsellors. There were forty-two of the first rank and I was bitterly reproached afterwards for having overlooked many others. Some of these nobles have still two or three families, sad débris of their tribe, which, nevertheless, is still distinguished by its name and the pride of its independent chief. But details would take too long and I distinguish only ten of them, the first of which on the list is the most numerous and the second next in number and so on.

---

servé, presque dans leur intégrité, les moeurs, les coutumes, les armes et les vêtemens de leurs ancêtres" (*Voyage dans les Deux Louisianes et chez les Nations Sauvages du Missouri, en 1801, 1802 et 1803*, p. 257).

[75] Plate 80 in Catlin gives a pictorial representation of an Arikara village as seen from the river and situated on its west bank, some two hundred miles below the Mandans (Ed. of 1850, I, 204). For a treatment, at once scientific and historical, of the Arikara and neighboring villages, see O. G. Libby, *Typical Villages of the Mandan, Arikara and Hidasta in the Missouri Valley*, North Dakota Historical Society *Collections*, II, 498 *et seq.*

[76] Although the name in the Washington version seems clearly to be, Pecosse, the same is rendered, "Pocasse (or Hay)," in the *Original Journals of the Lewis and Clark Expedition*, I, 185, and "pocausses" in the Montreal version.

On October 8th, 1804, Lewis, after a jaunt abroad, came back with some Frenchmen, we are told, "Particularly a Mr. Gravelines, a man who has acquired the language" (of the Arikara) (Coues, *Lewis and Clark*, I, 158) and, on the day following, three of the principal chiefs appeared, *Kakawissassa*, or Lighting Crow; *Pocasse*, or Hay; and *Piaheto*, or Eagle's Feather (*idem*, p. 159). Later, on April 7, 1805, came to Fort Mandan, bringing a letter from Mr. Tabeau, the Arikara war chief, "Kah-hah We-to, Raven brave" (*idem*, p. 252, n. 5). In all of these names is recognizable a counterpart in Tabeau's list; but it will be noted that his French equivalent gives a far better idea of the meaning of the Indian name in each individual case than does the English of the Lewis and Clark journals; viz., *Kakawissassa*, le corbeau en repos; *Pocosse*, La paille; *Piahito*, le plume d'aigle; *Kakawita*, le corbeau mâle. *Piahito* was usually called simply, *La Plume* (Drumm, *Luttig Journal*, p. 67, n. 105).

[77] "kahidjai" (Montreal version).

DIVISION OF THE RICARAS

	Chiefs	Signification
1. Rhtarahé	Pacosse[76]	The Straw
2. Sawa-haini	Kakawissassa	The Crow at Rest
3. Waho-erha	Piahito	The Feather of the Eagle
4. Awahaux	Kaydjai[77]	The Chief Robe
5. Toucatacaux[78]	Laitacas -taga	The White Kiliou
6. Touno-catacaux	Kaka-nechane	The Chief Crow
7. Laocata	Tailala	Le Chichikoi[79]
8. Tchinantacaux	Rha-nechane	The Chief Dog
9. Toucoustahane	Tchiri-Tiranihau	Great Wolf
10. Narh-karicas	Kakawita	The Male Crow

The Loups and all the different Panis[80] now on the river Platte, made, undoubtedly, with the Ricaras but one nation which time and circumstances have, without doubt, insensibly divided. The lan-

[78] "5éme toucatacaux — Laitacas-taga — le kiliou Blanc
6 éme touno-catacaux — Kaka-nechane — le corbeau chef
7 éme Laocata — tailala — Le chichikoi
8 éme tchinantacaux — rha-nechane — Le chien chef
9 éme toucoustahane — tchiri-tiranihau — Beaucoup de loup
10 éme narh-karicas — KaKawita — le corbeau mâle"

(Washington version).

"5 éme toucatacaux — kakanechane — le corbeau chef
6 éme tounaucatacaux — laita-castaga — le kiliou blanc
7 éme loakata — tainana — le chichikoi
8 éme tehinantacaux — rha-néchane — le chien chef
9 éme toucoustahane — tchiri-tironiaule — le loup en grand nombre
10éme norcaricas — kaka-wita — le corbeau mâle"

(Montreal version).

[79] *Le Chichikoi*, the Rattle. The *chichiquoi* was a sort of rattle made out of a gourd (Grinnell, *op. cit.*, II, 130) and was used in their ministrations by the medicine men. See John MacDonell's *Red River Narrative, Masson MSS*, Dominion Archives, Ottawa; Masson, *Les Bourgeois de la Compagnie du Nord-Ouest*, I, 276.

[80] Lewis and Clark, when at Fort Mandan, found that the Mandans were accustomed to refer to the Arikaras as "Pawnees" (Coues, *op. cit.*, I, 206) so that it is not to be marvelled at that Alexander Henry did the same. To all appearances he never once heard, when he was on the Upper Missouri, of the Arikaras as such. To him they were Pawnees. Nearly three decades later, Maximilian, being at the Mandans as Henry had been, accepted without question the idea that the Arikara and Pawnee are close of kin (*Travels*, p. 167). Thwaites came to be of the opinion that they must have separated from each other, however, in the seventeenth century (*Early Western Travels*, V, 113-14, n. 76).

guage was originally the same; but, like that of all the nations, it has undergone such great changes that it has left many different dialects.[81] Each of the tribes has its own particular one so that no one can say that he knows the Ricara language; for it would be necessary that he should understand in ten different ways the greater number of the words, in which the common etymology is scarcely to be recognized. The pronunciation especially differs markedly.[82] Among some it is drawling and among others hurried. The latter pronounce in the throat and pronounce the letter *v* in two ways, the pronunciation determining the meaning. The former do not use *v* at all, the letter *l* taking its place. The quantity especially is observed in all the syllables and a long in place of a short often makes a different meaning. For example, in tĭrĭhaū = grand and tĭrīhŏ = capable. The alliances among the tribes, in which each party is jealous of its idiom, causes every child to adopt its language. The grandparents, the aunts, the uncles, and the nephews, who are brothers among the Savages, have all their different *patois* and, as all live ordinarily in the same lodge as one family, it seems like the tower of Babel and as if all speak without understanding. If confusion reigns in the language of the Ricaras, the division of spirit is still more remarkable, as being more baneful to them. It can be well surmised that after what I have said of the Bois Brulés that the tribes of the Ricaras, still more savage, do not live on any better terms; that authority is not any more respected among them; that each chief earnestly desires the supremacy; that all this nobility, sprung from royal blood, wishes at least to have followers and tolerates no form of dependence. Thus insubordination and discord reign here still more than among the Sioux and make this nation infinitely more unhappy, as much by its internal and destructive quarrels, as by the number of enemies that it makes.

A particular dispute between two individuals is or becomes the signal for a party quarrel and sometimes for a civil war. The 25th. of July, 1804,[83] a young woman is kidnapped by a half-breed Ricara

81 *Original Journals,* I, 188; American State Papers, *Indian Affairs,* I, 710.

82 Brackenridge found much to wonder at in the great diversity of pronunciation among the Arikara (*Early Western Travels,* VI, 127). Their speech, reported Lewis, was "Pania, with a different accent, and a number of words peculiar to themselves" (*Statistical View,* American State Papers, *Indian Affairs,* I, 710).

83 The omission of this date, 1804, from the Montreal version may have been ac-

and Mandane. The father of the husband avenges the honor of his son by killing the horse of the father-in-law. At once the two rival hordes rush to arms. A man and a woman are killed upon the spot and the young man is dangerously wounded. The two parties, always growing larger, hold themselves for three days in check and war is upon the point of becoming general. Finally, mediations and ordinary presents seem to satisfy the angry ones; but this public peace merely retards individual vengeance, which was afterwards twenty times on the point of breaking out and which, still threatening today, merely awaits its opportunity.

The 31st. of August[84] the nation, wearied by its losses with the Mandanes and Gros Ventres, their superiors in number and especially in courage, proposes to accept the peace which is offered to them and arranges to send the peace pipe according to custom. A single tribe, the *Laocata*,[85] without other motive than that of showing its independence, raises a party which proceeds at once to make mischief by stealing some horses. Notwithstanding this treachery, the Mandanes, this gentle and peaceful nation,[86] renewed its offers and,

---

cidental. If not, it might be taken to imply that it, too, was written, at least partly, in that year, were it not for the fact that the date is supplied in the paragraph succeeding. In this connection, it would be well to note the allusion, a little later, to Captain Lewis's winter quarters.

[84] "Le 31 d' 8bre la nation fatiguée de ses pertes avec les mandanes & gros ventres leurs superieurs en nombre & surtout en courage, se propose d'accepter la paix qui leur est offerte & se dispose a envoyer le calumet suivant l'usage. ..." (Washington version).

"Le nation fatiguée de ses pertes avec les mandanes & les gros ventres leurs supérieurs en nombre & en courage, se propose dans une assemblée généralle, le trente-un d'aoust 1804, d'accepter la paix qui leur est offerte, & on prépare le calumet suivant l'usage. ..." (Montreal version).

Considering the matter of time reckoning in the two passages just quoted, Tabeau's method appears to be that of counting the months from January and of ignoring the Latin name of the individual months.

[85] It should be observed that one of the abandoned Arikara villages that Lewis and Clark saw signs of had borne the name of *"La hoo catt"* (*Original Journals*, I, 179). It had been occupied, they learned, as recently as 1797.

[86] It is quite evident that Tabeau, who could have had no intimate acquaintance with the Mandans, shared what was to become the traditional opinion of them. Such was not the case with David Thompson and Alexander Henry, who could boast at least a brief residence at their villages, neither was it with Francis A. Chardon, whose residence at Fort Clark, the American Fur Company post at the Mandans, lasted sev-

for the first time, the nine bands, unanimously deciding upon a public affair, threatened to cut off the *Laocata* from the Ricara body and to join themselves to the Mandanes in order to destroy them.[87] This threat seemed to produce its effect and our envoys departed. They were received with open arms and loaded with presents. Some days after the guilty secret of the *Laocata* leaked out and we learned that, with the design of removing all hope of reconciliation, they awaited some Mandane deputies, who, according to custom, ought to accompany ours, and sought to massacre them on arriving at the village. Happily, fear of the Sioux held back the Mandanes and thus deprived these Savages of a chance for the blackest perfidy.

Nevertheless, since the course of Capt[n] Lewis has aroused among the Ricaras terror and confidence, it seems that opinions are united and that all understand that peace with the Mandanes becomes more and more necessary for them, that it is the only means of escaping the slavery of the Sioux[88] by leaguing themselves against them, con-

---

eral years. Chardon's opinion of the Mandans was very like Tabeau's of the Arikaras and both attest the truth of the old saying that familiarity breeds contempt.

[87] One wonders if this was the decision that the American explorers heard about, as recorded in the following passage from the *Ordway Journal*:

"Saturday 6th April 1805 . . . . Some of the Mandans Indians informed us that the RickaRee nation was all comming up to their villages, as they Supposed to Stay and live with them. our officers wished to wait and know their business, as the indians sayed that they were near this on the opposite Side of the River. So our Interpreter one of the party and two frenchmen was Sent across the River in order to go & See if the report was true. the wind gentle from the South.

"Sunday 7th April 1805. clear and pleasant. about 9 oclock our Intrepter and them that went with him returned brought with them 4 of the RickaRee Savages. 2 of them Chiefs. they Informed us that only 10 of their nation had come up to the Mandanes villages to treat & Smoak a peace pipe with them &.C. they brought a letter from M[r] Tabbo who lives with (the) R.Ree to our officers with news that 3 of the Souix chiefs was going down on the Big barge to see their Great father and that Some of the Rick a Ree chiefs was going also . . . ." (Wisconsin Historical Society *Collections*, XXII, 189, 190).

[88] A forecast this, in a way; for, when a few years subsequent to the Arikara war of 1823, the Arikaras retreated to the Platte, retiring altogether for a period from the Missouri, it was largely fear of the Sioux that drove them. All things considered, the Arikaras were a rather unfortunate people. There was no especial prejudice against them in Tabeau's time, and they themselves were not especially unfriendly to the whites, and certainly never as generally hostile as the Sioux; but they became so before many years had passed, and the whites, in their turn, hated them almost to the point of detestation. The Arikara war of the early twenties was the outcome of this

vinced that these last will not stay to merit the punishments with which the disturbers of the general harmony are menaced. But, in spite of this resolution and this knowledge of the national interest, individual jealousy still disarranges all the plans which tend to bring about peace.

A man named *Kakawita,* chief of the tribe *NarhKarika,* prepared to carry the skin of the white cow to the Mandanes.[89] These latter had lately had two men killed by a party of *Okondanes* of the Sioux tribe. They suspected the Ricaras of this outrage and they had the Chayennes tell them that, if they did not come promptly to clear themselves, they would take their silence for confession and would exact vengeance on them. The Ricaras fear to see them descend upon them; but the discord and envy of the chiefs, even of those most zealous for peace, prevent the departure, so necessary, of Kakawita. They fear lest he receive too many great honors among the Mandanes and particularly some marks of distinction on the part of Captⁿ Lewis, who has his winter quarters there.[90] These chiefs, though, do not know that, during all these delays, the Sioux continue their incursions and always use their name and even their language in all the hostilities that they commit. They even carried off two horses[91]

---

state of things, and the *Horrid Tribe* figures, historically, as making the most determined resistance to the progress of the American traders up the Missouri, beyond which lay the coveted trade of the Rocky Mountains, of the Columbia, and of the Orient. On this subject, see Dale, Harrison Clifford, *The Ashley-Smith Explorations and the Discovery of the Central Route to the Pacific.*

[89] Citations without number could be made with reference to the high value put by certain tribes upon the skin of the white buffalo. For that of the Mandans, Soulliers, and Big Bellies, or Gros Ventres, see the journal of Alexander Henry, *Coventry Copy,* I, 335; also Abel, *Chardon's Journal at Fort Clark,* n. 301.

[90] At Fort Mandan. For Larocque's description of the American post, Fort Mandan, see his journal entry for December 16, 1804 (*Masson MSS, op. cit.*). It is as follows: "Sunday — 16ᵗʰ Arrived at Fort Mandan being the Name the americans give to their Fort, which is Constructed in a triangular form Ranges of houses Making two Sides, & a Range of amazing large Pickets; the front; The whole is made so Strong as to be almost, Cannon Ball Proof. The two Range of houses do not Join one another, but are Join'd by, a piece of fortification Made in the form of a demi Circle, that Can defend two Sides of the Fort, on the top of which they Keep a Sentry all Night, & the lower part of that building Serves as a Store, a Centinel is like wise Kept all day, walking in the Fort." For an index to additional information about Fort Mandan, see Abel, *Chardon's Journal at Fort Clark, op. cit.,* p. 76 and n. 432.

from Captⁿ Lewis and pillaged the men who are employed in the hunt. Finally, fortunately for them, I, having some important information to give to Captⁿ Lewis, sent off two Frenchmen.[92] My letters, assuring the Mandanes of the innocence of the Ricaras, stopped a large party who were ready to pounce upon them.[93] Then, some days before my departure, *Kakawita* carried the pipe to them, and peace is concluded in the presence of Captains Lewis and Clark who gave the medal to him.[94] He is perhaps of all the Ricaras the one who will make the best use of it. At least, he is the only one who will be able, when he wishes, to make himself respected through his bravery and his pretended magic. He is, besides, the most respected by all the unknown nations and the most renowned in his own village. It will be seen that without him I should not perhaps write these lines.

The Sioux on their part did all they could so that this peace should not take place, as much because the union of the three nations would become formidable for them, as because they would lose, in the Ricaras, a certain kind of serf, who cultivates for them and who, as they say, takes, for them, the place of women. Then,

91 For Ordway's corroborative account of the stealing of these two horses, see his journal entry, February 15, 1805 (Wisconsin Historical Society *Collections,* XXII, 181) and, for Clark's, see *Original Journals,* I, 261.

92 From Sergeant Ordway, we learn that these two Frenchmen were Mʳ Gravelleen and "Mʳ Roie" (Journal Entry, February 28, 1805, Wisconsin Historical Society *Collections,* XXII, 184); but Clark would have us think that Gravelines was an additional person. Under date of February 28th, he wrote:

"Mr. Gravelin two frenchmen & two Indˢ. arrive from the Ricara Nation with Letters from Mʳ. Anty Tabeaux, informing us of the peeceable dispositions of that nation towards the Mandans & Me ne ta rees & their avowed intentions of pursueing our councils & advice, they express a wish to visit the Mandans, & (to) know if it will be agreeable to them to admit the Recaras to Settle near them and join them against their Common Enemy the *Sous* . . . .

"Mr. Gravelen informs that the *Sisetoons* and the 3 upper bands of the *Tetons,* with the Yanktons of the North intend to come to war in a Short time against the nations in this quarter, & will kill everry white man they See. Mʳ. T. also informs that Mʳ. Cameron of Sᵗ Peters has put arms into the hands of the Soues ..." (*Original Journals,* vol. I, p. 267).

93 The American explorers had requested the intercession of Tabeau in the interest of peace (*idem,* I, 233) and he responded (*idem,* p. 267) in the way he himself indicates.

94 *Idem,* pp. 285-86.

too, war with them is never of long duration. The interest of the one, the weakness and stupidity of the other soon re-united them; but in such a way, nevertheless, that it can be said that they live together always in a state of war and in mutual distrust. The Ricaras cannot let their horses out of sight and are compelled at night to tie them to their lodges. Like cowards, they are traitorous and perfidious and have sometimes assassinated the Sioux, when occasion offered, without the running of any risk. *Kakawita* killed in this manner, some years ago, the brother of Black Bull, a Bois Brulé, who had come to pay a visit upon the faith of a recent treaty. Vengeance was not delayed and he cost the life of five or six Ricaras and the peace of all the others, who dared not leave their lodges. But the Bois Brulés themselves, at the maturity of the corn, made peace.

In this season, the Sioux come from all parts loaded with dried meat, with fat, with dressed leather, and some merchandise. They fix, as they wish, the price of that which belongs to them and obtain, in exchange, a quantity of corn, tobacco, beans, and pumpkins that they demand. They camp then near by on the plains, which they openly pillage without anyone opposing them except by complaints and feeble reproaches. They steal the horses and they beat the women and offer with impunity all kinds of insults.

Well provided with commodities[95] they wander for some time far from the village, while surrounding it and forming a barrier which prevents the buffalo from coming near. From there they still bring from time to time loads of meat and undressed skins which constitute the largest part of the robes which the Ricaras furnish. This nation, always destitute through its inertia and its idleness, buys from the Sioux even bows and arrows, although it is surrounded by woods suitable for supplying them. It hastens eagerly to a ruinous[96] commerce without one being able to make it understand that it deprives itself of permanent and assured objects of subsistence for precarious ones, which it could itself procure with much or little exertion.

But the Ricaras are the most simple and the most stupid of all

---

[95] "Bien munis danrées ..." (Washington version); "bien munis ensuitte de la meilleure partie des denrees, ..." (Montreal version).

[96] "ruineax" (Washington version); "ruineux" (Montreal version).

the Savages of the Upper Missouri. The Sioux, more shrewd, know them perfectly and consequently negotiate with them. The 22nd. of October a large camp of Sioux, established four leagues above the [Arikara] villages, closed the entrance to the buffalo cow, but fearing some attack from the Mandanes,[97] they fled under the pretext of kindness and of doing too much harm to the Ricara hunting. The Ricaras, who are their dupes, with gratitude see them station themselves below the last lodges. By this maneuver, the three [Arikara] villages lie between the Sioux and their enemy. They agree to circle for the hunt only in common; but the Sioux, who know the indolence of the Ricaras, keep the latter every day in activity, so as to force them to renounce the contract and let them have the right to hunt alone and where they please.[98] Indeed, after four or five days of unaccustomed work, the sluggards[99] pretend — soon that the wind is in the north and too cold; soon, that it is in the south and contrary to the practise of the chase; finally, that the cow (not a league away) is too far away and that, not being hunted, she will draw near. The Sioux, having attained their object, declare that they cannot await her, having only the hunt as their resource and that, as it may be that the hunt cannot be done in common, they will be compelled to hunt alone. At once they go on for half a league, whence making[100] their circles behind the village and before the rising of the Ricaras, they carry the meat thither. Upon it, greediness put a very high price

[97] "mais les ricaras sont les plus simples & les plus stupides de tous les sauvages du haut missouri. les sioux plus fins les connoissent parfaitement & agissent avec eux en consêquence. le 22. 10bre un camp considerable etabli a quatre lieues audessus des villages, fermoit le passage a la vache; mais redoutant quelqu' incursion des mandanes, ..." (Washington version).

"mais les ricaras sont les plus paresseux & les plus stupides de tous les sauvages du haut missouri. les sioux plus fins les connoissent parfaitement & se comportent en conséquence. le 22 10bre un camp considérable établi a 4 lieües audessus des villages, formoit un demi-cercle, qui ne laissoit aucun troupeau parvenir chez les ricaras; mais étants menacés d'une incursion mandane, ..." (Montreal version).

[98] In the Montreal version, a sentence corresponding to this, closes the paragraph, which is merged with the one preceding of the Washington version:

" ... mais les sioux qui connoissent la paresse des autres les tiennent pendant 4 — ou — 5 jours en activité continuelle, & après les avoir bientot lassés, font seuls le cerne avant le lever des ricaras, aux qu'els ils viennent ensuitte vendre la viande a un prix exhorbitant."

[99] "fénéants" for *fainéants*.

[100] "fesants" for *faisants*.

so that I am not able to procure it myself. Were it not for my host and the French who surround sometimes, I should live only on maize. But if, like imbeciles, they, [the Arikaras] are the dupes of the Sioux, as rogues they are yet more their playthings.

It seems that the Sioux approached the camp only to be nearer the [Arikara] horses which they carried off every day. But, still more, they helped themselves to them sometimes under the very eyes of the owners, who looked at them rushing to the circle with an eye of sorrow and regret. Nevertheless, it happens, although rarely, that some Ricaras make reprisals, but at once the alarm is general and the horse is given back at the first demand. The 14th. of February, a young man took secretly a horse from the Sioux who had taken two from him the same day. Hardly had he arrived when a brave, after having severely censured him, seizes it in order to restore it, believing that he will make a bold stroke by exacting from the Sioux some pieces of dried meat, which however he did not obtain.

Some braggarts also took it upon themselves to go to reclaim horses from the Bois Brulés and the Okondanes. They were scorned and sent away, fortunate in escaping with their lives. The 12th of January a man,[101] *We-hato,* Elk's Tongue, a kind of chief and one of the worst rogues among the Ricaras, accompanied by seven or eight men, takes some presents to the *Okondanes* who were wintering at the Fork near Mr. Valé, clerk of Mr. Loisel.[102] The Okon-

---

[101] *Langue de Biche,* Tongue of the Hind, popularly known as Elk's Tongue. Although a minor chief in Tabeau's time, he became a prominent one in the Arikara War of 1823, after the death of Grey Eyes, *Les Yeux Gris,* who was killed when Colonel Henry Leavenworth's artillery "shelled the Ree villages," in retaliation for the attack upon American traders and troops. It was Grey Eyes who enquired so anxiously of Lewis and Clark, in August, 1806 (*Original Journals,* V, 351, 352, 354), about the non-appearance of the Arikara who had gone to visit the Great Father in Washington, accompanied by Joseph Gravelines. Professor Morton translates the *Fils de la Biche* of Duncan M'Gillivray's journal as "Son of the hind or roe." See p. 50, n. 2.

[102] " ... Le 12..de janvier le nomé *Wa-hato,* la langue de Biche, espece de chef & un des matamores & des plus scélérats des ricaras, accompagné de 7 a 8 hommes, porte quelques présents chez les *okondanes* qui hyvernoient a la fourche auprès de mm. valé, commi de mm. loisel. ..." (Washington version).

" ... le nomé *wa-ha-to* la langue de biche, espéce de chef & un des matamores ricaras, accompagné de dix hommes va réclamer de la tribu *okondanas,* hyvernoit M^r valé commis de m^r loisel, quatre cheveaux volés quelques jours auparavant. Comme il portoit de grands présents, il les obtint, mais ..." (Montreal version).

danes give up to him four horses which he claimed and which had been stolen some days before. But he is hardly a league from camp when the Okondanes pursue him, kill the horses, and he escapes the same fate only by a hasty flight. On his arrival at the village, still all terrified and not knowing on whom to lay the blame, he turns his rage against me, accusing me of having armed and ammunitioned the Okondanes for the destruction of the Ricaras; of having given orders to Mr. Valé to trade with them at a low price while they themselves paid an exorbitant price. Finally, as the Partisan among the Bois Brulés, he gives feasts, he calls assemblies, he intrigues, and makes only too great an impression upon spirits already evilly-intentioned and bitter through his lies. *Kakawita,* in whose lodge I live, his son, according to their fashion, whether he was at first of his opinion or in order not to thwart his father, did not appear disposed in my favor. The band was resolved to compel me to make a reduction of 100% in the price. Happily, eight months' experience having given me some knowledge of the language and of dispositions to be cautious of, I first make *Kakawita* promise that he would observe the neutrality between his father and me, and, having assured myself that he would brook no violence in his lodge, and some leaders appearing openly in my favor, I saw the Elk's Tongue and his followers give up a project which resulted only in their disgrace. Nevertheless, I always believe that this affair, still fresh in their minds, has contributed not a little to the difficulties that I underwent with the trading sometime afterwards. Of those I shall speak elsewhere.

Stupidity, always brutal, far from detracting from malice, renders it more unruly, more deaf to reason, and, so to speak, invincible. That is what I found among the Ricaras. This nation, having already wasted great quantities, is accustomed to receive gratuitously. It looks upon the whites as beneficent spirits who ought, since they can, to supply all its needs and it looks upon the merchandise, brought to the village, as if destined for it and belonging to it. Furthermore, the great notion that they [the Arikaras] have of their buffalo robes, founded upon the price that they foolishly give the Sioux for them and still more upon the fatigue and dangers that we face in order to procure them, causes them always to imagine that they lose in the trade. Besides, their minds not grasping our ideas of

134

interest and acquisition beyond what is necessary, it is a principle with them that he who has divides with him who has not. "You are foolish," said one of the most intelligent seriously to me. "Why do you wish to make all this powder and these balls since you do not hunt? Of what use are all these knives to you? Is not one enough with which to cut the meat? It is only your wicked heart that prevents you from giving them to us. Do you not see that the village has none? I will give you a robe myself, when you want it, but you already have more robes than are necessary to cover you." All the logic and all the rhetoric in the world are thrown away against these arguments, and how hope for success in a nation, imbued with these principles and always destitute of everything.

In spite of these prejudices,[103] which make them troublesome, it is certain that the Ricaras would be more manageable if they were provided with peltries as the other nations. Then, the trader, being able to reduce his expenses by a proportional trade, could sell to them at a reasonable price. But my little equipment amounting in goods for trade to the sum of about sixteen or seventeen hundred francs, an ordinary venture in Montreal, having sustained a loss of a third upon the better articles, burdened with the expenses of two winter encampments, obliged to keep many people an entire year, required twelve or thirteen thousand francs in return in order to recover the capital and compelled me to trade in a way not suitable, certainly, for any nation. It was necessary to charge three piasters[104] for each

---

[103] "malgré ces préjugés pernicieux ..." (Montreal version).

[104] The Spanish or Mexican dollar, synonymous with *peso*. The Mexican is worth about fifty cents.

" ... il faloit (fallait?) tirer trois piastres de chaque couteau & cent écus pour livre de rassade Bleue. aussi l'annonce des prix que je voulois fixer a-t-elle dabord indisposé les esprits. mais le nécessité de ne me pas conformer a des coutumes abusives & ruineuses, y a contribué d'advantage. je fesois peu de présents contre l'ordinaire, & je prétendois même m'éxempter d'en faire un public, a des villages qui n'ont rien a offrir en retour. je refusois d'établir dans ma loge une tabagie publique, abus consacré par son anciennete & aussi dispendieux qu'importun. je ne payois pas les invitations en festins, encore moins les mets apportés dans des vûes interessées. je ne nourrissois pas vingt personnes dans la loge de mon hôte, & je ne partageois pas mon ordinaire avec vingt parasites. enfin mes Bénéfices ne me permettoient pas d'accepter les partis & les alliances qui m'étoient offertes." (Montreal version).

" ... a joutez a cela que je ne voulois pas me conformer a des coutumes établies depuis longtemps, mais abusives & ruineuses. je donois très peu & je prétendois

knife and a hundred crowns for a pound of blue glass beads. Thus the announcement of the prices I wished to charge estranged the people at first. But the necessity of not conforming to some abusive and ruinous customs contributed more to this estrangement. I made few presents beyond the ordinary and I even aspired to free myself from making them to villages that had nothing to offer in return. I refused to establish in my lodge a public smoking-room, an abuse consecrated by its age and expensive as it is tiresome. I did not pay back invitations with feasts, still less the dishes brought with interested designs. I did not keep twenty persons in the lodge of my host and I did not divide my daily fare with twenty parasites. Finally, my profits did not permit me to accept the parties and the alliances that were offered me.

I rightly gave to Kakawita, of whose lodge I occupied a part, certain gratuities which I deemed sufficient but which were not regulated according to custom or, without doubt, proportioned to his pretensions. Accordingly, this man, at first all enthusiastic in my interest, because of the choice of my home with him, gradually grew cold and, far from serving me, approved, at least, of the malcontents. This Savage, of whom I have often had occasion to speak, is proud, alert, ferocious, cruel and, consequently, a great man. He is known as the bravest of the Ricaras and as the foremost poisoner.[105] Although he is chief only of the weakest band, he is, none the less, listened to more than any other brave and enjoys no less the greatest consideration of all the nations that visit the Ricaras. His ferocity and his medicines render him formidable to all the nations and I have shown that, when he wishes, he can make his lodge respected.

---

même m'éxempter de faire le présent accoutumé a des villages qui n'avoient rien a doner en retour; je refusois d'établir dans ma loge une fumerie publique, abus consacré par son ancienneté & aussi dispendieux qu'importun. je ne payois pas les invitations en festin, encore moins les mets apportés dans l'espoir de retour. enfin je ne nourrisois pas vingt personnes qui composoient la loge de mon hôte, & je ne tenois pas table ouverte a cent parasites. ═ " (Montreal version).

105 Of the same class, though not so notoriously cruel, as Blackbird, (Wa-zhin-ga-ca-be, Ton-won-ga-he, etc.) the Omaha chief, for whom, see *Brackenridge,* Henry M., *Views of Louisiana,* pp. 229-30; Bradbury, John, *Travels in the Interior of North America,* pp. 63-64. For Truteau's account of Blackbird, who was a poisoner of the Medici type, using "arsenic or other poison to create fear of vengeance," see American Historical *Review,* XIX, 322-24 and n. 62.

He is firm and constant, when he has taken sides, more intelligent than he appeared at first, frank and without subterfuge, he declares at once his dissent. Although exacting as a Ricara, he waits until one offers to him and does not debase himself by continual begging. Finally, if there is some trader, wild enough to be determined on passing a year in a Ricara lodge, I counsel him to choose that of Kakawita, who declared only once against me — in the general uprising of which I am going to speak. Besides he had warned me.

The presence of more than fifteen hundred men — Sioux, Chayennes, Padaux,[106] Canninanbiches,[107] etc., restrained the Ricaras and I hastened to profit by this quiet in order to do some good trading. I was assured that after this affair it would not be so peaceful. In truth, immediately after their departure, the Ricaras, having themselves procured some robes from the strangers, a chief, known as the worst rogue in the three villages, brings me four robes for which he asks powder and balls. He is accompanied by five or six rascals, armed as he, from head to foot. I give him the quantity which I ordinarily gave and which I measure upon one of his robes. He looks at me with a hostile air and, signing to me to take back my articles, departs menacingly. I am told the next day that he had been upon the point of letting fly an arrow at me and had been restrained only by fear of Kakawita. However that may be, after a long talk outside of the lodge with the latter who had followed him, he gives me these robes and accepts that which he had at first so roughly refused.

He was probably sent to give the signal; for, during three consecutive days, I traded only a few trifles, while enduring, none the less, great difficulties and threats. Some double handfuls of maize are brought me for which is demanded, undoubtedly with design, ten times their value; quarrels arise the noise of which spreads itself everywhere to my disadvantage and end by provoking all the people. A Savage seizes a knife which I had refused him and flees with it;

---

[106] "Padaux," ["Padaucas" — Montreal version] Padoucas. In 1724 Bourgnont described the Comanches under the name of Padouca and they were known as such to the Osages and other Dakota and related tribes —) Mooney, James, *Calendar History of the Kiowa*, Bureau of American Ethnology *Report*, 1895-'6, pp. 161-62). For a good description of the Comanches, see Gregg, Josiah, *Commerce of the Prairies;* Thwaites, *Early Western Travels*, XX, 341-52.

[107] "Canninanbiches," for a discussion of whom, see p. 98, n. 18.

another, escorted by bandits, snatches from me a cloth cover and pays whatever price he pleases for it. Kakawita takes care always to be absent opportunely, which proves to me, as he himself has said to me, that the evil intentions are general and that he tacitly conforms.

In[108] the meantime some Sioux arriving from the St. Peter's River announce that merchandise is abundant and wonderful there, give in detail the price of each article and make the Ricaras understand that I treat them as slaves. They propose to beat down the side of the lodge in which I live and to carry off my effects which they will divide with the Ricaras without their helping in the pillage. This they would have done if Kakawita had cared to consent to it; but, whether from a point of honor, or politics, or good will, he turned them from it by giving some presents. In these critical circumstances I proved many times how imprudent it is to undertake to trade with some Savage nations without knowing their language and without an interpreter.

Finally, the 18th. of August a man named Graveline,[109] consenting to act as interpreter for me, I prepare an abundant feast and in-

108 This paragraph and some of the detail of succeeding paragraphs Tabeau passed over when he wrote for his friend in Montreal.

109 This must have been August of 1804 and, therefore, Gravelines could not have been long with Tabeau when Lewis and Clark appeared upon the scene. He probably succeeded Garreau in Tabeau's service and was first encountered by Captain Lewis the beginning of the following October (*Original Journals*, I, 184), a day or two before he, in Tabeau's company, appeared at the American camp one morning in time for breakfast (*idem*, pp. 185-86). He may have been one of the seven men that Loisel left under the orders of his "agent and man of affairs" when he himself returned to St. Louis (see Memorial, Appendix VII) and most certainly was the Joseph Gravelines, whose name, under date of 1806, occurs frequently in a *Letter Book of Pierre Chouteau, 1804-1819* (Missouri Historical Society) and to whom, in 1807, Frederick Bates had occasion to refer as "the Ricaras Interpreter" in a letter to Henry Dearborn, the United States Secretary of War (Marshall, Thomas M., *Life and Papers of Frederick Bates*, I, 168, n. 122. He was probably the man, reputed to have been with the Arikaras more than twenty years, whom Wilson P. Hunt's party fell in with on the Missouri in 1811 (Bradbury, John, *Travels . . . .*, *Early Western Travels*, V, 127). His knowledge of the difficult Arikara speech had so impressed Lewis and Clark that they, too, had employed him as an interpreter finally, engaging him, in March, 1805, as a substitute for Toussaint Charbonneau (*Ordway Journal, op. cit.,* p. 186), when it was suspected that the latter was inclining towards the service of Larocque, he having sought his help "as Interpreter in the trade to the big Bellies" almost immediately upon his own arrival on the Upper Missouri (*Larocque Journal*, November 27, 1804, *Masson MSS, op cit.*). Charbonneau kept his prior engagement with the Ameri-

vite the chiefs and counsellors of the village in which I live. I wait for an opportunity to do as much for the others, as I am persuaded that they would not dare to go contrary to the decisions of the first. But the Savage, La Paille,[110] chief of the *Rhetarahé,* probably warned, is one of the first to arrive at the meeting. I drew no good augury from it. I showed first that up to that day the measure of powder had not been very large, because the strangers were the only ones furnished with peltries and that I had done this so that there might remain for them a larger quantity, that I would increase it presently for them. I cite the example of the Bois Brulés, who, in punishment for their conduct, had been compelled this year to implore the pity of the Okondanes to obtain a knife and a charge of powder. I hope for a different treatment for the Ricaras; for their customary mildness, long known, would induce the government and the traders to provide them constantly in the future. They listen to me thus far attentively and applaud; but when I came to fix the prices, La Paille interrupts me, fixes them himself to my complete loss and, growing angry at my remonstrances, declares to me that the Ricaras have no need of a trader who brings merchandise in order to preserve it;[111] that, since my arrival, although I had seen them without breech-clout, without powder, and without knives, I had not given the articles to them; that, in consequence, they were resolved to send me away. "Go, this instant," added he, "And do not be here at sun-

cans, after all, but Gravelines was retained also and Lewis and Clark, finding him, not only a good Arikara interpreter, but also "an honest discrete man and an excellent boat-man," soon employed him to conduct, as pilot, their barge to St. Louis (*Original Journals,* I, 283), the same upon which Tabeau had obtained permission to be a passenger. Some of the Arikara chiefs expressed a desire to visit Washington (*idem,* p. 286) and Gravelines was selected to accompany thither the only one that finally ventured to go. It was his misfortune to have his charge die on his hands on the return journey, at Richmond, Virginia. To that untimely death has been sometimes attributed the alienation of the entire Arikara tribe from the whites. For Gravelines's commission, which he brought with him from Washington, to teach the Arikaras agriculture, see *Original Journals,* V, 383. In his Montreal version, Tabeau neglected to mention that Gravelines had consented to act as his interpreter when he gave his feast.

110 " ... mais le nome *la paille* l'un des chefs des autres villages, averti sans doute, ..." (Montreal version). This was Pocosse, called in the Lewis and Clark journals, "Hay." See Coues, *Lewis and Clark,* I, 159.

111 "Brayets," (Brayettes?), not mentioned in the Montreal version.

set. And you, Graveline, who are here worthy of pity, return with your Mandanes at once."[112] It was impossible for me to follow out this order and, besides, I was certain that the plan was to pillage me if I left and to conceal this brigandage under the pretext of my flight. Besides I was not given time to announce my decision, all having quickly filed out at the last words. The kettle remained full and, notwithstanding the alarming crisis of affairs, I could not keep from laughing on seeing the look of the hungry old men who left slowly, casting upon the rich meat an eye of regret and who, secretly, surely consigned the haranguer to all the devils.[113] A couple of hours after I summoned La Paille and Kakawita, from whom a small present drew great promises. The latter, having remained alone with me, gave me to understand that he would always prevent the pillage, but that I should take away my goods and I should look for peace only by increasing the powder by half and by appeasing the men with a present to the three villages.

Resolved to come to this only at the last extremity, I endured for eight days quarrels and threats without number and Kakawita showed himself only when they were pushed too far. The haranguers forbid anyone to trade any kind of provisions with me. A man, Garau[114], laden with some trifles so as to buy from me corn for the

112 Gravelines and the Mandans are not here referred to in the Montreal version.

113 " ... les chaudiéres ont restés pleines & malgré la conjoncture inquiétant, je n'ai pu m'empêcher de rire en voïant la mine des vieillards affamés, qui sortoient a pas lents, & jettants sur les viandes grasses un coup d'oeil de regret & qui interieurement donoient seurement le harangueur a tous les diables. = ..." (Washington version).

" ... mes chaudiéres sont restées pleines & malgré la conjoncture inquiétante, je n'ai pu m'empêcher de rire, en voïant la mine comique des vieillards affamés, qui suivoient par politique, en jettant sur les viandes grasses un oeil de regret, & qui dans leur ame donoient certainement le harangueur a tous les diables. notez qu'ils jeunoient depuis longtemps. = une coupple d'heure après *kakawita* entre dans ma chambre & me déclare franchement que je ne dois attendre aucune tranquillité, qu'en doublant ma mesure de poudre, & en appaisant les esprits par un présent aux trois villages, tel qu'avoient fait tous ceux qui m'avoient précédé. — " (Montreal version).

114 " ... le nomé garau" (Washington version); but not appearing in the Montreal either in this or the following paragraph. This was, undoubtedly, Joseph Garreau, for an account of whom, see Drumm, *Luttig Journal,* p. 64, n. 97. In the Lewis and Clark journals, he is "A Mr. Garrow, a Frenchman who has resided a long time among the Ricaras and Mandans" (Coues, *op. cit.,* I, 245) and a "Mr. Garrous," in the attempt to identify whom, Thwaites says, "Little is known of this Garreau, save that it is prob-

villages above, is insulted and is told that his horses will be killed. To escape pillage, he is forced to bring back to me my articles and is told to tell me to depart if I wish to live a few days longer. At last, seeing that obstinacy is becoming more and more dangerous, I yield to necessity and, on the 26th. of August, I call an assembly of all the nobles of the three villages.[115]

Two great kettles are on the fire, important prelude of etiquette. I display at first a suitable present of powder, balls, knives, vermilion, and hardware, and the man Garau, serving me as interpreter, I represent to them my sad position among them — how I have already exhausted much of the merchandise in particular gifts with no return, and especially for their commodities, that, nevertheless, I still offer this trifle to them, hoping in turn they will be charitable to me, and that for the few goods that remain to me they will bargain peaceably, under reasonable conditions. Then I enumerate the number of all the articles that remain (lying about more than half), and I fix prices which are suitable to them. I close by informing them of the change of government which will certainly be favorable to them if they behave well. Kakawissassa, chief of my village, speaks first in my favor[116] and, after many exhortations, leaves to the two other villages to divide the share of the present, alledging that his people have the advantage of possessing the trader always. All the others,

---

ably his son Pierre (whose mother was an Arikara woman) who was long an interpreter at Fort Berthold; see Coues's *Narrative of Larpenteur* (N.Y. 1898), I, 125, 126. Clark's Garreau may be the Jearreau (of Cahokia, Ill.) mentioned by Pike in 1806 . . . ." (*Original Journals,* I, 7, n. 1). Had Thwaites known of the *Chardon Journal,* it would not have been necessary to seek for Pierre Garreau at Fort Berthold; for he was at Fort Clark among the Mandans through all the years of Chardon's incumbency. It is worth noting that a Garreau is repeatedly mentioned in *John MacDonell's Journal of 1793-1795* (*Masson MSS,* Photostat, Dominion Archives, Ottawa). See, for instance, the entry for January 5, 1795, where he is spoken of as on River la Souris.

115 " ... si je veux vivre encore quelques jours. enfin voyant que l'opiniatreté devient de plus en plus dangereuse, je céde a la nécessité & le 26 d'aoust je forme une assemblée de toute la noblesse des trois villages. = " (Washington version).

" ... si j'aimois encore la vie. ce trait & plusieurs autres me prouvants qu'il faut enfin céder a la nécessité, je forme une nouvelle assemblée de toute la noblesse des trois villages. — " (Montreal version).

116 " ... je détaille ensuitte le nombre de chaques articles qui me restent (en mentant de plus de moitié) & j'établis des prix qui leur conviennent. je finis par les instruire de changement de gouvernement qui leur deviendra certainement favorable,

at his example, make the most beautiful promises and particularly admonish Kakawita to watch over my sleep and my safety, a duty which he afterwards always performed well.

These public promises on the part of the chiefs bound individuals so little that the next day a counsellor named Shoulder of the Bear,[117] piqued because he had not been invited to the council, wishes to compel me to give him a knife for some pounds of lean beef and, upon my refusal, threatens to stab me then and there. I did not listen to this threat and he did not think he was so near to my guardian, who heard him through the partition and who cries to him to leave at once and that he would not live a moment longer were he not related to him so closely. The boaster did not take time to carry away his meat.

The Ricaras having nothing to trade before spring I was left in peace up till then as regards trading and abstraction made for exigencies. But, from the end of February, all the promises of the chiefs were forgotten and it would have been astonishing if the Ricaras had remembered a present of six months back — they who forget benefits immediately upon receiving them. I do not wish to weary one by a recital of a thousand difficulties, to overcome which one would have to be a new Job. It is true that, depressed by ten months' insupportable importunities, I lost patience sometimes and stirred up the fire. I ought to have been relieved in March by another trader, who would have had less reason to detest them, just as fresh troops are employed at need.

The 18th. of March, the balls gave out and the evil-intentioned, in the absence of Kakawita,[118] seized this opportunity for wrang-

---

s'ils se comportent Bien. KaKawissassa chef de mon village, parle le prémier, en ma faveur ..." (Washington version).

" ... j'établis ensuitte des prix sur chaque objet & l'on applaudit. Le chef de mon village parle le premier & après ..." (Montreal version).

117 "l'epaule d'ours" (Washington version). The Montreal version avoids mention of this second-rate chief altogether and the paragraph, while concerned with Tabeau's trade difficulties in general differs considerably from its counterpart in the Washington version, merging itself with the two succeeding paragraphs of that version.

118 This absence would seem to have been occasioned by Kakawita's having gone on the mission to Fort Manden.

ling by demanding, in their place, an unreasonable amount of powder. Kakawissassa, now first chief of the Ricaras,[119] whom I have so illy understood, was convinced that, at my departure, I would become lavish in his favor and that was the object of his good conduct on my regard. But, although I gave him more presents than a reasonable chief ought to expect, the knave, seeing himself bereft of his limitless hopes, reveals his character as interest alone had made him hide it. He increases the ill-will of the disaffected by most pernicious talk; he avails himself of every circumstance in order to stir up difficulties for me; and, seeing that he is not succeeding satisfactorily enough, he comes himself, armed, contrary to his custom. On entering he makes some Savages, who had come to trade, leave my lodge and compels many who accompanied him to remain outside. Then he throws me a robe for which he demands the price of two. I saw that he was determined to obtain it. The distinct threats of a Savage are less dangerous than ambiguous words and certain glances which experience alone can make intelligible. My men were at the hunt; I was alone, not only in my lodge, but even on the island, the families of which had left through fear of the flood. Kakawita had confidently assured me that his lodge would be respected in his absence; but it seemed to me as imprudent to trust myself there as to expose myself to pillage for a pound of powder. Consequently, not being the bravest, I yield in spite of my teeth and, as his followers come in again immediately, I content myself with the slight satisfaction of boldly making them understand that, if the young men are in want of merchandise, they should put the blame on their chiefs, all of whom have demanded it gratuitously; that, from the time of my arrival, finding themselves the only ones provided with peltries, they had fixed munitions at a low price, only to take them all, despite my remonstrances; that, all the winter, they had not given over exhorting that meat should not be furnished except for balls, knowing well that there would remain none in the springtime for the robes of the young men; that today they wished to do likewise in the case of powder, of which I had very little left and of which a chief, in trading a robe, carried away the portion of a young man with his own. My

119 " ... Kaka-Wissassa presentement premier chef des ricaras. ..." (Washington version); "Le premier chef de mon village nome *Kakawissassa* ..." (Montreal version).

visitor left, furious, and I learned that he had been restrained only by the fear of the vengeance of Kakawita. I confess that I would not have spoken so strongly without this same confidence and especially if I had known then the plots of this rogue.

Some days afterwards, Kakawita, having returned, remained most assiduously indoors, without my knowing why — he, who had said to me that he absented himself to avoid more serious difficulties, who, finally, would always cast reflections upon me; but who had said I had nothing to fear, either for my merchandise or for myself when he was absent and as long as he was known to be alive. He repeated then to me these assurances and said he did not know I had been molested and that he would act in this matter as should seem proper to me. I learned afterwards, in a way not to doubt it, that a pipe had been prepared to invite him to connive at it so that I could be assassinated in his absence. Garau knew the plot, as I did; but Kakawita did not wait until the pipe was offered to him. He said, in a whisper, that his spirit was always about me, but that it was known that it was not much attached to life. I admired his discretion and his policy did not compromise his nation as Kakawissassa was, without appearing to be, the head of the conspiracy. I knew it only at his absence and I did not see him again. That was then the cause of his recent industry and every other Ricara would certainly have sacrificed his father to take advantage of this unusual service.

The gratuitous exactions of the Ricaras are, far more than the trading, sources of sulking, enmities, and dissensions, as fatiguing as they are repeated. Kakawita, without pretensions for himself, found fault in that I had not been very generous and the Ricaras persuaded him that I ought to enable him to be so himself. The most foolish of them astonishes one by his cleverness in giving birth to and seizing a circumstance where one cannot reasonably refuse. The worst is that he never begs without being persuaded that he is justified in doing it and, consequently, he is firmly resolved to obtain his object by importunity. Really, who could constantly resist for ten whole months prayers, supplications, and servilities, while hoping that the Savages would be in a condition to buy? However tenacious a trader may be, it is impossible for him to escape having to give, sometimes, a knife, a mirror, an ounce of vermilion, some charges of powder and balls, and gradually these gifts have an effect upon a store so moderate.

In order to derive some advantage from the slight trade of the Ricaras, it is necessary: first, to appear among them in the spring-time, after having informed them in the fall; 2nd. to bring only objects, the value of which does not exceed that of a single robe, for a Ricara cannot conceive of two articles being asked for one and every time one of them wished to trade for cloth, upon which I lost half, he always offered his robe as a measure. This foolish idea resists all reasoning, to which he listens attentively, but to which he always makes reply, steadily and sulkily, "My robe is larger."

Hospitality and the protection of one's hosts, according to established usage, give an incontestable right to exactions without limit and entail excessive expenses. All the families residing in the lodge do not fail to give to the trader who lives with them all the meat that they may have in common and a part of that which they have cooked. He is in the habit of paying those who have given it uncooked and of recognizing the offer of others by a similar courtesy. But the day after, the trader finds himself alone provided with provisions and consequently bound to divide, with fifteen or twenty mouths, the provisions he already had as well as those which he received from them, the first, through pity, and the other, in recognition of the fact that they left themselves unprovided in his favor, although they had been well paid. It is useless to call it an abuse, the custom is beyond reason, and, to escape it, I separated myself from my hosts by a partition of upright stakes, in which I left only a single opening for a door which was always locked on the inside. Having then made a chimney in my apartment, I ate alone there every day and, refusing all the presents of meat, except those of Kakawita, I had no longer anything in common with the others. This innovation at first caused murmuring. I was a miser, a hard man, a glutton; but time caused their claims gradually to be forgotten. It is true that the correction of this ruinous abuse was noticeable. I could scarcely help inviting Kakawita and sending pieces of meat to his wife, who, in her turn, gave me regularly a share of the largest parts of the best pieces of all the hunt of her husband.

Among the Ricaras, as elsewhere, one could dispense with the inconvenience, or rather, free oneself from the servitude of dwelling in their lodges by building a separate house enclosed by a fort. It would have to be built in the village because of the Sioux and would have to be under the protection of a chief whose lodge a trader on arriving could enter. This protection would not be very expensive, particularly as regards Kakawita, who would be in honor bound to protect him. But, although it would cost more, an honest man has enough trouble to undergo there without depriving himself also of the sight of the sun, burying himself alive, and wallowing in the dirt. These lodges should be inhabited only by Ricaras, dogs, and bears.[120] I live in one of the largest lodges, which is one hundred and eight feet in circumference. A lodge is built in this way:

Four posts, thirteen feet above the ground, are fixed in a square, twelve feet apart, and hold up in their notches four joists. Eight other poles, five feet long above the ground, are then fixed in an octagon twelve feet from the first and hold up also eight joists.[121] These latter sustain the frame of little stakes and, being themselves inside

[120] With respect to the foregoing, the two versions again become nearly parallel. The differences are largely a matter of literary phrasing and choice of words:

"On pourroit chez les ricaras, comme ailleurs, se dispense de l'incommodité, où plutot s'affranchir de la servitude de résider dans leurs loges, en construisant une maison particuliére, entourrée d'un fort. il seroit seulement nécessaire qu'elle fut dans le village par rapport aux Sioux & sous la protection d'un chef, dans la loge du qu'el on pourroit entrer en arrivant. cette protection ne seroit pas fort dispendieuse, particulierement avec Kakawita qu'il faudroit seulement piquer d'honneur. mais quand il en couteroit plus, un galant homme a assez de désagrements a essuyer ici, sans se priver encore de la vuë du soleil, s'enterrer vivant & se vautrer dans la poussiére. ces loges ne doivent être habitées que par des ricaras, des chiens, & des ours. J'habite une des plus grandes, qui a cent huit pieds de circonference. en voici la construction. =" (Washington version).

"On pourroit pourtant, chez les ricaras, comme chez tous les Sauvages, s'affranchir de la servitude qu'entraine la résidence dans leurs loges, en construisant une maison particuliére. Il seroit seulement nécessaire qu'elle fut entourée d'un petit fort, mais toujours dans l'interieur du village, & sous la protection d'un chef, (& kakawita est le seul alors convenable) dans la loge du qu'el on seroit dabord entré en arrivant. cette protection seroit un peu dispendieuse par les dons gratuits, mais quand elle le seroit beaucoup plus, un galant homme a assez de désagrements a essuyer ici, sans se priver encore de la vuë du soleil, s'enterrer vivant dans ces cabanes & se vautrer dans la poussierre. ces loges ne sont reellement propres, qu'a des chiens, des ours, des pourceaux & des ricaras. j'habite une des plus élégantes & des plus grandes, dont voici la construction." (Montreal version).

[121] "sauliveaux," changed to "soliveaux" in the Montreal version.

and outside propped upon the forks, which prevents them from falling, they serve as a support for the rafters. The rafters touch each other by being joined at the top and they also rest upon the four joists which form the inner square. Only one opening is left. This, being in the middle, forms a point which, consequently, allows only one fire in the center of the lodge. Upon this frame are spread mats of willow or of osier, covered first with a layer of straw and then with earth five to six inches deep. Thus, at a distance, all these cabins, built without order, appear to be small natural elevations. Notwithstanding this triple covering, which would be sufficient were it not for the poor workmanship of the builders, the rain comes in a great deal in all the lodges and each one is obliged to make a camp above his bed. There is but one door and the opening at the top is in place of window and chimney.[122]

[122] Patrick Gass's description of an Arikara lodge, or hut, herewith quoted is sufficiently different from Tabeau's to justify the opinion that he trusted to his own eyes and made a personal examination. The building that Tabeau had in mind, as we learn from the Montreal version, was Kakawita's dwelling, where Tabeau resided. Gass's entry in his journal for Wednesday 10th, 1804, is as follows:

"This day I went with some of the men to the lodges, about 60 in number. The following is a description of the form of these lodges and the manner of building them.

"In a circle of a size suited to the dimensions of the intended lodge, they set up 16 forked posts five or six feet high, and lay poles from one fork to another. Against these poles they lean other poles, slanting from the ground, and extending about four inches above the cross poles: these are to receive the ends of the upper poles, that support the roof. They next set up four large forks, fifteen feet high, and about ten feet apart, in the middle of the area; and poles or beams between these. The roof poles are then laid on extending from the lower poles across the beams which rest on the middle forks, of such a length as to leave a hole at the top for a chimney. The whole is then covered with willow branches, except the chimney and a hole below to pass through. On the willow branches they lay grass and lastly clay. At the hole below they build a pen about four feet wide and projecting ten feet from the hut; and hang a buffalo skin at the entrance of the hut for a door. This labour like every other kind is chiefly performed by the squaws . . . ." (Third Edition, 1811, p. 52).

Of equal interest with this description of Gass's is one that Perrin du Lac attempted with respect to the dwellings of the sedentary tribes generally. It reads as follows:

"Les peuples sédentaires se construisent des cabanes dans le lieu de leur résidence, et portent des tentes lorsqu'ils vont à la chasse. Les cabanes sont rondes, terminées en forme de cône, et grandes à proportion du nombre d'individus qu'elles doivent contenir. Il n'est pas rare d'en voir qui ont au-dela de cinquante pieds de diamètre. Lorsqu'une famille Sauvage veut se construire une demeure, elle en trace le contour

The women work alone on these buildings, as at all other work. This sex is much more unfortunate and debased here than among the other Savages. It is reduced to the most humiliating slavery by tyrants, who enjoy all the fruits of its labors.[123] Thus, the more women a Ricara has, the more opulent is his lodge. Beasts of burden of these inhuman monsters, they (the women) are loaded with all the work. They endure alone all the labor of farming, a resource, however, without which the men would probably not be able to live; because of their sloth and laziness; for it is only by its means that the women procure their food and the clothes that the men buy[124] from strange nations. Still, if the men would assist the women a little by furnishing, at least, the raw material, the undressed skins, the latter would certainly be always well provided; but, on the contrary, all

---

avec des poteaux fourchus, de six à sept pouces de diamètre sur sept pieds de hauteur. Ces poteaux sont distans les uns des autres de dix pieds environ. L'on pose sur les fourches des pièces de traverse de quatre à cinq pouces de diamètre, et l'on garnit les intervalles entre chaque poteau avec de petits bois qui se touchent presque tous; ces bois sont recouverts et mastiqués en dehors et en dedans avec de la terre foulée avec force jusqu'à la hauteur des traverses, qui peuvent être considérées comme le premier étage de la maison.

"Cette première opération terminée, l'on creuse au centre de la cabane une place quarrée d'environ dix pieds sur chaque face, aux angles de laquelle on élève un fort poteau de dix-huit à vingt pieds de long que l'on enfonce en terre, le plus solidement possible. Au sommet de ces poteaux, on attache de fortes traverses, destinées à soutenir la couverture; elle est faite de longues perches grosses comme le bras, dont une extrémité est appuyée sur les premières traverses, et l'autre sur celles dont je viens de parler et qu'elles excèdent en hauteur de plus de quatre ou cinq pieds, de manière à ne laisser qu'un petit espace pour donner passage à la fumée. Ces perches sont recouvertes de jonc ou de petites branches de saule, mastiquées avec de la terre, de cinq à six pouces d'épaisseur qu'ils pétrissent et foulent de la même manière que celle dont leurs cabanes sont enduites." (*Voyages dans les deux Louisiana, op. cit.,* pp. 339-41).

123 This was the almost universal observation made by white men. Perrin du Lac wrote, "Les femmes qui sont généralement tenues dans un état de servitude, ont beaucoup plus de peine que les hommes, à qui elles obéissent aveuglément: elles n'entrent jamais dans les salles de festin; celui qui traite, a soin de les en faire sortir, ainsi que les enfans, qui ne peuvent y rentrer avec leurs mères, que lorsque le repas est entièrement achevé et que les convives se sont retirés" (*op. cit.,* pp. 353-54). For the debased position of Indian women the length and breadth of the continent, see Thévenin, René et Coze, Paul, *Moeurs et Histoire des Indiens Peaux-Rouges,* pp. 85 *et seq.* Nowhere in a contemporary account can the squaw's case be better stated than it was by Duncan M'Gillivray, for whose account, see Morton, *op. cit.,* pp. 33-34.

124 "achentent" is corrected to "achetent" in the Montreal version.

that they obtain by their work is employed for the use and for the dissipation of these idle barbarians and they cannot even procure the iron tools necessary for their work. Shoulder blades of cow or deer serve them for pickaxes; reeds curved at the end, separated from each other by interlaced rods and bound in a bundle for a handle, are their rakes;[125] a sheet of tin drawn from old kettles furnishes them with knives with which they jerk their meat, cut the skins and other articles. By means of a buffalo horn, they split their wood, which the floods wash up on the bank. However, some are now provided with hatchets. They readily see their own abnormal servitude and the laziness of their husbands and say very often, if enough whites come, the Ricaras would have no women. A Spanish prisoner taught them how to melt our glass beads and to mould them into a shape that pleases them. This art which is as yet unknown to them is practised only secretly and still passes for a supernatural and magical talent. They make a very hard but very coarse pottery which stands heat well and suffices for all their cooking.

The lands which the women cultivate are subject to inundation and, in 1803, a flood destroyed all the crops. The island alone escaped; but, as it is not large enough to furnish subsistence for the nation, it became a wandering one up to the time of the maturity of the corn the next year and was obliged to hunt at a distance. It could not hunt with impunity near the villages because the Corbeaux, the enemies of the Ricaras, make frequent incursions there. The 15th. of June, 1804,[126] two lodges ventured to hunt alone three or four

[125] Alexander Henry testified to much the same state of affairs as prevailing among the Indians farther up the river. He was writing of 1806 and, speaking of the improvised hoe, he said that the nature of the soil made it a not inadequate tool:

". . . . Early this morning I set off on horse back with part of my people towards the upper Villages. On our way we passed some very extensive Villages fields of Corn, Beans Squashes and Sunflowers. Many of the women and children were employed cleaning and hoeing their plantations, although very early in the morning. Their hoes are nothing more than the shoulder blade of a Buffalo to which is fastened a crooked stick and serves for a handle, the soil being but little interrupted by stones, renders this slight utencil of every use of a real hoe" (*Coventry Copy, op. cit.,* I, 483-84).

[126] The phrase, "pendant mon séjour chez eux," is introduced into the Montreal version. Other changes are revealed in the following:

" ... mes hommes etoient alors occuppés a faire des pirogues & si ces deux familles ne se rencontrent pas sur le chemin des énemis, qui venoient droit au missouri, ils devenoient infailliblement victime de la fureur de ces barbares, qui n'avoient plus qu'une lieuë a faire pour arriver au chantier. — "

leagues from the village and were destroyed by a party of that nation [Crows]. Some men, while defending themselves, nevertheless, aided the escape of two women, who also saved their two children by plunging into a little river. There, keeping only their noses above the water among the rushes, they saw six women and children, their relatives, carried off into slavery, and their husbands and their brothers killed. My men were then with Mr. Valé making pirogues and, if these two lodges had not met on the path of the enemy, who come to the Missouri, they (my men) would certainly have fallen victims to the fury of these barbarians, who were only two or three leagues away and coming directly towards their wood-yard.

The Ricaras, as much by their extreme laziness and their intractable[127] nature as by the want of peltries in their territory, are not a fit subject for a special trade expedition. Their pressing needs always require a large consumption of merchandise and the cost always exceeds the value of the peltries which they can furnish. If some one has the temerity to succeed[128] me for a year among them, he will find, perhaps that they will wish, by force or without it, to enjoy things as do the better provided nations, unless the fear of the new government restrains them. I confess that I myself owe, perhaps, my safety to this fear, already instilled, and to the meditated voyage of one of their chiefs, who is to go down to the Ilinois.[129]

[127] The subject matter of this paragraph is merged with that of the next in the Montreal version. Such verbal differences as occur are of little moment. Twenty-six degrees have become twenty-nine and the concluding sentence of the second paragraph has been dispensed with.

[128] It may be safely assumed from this that Tabeau had no intention of returning himself. "Reeved & Greinyea" (Rivet, or La Riviere, and Grenier?) went back (*Original Journals*, V, 349-50), apparently as free trappers. This is Sergeant Ordway's account of a meeting with them, August 21, 1806:

"a fair morning. we set out eairly and proceed on soon met three frenchmen one by the name of Revey they have been trapping as high as the river Roshjone (Yellowstone) but have made out but poorly and have been living at the Rickarees and are now going to the Mandans for their traps and then they Say they will return to St Louis . . . ." (Wisconsin Historical Society *Collections*, XXII, 391-92) and Clark adds,

". . . . they also informed us that no trader had arived at the Ricaras this Season . . . ." (*Original Journals*, V, 350).

[129] "Reeved & Greinyea" gave Lewis and Clark their first news of the death of this Arikara visitor, not simply "to the Illinois," but to Washington (*idem*).

This country is, moreover, certainly less adapted to settlement than to trade. It seems to have received from nature only the boon of climate, which, if the winter were a little less rigorous, would be, methinks, one of the most beautiful in the world.[130] The sky is almost always serene and cloudless; rains are very rare, also hurricanes, although winds are frequent and, in the springtime, wellnigh constant. The cold in winter is usually from ten to eighteen degrees and once it was twenty-six. The heat is from twenty to twenty-eight and one time thirty-five. The change of temperature, according to the seasons, advances by a progression so regular that it is unnoticed and has none of the deadly variation that is found in the Ilinois. Consequently, inflammation of the lungs, ague, jaundice, and other maladies are here absolutely unknown. Strangers, like the natives of the region, enjoy perfect health and I believe that, were it not for accidental illnesses and especially the venereal diseases,[131] one would be ill only to die.

THE CHAYENNES
AND OTHER NEIGHBORING NATIONS

The commodities of the Ricaras attract almost all the year a large crowd of Sioux from whom the Ricaras have to endure much without deriving any real benefit. It is not so with the Chayennes and many other wandering nations, whom they supply with maize, tobacco, beans, pumpkins, etc. These people visit them as true friends and the advantage of the trade is almost equal. The Chayennes, having themselves been farmers put a higher value on the commodities and, with more difficulty, go without them.[132] This nation was

---

[130] So thought the representatives of the Chicago, Milwaukee, and St. Paul Railroad when in the seventies of the last century, the railway companies of the United States were constituting themselves the chief agents for its further colonization and settlement. A writer of only a few years back expatiated fully upon the theme, that, to the railway advertisers, the Dakota country did, indeed, have a supremely "healthful climate." (Farmer, Hallie, *The Economic Background of Frontier Populism, Mississippi Valley Historical Review*, X, 408). The terrible droughts of recent years they never even dimly visualized.

[131] For Truteau's remarks upon this distressful subject, see *Seconde Partie*, Missouri Historical Society *Collections,* IV, 31.

[132] Perrin du Lac, writing only a few years before, had acquired information to

for a few years established on the Missouri;[133] but, having neither the patience nor the weakness of the Ricaras to endure the insults and the vexations of the Sioux, it had to resort to open war. The Sioux, always wandering, left little for capture to the enemy, who often knew not where to find them, and the Chayennes, settled there, were every day exposed, in spite of their superior courage, to some particular catastrophe. To lessen this disparity more, they abandoned agriculture and their hearths and became a nomadic people.[134] In a short time, they reduced the warlike ardor of the Sioux, who willingly consented to a peace, which still exists. But, since it is only the fruit of necessity, the truce is not very sincere and these two nations live in mutual fear of treachery and always, potentially, in a state of war. At their meeting with the Ricaras,[135] the Missouri separated the two camps and, as the Chayennes occupied the bank where the Ricara villages are, the jealous Sioux wished to cross in order to camp near them. The Chayennes opposed this with firmness and with threats and the Sioux manifested neither obstinacy nor offense. They contented themselves with saying to the Ricaras that they would be avenged for this noticeable favor.

Now that the Chayennes have ceased to till the ground, they

---

the effect that the Cheyennes were agriculturalists a part of the year and wanderers the remainder. They combined the nomadic and the sedentary life thus:

"Les Chaguyennes, quoique errans la plus grande partie de l'année, sèment près de leur village du mais et du tabac, qu'ils viennent récolter au commencement de l'automne. Ils sont généralement bons chasseurs, et tuent beaucoup de castors dont ils trafiquent avec les Sioux" (*Voyages dans les deux Louisianes*, pp. 259-60).

133 " ... cette nation étoit autrefois fixée sur le haut d'une petite rivierre, rive *est*, & ensuitte sur le missouri même ..." (Montreal version). Truteau must have had reference to this same time and possibly to the same general location, when he wrote,

"a trente lieux environ de son Embouchure sur une de ses fourches, nommè la riviere au Cerize a Grappe, les Chaguiennes yont Batie quelque Cabanes fixée, a lentour des quelles il cultivent des petits Chams de mays & de tabac, .." (*Description du haut Missouri*, Mississippi Historical *Review*, VIII, 165-66).

134 Compare Tabeau's account of Cheyenne wanderings with that given in the Lewis and Clark narratives. See Coues, *op. cit.*, I, 147.

135 " ... a leur entrevuë chez les ricaras, les missouri séparoit les deux camps & comme les chayennes occupoient la rive ou les villages sont établis, les sioux jaloux ..." (Washington version).

" ... a leur entrevuë chez les ricaras, ou j'étois, le missouri séparoit les deux camps. comme les chayennes occupoient la rive ou les villages ricaras sont établis, les sioux jaloux ... (Montreal version).

roam over the prairies west of the Missouri on this side of the Black
Hills, from which they come regularly at the beginning of August
to visit their old and faithful allies, the Ricaras. The Chayennes, who
have always visited either the whites or the Savages of the St. Peter's
River, are, at least, as difficult to trade with as the Ricaras and a man,
Guenneville,[136] who came from among them, says nothing good of
them. The nation has only a half-knowledge of the value of merchandise and prides itself, none the less, on being ignorant in this
respect. This vain-glory has been conducive to my detriment in the
slight trade of the Caninanbiches and others who obstinately defer
to its judgment. Happily, according to a principle and general policy among all the Savages, a stranger is obliged to trade peaceably
and to find no fault with that one who consents to let him share his
profits. I proved the force of this custom even as regards the Sioux,
who traded with me among the Ricaras. They scarcely dared to bargain. Although accustomed to the easy trading of the St. Peter's
River, the Savages, who would have compelled me to conform to it
had I been their trader, were content, after mentioning it slightly, to
accept, without question, the quantity or the number I had already
fixed. However it may be, it is certain that, if it had not been for the
interference of the Chayennes, I should have made better use of the
nations who accompanied them this year for the first time on their
visit to the Ricaras. They would probably have left to my discretion
the price of the trifles they brought. A new nation is always disposed in favor of the whites; it worships[137] them, sometimes, up to
the point of superstition and especially fears to displease them. A little familiarity destroys the illusion; the first ray of light convinces

---

136 This citation of Quenneville as an authority is lacking in the Montreal version.

137 Compare with Truteau:

"Tout les peuples sauvages dont jai fait mention dan cette description, c'est-adire
ceux qui habitent à l'occident du missouri, sont les plus doux et les plus humains pour
nous de tout les peuples de l'univers. Ils ont un grand respect et une Grande vénè-
ration pour tout les hommes blancs en Général qu'il mettent au rang de la divinitee,
et tous ce qui provient deux est regardés par ces mêmes peuples comme des Chause
miraculeuse. Il ne scavent point faire la distinction des nations policées, anglaise,
francaise, Espagnoles &c. qu'ils nomment tous indifferemment hommes Blanc ou
Esprits." — (*Description du haut Missouri, op. cit.,* pp. 177-78) See also his *Seconde
Partie,* where he had particular reference to the Arikara (Missouri Historical Society
Collections, IV, 24).

them that they are enlightened and that period is the most critical for the trader. Intercourse with the Savages has three ages: — the age of gold, that of the first meeting; the age of iron, that of the beginning of their insight; and that of brass, when a very long intercourse has mitigated their ferocity a little and our trade has become indispensable to them.

The Ricaras, before this year, carried to the foot of the Black Hills, tobacco[188] and maize. They accompanied the Chayennes and found, at the meeting-place, eight other friendly nations — The Caninanbiches, the Squihitanes, the Nimoussines, the Padaucas, the Catarkas, the Datamis, the Tchiwak, and the Cayowa.[139] The first

[138] The Arikaras, so the Biddle edition of the Lewis and Clark narratives has it, cultivated "a species of tobacco peculiar to themselves" (I, 406); apparently, the Mandans and other Indians shared the secret with them. Their tobacco was peculiar only in that it differed from the trade tobacco of the whites, being made of buffalo tallow mixed with the corolla of a plant. For accounts of its preparation, see *Original Journals*, VI, 149-51, 157; *Coventry Copy*, I, 593; Burpee, L. J., *La Verendrye*, p. 309, n. 1; *Second Journal of Simon Fraser*, May 31, 1808.

[139] "les ricaras avant cette année portoient jusqu'aux pieds des cotes noires du tabac & du mahy; ils accompagnoient les chayennes & trouvoient a un rendez vous huit autres nations amies, les caninanbiches, squi-hitanes, nimoussines, padaucas, catarkas, datamis, tchiwâk & cayowa. les deux premieres parlent la même langue, mais toutes les autres n'ont entre elles aucun rapport, celle des tchiwak est peut-être la plus singuliére du monde. ..." (Washington version).

"les ricaras avant cette année 1804 portoient, jusqu'aux pieds des côtes noires leur tabac, mahy &c. ils reconduisoient jusques là les chayennes & y trouvoient a un rendez vous huit autres nations amies, les *cani-nan-biches*, les *ski-hi-tanes*, les *ni-moussines*, les *padaucas*, les *catarcas*, les *datamixes*, les *tchiwâks*, & les *kayo-was*. = les deux premieres parlent la même langue, mais toutes les autres ont leur idiôme particulier. la langue des tchiwâk est peut-être la plus siguliére du monde ..." (Montreal version).

The above-mentioned bands or tribes, in so far as they have been identified, prove not to be mutually exclusive. For example, the Datamis and the Cayowa, or Kayo-was, are represented by the modern Kiowa; the Nimoussines, the Catarkas, and the Padaucas, by the modern Comanche. The Ski-hi-tanes, or Sequihitanes, may possibly have been, like the Alitanes, or Aliatans, elsewhere commented upon, a branch of the Shoshoni, or Snake, Indians. Then again they may have been the Sissiton, a branch of the Sioux (Hodge, Frederick W., *Handbook of American Indians*, Bureau of American Ethnology *Bulletin*, No. 30). For the equivalents of nearly all mentioned by Tabeau, see Lewis, Meriwether, *Statistical View*, American State Papers, *Indian Affairs*, I, 707 *et seq.* and *Original Journals*, I, 190, and VI, 100-108. Mooney identifies the Catarcas, the Catoha of Lewis and Clark (*Original Journals*, VII, 316), with the Kiowa Apache (*Calendar History of the Kiowa*, Bureau of American Ethnology *Report*, 1895-'6, p. 166). They lived on the headwaters of the two branches of the Cheyenne. The Tchiwak may have been the Chaui, a tribe of the Pawnee confeder-

two speak the same language, but all the others speak a different one. It is a kind of song or rather a modulated croaking, in which the syllables and even the words are not pronounced distinctly. Although constant visiting helps these nations to understand the speech of each other, no one understands a word of Tchiwak. But the need of communicating their ideas has given to all these people, far more than to the Sioux and to the Ricaras, a gesticulation so regular and so expressive that it could be said to be conventional.[140] These are true pantomimes which can express anything; but the gestures of which, not being always natural, are significant only to the eyes of the experienced and were at first for me as unintelligible as the Tchiwak language. Nevertheless, it can be rightly conjectured that it demands little practice.

The territory, which these nations ordinarily roam over in their wandering hunt, lies between the River Platte and the Yellowstone, which at their sources are quite near together. These nations live there in perfect harmony and form a league against the Mandanes, the Gros Ventres, and all the nations above.[141] I believe I have al-

---

acy (Hodge, Frederick W., *Handbook of American Indians,* Bureau of American Ethnology *Bulletin,* No. 30, Part I, p. 238) and the Datamis, the Detain of Lewis and Clark (*Original Journals,* VII, 316). The Nimoussines would be their Nemousin (*idem,* VI, 102).

[140] Mr. William M. Ege, who, from January 1, 1902 to March 6, 1917, taught among the Teton Sioux at the Camp School of He Dog (Sunkabloki), Rosebud Agency, says that among the northern tribes this conventionalized sign language is yet in use. There are numerous references to its earlier vogue, see, for example, *Coventry Copy* of the Henry Journal, I, 467-68, 557; Coues, I, 335; *Reputed Journal of John Filson,* Mississippi Valley Historical *Review,* IX, 326; Murray, Charles Augustus, *The Prairie-Bird,* p. 100. From the Reverend Timothy Flint's *Recollections,* p. 137, comes a suggestion as to the wide extent of its adoption: "They have a language of signs, that is common to all from Canada to the western sea." The standard work on the Indian sign, or gesture, language is, Clark, W. P., *The Indian Sign Language.* The allusion that Tabeau makes to the use of gestures to communicate ideas is noteworthy; because, according to Clark (see p. 11), Lewis and Clark, his contemporaries on the Missouri, made no remark on the subject until they reached the domain of the Shoshoni.

[141] At this point, the two versions part company for a time, at first partially and then completely:

" ... audessus, je crois avoir deja dit que les chayennes en comptent trente deux, mais je scais de puis peu qu'ils y comprennent les peles & tous les differents alitanes, tant sur le haut de la rivierre aux roches jaunes, que du cote du mexico. il paroit qu'ils

ready said that the Chayennes count thirty-two of them; but I have lately learned that they count the Pelés[142] and the different Alitanés,[143] as much upon the upper part of the Yellowstone River, as from the Mexican side. It appeared that they easily obtained an advantage over these last, if one judges them by the number of slaves they bring in, all of them speaking different languages. A Chayenne told a very singular story [144] about a Canninanbiche and a Pelé: —

ont Bon marche de ces derniers, si on en juge par la quantite d'esclaves qu'ils en amenent, tous de differents langages. un chayenne racontoit une anecdote ..." (Washington version).

" ... audessus. celles font aussi la guerre aux *pelés* & autres *alitanes* du coté du méxique, dont ils ont bon marché, si on en juge par la quantité d'esclaves jeunes qu'ils en amenent & presque tous de differents languages. ils ne font pas si bien leurs affaires avec ceux du haut missouri, mandanes & autres, car dernierement dans une incursion des seuls *corbeaux,* qui passent il est vrai pour les premiers guerriers du nord, ils ont perdu plus de trente persones, sans même blaisser un énemi. depuis cette expédition, les chayennes au nom de tous les alliés, ont porté le calumet chez les mandanes & gros ventres qui l'ont accepté. les entrevües ont été depuis réitérées, & j'ai sçu après mon départ que le paix géneralle étoit conclue. — en présence des cap[tnes] lewis & clark." (Montreal version).

[142] It would seem from the wording here that Tabeau, unlike Truteau, for whose opinion in detail, see p. 160, n. 156, considered the Pelés as distinct from "the different Alitanes." They may conceivably have been the Paloos of Lewis and Clark, a Shahaptian tribe formerly occupying the valley of the Pelouse River in Washington and Idaho and that of the Snake; but this idea is quite at variance with Perrin du Lac's understanding; for he wrote, from what he had heard, that "The Halisanes or Bald-heads, are a wandering people, who hunt on the opposite side of the Plate River, as far as that of the Arkansas, and extend to the foot of the mountains of New Mexico" (English Translation, p. 63).

[143] Shoshoni, formerly occupying the western part of Wyoming. Lewis and Clark met them in 1805 on the headwaters of the Missouri. See Hodge, *Handbook of American Indians,* II, 556.

[144] This anecdote is reserved, in the Montreal version, for the concluding paragraph of the section and, by reference to it, it will be obvious that Tabeau could not have been entirely sure of the derivation of his story. In the one case, it came from "several Caninabiches," or Arapahoes, in the other, from a Cheyenne. The same anecdote, with modifications and additions, to be sure, but only such as the lapse of almost half a century might easily account for, is to be found in Ruxton, George Frederick, *Life in the Far West* (1849), pp. 112-13; (1851), pp. 128-29. The luckless one, as Ruxton heard the story, was not a Pele, but a Sioux and the lucky, not an Arapaho, but a Crow. They played again, however, "and both the warriors stood scalpless on the plain." The whole affair is not unlike the risks taken by the early Germans, at approximately the same stage of civilization, in their games of chance, when they parted even with their freedom, selling themselves, as Tacitus tells us, into perpetual bondage.

Two hostile parties, without knowing it, were preparing to camp a little distance apart and two scouts met within arrow range. The one threw down his arms, the other did likewise, and they drew near to one another. After an account of their mutual dispositions and of the position of the two camps had been given, the Caninanbiche proposes to stake his leggings and his shoes, the general combat being put off till the morrow. The necessary articles are laid down at once. The Pelé having lost, pulls off shoes and leggings and pays. He demands revenge, loses his weapons, his garments, and stands naked. Then, furious at seeing the enemy carry off as a trophy all his wardrobe, he proposes to stake his hair and, having lost again, he seats himself tranquilly to suffer in grand style the entire operation, and retires. The Caninanbiche returns triumphant to his camp and, in the morning, comes back with his party to the place designated; but the Pelés, terrified at this mutilated head of evil omen, had not waited for them.

They [the Chayennes] do not manage their affairs as well with the Mandanes and others of the upper Missouri and they lost the past year twenty-five or thirty persons in a single affair with the Corbeaux, who are considered, it is true, the best warriors of the nations of the north.[145] Some small parties of Chayennes afterwards went to avenge themselves on the Mandanes but were unsuccessful. Nevertheless, a young man alone entered the village in the night. His companions feared that he was dead and, after having waited for him three days, fled through fear of being discovered. Some days after their return to the camp, the young man arrived with two superb chargers. He had remained four or five days among the enemy without being detected and had picked out the fleetest horses. After this expedition the Chayennes carried the pipe to the Mandanes and the Gros Ventres and, with the arrival of all these nations among the Ricaras, a large embassy ought to be formed so as to make with the nations above a general and lasting peace.[146]

[145] And Kenneth Mackenzie, "King of the Missouri," "Emperor of the West," who had opportunity to know them well when he was stationed at Fort Union, near the mouth of the Yellowstone, as head of the *Upper Missouri Outfit,* declared to George Catlin that they were "the finest Indians of his acquaintance" (Catlin, *op. cit.,* I, 47).

[146] The Montreal version adds that this was done in the presence of Lewis and Clark.

With the exception of the Chayennes, all these nations, although always at peace with the Ricaras, never approached the Missouri; but the warm welcome they received and the inducement of finding a trader there will pledge them probably to an annual visit, as they promised, at the maturity of the corn. According to their statement, the Spaniards[147] whom they see at St. Antonio or Santa Fé make light of their peltries and offer them only some hardware in exchange. In reality, they let me see only crosses, tears of Job, and Agnus dei.[148] In return, they buy there at a low price as many horses as they wish and rob them at their discretion. The horse is the most important article of their trade with the Ricaras. Most frequently it is given as a present; but, according to their manner, that is to say, is recalled when the tender in exchange[149] does not please. This is an understood restriction. This present is paid ordinarily with a gun, a hundred charges of powder and balls, a knife and other trifles. Deer leather, well-dressed, shirts of antelope-skin, ornamented and worked with different-colored quills of the porcupine, shoes, and especially a quantity of dried meat and of prairie-apple flour are traded for certain commodities, particularly for the tobacco, which the Ricaras sell to them very well, because of this value. It is a plant which has little resemblance to our tobacco. The Savages put it to dry at full length and so make rolls of it that long. The French smokers say that when they lack other tobacco this satisfies them.

[147] For references to the intercourse of the western Indians with the Spaniards to the southward, see Nasatir, Mississippi Valley Historical *Review*, XIV, 49, n. 15 and, for Kiowa raids upon the Spanish frontiers and the resulting trade in horses with the Arikaras and Mandans, see Mooney, *Calendar History of the Kiowa, op. cit.,* pp. 160-61.

[148] Alexander Henry, speaking of the "Rocky Mountain Indians," said, " ... some of them indeed go down towards the spanish settlements in company with the Flat heads, but what they get in this way is very trifling and cannot answer their purposes ..." (*Coventry Copy,* I, 586). The things shown Tabeau were all of some religious significance.

[149] Here is an instance of a definite emendation in the Montreal version. The Washington text, as it stands, is incomplete and fails to make sense until words found in the Montreal are added.

" ... le plus souvent ils sont donés en présent, mais suivant leur maniére, c'est-a-dire que si la rétribution ne plait pas lieu. ..." (Washington version).

" ... le plus souvent ils sont donés en présent, mais suivant leur maniere, c'est-a-dire avec cette restriction sous-entenduë, que si la rétribution ne plait pas, *le présent n'a pas* lieu." The words italicized, *le présent n'a pas,* are those meant.

THE MANDANES, GROS VENTRES
AND NATIONS ABOVE

I should not dare to be too positive concerning that which I am going to relate about the nations I have not visited; but the accounts which I have been able to get from the whites and the Savages conform so closely that I am persuaded I cannot err greatly and, as these nations ought to become the most important object of the speculations of merchants I deem it necessary to give an idea, at least, of them. Besides the error into which I may be led will probably not be of long duration since accurate information as regards them will soon be given in the narrative of Captains Lewis and Clark if they who were sent by the government on a tour of the west agree to share their knowledge.[150]

The Mandanes, who are established on the Missouri, are tillers of the soil.[151] They are said, even by their enemies, to be a mild and peaceable people.[152] The Ricaras now confess that they for a long time abused this goodness and that they always regarded as weakness and cowardice what was really only love of peace. The Ricaras having been a long while their neighbors had tried the patience of this easy-tempered people upon whom they inflicted all the evils that they themselves receive today from the Sioux; but, eventually, the Mandanes lost all patience, after having had some of their nation

---

[150] This concluding sentence is wanting in the Montreal version, the paragraph there ending thus: " .. j'ai cru nécessaire d'en doner au moins une idée. = "

[151] "les mandanes sédentaires sur le missouri a 500 lieuës de son embouchure sont cultivateurs ..." (Montreal version).

[152] This was not the opinion that Alexander Henry had formed of the Mandans. In a passage of his journal, significantly omitted by Coues from *New Light on the Early History of the Greater Northwest,* he says, ". . . . as no manner of lenity can be expected from those Mandan savages, they have already given too many instances of their barbarous behavior to white people when meeting them in the plains . . . ." (*Coventry Copy,* I, 435). They could boast none of the cleanliness to be expected from their twice daily dip in the Missouri (*idem,* p. 450), their personal habits were very disgusting, their lasciviousness, most gross (*idem,* pp. 452-53). Neither David Thompson nor Alexander Henry had anything of the traditional view of the Mandans. To the former they were as repulsive as they were to the latter. See Tyrrell, J. B., *David Thompson's Narrative of His Explorations in Western America, 1784-1812,* Chapter XIV. That Francis A. Chardon shared their opinions, although he was writing in the later thirties, his journal fully attests. See *Chardon's Journal at Fort Clark, 1834-1839,* edited by A. H. Abel and published at Pierre, South Dakota, 1932.

murdered yet, not wishing to take the Ricaras by surprise, declared war and killed thirty-five of them. Since then they have maintained their superiority and the Ricaras, after many losses, now accept the peace that was for so long a while offered to them.[153]

The Gros Ventres,[154] more numerous than the Mandanes, are their neighbors and till the soil also. All live about fifty leagues from the Ricaras and about as many below the mouth of the Yellowstone River. Their language is the same as that of the Corbeaux,[155] a nation that can count more than two thousand men, the reputed heroes of the north. The latter are a wandering people and ordinarily roam along the branches of the Yellowstone where they often meet the Pelés, the Alitanes, and the Serpents, their allies.[156] These last

[153] In his Montreal version, Tabeau added the remark: " ... j'ai dis haut que captnes lewis & clark ont présidé au conseil de paix. = "

[154] Henry's opinion of the Gros Ventres was very like Tabeau's of the Arikaras. When he "bid a last adieu to the Borgne," he wrote, "We now bid him farewell, and for my part I never wished to see this great man again, nor any of his clan as I was heartily tired of them all, and felt my mind much at ease by the prospect of pursuing our journey according to our own free will and pleasure, and not being subject to the capricious will of these mercenary Savages" (*Coventry Copy*, I, 598). He regarded them as more lascivious than even the Mandans and was repelled by rumors of their indulgence in unnatural vices (*idem*, pp. 488-89) and of their depraved tastes in the matter of preparing their food (*idem*, p. 584). What he would have said had he seen, as Palliser did (*Solitary Rambles . . . .*, p. 286), Gros Ventre women broiling and eating human flesh, the body of a slain Sioux, can best be imagined. Le Borgne, in the rôle of jealous husband, was a monster of cruelty (*Coventry Copy*, I, 552; Coues, I, 380-81). For a composite picture of him as he was seen by Henry and Brackenridge, consult Drumm, Stella M., *Luttig Journal*, p. 73, n. 112 and, for further proof of his brutal treatment of women, Bradbury, *Travels*, p. 149. The pilfering tendencies of Mandans and Gros Ventres alike was a matter for comment on the part of nearly every white man that came their way. Larocque's experience was the experience of all:— "The Indians appeared to be of a very thievish disposition" (*Journal*, November 27, 1804, Dominion Archives, Ottawa).

[155] Palliser seemed to think that their record of unbroken friendliness with each other was, in a measure, proof of their having been originally one people (*Solitary Rambles . . . .*, p. 244). Henry noted the great similarity in the language of the Crows and of the Big Bellies, as he invariably called them (*Coventry Copy*, I, 588), likewise in their perverted appetites.

[156] In previous notes, notes 142 and 143, some discussion has been given to these three tribes, conceded, by most authorities, to be virtually the same. Truteau certainly regarded the Pelés and the Alitanes as identical unless the following passage from his *Description du haut Missouri* is to be discounted:

"les hahitannes ou Tête pelée peuple errant occupent tout le pays au dela de la grande riviere platte, jusque sur les bords de lariviere des arkansas; et setendant le

three have the same language. All these people come every year to the Mandanes with whom they trade horses for merchandise of various kinds, for guns and ammunition. The Serpents have only garments of beaver. Nevertheless, they make for their children some clothes from rabbitskins. The women cut the skins into thongs which they plait in such a way as to make them very warm. The weapons are the bow and arrow, barbed with bone or sharpened stone.

The Asseniboanes,[157] the Pieds Noirs, the Chrystinaux,[158] the Têtes plattes, the Leaves,[159] the Panses,[160] and an infinity of others hunt upon the east bank of the Missouri, more or less above the Yellowstone River. They furnish the most beautiful peltries to the companies of the North West and Hudson's Bay which come to seek them with unbelievable labor and expense.[161] These nations, friendly to the Mandanes, also visit them every year. They bring merchandise and receive commodities and horses.

In short, all the rivers, which empty into the Missouri above the Yellowstone, are frequented by a swarm of nations with whom, at the post of the Mandanes, a trade, as extensive as it is lucrative, can be carried on.

---

long des grande montagnes qui separent le nouveaux mexique de cette partie de la merique meridional" Mississippi Valley Historical *Review*, VIII, 168).

[157] The Assiniboines, Stone Indians, were an offshoot of the Sioux.

[158] Kristineaux, Kinistinoes, Knistanoes, Cristanoes, Christineaux, Kris, etc. were all names applied to the Indians now universally known as Crees.

[159] These were probably the same as the *Gens des Filles,* a band of Assiniboines, with whom John MacDonell had dealings. See his *Journal, 1793-1795 (Masson MSS,* Photostat, Dominion Archives, Ottawa). In the existing Sioux groups, the Wahpeton were the People of the Leaves.

[160] Probably Pawnee, whose habitat was in the valley of the Platte River, Nebraska. Lewis and Clark refer to them as the Pansas. Their more common name was Panis.

[161] For a yet stronger statement to this effect, see Truteau's *Seconde Partie,* Missouri Historical Society *Collections,* IV, 33.

CONCERNING TRADE

O N seeing this great gathering of different nations[1] which assembled at the Ricaras, at the beginning of August, to the number of fifteen to sixteen hundred men, one surmises that the post would be capable of a large trade; but, on the contrary, this multitude, destitute of everything, is only a burden to the trader, who gives, indispensably and to no purpose, without means of idemnifying himself by trade. Forty pounds of beaver, four bear skins, and fifty buffalo robes comprise all the wealth of about six hundred lodges. The Chayennes, however, could not pretend that they did not expect to find a trader among the Ricaras; for they had been informed of this fact a long while before by Mr. Henney and one of their chiefs had promised Mr. Loisel, the preceding autumn at the Isle of Cedars, to bring his people in the spring, either to the Fork or to the Ricaras. This plan and the certainty of finding goods must have been communicated to the other nations and yet all came without peltries. Here are some reasons that prevent one from hoping that the trade of these nations could soon be profitable:[2]

1st. All the wandering nations which subsist only on the buffalo do not dwell very long in the places suitable to the beaver, the otter, and the bear, all animals[3] hostile to the prairies.

---

[1] Clark gives a list of the "Names of the nations who come to the Ricaras to traffick and bring Horses & robes" (*Original Journals*, I, 190).

[2] " ... les chayennes ne pouvoient pourtant prétexter, qu'ils ne s'attendoient pas a trouver un traiteur chez les ricaras, en étants prevenus depuis longtemps par mm. henney, un de leurs chefs s'etant engagé l'automne précedent avec mm. loisel a l'isle aux cédre d'amener ses gens le printemps, soit a la fourche, soit chez les ricaras. ce projet & la certitude de trouver des merchandises ne peuvent non plus n'avoir pas été communiqués aux autres nations & cependant toutes sont venuës sans peleteries. en voici quelques raisons qui ne laissent pas esperer qu'on puisse sitot tirer avantage du commerce de cette nations. == " (Washington version).

" ... les chayennes que j'avois vu l'automne précédent a l'isle aux cédres, avec qui j'avois *rendez vous,* avoient pourtant prévenu toutes ces nations qu'elles trouveroient un traiteur chez les ricaras, & cependant toutes sont venu sans peleteries. pourquoi? je vais hasarder quelques raisons, qui a ce que je crois, ne laissent pas asperer qu'on puisse sitot tirer quelqu' avantage du commerce de ces nations. == " (Montreal version).

[3] The Montreal version adds: "a la martre, &c, tous animaux énemies des grandes prairies ou se tient la vache."

2nd. They disregard all other hunting and are unskilful at it.[4]

3rd. The facility of buffalo-hunting with the arrow, as it requires only going to meet the animals, makes them dislike all fatigue. The beaver can be obtained only by activity and industry[5] as they are nowhere common enough to be hunted with the arrow or the gun.

4th. None of these nations values our merchandise highly and, if we except some iron implements, they have more liking for their skins, white as alabaster, which they work upon and ornament in different ways and which are, throughout the Upper Missouri, the foremost fancy goods.[6]

5th. They find in the buffalo cow, as I have elsewhere remarked, everything necessary to them and much that is superfluous and, for this hunt, they rightly prefer the bow and arrow to our guns and ammunition. If they desire the latter, it is for war alone, as they do not even dare to use them against the black bear which is very common in the Black Hills. This animal, dreadful to all, is an object of superstition, for the most part, and will be for a long time invincible.[7]

Nevertheless, all these difficulties have, doubtless, been met with everywhere where trade has opened up new routes among the Savage nations and everywhere they have been overcome, especially under our eyes by the English companies. They flourish more and more and, by their constancy and activity, deserve the great success that they attain.[8]

[4] Here the Montreal version expands with literary effect: "les sauvages habitués a suivre la vache, négligent toute autre chasse, la dédaigne (dedaignent?) même, & y sont inhabiles faute de pratique."

[5] Close of the passage in the Montreal version.

[6] The Montreal version adds: "au mépris de nos rubans, indienne, &c."

[7] The addition here is, "le castor l'est aussi pour quelques uns."

[8] This concession to the well-merited success of the British companies is omitted from the Montreal version, the passage there ending with, "particulierement sous nos yeux par des compagnies qui florissent de plus en plus;" but Tabeau then goes on to enlarge upon the trade prospects with possibly those companies particularly in view:

" ... je ne m'étendrai pas sur les moyens beaucoup plus faciles qu'offre la communication du missouri, pour tirer des peleteries précieuses des nations que je viens de nomer (nommer?), & particulierement de celles qui habitent ou parcourent les sources de cette grande rivierre. on voit assez que les voies d'exportation du canada au nord par des portages multipliés, par des montagnes & des parages dénués de toute ressources pour la vie, entrainent une immensité de frais, que peuvent épargner de grandes barges, toujours sur une même rivierre, & qui transporteroient ainsi les mêmes objets aux mêmes lieux. audessus des mandanes on peut se servir de pirogues dans la

Without expatiating upon the easier ways that we have at hand
to draw a quantity of valuable peltries from the nations which I have
just named and particularly from those which wander near the
sources of the Missouri, I shall only say that a company, well enough
established to sacrifice some capital for a couple of years, would surely open up a source of fortune.[9] The beaver, the otter, the martin,
the lynx, the wild cat, the pekan,[10] the red and silver fox, and the
bear of the first quality are certainly not rare for some hundreds of
leagues above the Mandanes, where our neighbors imperceptibly penetrate every day; but, enjoying now as then, the advantages and the
protection of a government friendly to trade, who can prevent ours
being freed of their shackles[11] and having the same energy and the

---

rivierre aux roches jeaunes & plusieurs autres, & presque jusqu'aux sources du missouri. je ne parle pars de la facilité avec la qu'elle on rapporteroit les retours, on le
pourroit faire même en médiocres chalants, dans les grandes crües d'eaux $=$ la plus
grande partie des articles nécessaires a la traite, dont il est question, se fabriquent aux
ilinois, ou dans la belle rivierre; & ceux qui manquent peuvent être apportés d'europe
a la nouvelle orleans, au même prix qu'a montréal. $=$ partout audessus des mandanes on pourroit tirer des engagés en les employants a la pêche au castor, ce qui se
pratique dans tout le missouri, & ou plusieurs font plus que leurs gages. $=$

"après cela je hasarderai de dire, qu'une compagnie formée aux ilinois, capable de
sacrifier quelques capitaux pendant une coupple d'année ..." (Montreal version).

[9] As much out of this, perhaps, or the same kind of information that Tabeau
could with even stronger emphasis have given *vive voce* when he reached St. Louis,
as out of Lewis's report, came very probably the American *Missouri Fur Company*.
The *Gratiot Letters* at the Missouri Historical Society show with what insistence
Charles Gratiot, Senior, a Swiss by birth, urged the matter of the Upper Missouri
trade upon John Jacob Astor. "You are without a doubt," wrote he as early as April
29, 1800, "the one who can do the most in the fur trade. Your domestic and foreign
relations put you in a position to do what no other House in the United States could
do, and you are residing in the most alive and flourishing town on the Globe." For
years and years he dangled before the eyes of the ex-German the alluring prospect of
the Upper Missouri commerce; but, in its beginnings under American auspices, that
particular part of the great traffic was to go to men who, by a sort of preëmptive right,
had a better claim to it. Chief among them were the Chouteaus, and Manuel Lisa,
the Spaniard, also Pierre Menard, a relative of the Vallé family, as were both Tabeau
and Loisel. Had Loisel lived he would have assuredly been one of them as well and,
therefore, why not Tabeau, if yet alive? It is interesting, in perusing the Tabeau narrative, to realize how exactly in its section on *Trade* it anticipated what Lisa attempted.

[10] A mustelline carnivore of the northerly wooded parts of the continent.

[11] A sarcastic allusion to the Spanish system of trade, a system of restrictions and
of special privileges.

same activity as that of our rivals? The greater part of the articles necessary for this new trade is made among us and those which we lack could be brought from Europe to New Orleans at the same price at which they come to Montreal. The large concourse of strangers in our ports insures a sale, equivalent to that of London, for peltries sought everywhere.[12] Our competitor's ways of transporting by portages multiplied in the mountains and waste places entail great expense, which we avoid through the facility of our communications. We transport always upon the rivers themselves and in large boats.

A post[13] among the Mandanes would be a gathering-place for more than twenty nations and would be the means in determining the Ricaras to take up a station nearby, as they already plan to do without this new attraction. If the latter should remain separated from the Mandanes, they would no longer receive an annual visit from remote people who would doubtless prefer to sojourn with the traders. In this case, by sending out a small canoe in the spring, one could trade with the Ricaras without additional expense and the peltries could be picked up by the passing boats.

The nations above would come to welcome their trader as do the Panis upon the river Platte and, on his ascending the river, could convey him to his destination.

A venture on the Yellowstone River would gratify the Corbeau, Serpents, and others and would even receive all the peltries of the Chayennes, etc., by sparing them the hardship of transportation, the greatest obstacle to their hunting.

The main thing would be to keep the peace among these nations. They are already well on the road to it; all desire it; and such a peace is never broken except in passion. A man, who, by wise and prudent conduct,[14] will deserve the respect of the Savages, who, by

[12] The Montreal version, already quoted, is decidedly an improvement in expression.

[13] This idea was an ever-recurring and persistent one. It did not, of course, originate with Tabeau. In recommending both the Mandans and the Yellowstone as sites for trading posts, he foresaw advantages that the *Upper Missouri Outfit* later enjoyed.

[14] "un homme qui par sa conduite sage & prudente (que je suppose sédentaire a l'entrepot chez les mandanes) sçaurra mériter le respect des sauvages, ..." (Montreal version).

mild and ingratiating ways, will gain their friendship, and who, by never deceiving them, will learn to gain their confidence, will easily make them perceive their interest in a general union and, if the government[15] establishes a small garrison there, order will reign everywhere.[16] This main point obtained, it is not to be doubted that custom, intercourse, the spirit of imitation, rivalry, the idea of luxury will give birth among the Savages to new needs; and the necessity of enjoying will produce the activity required to procure the means for them.[17]

In this supposition of peace, much could be hoped for from the hunt of the whites upon the branches of the rivers above the Mandanes by means of horses or, afterwards, by ascending the Missouri itself. The beaver has never been hunted in the greater part of these places and only imperfectly in the others, as the iron trap is the only real destroyer of this amphibian. Up to this time, the whites have not felt secure enough to encourage them in their work and, as they are often obliged to avoid the most productive places. The result has not paid them for their expenses, overcharged, it is true; but which can be reduced very much. The hostile nations are such near neighbors to one another that war parties follow each other without interruption and their meeting is not deemed fatal, although one be subjected to pillage. A white man who lives with or who leaves the enemy is regarded as an enemy and, accordingly, his life is rarely granted him. If the nation which he leaves is only a strange one, or even an ally, the warriors content themselves, ordinarily, with despoiling the captive of arms, munitions, and garments and with send-

[15] This phrase, a reference, presumably, to the United States government, does not appear in the revised version.

[16] A backward glance this and a forward view as well. It brings to mind all that James Mackay must have dreamed of since first he visited the Mandans, perchance in 1787, of all that he must have recommended to Clamorgan and to the Spanish Company of Commerce and Discoveries, and it likewise brings to mind the later "Yellowstone Expedition," a project designed to accomplish just what Pierre-Antoine Tabeau here outlined and, incidentally, to make good the American claim to the country, "where rolls the Oregon."

[17] Repeating the idea that he himself earlier advanced, Tabeau was but expressing the opinion that all the leading traders had and that historians admit the truth of, when they recognize in commerce the handmaid of civilization and peace as essential to it.

ing him away, after having sometimes beaten him well. A man, Souci,[18] equipped by Mr. Loisel, [19] met the Poncas on some territory of the Sioux and, after receiving many wounds from them, owed his safety to an unusual strength which sustained him in a long flight.[20] Menard, who lived for thirty years among the Mandanes, was massacred lately on returning from the English forts, although he was well known to the Asseniboanes, his assassins.[21] A man, named

[18] This was, no doubt, a member of the family, *Roussel dit Sans Soucy* of which there were representatives both in St. Louis and Ste. Geneviève, as also in Chateauguay (see Transcripts of Church Registers, *op. cit.*). In the trade licenses, issued at Quebec, there is at least one reference to each of the following: Antoine Sansoucis, Bte Sans Souci, Benjamin Sans Souci, Claude Sans Soucy, Gabriel Sans Souci, Ignace Sansoucy, Jean Baptiste Sanssoucy, Joseph Sans Souci, Louis Sans Soucy, and Pierre Sans Soucy. For one reason or another, however, all these are made to yield in preference to François Sanssoucy, described as an habitant of Vaudreuil, who, in 1769, was an engagé under "Monsr Blondeau," a later partner of James McGill and Benjamin Frobisher. In 1774, François Sanssoucy engaged himself to Étienne and Alexis Campion, also to J. Bte Tabaux and Jean Calvet. At some subsequent time, a man of the same name appeared in Upper Louisiana and was, no doubt, the "Francis Sauci," who obtained a grant of 8,800 arpens from the Spanish authorities (*Pierre Chouteau Collection, op. cit.*). *Either* he or a son may have been the man equipped by Régis Loisel. A certain "Pierre Roussel" had land in Florissant in 1785 (Houck, *History of Missouri,* II, 67) and a "Sanssouce," Christian name unascertained, was with John MacDonell at Fort Esperance. See *Journal for 1793-1795, March* 3, 1794.

[19] The Montreal version, as so very often before, omits the name of Loisel:

"... un nomé souci équippé de mm. loisel, recontré par les poncas sur les parages des sioux a reçu plusieurs Blaissures & n'a du son salut qu'a une force extraordinaire qui la soutenu dans une longue fuitte. menard résident depuis trente ans avec les mandanes, a été massacré dernierement revenants des forts anglois, quoique parfaitement connu des asseniboanes ses assassins. un nomé grenier parti de chez moy au village des ricaras & chassant en montant le missouri, rencontre des guerriers mandanes, qui eu egard a la paix se sont contenté du pillage presque complet. heureusement que les captnes lewis & clark a leur arrivée chez cette nation leur ont fait rendre leurs piéges & quelques articles. mais tout son castor étoit déja traté par les voleurs." (Washington version.)

"... un nomé *souci* chassant chez les siouz, & étant rencontré par des *poncas,* a reçu plusieurs blaissure & n'a du son salut qu' a sa force extraordinaire qui l'a soutenu dans une longue fuite. = *menard* résident depuis trente ans chez les mandanes, a été massacré dernierement, quoique parfaitement conu (connu?) des asseniboanes ses assassins. le nomé grenier parti de chez les ricaras, ou je l'avois équippé, & chassant en montant le missouri rencontre des guerriers mandanes, qui eu égard a la paix nouvellement conclue se sont contente du pillage presque complet. = " (Montreal version.)

[20] Is this at all reminiscent of the Lécuyer expedition?

[21] In the *Journal of Duncan M'Gillivray* occurs the following reference to a

Grenier,[22] leaving the Ricara village and hunting on his ascent of the Missouri, meets some Mandane warriors, who, out of regard for the peace, content themselves with robbing him of almost everything. Happily, Captains Lewis and Clark, on their arrival among this nation, made them give back the traps and certain articles; but the robbers had already traded away all his beaver skins.

As for the trade with the Sioux, only the buffalo robes can be counted upon, of which an extra quantity could be obtained, as also

---

murdered Ménard: ". . . . The Murder of old *Minard* is amply revenged (if it has been committed by them which is only suspected) by the death of 5 Gros Ventres killed at Pine Island & S. Branch so that it only remains for us to recover the value of the horses and baggage, which they have pillaged at those places" (Morton, Arthur S., *The Journal of Duncan M'Gillivray of the North West Company at Fort George on the Saskatchewan, 1794-5,* p. 57). A. P. Nasatir says that D'Eglise obtained his information about the Mandans from a Frenchman, who had been living among them fourteen years. D'Eglise went up the Missouri, for the first time, in 1790. Fourteen years anterior to that date would give 1776; but, if Ménard were already dead when M'Gillivray wrote, he could not have lived Tabeau's "thirty years" among the Mandans. It will be recalled that Truteau said, "sixteen years" and Collot, "more than sixteen years." For the possible identity of the murdered Ménard with a François Ménard who lived at Florissant in 1787, see Mrs. Beauregard, Missouri Historical Society *Collections,* IV, 36, n. 36; but why, having been of the North West Company, he should be looked for in Upper Louisiana is not stated. The Christian name of the murdered Ménard is not yet certainly known. There was a François Ménard in Detroit in 1791. See Riddell, *Michigan under British Rule,* p. 176. If there were only the one murdered Ménard, Alexander Henry must also have been misinformed as to date of his death; for, when on his way to the Missouri, he wrote that, having crossed a little stream, the Rivière Plé, a tributary of the Souris, he soon came to the place where "Old Menard was pillaged and then murdered by three Assineboines in the year 1803. On his way to the Missouri . . . ." (*Coventry Copy,* I, 425; Coues, I, 311-12). For the allusion in narratives of the Lewis and Clark expedition to Ménard and to his recent assassination by Assiniboines, see Coues, *Lewis and Clark,* I, 195 and, for Nasatir's article, *Jacques D'Eglise on the Upper Missouri,* see Mississippi Valley Historical *Review,* XIV, 47-71.

[22] Clark's scarcely recognizable, but almost phonetically correct *"Greinyea"* (*Original Journals,* V, 350) must, of a surety, be Tabeau's "Grenier" because of the circumstances attending the first meeting with him. "Greinyea" was one of the two men and "Reevey" the other, who had been plundered "by a hunting party of the Mandens" (*Ordway Journal, op. cit.,* p. 155). From Collot's Index to the Church Registers of St. Louis, it seems possible that a *Francis Fleury dit Grenier* was the hunter Tabeau knew. There was, however, a Joseph Grenier of the Parish of Pointe aux Trembly and, in an anonymous journal for 1804-'5 (*Masson MSS,* Dominion Archives, Ottawa), a Grenier, who received frequent mention, as did also a Grenier in the *Charles Chaboillez Journal,* 1904-'5 (*idem*).

of fat. A post maintained at the Fork would receive all the Titons and a part of the Yinctons of the north. Although the beaver cannot be an object of speculation in this trade, a moderate quantity of them could always be obtained, at least, for some years, if the price should encourage beaver-hunting. The trader has not been able to do this thus far, finding no profit in it proportionate to his contracts among the Ilinois. It is necessary to remark that a beaver skin in trade costs as much as a buffalo robe and is worth to the trader only three-fifths as much.[23]

Many Yincton tribes of the River of the Mohens could be induced to settle on the James River. Some have been already tillers of the soil and all are familiar with the hunt of the beaver, the deer, and other animals, yielding peltries, with which this river is said to be well supplied. The only thing that holds them back is the high price of our merchandise; but this obstacle ought now to disappear if the trade of the River of the Mohens, of the St. Peter's, and of the Missouri has no longer but one and the same source.[24] Expenses being everywhere almost the same, there should result a trade traffic susceptible of little difference. If there should be found a considerable difference, it could come only from the incapacity or from the evil

---

[23] "pour le plus" added in the Montreal version.

[24] This points to the exclusion of all but American traders and yet when, on November 29th, 1804, Larocque, having gone up to the American encampment to see why Charbonneau had failed him, had an extended visit himself with Lewis and Clark, they assured him "that it was not the Policy of the United States to Restrain Commerce & fetter it, as was the Case when Louisiana, belonged to the Spanish, that we & all persons who Should Come to their territories, for trade or for any other Purpose, will Never be Molested by an american, Officer or Commandant, Unless his behaviour was Such as would Subject an american Citizen himself, to Punishment — Nor will any trader be obliged to pay for Permission to trade, as was formerly the Case Under the Spanish, as no Exclusive Privilege will be granted, Every one Shall be free to trade after his own Manner — One thing that Government may do, as it has already done, about Detroit & other places, where Opposition in trade Ran high, is to have a Public Store, well assorted of all Kind of Indian Goods, which Store, is to be Open'd to the Indians, only when the traders, in Opposition Run to Excessive lengths; for the purpose of Under Selling them, & by that Means, Keep them quiet, No (?) to take place, No Liquor to be Sold (that is, of a Spirituous Kind) &c &c. In Short, during the time, I was there, a very Grand Plan was Schemed, but its taking Place is more than I can tell although, the Captains Say they are well assured it will." (Larocque, François Antoine, *Missouri Journal, Winter 1804-5, Masson MSS*, Dominion Archives, Ottawa).

conduct of the trader. Opposition itself never leads an honest, sensible man to sacrifice his interests to the wild desire of getting more custom.

Those who are not versed in the Savage trade cannot imagine how important is the selection of articles and how far an individual, unfit or evilly-intentioned, can be harmful to the success of commerce and to good order. The envenomed tongue of the greatest idiot, object even of the scorn of the Savages, pours, none the less, its poison into minds on every side open to evil impressions. How many thefts, quarrels, pillages, and murders, committed every day under other appearances, have, as their true cause, only the ineptitude or the wickedness of the whites! This multitude of evil things in every post should certainly merit the attention of the government and a law, which would allow no one to dwell or to journey among the Savages without giving a pledge as to his character and his conduct should be most necessary.[25] Another law, relative to the *engagés* who fail in their duty, and punishments, proportioned to the harm which they do, would truly do away with the baleful results of their insubordination.[26] The selection of persons is of far more moment for these remote expeditions as these men are sure to be seconded by the Savages in their dishonest practices and favored especially by the ease of desertion.[27]

I shall not go into detail concerning the articles suitable for traffic with the Sioux and the Ricaras. The articles for the former can be arranged with careful proportion to those for the Osages and the Kans.[28] Only there should be added many blue glass beads, brass

[25] No doubt Tabeau knew of the *Reglement pour la traite des Illinois,* which had been issued at New Orleans, July 20, 1793, and which, in respect to this matter, had been most excellent. For the text, see Houck, *Transcripts from Spanish Archives,* Missouri Historical Society.

[26] This would suggest the drastic measures that Ramsay Crooks would have had enacted in the interests of the American Fur Company. See *Cass Letter Books,* United States Office of Indian Affairs.

[27] Here is a case where Tabeau, in revising his narrative, re-organized his material with a view to a more logical arrangement. The number of paragraphs towards the end of this chapter is slightly reduced and the equivalent of this paragraph is put at the very end.

[28] One might argue from this that Tabeau was familiar with trade conditions on the lower Missouri.

wire, iron for arrows, and spears. There is no need, as I have already
said, to consider for the Ricaras any object the value of which exceeds that of a buffalo robe. They make great use of vermilion,
which is mixed with an equal measure of flour; but it is regarded
merely as an accompaniment to each article traded. Nevertheless, it
is very useful in the purchase of provisions, shoes, and other trifles
of which there may be need. Ammunition, knives, spears, blue
beads, tomahawks, and framed mirrors are the only articles for
which they are willing to exchange their robes. Hardware of every
kind can procure skins of the common fox and, among the required
presents, they save articles much larger. One should not neglect, on
ascending the river, to hew roughly bows of walnut, for which the
Sioux will trade much fat and the Ricaras, dressed leather, and to
gather turkey feathers, which will suffice, perhaps, for the supply
of maize, beans, etc.

Intoxicating liquors would be merely useless, up to the present,
among the Ricaras, who are not willing to drink them, unless they
are paid. "Since you wish to laugh at my expense," they say to that
one who offers them liquor, "You ought at least to pay me."[29] The
Titons have not yet used intoxicating liquors enough so that they
have a passion for them and, if some drink, it is less from taste than
from imitation and to show that they are not ignorant of that which
it is the fashion to know. But this evil of savage trade will increase
only too easily, if nothing opposes its introduction. Long experience
has made it known more by its ravages than by its benefits. Certainly, opposition and a very unintelligent estimate merely waste it;

[29] This story, practically unchanged, is related by Lewis and Clark; but it does not
appear in the Montreal version of the Tabeau narrative. For the Arikara distaste for
spirituous liquors, see *Original Journals,* I, 186, 199. In this same connection it
might be observed that three decades after this the tribes of this particular part of the
Upper Missouri had developed no over-mastering appetite for whiskey or rum. In all
the time he lingered at Fort Clark, which, situated on the right bank of the river,
was almost directly opposite the site of Fort Mandan, Maximilian never saw a Mandan
under the influence of liquor; but it was the corn, or maize, which the Indian agriculturalists of the region produced, that suggested to Kenneth Mackenzie the practica-
bility of running a distillery at Fort Union and that kept it supplied (Coues, *Larpenteur: Forty Years a Fur Trader on the Upper Missouri*, I, 58). The Assiniboines, who
were reported by Lewis and Clark to be, in their day, the only Missouri River Indians
that cared for intoxicating beverages (Coues, *Lewis and Clark,* I, 271) still created a
demand for it thirty years afterwards.

for the rivals giving equal bounties, the customers remain in the undecided state relative to preference. But why should it not give birth to evils among nations where internal dissensions and individual hatreds are general and inveterate?

MANNERS AND CUSTOMS

IF the Ricara, if the Sioux, is the man of nature so much praised by poets, every poetic license has been taken in painting him; for their picture makes a beautiful contrast to that which I have before me.[1] All that one can say is that, if these barbarians leave no doubt that they are human, intelligent beings, it is because they have the form, the face, and the faculty of speech of human beings. Stupid, superstitious, gluttonous, lewd, vindictive, patient by principle, fierce of temper, cowardly with men of like strength, fearless in assassinations, ungrateful, traitorous, barbarous, cruel, lying, thievish, etc. I add the "and so forth" in the fear that these epithets do not wholly comprise their vices and that I may be free to add to them.[2] That is, it seems to me, a beautiful national character,[3] in which I believe that

[1] What would Tabeau have said of Catlin, who, seeing the Upper Missouri tribes a quarter of a century later, thought so well of them that he must surely have viewed them as if through magic spectacles? To him everything was picturesque, every Indian brave, a stalwart warrior; every squaw, a veritable Pocahontas and, of necessity, pretty, handsome, or beautiful. Catlin was either bent upon writing and featuring something so attractive that it would make its own appeal or he, personally, was still very much under the influence of that idealization of primitive man that characterized the thought of the later eighteenth century and to which Tabeau refers.

[2] The experience of Francis A. Chardon among the Mandans would have put them without reservation in this same category. Patrick Gass had found them great pilferers (*Journal*, p. 252), as had Alexander Henry, and Captain Sire, who had far better opportunity to know them well, declared to Audubon that they were the "ne plus ultra of thieves" (Audubon, *Journals*, II, 11).

[3] This sweeping depreciation and disparagement of the Indians was hardly justified. The very low opinion that Lewis and Clark had of the Teton Sioux, whom the former, in his *Statistical View, op. cit.,* p. 714, denounced as the "vilest miscreants of the savage race," was probably derived, partly at least, from Tabeau. Others before and since have had a quite different opinion. Caleb Atwater thought the Sioux on the whole an exceptionally "fine race" (*Antiquities of the Western Country*, p. 332) and George H. Kennerly, who had rare opportunities of studying them at close range, pronounced them "proud samples of men in a savage state." Not all thought so

the facts already related and those to follow ought to prove sufficiently that nothing is exaggerated.[4]

They have as a recompense all physical advantages, although generally of medium height. Well-built, active, agile, they excel in all sport and, in the race, are as active as they are unwearied. Thus the quickness with which news is communicated is astonishing. To go eighty or a hundred leagues is a walk, which the young people make in winter, as in the finest weather, often needlessly. It is only to take the air. The Ricaras, especially, are considered the best runners of all the nations and it is probably before the enemy that they have gained this great reputation. It is certain that they are, perhaps, the best swimmers in the world.[5]

Among the Sioux, the Ricaras, and others, whom I have had opportunity of seeing, a national aspect is not noticeable, generally so distinctive among civilized peoples and among the nations of the lower Missouri and those of the Mississippi. Nevertheless, the Caninanbiches and the Padaucas are distinguished by their fairness and their reddish hair; but, notwithstanding this advantage, to which the features do not correspond, the women have nothing agreeable and are not comparable to the Chawoinones,[6] Abenacquises[7] and others

---

badly of the Arikaras, either, as did Tabeau. Clark, it is true, thought them dirty (*Original Journals*, I, 188); but Gass, who had identically the same, if not better, means of judging, evidently considered them, in comparison with other Indians, an improvement on the breed (*Journal*, pp. 52-53). The much earlier acquaintance of Truteau made him their admirer and their apologist (*Seconde Partie, op. cit.*, pp. 24 *et seq.*). At the beginning of the nineteenth century, the bad reputation of the Sioux must have been very widespread. Harmon recorded in his journal that they were "said to be the greatest villains in this part of the world" (*op. cit.*, p. 165). With Americans their friendly attitude towards the British was not likely to make for their greater popularity, it being one of the several admittedly anti-British periods of United States history.

[4] In his revised version, Tabeau made the addition after "outré":

" ... je crois pourtant n'avoir rien outré, & si l'on veut faire attention aux faits que j'ai déja rapporté & a ceux qui vont suivre, j'espere qu'on en conviendra avec moy. je voudrois avoir trouvé chez eux quelques vertue, qui pussent un peu voiler l'horreur de ce tableau, mais je ne puis offrir que leur extrême amour pour leurs enfants, & si je les appelle dénaturés, c'est eu égard a leurs peres, meres, ayeux & autres dans leur vieillesse, qu'ils n'attendent pas toujours pour les mépriser. = "

[5] The last three lines are omitted from the Montreal version.

[6] "Chawoinones," one of the many variants of Shawnee. For others, Chawanons, Chiouanons, Chaouannons, etc., see Hodge, *Handbook, op cit.*, II, 536-38.

who are seen in the Ilinois country. The Sioux women are the only ones among whom there are many who are passable and some who are very pretty.[8] As for the Ricara women, I have reason to believe that it is, in derision or in irony, that some travelers have called them the Circassians of the Missouri or else the present race has degenerated greatly. This is difficult to believe on seeing the old women. They are certainly the most ugly and have the advantage of surpassing all the others in slovenliness. They generally have a color as of death, as far as one can judge through the layers of dirt, in which sweat or the rain has traced lines. And I would not be accused of exaggeration here, if decency did not forbid a detail, too repugnant. I shall say only that, after having eaten almost a year with the Ricaras, one ought not to be allowed to be fastidious or disgusted.[9]

The clothing of the Ricaras is: One cannot be more unadorned. They are naked and wear carelessly over the shoulder a robe or a dressed skin.[10] Leggings of antelope-skin and shoes of buffalo hide are worn, in summer, only at ceremonies[11] and, in winter, for protection from the cold, to which habit has rendered these Savages almost insensible. The 17th. of December,[12] when it was 26° below zero, many, quite naked, played, at daybreak upon the ice, a game

7 "Abenacquises," (Washington version); "Abenakises," (Montreal version), the Abnaki, or Abenaki, with a broader application than that usually given to the name. The tribal name, Abnaki, was applied at one time to certain emigrant Oneidas, Stockbridges, and Munsees settled about Green Bay, Wisconsin.

8 For a recognition of the beauty of Sioux women, see Boller, Henry A., *Among the Indians: Eight Years in the Far West*, p. 169. John C. Frémont remarked that the Sioux girls at Fort Pierre were "noticeably well-clothed" (*Memoirs,* p. 39).

9 Again do we find an unpleasant detail omitted from the revised version, a pretty clear indication of re-writing.

10 "Les Sioux des Prairies, les Chaguyennes et les Tocaninambiches, sont les plus propres de tous les peuples Sauvages. Leurs habillemens sont faits avec plus de soin, leur chevelure mieux entretenue, leurs tentes plus régulierès. Les Ricaras, au contraire, sont si mal-propres que l'on ne sauroit toucher à rien chez eux ou sur eux, sans la plus grande répugnance" (Perrin de Lac, *op. cit.,* p. 339).

11 Espèce de pantalons divisés en deux parties, qui les couvrent depuis les pieds jusqu'au dessus des hanches; ils ne s'en servent qu'en hiver ou les jours de fête" (*idem,* p. 327, n.).

12 "le 17 — 10bre" — both versions. Were it not for the added fact of the intense cold at the time there would be little doubt of the fact that here, as elsewhere, Tabeau was counting in consecutive order from January and ignoring the Latin numeral.

that the French have called billiards[13] without it having the least
resemblance to our game.[14] The Savages are passionately fond of
this game; but, although it gives much exercise, the weather was
hardly suitable for this amusement and, as I thought I saw that there
was bragging, I judged that they paid somewhat dear for the renown
of man above pain. Perhaps, all these old partisans of physical im-

[13] " ... le 17 — 10bre par un froid de vingt six dégrés, plusieurs dès le point du
jour jouoient le corps nud, sur la glace, a un jeu que les françois ont nomé Billard,
sans qu'il ait le moindre rapport au nôtre ..." (Washington version).

" ... l'habitude a tellement endurci ces sauvages que je les au vu le 17 — 10bre
par un froid de 26 dégrés reaumur jouër a la crosse sur la glace, parfaitement nuds,
pendant près d'une heure. c'étoit payer bien cher la renomée d'homme dur & insensible, unique motif qui les fasoit agir." (Montreal version).

[14] Lewis and Clark went on record in support of the resemblance of this Indian
game to European billiards (Coues, *Lewis and Clark*, I, 213) and it may have been
their insistence upon that fancied likeness and their ascribing of it to an "ancient intercourse with the French of Canada" that made Tabeau so emphatic in the opposite
direction. It was in December, 1804, after the American captains had come to know
the Frenchmen at the Arikaras, that they saw the game played. As if to make it very
clear that he knew whereof he was speaking, Tabeau, in his revised version (see preceding note), calls the game *Lacrosse;* but, in spite of his dissent, the practice has continued of likening it to billiards. See Quaife, Wisconsin Historical Society *Collections,*
XXII, 172, n. 1; Burpee, *Journals and Letters of Verendrye,* pp. 343-44, n. Thaddeus
Culbertson, who was a serious-minded, discerning man, took the same exception that
Tabeau did, saying, "it is entirely different from our game of that name" (*Journal of
an Expedition to the Mauvaises Terres,* 1850, Senate Document, Special Session, 32nd
congress (1851), I, 98). If Tabeau had reference to the same game in his two narratives, there ought to be no confusion and nothing to mislead, since Lacrosse is
played by twenty-four and Billiards by two or four. At Fort Tecumseh, where, as at
all the Upper Missouri Outfit posts, Scots from Red River of the North and French
Canadians were well represented, a game was played, called as in the following:

(1830, March 19th) ". . . . In the afternoon Mess. Laidlaw, Holliday and myself (Halsey) played at cross ball with the squaws — they bet Moccassins against
beads — we came off victorious . . . ." (*Fort Tecumseh Journal,* 1830). Latrobe, referring to the time when he was on the St. Peter's with Sioux Indians around him,
said, "To while away the time, arrangements were made as well as circumstances
would admit, to get a sufficient number of Indians together to form a ball-play, one of
the most celebrated games of the North American Indians, and frequently played with
great effect by several hundreds ranged on either side . . . .

". . . . The game is precisely that which we call hockey, with the exception, that
a stick with a kind of netted scoop at the end is used . . . ." (*The Rambler in North
America,* II, 298-99). For a treatise on the entire subject, see Culin, Stewart, *Games
of the North American Indians,* Bureau of American Ethnology *Report,* 1921-'3 and,
for other minor allusions, see Abel, *Chardon's Journal at Fort Clark,* n. 505.

passiveness would have hesitated about giving a proof of their system in this way.

The women are covered with a skin of the cow or of the doe, bound around the middle of the body, sewed on the two sides, and ornamented with long fringes at the bottom and down the seams. They wear, also leggings of antelope-skin. They cover the shoulders and the upper part of the arms with two kinds of wings. From the elbow to the wrist the sleeve is very narrow and is also ornamented with threads, which are everywhere a great adornment. The blue bead, as precious here as the porcelain among the nations of the Mississippi, is used to trim all the seams of these sacks called Roman by some Frenchmen. The Sioux women are dressed almost in the same fashion and are distinguished only by rolls of brass wire in the ears and by huge locks of hair, covered with blue beads and tied on the temples in the shape of cushions.

The Sioux men wear commonly below the buffalo robe a chemise of leather with long fringes, and are always modestly covered. The number of feathers and the buffalo heads give to these Savages a truly Savage air, which is becoming to them and suits them perfectly. Among these nations hair is the greatest ornament[15] and, not only is every means taken to preserve it, but tresses of hair of buffalo wool, long and furry, are pasted together and arranged in such a way that the coiffure resembles, as much as it is possible, the head of the buffalo. But all this attire is common. Here is the dress of a dandy whom I observed:[16]

---

[15] "le plus grand ornement." Greatest, therefore, in the sense of most beautiful. See the Montreal version where the corresponding phrase is, "le plus bel ornement."

[16] Tabeau's description of the dandy in his revised version, though shorter, is equally effective:

" ... violà l'habillement général & commun, mais comme tous les petits maitres ne sont pas a paris, les jeunes gens ont mille colifichets de peau de bêtes puantes (putois), de guenilles d'écarlat, de coquillages, de griffes d'oiseaux, de manchettes pendantes & garnies de petits grelots. ils portent du grandes épaulettes & un long rabat garni en porc-épic & peints de diverses couleurs, tripple rouleaux de fil de leton aux oreilles, & le visage peint de bleu, blanc, rouge & noir. dans la main gauche est un sac de pe-cant & une lance, le tout enjolivé & accompagné d'un *chichikoi* sonore. l'autre main est réservée pour la gesticulation. ainsi enharnachés on se proméne a pas lents, deux a deux, en ricanant, papillonant, & favorisant les dames de quelques coups d'oeil gracieux. qu'on juge de leur vanité, par celui qui s'appercevant que le l'observois at-

He has shoes fully ornamented, with a skunk skin trailing at each heel and decorated with a piece of scarlet. The lower part of the leg is bound with two narrow cords, trimmed with quills of the porcupine. Leggings of very white antelope-skin, of which one has a cut-out fringe, and the other, streaked with black, are joined and crossed above and are like Bavaroises.[17] These fringes are ornamented with shells and with various spurs, the little clashes of which are sonorous enough to attract attention. A long, wide chemise of antelope-skin, all its edges fringed, perforated and festooned below with different figures, has two narrow points which trail under the arms and is closed only from the elbows to the wrists where there are wrought and pendant cuffs. All this is trimmed with little bells. Upon the shoulder straps, diverse shells are fixed, and a band of fine leather, ornamented with porcupine quills and painted with figures of different colors, covers the throat and the stomach. Above it, is a collar of bear-claws, between which are little tassels of blue beads. Triple rolls of brass wire are in the ears, which are also trimmed with a double row of shells and feathers. Upon the head are scattered, without order, little balls of swan's down. The hair, separated into two tresses, covered with fine red leather, hangs very low in front. The face is daubed with white, blue, black, and vermilion. In the left hand is a spear, of which the long handle, gay with rags and fine leather and ornamented with porcupine, is held in the middle and kept in countenance with a pouch of the pekan. The head and tail of this animal, being the most brilliant and ornamented parts, hang side by side. A chichikoi, filled with small pebbles which make a noise, is attached to the left wrist. The other hand is reserved for gestures. Thus accoutered, the dandies promenade, two by two, with slow steps, fluttering about, chuckling, and favoring the ladies with sheep's eyes. It is clear that all the dandies are not in Paris and one can imagine the vanity of him who gives me time to make this examination, on perceiving that I am looking at him attentively.[18]

---

tentivement en écrivant, m'a laissé tout le temps d'éxaminer son attirail, que j'ai abregé des trois quarts. — "

[17] A kind of trowsers, worn in the early part of the nineteenth century, with fore and aft flaps that buttoned around the waist.

[18] Indian vanity was early commented upon by Europeans coming into contact

The Sioux women, although not very strict, are more reserved than the Ricara women. It could be said that the latter do justice to themselves and know the value of their favors, if their facility in granting them is any criterion. The most inflexible is not proof against a prize of vermilion and of twenty strands of blue beads. There are, nevertheless, a few prudes who greatly wish to pass for cautious ones; but who surrender themselves, moreover, with discretion and secrecy.[19] All are generally hostile to ceremony and, to avoid the embarrassment of an intrigue, they ordinarily make the first advances in a less equivocal manner and it is here where one truly takes the romance by the tail. The most peculiar thing is that all goes on often in the presence of and even by order of a jealous husband. This paradox will be no longer a paradox when it is understood that a Sioux, as a Ricara, is alive to this affront only when his wife, by a secret infidelity, departs from his house. Therefore, all that which meets with his approval, being in order, is not offensive and such a man, who would kill or at least turn out his wife up-

---

with the red men. The instance recorded by Creuxius (*Historiae Canadensis seu Novae Franciae*, p. 63) of the Indian husband, who decked himself out in the Parisian costume that the Ursuline nuns had presented to his bride and strutted pompously about quite oblivious of the fact that particular garments belonged to a particular sex, is the most famous; but there are many others and not a few travelers have fallen in with Indian dandies and described them. Murray's Pawnee dandy (*Travels in North America*, I, 317-21), Catlin's Mandan (*North American Indians*, I, 112-14), and Mrs. Jameson's Potowatomi (*Winter Studies and Summer Rambles in Canada*, pp. 43-46) are all comparable to and very like Tabeau's Arikara. These professional beaus were a little different, in tribal estimation, from such men as the Assiniboine chief, *Wijun-jon*, and the Mandan, *She-he-ke*, who, puffed up with pride because they had had the privilege of a trip to Washington, paraded about and affected airs that brought down upon themselves the derision of the onlookers. For the disrepute into which *She-he-ke* fell, see Brackenridge in Thwaites, *Early Western Travels*, VI, 137. The Assiniboine, *Le fils du gros Français* (Maximilian, *idem*, XXIII, 21), called "General Jackson" because he had been to the American capital city and seen that particular "Great Father," killed himself the year subsequent to his return (Larpenteur, *Forty Years a Fur Trader on the Upper Missouri*, II, 412-15).

[19] Though in agreement with Tabeau in the main, as with Truteau (*Seconde Partie, op. cit.*, pp. 30-31), Brackenridge would not have said that all Arikara women had a price. Indeed, he gave in his narrative some very notable instances of feminine chastity among the Arikaras that came under his own observation or were recounted to him (*Early Western Travels*, VI, 131-32). They were revealed in what might be called, not inappropriately, a running of the gauntlet.

on the slightest suspicion, prostitutes her himself for a very small reward and it is seen that a wife has not yet been chastised for having failed in submission in like case.

I have seen among the Bois Brulés a secret infidelity punished and a husband order his wife to be unfaithful.[20] Here are the two cases: The 6th. of August a man surprises his better half in flagrant wrongdoing and, in order to avoid all proceedings, he takes it upon himself to pronounce and to execute sentence. He commences by removing her hair from the nape of the neck up to brow and, stopping near the ears, he allows the hair and skin to hang down each side. He continues his work by mutilating her arms and hands and ends by a cut of the knife on the shoulder-blade.[21] The wife having wholly

[20] The revised version introduces some differences of detail:

"j'ai vu chez les bois brulés punir une infidelité secrette, avec barbarie, par un mari, qui quelques jours après prostitua une autre de ses femmes. voici les deux faits. le 6 8bre 1803, un brave surprend sa femme en flagrant délit, & suivant l'usage, prend sur luy de prononcer & d'éxécuter la sentence. il commence par lever la chevelure depuis la nuque jusqu'au front & ne s'arrêtant qu'aux oreilles, ils laissent pendantes les peaux & les cheveux ensanglantés il mutile ensuitte les bras & les mains, & finit par un coup de couteau sous l'omoplatte, elle en est cependant revenue & le mari nous disoit; que si elle y retournoit, il la regarderoit comme incorrigible. un sauvage trouve l'infidélité en faveur d'un blanc moins outrageante, en ce que la femme est entraînée par l'appas du gain, & que d'ailleurs il ne suppose pas que ce rival présume luy être preféré. =

"le 14 du même mois, cet homme qui vient de doner une si grande preuve de sa délicatesse, améne au fort sa femme bien aimée, une des plus jolies du canton & de plus réputée sage. un cavalier offre dabord un couteau fin, une once de vermillon & six pouces de tabac filé. le présent paroissoit modique, en raison des charmes, que le mari fesoit étaler, en dépit de quelques minauderies. on balançoit lorsque la prude, (qui ne vouloit pas négliger l'occasion de prouver sa soumisson) fit remarquer la beauté du vermillon, la belle qualité du tabac; elle ajouta que les couteaux a manche vert, n'étoient pas communs. enfin elle dit tant & si bien, que le mari tomba d'accord, & fit sentinelle. = " (Montreal version).

[21] There are many instances, well-known because already often told, of the cruel treatment of Indian wives. For two of them recorded by Alexander Henry, see *Coventry Copy*, I, 329, 382. In one other case, pp. 126-28, a variation of the theme is introduced, in that the aged husband is shown, weeping tears of remorse, and the wife, relentlessly unforgiving. That Indian women sometimes took revenge for the cruelties and indignities heaped upon them and sometimes, too, exhibited jealousy on their own account, punishing its cause, there is ample proof. See, for example, Morton, *Journal of Duncan M'Gillivray,* p. 34, and, for one case yet more terrible, see *Anonymous Journal, 1804-'5.* (*Masson MSS*, Dominion Archives, Ottawa), August 11, 1804.

recovered from the wounds, he said that if she did wrong again he would regard her as incorrigible. A Savage regards the infidelity of his wife in favor of a white man less of a sin, in that she is won by the allurement of gain and he does not dream that this rival presumes to think that he is preferred to himself. This opinion, elsewhere, is perhaps often the hidden cause of jealousy and it cannot be otherwise among the Savages, who know neither love nor delicacy.

A Sioux brave, wishing to prove that he is brave-hearted, comes, in open daylight, to find a Frenchman at the Isle of Cedars. He is followed by his young wife, one of the prettiest of the village and, moreover, reputed discreet. He offers the favors of this well-beloved, demanding only a few small articles in return.[22] The cavalier, although surprised, is not the man to give up his cloak and offers at first a fine knife, a prize of vermilion, and about six inches of tobacco. As the present appeared small because of her attractions, the husband pulls off the robe in which the Venus is wrapped through modesty and, in spite of some affected manners, increased, of course, the price of his goods by exposing it. The cavalier still hesitated, when the victim to whom the sacrifice was doubtless painful, but who feared, nevertheless, to lose the occasion of proving her submissiveness, remarked that knives with a green handle were not common; that the vermilion was a beautiful red; that the tobacco — in short, well, what else? At least, she speaks so well that they agree and the husband firmly holds the door.

This politeness is carried out every day among the Ricaras, and always the more readily in the case of the whites; but infidelities, un-

---

[22] For cheapness of this deplorable sort, take note of the story told by Patrick Gass relative to "the daughter of the head-chief of the Mandan nation" (*Journal of Patrick Gass*, p. 75), whose honor was sold "for an old tobacco box" and, likewise, the observation of Alexander Henry that the Mandan men offered their wives to the strangers within their gates "without any solicetation and are even offended if their offers are not accepted of unless you can convince them of there being some good reason for your refusing to comply with their wishes, and that it is not out of contempt, they always expect payment for their complaisance, but a mere trifle will satisfy them, even one single coat button . . . ." (*Coventry Copy*, I, 481). John MacDonell tells of declining the gratuitous offering and of, thereby, giving offence to the husband (*Journal, 1793-1795*, entries for March 26 and April 5, 1795). The scribe of the *Fort Tecumseh Journal, 1830* wrote of the Mandans, "The men do not scruple to lend their wives to the whites without solicitation."

avowed, are not always punished severely and the braves ordinarily content themselves with repudiating the wives. This is, often, only a momentary divorce. Besides, the intrigues are so common that they are generally made light of. Furthermore, reciprocation of injury suffices in a nation, where immodesty is carried to its highest pitch.

The word, modesty, is not even known among the Ricaras. The Chayennes and the Caninanbiches are reserved in this respect, even in their conversation. The Sioux are, at least, modestly covered; but the Ricara men are absolutely nude. Through force of habit, though, no notice is taken of it. The women and the young girls mingle with the men and laugh, inconsequently, at the most obscene things. The men, nevertheless, would think it immodest to be without a loin cloth made of blades of curled grass. To neglect this is here a great fault. The 2nd. of August I saw all the women and girls of the vilage, spectators of a comic dance, where the men, attached thus, two by two, drew backwards and offered, in their gambols, attitudes which drew great applause. After that, it would surely astonish one to hear it said that the girls are virtuous before marriage and that there are virgins, eighteen to twenty years old. Truth exceeds probability here. It is true that the mothers and all the relatives watch with the greatest care and that they carry watchfulness up to the point of fastening at night the petticoats of the girls who lie thus tied down. Nevertheless, these bonds are not proof against a lover who pleases; but, according to their law, that is a marriage and, even if it last only an hour, the girl becomes, none the less, an honest widow.

Incest[23] is not recognized till the third degree and the brother and the sister in my lodge are considered to be beyond criticism. It is needful to confess that they save appearances as much as they can. The seventy-year old man and his eldest sister, being unable, doubtless, to find better fortune elsewhere, mutually gratify themselves. It does not appear that there is much to say about it. Incest, on the contrary, seems infinitely applicable to the son-in-law, who often marries

---

[23] Of this, George Keith gave a quite different idea when writing about the Beaver Indians to Roderick McKenzie, January 7, 1807 (Masson, *op. cit.*, II, 69); but he was in substantial agreement with Tabeau when referring to the Filthy Lake, or Grand River Indians (*idem*, p. 115).

all the sisters and, were his mother-in-law a hundred years old, he would fail in good manners and filial respect if, from time to time, he did not secretly gratify the old woman.

Women are of so little importance among the Sioux and the Ricaras that it would be astonishing if the husbands were fastidious about their conduct from any other motive than that which I have already explained. They are, in the fullest sense, slaves; for, being bought, they become property that the husband can lend, give away, and sell when it pleases him. A Ricara[24] lost at play the enjoyment of his wife for some days and he lay tranquilly at the foot of the bed, while the young man who had won received, in his sight, a thousand caresses. I know not if this was in order to be revenged on her husband or to pay honestly his debt; but she did reproach him for being a great gambler and she made much more fuss the next morning over a basket he had lost in play.

A monster, whom I looked upon every day with horror, had a pretty wife. He learns that she is unfaithful to him and, to hide his plan of vengeance, he says many times to his friends, that repeatedly in his dreams the French demand his wife of him. The barbarian, at length, takes her aside one day and, after having stabbed her, dismembers her and sacrifices her limbs to the French and the four points of the compass. He then carries the tongue to the village and coolly tells of his execrable crime. The relatives murmured at first; one spoke of vengeance; but everything is easily quieted. What could one say? She was his wife and he could dispose of her.

The women do not assist at any ceremony and are not present at the feasts where the husbands alone eat greedily all that which the women are able to procure.[25] In their lodge even, they do not always taste the daily fare which is divided generally among the masters, the guests, and the parasites. They have, none the less, charge of the cooking. This is not displeasing to them as this is their only opportunity of approaching the fire which they replenish. There is in these lodges an insupportable cold as there is in the center only a single fire of little dried sticks, always surrounded by men crowded

24 " ... un jeune homme de ma loge ..." (Montreal version).
25 For a contrary opinion, see Culbertson, T. A., *Journal*, Senate Documents, Thirty-second Congress, special session, I, 106-7.

together, who prevent heat passing beyond and reaching the women behind them.

The Ricara women appear to endure their hardships with more fortitude than the Sioux whom their hard lot often drives to suicide.[26] I saw many cases of suicide during the six months I lived on the Isle of Cedars.[27] A young woman hanged herself; some days after, a very pretty girl followed her example; a third did likewise; but her mother, who suspected her plan, arrived soon enough to save her by cutting the rope. It is always this kind of death that they choose and they are often found strangled without being suspended, madness giving them the courage to draw, until death comes, upon the cord tied to a tree.[28]

The venereal disease makes terrible ravages here and, from the moment it attacks a man, it makes more progress in eight days than elsewhere in five or six weeks. These Savages are too ignorant and too lazy to profit from the gifts of nature and to find in plants remedies for their ailments. They do not know one purgative root as this treatment is not in use. Blood-letting, resorted to at every accident and on every occasion, is the universal remedy. Although the soil is not capable of producing a great variety of plants, there are certainly some medicinal ones. The ginger, anise, maiden's hair, the beautiful angelica, the ginseng,[29] and many others are common; but, as among the Sioux and still more among the Ricaras, there prevails no natural sickness, as all illness is either the result of the vengeance of some angry spirit or a succession of evil deeds of a magician, diviners are

[26] Bradbury says that so hard was the lot of Sioux women and so vivid their realization of it that they not only frequently killed themselves but frequently destroyed their female children to save them from a like stern fate (*Early Western Travels*, V, 109); Henry found suicide "not uncommon among the Soulteux women" (*Coventry Copy*, I, 349); and Long was informed that it was quite the usual thing among the Sauks, especially among the women (Keating, *op. cit.*, I, 227). Hanging was most often the means taken to accomplish the end (*idem*, p. 394). See also, on this point, the *Harmon Journal*.

[27] " ... deux femmes & une fille se sont pendues pendant que j'étois a l'isle aux cédres. ..." (Montreal version).

[28] At this point begins, in the Montreal version, Tabeau's treatment of *Des Médecines ou Charlataneries*, the introductory sentence of the rough draft being dispensed with.

[29] " ... le gingembre, l'anis, le capillaire, la Belle angélique, le ginsseing & plusieurs autres ne sont pas rares. ..." (Washington version).

the only recourse. They are called *medicine men*,[30] which signifies supernatural power. These charlatans are here in their midst, admired and feared with the most stupid crudity. What is more singular is that often the doctor, far more foolish than the patient, is himself the dupe of his professed knowledge and, if after songs and invocations, the illness persists, he is convinced that it is the moral disposition or sorcery which opposes the cure. Songs of a particular medicine (of which each doctor possesses a certain number, that properly belong to him and that no other can sing, at least, with success, only after having bought them[31]) produce a marvelous effect. They precede and accompany all cures. The cures are made by friction with the hand, with magic feathers, beaks and talons of birds, and with a thousand other mysterious objects. Then come sprinklings upon the stomach, upon the neck, upon the sides, of a decoction of powder made of different leaves. Finally, this charlatanism having lasted whole nights and days and having been repeated a hundred times, the doctor puts his mouth firmly to the skin and, with a strong breath, with a great cry, he draws from the body of the sick one, shells, pieces of iron, of horn, of grass, which he declares are the source of the evil.[32] Then he promises a speedy cure and, as the payment, always very large because of knowledge, has preceded the treatment, if the sick man dies, he is greatly in the wrong.

All the medicine men are not foolish enough to believe sincerely in their own nonsense. Some have in view only that of others. Guided by greed, vanity, and the allurement of gain, they wish only to profit from the general imbecility; but, although by their own experience they ought to know that the others, whose operations are similar, are not greater sorcerers than they, they have as much confidence as the common people and believe themselves the only ones obliged to have recourse to knavery. Accordingly, each one in partic-

30 " ... que l'on nome *gens de médecine,* (tai-wa-rous-tés), ou *hommes de pourvoir surnaturel. ...*" (Montreal version).

31 Parentheses as in original.

32 Henry Kelsey has something to say on the removal of the cause of physical disorders by suction, see *Kelsey Papers,* p. 21, so also has Alexander Henry. For comparatively recent remarks upon the subject, see Densmore, Frances, *Teton Sioux Music,* Bureau of American Ethnology, *Bulletin,* No. 61, pp. 245-48.

ular, persuaded of his own ignorance, admires his colleagues and all revere and fear mutually their magic power.

It is impossible to conceive up to what point a professed sorcerer is jealous of the opinion he can give of his power. A sorcerer, named *Kahid-jai,* was accused of evil-doing in regard to a young man taken suddenly ill at a village more than a league away, where the charlatan had not been for six months. It was not difficult for him to clear himself, but vanity was not satisfied and, rather than deny a crime that gave a great idea of his ability, he preferred to remain exposed to the vengeance of a family of braves by preserving a mysterious air that seemed to give a silent assent. His vanity would, perhaps, have cost him his life, but for the intervention of my host, Kakawita, a still greater rogue than he, who, seeing the young man convalescent, told the family that the only remedy was to appease the magician. In effect, he extorted a horse by this means and the sick one, readily recovering, everything was satisfactorily arranged without compromising the honor of the medicine man.

Medicine men, diviners, and jugglers are here of the same rank. As all these professions have the same supernatural foundation, one presupposes another and takes its place, and all are comprehended under the term, medicine men. Kakawita does not foretell the future, but he does some wonderful things. By a powder, which he prepares, into which as he revealed to me in confidence, there enters the pulverized head of the green woodpecker, and which he blows through a constelled corn-stalk, he can scatter an epidemic at a distance and upon villages that he wishes to harm. Once smitten by the fatal powder, a man has no more than a dozen days to live. One day some Saones report that a mortal sickness has greatly ravaged the Bois Brulés after their inroads upon the Poncas. Immediately, Kakawita whispers mysteriously to me that undoubtedly among the latter there are to be met makers of pivart powder.

Each medicine man carries a little mat in which are wrapped all the implements of sorcery. This mat is the wand of the fairies, with which alone the magician can work. It is hung up and reverenced by all and opened only for important cases. Kakawita believed that the powder of his was weakened if some one broke a bone in his lodge, took out fire, burnt horn there, or touched the meat on the

185

fire with the point of a knife. Great evils generally follow these betrayals. A young man is wounded by a cow; another, on the same day, has a bad fall; and the two accidents are attributed — the one, to Marié, my *engagé,* who had pricked the meat, and the other to a man, named Cadien, who was seen to leave while smoking.[33] Kakawita has in his mat a little whip which makes a famous courser out of a draught horse and, when he hangs it on his wrist, while singing a certain song, all the horsemen who accompany him fall from their horses. And, inconceivable thing! the Ricaras are so far blind that they themselves are convinced so that he has made them prove it many times.

During the greatest famine, the soothsayers never fail to revel at their ease. Some one wishes to learn where the buffalo cow is; another is disturbed over the fate of the warriors; another desires news; another rushes to the oracle, which reveals itself after feasts that the priest causes to be repeated by answering only at the third or fourth consultation. The man, named the Tongue of the Hind,[34] exceeded by far the time that he had fixed for the return of a war expedition. The well-nourished soothsayers promised every day to tell on the next day. Finally, the party arrived unexpectedly and mourned upon a high hill from whence all the village heard them. Immediately, a bold diviner, whom I had seen mount upon a lodge in order to see better, descended and had the effrontery to rush through the streets and to predict with a thousand contortions that the Tongue of the Hind ought to be on the point of arriving. I was still more incensed at seeing the Ricaras marvel at and boast of his knowledge. I believe, nevertheless, that all the travelers, who recount such exploits of these pretended oracles, have wondered at them as they have (the Arikaras).

[33] " ... Le 5 de fevrier 1804, un jeune homme au cerne est blessé par une vache, un autre tombe de cheval & s'estropie; ces deux accidents sont aussitot attribués a deux de mes engagés, dont on a vu l'un sortir de la loge, la pipe allumée, & l'autre piquer un morceau de boeuf dans la chaudiére." (Montreal version).

" ... un jeune homme au cerne est Blaissé par une vache, un autre fait une mauvaise chute dans un meme jour & les deux accidents ont été attribués l'un a marié mon engagé qui avoit piqué la viande la veille & l'autre au nomé cadien qu'on avoit vu sortir en fumant. ..." (Washington version).

[34] "le nome la langue de Biche" (Both versions).

A soothsayer, who has had the good luck to guess rightly a time or two, can risk much without endangering his reputation. Obstinacy as to his infallibility rises so high that in vain the event contradicts his predictions. The observer believes him rather than his own eyes. I saw an instance of this among the Bois Brulés. One of these Delphic[35] men, judging by great fires built along the route that our warriors should take that they are returning victorious, declares that his familiar spirit has informed him of the near return of the braves, who have killed many people or who bring in prisoners. He enters with an astonishing impudence into the details of the battle and makes so great an impression upon the people that the warriors, having arrived, can undeceive no one. In fact, they themselves are almost uncertain about the fact and, at least, believe that the number of enemies of which the oracle has spoken is lost in some way but always from a result of the expedition.

Each medicine man possesses also for his own benefit some knowledge of the subtle tricks by which he performs his magic works and, as these physical wonders appeal to the senses, they draw forth more admiration and reverence than all the other knowledge.[36] Every year in the month of September a great performance begins among the Ricaras and lasts from fifteen to twenty days. Comedians, jugglers, sorcerers of every kind assemble in the evening in a large main building, called the medicine lodge, where they have gourmandized all day at the expense of the spectators. In order to learn something on this subject, I thought I ought to assist at it for once and I confess that one must be a little *Ricararise*[37] to endure the foolishness of most of the performers. One put a handful of ashes into a

---

[35] " ... un de ces delphiens jugeants par de grands feux élevés sur la route que devoient tenir nos guerriers, qu'ils revenoient victorieux, declare que son genie familier l'a informé du retour prochain de nos Braves, qui ont tué plusieurs personnes ou amenent plusieurs prisoniers. ..." (Washington version).

" ... Un prophéte jugeant par de grands faux allumés sur la route que devoient tenir nos guerriers a leur retour, qu'ils revenoient victorieux, déclare que son genie familier l'a informé du retour prochain de nos braves, qui ont tué ou amènent plusieurs personnes. ..." (Montreal version).

[36] For tricks of legerdemain among the Sioux, see Keating's Long, I, 407.

[37] By this word of his own coining can be determined the measure of Tabeau's contempt for these poor Indians, whose chief fault seems to have been that they made trading for him very difficult.

hat, which he turned to vermilion after having put the latter into the lining of the frame. Another drove a pointed horn into a flint and one has to be blind not to see that he made a hole beforehand. This man put on the fire an old, dry bone and, after having broken it easily, if one judges correctly, draws fresh marrow from it, which he swallows. That man breaks a whistle into pieces, much to the regret of a youth, who hurries out crying and finds it again at the bottom of the river. True he could have had under his belt a dozen of them similar to the broken one. I was indignant at having come almost two leagues to witness such nonsense. The most trying thing is that this beginning of great acts occupies half of the night because of their being repeated and the suffering one endures is doubled on witnessing the applause; but I thought I was compensated at the sight of the tricks which I certainly did not expect from the most dull-witted of all the Savages. I saw a man, named *Scarinau,* absolutely naked, his hands empty, the lodge well lighted, show to me, nearby, a leather garter[38] and, after having rolled it in his hands, throw it on the ground, changed into a living adder. He took it up and showed it to me again, a garter. He repeated the same trick ten times without giving the least hint as to the means that he employed.

A man all in black comes stealthily behind one of the actors and, with all his force, deals him a blow with a hatchet upon his head. The sound of the blow leaves no doubt[39] that he really received it. All the spectators and the medicine man yell horribly; but, after many contortions, one of them undertakes to cure him and the dead is brought to life.

Another shoots a gun through the body of his companion who falls down upon his back, dead. The blood gushes forth from two openings, showing that the bullet has gone through the body; but, after a great many grimaces and lamentations, he also is mysteriously healed.

---

[38] " ... j'ai vu un nomé *Scarinau* absolument nud, les mains vuides, la loge Bien éclairée, me montrer de très près une jarretiére de cuir, ..." (Washington version).

" ... j'ai vu un nomé *scarineau,* absolument nud, les mains vuides, la loge étant bien éclairée, m'apporter une jaretierre de cuir, que je détachai moy même, ..." (Montreal version).

[39] "le son du coup de laisse pas a douter ..." (Washington version). *de* is evidently the result of a slip of the pen (Tr.). It is corrected to *ne* in the Montreal version.

Some thrust a knife blade through the hand, pierce the arms, the thighs, the tongue, and all these wounds, so apparent, merely result in making the power of the doctors shine.

Finally, to crown the work, an elderly man, showing all the symptoms of despair and transported by rage, plunges a barbed arrow into his heart. He falls weltering in his blood. The actors, not being able to withdraw the arrow without leaving the barb in the body, seize the point to make it pass through.[40] The spectator really believes that he sees the feathers gradually enter and the arrow, all bloody, come out on the other side under the shoulder-blade.

I cite only these five cases as they are the most striking and could scarcely be better done. The man, *Scarinau,* who changed so well the adders shows the next morning that his powers extend likewise to real snakes. Two Frenchmen,[41] who are walking at some distance from him, see a rattlesnake before them. They warn the Savage, who cries out to them not to harm it, and, on reaching the spot, seizes it himself by the neck and draws from the little sack that he wears around his neck a root which he chews and which he then makes the snake swallow. Then he lets it go and, after a moment, takes it up, very mild. He sings to it; he talks to it; he caresses it; he even irritates it; but the snake in his arms, encircling him, hisses, sounds its rattles, and threatens, and yet does not bite him. Finally, he wraps it in a cloth band and hides it in a hole in order to take it up again on returning and to make it, as he said, his slave; but I know that the slave deserted in the night. I know that some Savages cherish snakes in this way as domestic animals; but I know, also, that a Ricara, while playing thus with his own, was bitten on the neck and that, in spite of medicine and of all the sorcerers, he died the next morning.

[40] "... faire passer de parc en parc." (Both versions). An error, possibly, for *de part en part* (Tr.).

[41] " ... deux de mes engagés qui nous précedoient de quelques pas ..." (Montreal version).

[42] "j'ai scu de luy même son secret & c'est La racine de Bois blanc de prairrie" [I learned his secret from him and the root is from the white wood of the prairie]. In the margin of the Washington version.

RELIGION, SUPERSTITIONS, ETC.

IT would be difficult to give an account of the religion of the Savages of the Upper Missouri, if they had any. These men, incapable of reasoning, too limited to formulate principles and to draw inferences from them so as to develop a belief, have no religion that is fixed or established.[1] Their mind, analogous to their intelligence, not being susceptible to any metaphysical ideas, and not having, perhaps, once reflected upon this matter, naturally takes as an object of its worship that which it sees most striking in nature. Consequently, the gods are the sun, the moon, Venus, and the thunder; but I do not know yet if the idea which they conceive of them and the worship which they give them can be called adoration. They speak commonly of a master of life; but it is in so vague a way and he bears so much resemblance to these first four that he appears rather to depend upon them than to be the author of them. After these gods, the earth, the stones, the four principal winds receive invocations and vows. Then, buffalo heads, snakes, claws of bears and of birds, some roots, flints of peculiar form, are household gods, or particular genii, that each one has a right to take for guardian angel and whose power and protection work every day supposed miracles that affirm and strengthen the superstition.

The thunder is a great bird, the two wings of which have each four joints from five to six feet long. It is always enveloped in a cloud which it pierces with its eyes from time to time and thus causes the lightning. It is armed with fire, stones, hail, and a spear. It carries also a parfleche[2] which appears very useless and of which I have not been able to learn the symbolic significance. It sometimes strikes men and of the animals that it has killed it takes only the tongue, its favorite morsel.

[1] Truteau would appear to have been of like opinion. See *Seconde Partie, op. cit.,* p. 30.

[2] "un parc-fléche" (Washington version); "un pare-flêche" (Montreal version). "A raw-hide case used for packing in horse transportation and also as a trunk, or receptacle, for use inside the tipi" (McClintock, *The Old North Trail*, Appendix, p. 518). See also, Upham, C. W., *Life, Explorations, and Public Services of John Charles Frémont*, p. 85.

Among all the superstitions, confidence in dreams is most credited. As they are always of figurative meaning, they are more susceptible of an equivocal and arbitrary interpretation. In that way
they lend themselves more easily to charlatanism and they offer further this advantage: that it is not necessary to be a medicine man in
order to pretend to inspiration by their means. The most obscure
warrior by a dream, true or pretended, spreads terror on every side,
so that the warrior runs away when about to attack with every possible advantage; but a dream of happiness presages infinite courage
in critical circumstances and the victory is often the result of the
courage which the dream inspires.

In order to obtain a revelation a long and rigorous fast is first
observed. The mind, empty, does not usually lack images to choose
from and the dreamer retains that which pleases him most or which
offers him more of the marvelous. If a buffalo or a deer or a bear
presents itself many times in the night to his imagination, always
occupied with other objects, he doubts no longer the favor and the
protection of a genie transformed into this figure. Invocations, vows
and a special worship follow this belief, especially in times of distress. For example, a wounded warrior sacrifices all his possessions
in favor of a medicine man who will know the right song for the
animal protector. He makes him sing and feast day and night. He
beseeches him to send him his good medicine which he believes he
has certainly received if he recovers from his wounds. First of all, he
makes a vow, whatever may be, to the sun, the moon, etc.

These vows, which are never given except in important cases,
such as that of which I have just spoken, or in a war expedition, or
in famine, or for the safety of some dear one who is believed to be in
danger, bind sometimes, not only not to leave the guns and the
horses in a state *deserving of pity*, but, on the contrary, to look well
after both. Some promise to dance four or five days without intermission,[3] without rest, without smoking, without food and especially
without intercourse with women. Finally, others engage to cut a
finger, to drive knife-blades, arrows, spears, into the arms, the legs,
and the thighs, to mutilate themselves, and to practise upon them-

---

[3] Suggestive of the present-day practice, or epidemic, of dancing marathons in
various American cities.

selves unbelievable cruelties, and all these vows are scrupulously carried out.[4]

I saw among the Ricaras one of the brothers of Kakawita drag two enormous buffalo heads, attached to the ends of a broad strap that cut into the flesh of his chest, and go thus through the village many times, singing and weeping alternately.[5] The horns were often impeded, the heads themselves fell into hollows from where he could lift them only by lacerating jerks, as he did not have the right to help himself with his hands. Notwithstanding the impossibility of succeeding, he, none the less, reiterated his grievous efforts so that the blood gushed from the wounds always growing larger, until some one was willing to aid him; otherwise, he was bound to tear the flesh apart or to die there. The next day he went through the same ceremony again with as much firmness and certainly with more suffering. The entrance of a large strap from an inch and a half to an inch and two-thirds, in width, into the half-closed wounds, the resistence of the weight, and especially the shocks from the inequalities of the ground, doubtless caused pain that fanaticism alone could endure. The blood flowed and yet, in order to finish, he had some

---

[4] Self-torture among Indians, any more than among many primitive people, was not always, as here implied, a mere pretense. For examples of its genuineness among the Arikaras, see Brackenridge (*Early Western Travels,* VI, p. 126). A very realistic account of the custom is to be found in Catlin (*North American Indians,* II, 170 *et seq.*). For self-mutilation among the Beaver Indians, see Harmon, *op. cit.,* p. 182.

[5] For a description of just such an exploit as indicative of a young man's attaining his majority, see Henry's journal (*Coventry Copy,* I, 519-21; Coues, *New Light . . . . ,* I, 364-65; McClintock, *The Old North Trail,* pp. 318-19). Henry introduces the subject by saying, "When a young man has attained to the age of Twenty Years, he generally in the depth of winter performs his penitent progression ..." Jacob Halsey, if, indeed, he were the scribe of the *Fort Tecumseh Journal, 1830,* says therein, "A young man before going to war will have two holes cut in his back near the shoulders, through these holes a cord is passed, at the two ends of which a Buffalo Bulls head is attached — thus arrainged he will proceed out a little before Midnight, without anything to defend him from the Bulls head after him till the weight of it tears his flesh away, alternately crying, and imploring the Great Spirit or Master of Life, to grant him success in war, and not to let him return to his village without bringing trophies of his having been victorious. They (Mandans) have many other modes of torture equally severe all of which they sustain with extraordinary calmness." Fort Tecumseh, where Halsey at the time of this writing resided, was the post for the Teton Sioux; but Halsey had lived among the Mandans in the winter of 1828-'9 and it is about them he writes.

one attach the two ends of the strap to a post where, by dint of jerks, rending what remained of flesh, he found himself free and religiously acquitted.[6]

Vows that bind for life are also made in two orders, or brotherhoods, which are based on superstition.[7] Men, distinguished by two long locks of hair and by other special marks, are called pirains. These braves vow never to retreat before the enemy; but I believe the vows are not kept to the letter. Either the sacrileges are common or, in acting according to vow, much indulgence is given for human weakness. At all events some transgression must have happened among the Ricaras and the pirains must have cast off the rags which hindered their flight, since some in derision call them, *those whose garments do not retreat.* However that may be, they are many in number and accompany the warriors without other arms than a whistle and a chichikoi, with which, new prophets, they mean to cast down the walls of Jericho. They sing and whistle during the battle as exposed as the combatants and, in defeat, they are really found foolish enough to remain still, to allow themselves to be killed and to utter a sound only at the last sigh.

The second order is that of the dogs. To have the honor of being received into this order, it is necessary to give proof of some warlike deed, if it be only the theft of a horse. After these honorable proofs, the candidates are admitted to a novitiate and, while it lasts, they

---

[6] " ... le sang ruisseloit, & cependant pour terminer, on a attaché les deux extremités de la courroye a un poteau, ou déchirant a force de secousses cequi restoit de chaire, il s'est trouvé libre & religieusement acquitté. ⹀ " (Washington version).

" ... le sang ruisseloit sur son corps, & cependant (suivant la rubrique) il faloit paroitre insensible. aussi avoit-il tout l'air d'un vrai stoicien, qui veut prouver son système par pratique & par expérience physique. ⹀ " (Montreal version).

[7] Scattered here and there throughout the *Chardon Journal* are allusions to the Dog Band of this tribe or of that, as, for example, the *Sioux Dog Band,* September 15, 1834; the *Gros Ventre Little Dog Band,* August 25, 1835; the *Sioux Big Dog Band,* September 13, 1835; and the *Arikara Dog Band,* May 7, 1837 (Abel, *op. cit.,* pp. 8, 45, 50, 111) and Major Long, when in the Sioux country, heard of young men banded together not to retreat, "the Dauntless," as he called them (Keating, I, 418-21); but, according to Mooney, the two — and they were the very two described by Tabeau — were one and the same part of a huge social and military organization. The sixth order, in this organization, were the "Dog men," those who did not retreat (*The Ghost-Dance Religion,* Bureau of American Ethnology, *Report,* 1892-'3, Part 2, pp. 988-89).

have the entire body painted red, as also the few garments that they wear. They have at hand, as the pirains, the whistle and the chichikoi,[8] of which they make a very different use. Having become dogs by profession, they appear to have acquired their instinct. They imitate them in everything; they steal around furtively everywhere; and enter the lodges softly, from whence they carry away what they can, sometimes the kettles with the food. They return all that is not eatable, although everything is lawful prize, as everyone, being warned, can keep himself upon his guard and pursue them with great blows of the stick, without which they would be offended. On the contrary, although they flee at the first threats, they return cautiously from the rear to the attack. As they are always many times dispersed, a blast of the whistle, while they flee, announces something seized and, instantly, from every side comrades come and follow the thief. The most comic thing is to see all the real dogs of the village, trained to recognize the whistle, rush forth as the others, mingle indiscriminately with them, and receive their share. If anyone is disposed to treat them kindly, he allows them to enter the lodges where, without saying a word, they glide into the corners in the posture of dogs and show only the nose outside of their covering. If pieces of cooked or raw meat are thrown to them, they throw themselves pell-mell upon them and quarrel voraciously over them.

This metamorphosis generally lasts many months, after which only certain distinctive marks and ways of acting are retained that show a man to be of the order. For instance, they often mount upon the roofs, where they sing, or rather, shout for a part of the night. Their women follow them sometimes and join in at the end of each couplet, which is always the same, a hundred times repeated.[9]

The white cow, being very rare, is particularly worshipped as of

8 See p. 125, n. 79.

9 "cette métamorphose dure ordinairement plusieurs mois après les qu'els on ne conserve plus que quelques marques distinctives & quelques maniéres, d'agir qui pruvent qu'on est de l'ordre. par éxample, ils montent souvent sur les toits ou ils chantent, ou plutot heurlent une partie de la nuit. leurs femmes les suivent quelquefois & accompagnent sur la fin de chaque couplet, qui est toujours le même cent fois répeté. ==" (Washington version).

" ... cet éxercise dure un mois, après le qu'el, ils conservent quelque marques distinctives, & passent quelquefois des nuits entierres a heurler sur les toits. les femmes font *chorus.* ==" (Montreal version).

medicine and this superstitious idea gives to the skin an extraordinary value. Ten and a dozen horses, guns, kettles, and a quantity of other articles are, among the Mandanes, the usual price of the skin of a heifer.[10] The younger she is, the more precious she is, and it is hardly possible for old ones to be met with, as she is sought by all the nations and always followed to the death by the first persons who discover her. The skin of the white cow, the formal sale of which would be a profanation, is always given gratuitously; but that one who offers it, commonly himself a medicine man, finds a way for the reception of each article given in remuneration by making some part of the skin move and by concluding that the spirit is not yet satisfied.[11] Thus the discretion of the charlatan is the measure of the offering.[12]

In general the bear, the deer, and the cow are the kinds of genii that take pleasure in this form and lead this wandering life through kindness for the Savages, in order to furnish subsistence for them. Accordingly, the Savages hunt only with consideration and with a sort of religious respect and are subject to laws that no one would dare to break. This is especially the case when the soldiers are strict

10 " ... dix & douze cheveaux, des fusils, des chaudiéres & quantité d'autres marchandises, sont le prix commun d'une peau de genisse, chez les mandanes. ..." (Washington version).

" ... dix cheveaux, accompagnés de fusils, chaudiéres &c, en font le prix commun chez les mandanes. ..." (Montreal version).

"Les Mandanes et Gros-ventres ont une grande vénération pour les peaux de vaches blanches, pour lesquelles ils donnent souvent huit ou dix chevaux. Ils pensent qu'aussi long-temps qu'ils pourront les conserver, les boeufs et vaches seront en abondance dans le pays qu'ils habiteront. Ces mêmes peuples font, en certain temps de l'année, des assemblées générales de la nation hors l'enceinte du village, et passent plusieurs jours et plusieurs nuits sons des tentes de peaux de boeufs, à chanter, danser et manger en l'honneur du grand Esprit" (Perrin du Lac, op. cit., p 272).

11 Alexander Henry tells of the shaking of the tail to denote insufficiency of price. See Coventry Copy, I, 498; Coues, New Light . . . . , I, 353.

12 " ... de façon que la discretion du charlatan est la mésure des sacrifices." (Washington version).

" ... de façon que la discrétion du charlatan est la mesure des sacrifices, qui tous luy appartiennent." (Montreal version).

In the Montreal version, the paragraph, coming immediately after the passage just quoted, corresponds in substance to one coming much later in the Washington version. It has to do with the Indian awe-like attitude towards white people and takes note of York, the negro attendant of Clark.

and severe in the execution of their duties. In reality, these laws are an absolute necessity, especially among nomadic peoples, who would not be able to subsist, if an individual had the right to kill a cow, to put to flight an entire herd, and to destroy the source of their common food. Thus all possible pains and precautions are taken to prevent these things.[13]

A certain number of young people are always upon the watch and ride in circles, seven or eight leagues distant from the village or the camp, and that one who discovers a herd is obliged to come and give warning without pursuing it or showing himself. One must trust blindly to the declaration of the discoverer since the least doubt upon the truth of his information affects the cow infallibly. It happens, however, very often among the Ricaras, the greatest liars of the universe, that all the village rush away in vain for entire days. A remarkable thing is, that he who deceives them often goes to the hunt in good faith, as he is persuaded that upon his word the cow has returned to the designated place. Not finding her, he brings forward causes and reasons which satisfy everybody and convince even him himself.

The superstitious means used to attract the cow are infinite and, as they are without effect, the blame is laid to the wickedness of the nation, to the quarrels of the village, to the divisions of the tribes, to those who do not gourmandize — the soldiers and the old men — and often to the stay of the French in the village. The cow is called by the buffalo heads set up around the camp, upon the ridges, and each lodge. These heads, surrounded and enclosed by sacrifices, look to the east or the west and display some dry grass which they eat. The festival of the buffalo is solemnized particularly by dances and feastings. Then a thousand senseless ceremonies that I will now describe are carried out.

The *engagés* of Captains Lewis and Clark were actual witnesses of a curious and singular ceremony among the Mandanes which was performed in order to draw the cow near to the village.[14] The old

---

[13] Compare the sociological significance of the *tabu* among the Polynesians of the South Seas.

[14] "Les engagés des capt^nes lewis & clark ont été témoins actifs chez les mandanes

men assemble in the evening in the medicine lodge and announce through the heralds that the cow is not very far away; but that she waits until the braves shall make sacrifices in her honor. At once the men bring in their wives to this altar of Paphos,[15] clad only in a single garment which covers them. While the master of ceremonies arranges them at the farther end of the lodge, the nude old men touch them, bellow, roar, paw the earth, strike it with their heads and make the dust fly. At last, they imitate the bull pursuing the heifer. During this performance, a small fire is lighted in the center of the lodge in which some odoriferous herbs are burnt and, in the smoke of which, the victims themselves come to be perfumed without observing decency very much. They defile then before a number of young men seated in a row. Each husband has put into the hands of that one who has pleased him a little stick, which his wife recognizes in passing and which she seizes as if to take it away; but, the cavalier resisting, she drags him outside the lodge and, all the others doing the same, the company finds itself in a moment in couples on the prairie, where the old men, always bellowing and keeping at a distance, seem to censure their weakness and to manifest their sorrow. On re-entering the lodge, the husbands thank them very humbly, and the ceremony continues all the night, the actors only changing partners at each scene. Among the Gros Ventres, they are paid. The cavalier, requesting a favor, the husband weeps upon his head, brings him that which he holds most precious, entreats him to do good to him and, if he can prevail upon him, he is very grateful still for this marked service. The fête lasts from ten to fifteen days; but, as the cow is really near, the herds have arrived two or three days after the first performance. This early success the Mandanes attributed to the captains' people, who were untiringly zealous in attracting the cow.

---

d'une cérémonie curieuse & singuliere, éxecutée pour atirer la vache auprès de village. ..." (Washington version).

So far as can be ascertained, the detail of this is not recorded in any of the original narratives of the Lewis and Clark expedition. The occasion is, however, discussed and reference made to the excessive indulgence in dancing. See *Ordway Journal, op. cit.,* p. 175; Biddle edition, I, 150-52; *Original Journals,* I, 245.

[15] An allusion to the ancient "cult of the 'Paphian goddess' . . . . a nature worship like that of the Phoenician Astarte . . . ." *Encyclopaedia Britannica,* XVII, 238.

Autumn and spring, seasons for the annual passage of the cow, no one is allowed to meet[16] her and, even if there is the greatest distress, she is allowed to approach and even the first herds are allowed to pass as they serve as guides to others, since all follow the same route. When the soldiers judge that the cow is sufficiently invited, they make speeches and order the surround. This hunt is made in partnership and this is how it is undertaken: — As great a number as is possible advance within a certain distance from the animals and to a place designated by the soldiers. The best archers, runners, and horsemen have their places assigned. The old men begin the ceremony. They offer the pipe to the sky, earth, and the four cardinal points; then they present all the shanks of the pipe to the cow. While she is supposed to smoke, the old men bellow very softly and make the same grimaces as at the festival for attracting her. The partisan of the circle (for there is one for it as for war) then speaks thus to the herd, "O, you cows, you learn every day from the talk of our old men that you are our only resource. Have pity then on us today. You know that we are hungry; grant us some of your young ones. You see that ours are weak, that our horses are poor and will not, perhaps, be able to join you; flee not then with all your strength, and, you others, lands, winds, and especially rocks, grandsires of the Savages, aid us today, give courage to the cow. Tell her not to be foolish and not to harm our young men!" After this bit of eloquence, he gives the signal to the others, who leave him and advance in a way to surround the herd that is to be attacked. The circle closes in gradually, until the soldiers, being very near, send some young men to windward to spear the animals. As soon as the scent comes to them, the herd take to flight and, seeing themselves surrounded, do no more than turn and get in one another's way. The horses and the runners, much more quickly, everywhere close the way for them and bring them back to the center where the arrow and the gun kill sometimes as many as two or three hundred of them. At last, pressed on every side, these animals seem to make a hopeless resolution and force the ranks to open in one place. In the *melé* the hunters are very bold in penetrating among the herd and in selecting the fattest cows there. It is true that they pretend to distinguish those which

16 "racontre," a slip of the pen for *rencontre* (Tr.).

are evil-tempered and they do not attack them unless they have a place of refuge. Certainly, accidents are rare. It is true that an arrow sent by a good archer, passing through the animal and sometimes, moreover, falling far from it, does not leave it great strength; but, with the largest number, the arrow penetrates only up to the feathers. Some (of the hunters) are armed with a gun, the barrel of which has been shortened[17] in order to make arrow heads, and the stock shortened to make the gun more portable.

The largest number, as the old men and the young boys, are without arms; but, having aided in closing the exit to the animals and having contributed to the success, they have the same right in the division of the hunt. This also is done according to fixed rules.

The remainder of the herd has barely escaped before each hunter hastens to go to the prey and to arrive first at a cow, which the law divides into five parts, according to fixed and recognized rights of the first (arrival), who has for himself, — half of the rump, the paunch, the fat that covers it, the calf, and a shoulder and thus with the others. This still-born calf is the piece preferred and sought after. Yet difficulties arise very often, either some one profits from the occasion to satisfy a secret resentment or disputes arise respecting the moment of arrival; but these last can happen only when the hunt is not sufficient for everyone or when there are few fat cows. Yet, in these cases, each one almost always yields his claims and all return contented. The soldiers, independently of their common rights, have yet great privileges, can claim a certain number of humps and sometimes all the tongues. Any person, having to perform some ceremony, such as naming a child or having his ears pierced or something else, chooses the fattest of the cows and, declaring it medicine, prevents it from being divided.

In the simplest operations, as in the most serious, among the Savages of the Upper Missouri, everything bears the imprint of superstition and of credulity, its mother. It suffices that a thing is marvelous to the imagination to gain public belief. Although all may not be done in good faith and although malice hide itself oftentimes under the garb of foolishness, it can, nevertheless, be said that, in general, the Savages easily credit the most absurd things and the

---

[17] "racourci," a slip of the pen for *raccourci* (Tr.).

most impossible, physically. Kakawita, one of the most intelligent of the Ricaras, told me in all seriousness, after the visit of the Captains, things which I would not repeat if I had not wellnigh got myself into a bad scrape by treating them as ridiculous. He maintains (and it is an opinion generally accepted) that these gentlemen, while journeying among many nations, met obstacles perhaps invincible, of which I shall cite only two, certainly very singular. The one obstacle is without a mouth and is nourished only by breathing the smoke of the meat through the nose. It gains greatly in weight in the springtime and the autumn by its victories over the swans and bustards that obstinately make war upon it in these two seasons. The other is a troop of Amazons who kill all their male children, pulverize their genitals, and conceive again by the injection of the powder obtained. The girls, when born, are put into a cradle and hung on a tree where the air nourishes them, until each mother, when she judges her child large enough to be useful, claims her own.

It is[18] only a little while since the Ricaras deified the French, who, unhappily, have only too well disabused them by their conduct and

[18] This is the early inserted paragraph referred to in n. 12:

" ... il n'y a pas encore bien long-temps que les ricaras poussoient la superstition jusqu'a diviniser les pirogues des blancs & leur offroient des sacrifices. encore aujourdhui tous les meubles ou instruments, dont l'art est audessus de leur conception, sont regardés comme de médecine. peu d'hommes s'exposoient a toucher ma montre ou mon thermometre métallique, dont les rouages sont visibles; mais les instruments mathématiques, l'octan, l'aiman, quelques phosphores, un fusil a vent que leur a montré le cap[tne] lewis, l'ont fait regarder comme le maitre des magiciens. un me demandoit si c'étoit par le moyen de tous ces diables, qu'il avoit fabriqué un gros & grand animal, noir comme un ours, semblable a l'homme, qui parloit, agissoit, & paroissoit soumis. c'était un négre. = " (Montreal version).

The Washington version is sufficiently different from the foregoing to justify its quotation in full, likewise:

"il n'y a pas encore Bien longtemps que les ricaras divinisoient les françois, qui malheureusement ne les ont que trop Bien désabusé par leur conduite & leurs discours. aussi sont-ils passés aujourdhui d'une extrémité a l'autre & nous sommes Bien peu de chose a leurs yeux. ils reverroient jusqu'aux voitures qu'ils entrainoient dans leur village pour leur faire des sacrifices & des festins. tous les meubles & instruments dont l'art est audessus de leur conception sont encore aujourdhui des objets d'un respect superstitieux. peu d'hommes se sont exposé a manier mon thermométre métallique; l'octan, les phosphores, l'aimant ont été regardé chez les capitaines comme de médecine, c'est a dire comme surnaturels & puissants. le plus étonnant étoit cependant un gros & grand homme, noir comme un ours, qui parloit & agissoit comme un autre." (Washington version).

their talk. Thus they have passed today from one extreme to the other and we are, indeed, nothing in their eyes. They worshipped the very vehicles[19] which they brought into their villages to make sacrifices and feasts to them. All the furniture and instruments, the art of which is beyond their conception, are today objects still of superstitious respect. Few men are likely to touch my metal thermometer. The quadrant, phosphorus, and the magnet were regarded at the Captains' as medicine; that is to say, as supernatural and powerful. The most marvelous was, though, a large, fine man, black as a bear, who spoke and acted as one.[20]

The *ignis fatuus*[21] and other meteors have given birth, not only to ideas akin to transmigration of souls, but to positive ideas upon men-wolves, aerial spirits, and the return of the dead. Without distinguishing clearly the spirit of matter, with no conception of the immortality of the soul, these Savages are convinced that, after death, there remains a kind of shade that hovers a long time about the tomb.[22] It is, perhaps, for this reason that the corpses are often ex-

[19] Clark entered in his journal a remark with reference to the effect that the approach of the Lewis and Clark party had upon the Gros Ventres ". . . . we made up the presents and entertained Several of the Curious Chiefs whome, wished to see the Boat which was verry curious to them viewing it as great medison, (*whatever is mysterious or unintelligible is called great medicine*) as they also Viewed my black Servant . . . ." (*Original Journals*, I, 209).

[20] This was, of course, Clark's body servant. For the astonishment created among the Arikaras by his appearance, see *Original Journals*, I, 185, 186; Quaife's *Ordway Journal*, Wisconsin Historical Society *Collections*, XXII, 31, n. 2; Biddle edition, I, 101-2.

[21] "Les feux folets" in both versions, instead of *follets*.

[22] George Keith, writing of the Beaver Indians, he being then among them, said, "They appear to have no idea of a supernatural being, however they seem to entertain some conceptions of a future state — alleging that the shade must penetrate through the earth — after which they find a large lake — after crossing it they land in a new world — when they join their ancestors (with) whom they begin the world anew" (*Masson Papers*, Dominion Archives, Ottawa; Masson, *Les Bourgeois* . . . . , II, 69). From a letter of "Dr. John MacLoughlin," dated Fort William, 6 June 1808, the following extracts are taken:

"In their religious sentiments the Indians of this quarter (Chepewas) suppose a *Good Being* whom they name *Kitchemanetou* — and an Inferior Evil Being whom they stile *Matchimanetou* or Evil Spirit. In is certain that they pray to the first — but I could not learn to whom they sacrificed — Their sacrifices or what they name so consist in hanging up guns, Tobacco, Goods &c. This they do upon the death of any

posed and placed upon a scaffold upon trees where the open air leaves a beautiful space for a promenade. Some great medicine men are privileged and return in their own form and with the same habits. Thus they become still more formidable after death. During our stay with the Bois Brulés, a secret rumor spread that we had in a casket one,[23] named *Bateur de Chaudiere*,[24] whom they themselves had killed and whose limbs they had scattered upon the prairie, nine or ten years before. This man, the terror of his nation through his cruelty and his medicines, had expressly commanded his mother that, in case he should be assassinated, she should not fail to dismember him after his death and to throw his limbs into the Missouri, asserting that all would be gathered together at the Ilinois, from whence he would return to wreak vengeance upon his murderers. It was known that, in reality, the old woman, finding the work of dissection most painful, was acquitted of this duty. Terror spread throughout the camp and the fearful chiefs followed us without rest; in order to make us confess if it were true that Bateur de Chaudiere had made use of us.

Death itself, especially when it is premature, is a source of superstition. In it is always found some supernatural cause and, if there is in the camp a Frenchman supplied with merchandise, it is unusual

---

of their relatives — for it is certain they allow the immortality of the soul and a different state either of happiness or wretchedness in the other World —

"The state of happiness they suppose to be a country where they will find all they want — while the only preparation necessary to get into this region of Bliss is to live quietly, shew charity and be a good hunter — As for those that do not follow these rules and are lazy — they are condemned to wander in a Wild, dreary, barren country and of course be always starving.

"They are likewise so very superstitious as to attribute all their good or bad luck to the agency of some invisible being — which makes them have an aversion to certain parts of several animals believing that eating these parts would bring bad luck &c.

"They bury the dead with all their hunting implements on the top of the coffins or graves — the chiefs are placed in scaffolds six feet from the ground. They take a lock of hair from the deceased which the morose relatives carry about in safety for a year" (From *Odd Papers of Roderick MacKenzie's* in *Masson Papers*, IV, Dominion Archives, Ottawa. For ideas of a Supreme Being among the Sioux, see Keating's *Long*, vol. I, pp. 391 *et seq.*

23 "cassete" for *cassette*, the form of the word that appears in the revision.

24 "*Bateur* de chaudiere" (Washington version); Bateur de Chaudiere, — Montreal version.

for him not to suffer for it. Either suspicions really fall upon him or spitefulness and the hope of presents under the guise of credulity have the greater share in the accusation.[25] The rogue, the Tongue of the Hind, of whom I have already spoken, lost within forty-eight hours, two boys from seven to eight years old and, as he had stolen considerably from two French hunters living in his lodge, he attributed to their witchcraft these almost unexpected deaths, which happened a short while after their departure. In default of them, he turned upon me and all the relatives, boldly showing the most evil intentions, weep and threaten day and night around my lodge. I am told that the father has put into the hands of a brave as wicked as himself the bow and arrow of his eldest son so that he may be followed by a French shade. Finally, seeing that I was resolved to offer nothing (which would have been a kind of confession) he changes his tactics and comes weeping into my quarters. He assures me that he shall learn soon the cause of his misfortune, that the French have nothing to do with it, and, having cited to me a thousand superstitious reasons, he declares that he leaves with good augury to avenge himself upon the enemy. He had the worst of it; he came back frightened two months afterwards. But this is the customary expedient of the Savages. The enterprise alone is a sort of consolation and success makes them forget the greatest calamities.[26]

---

[25] The two sentences just preceding are not found in the Montreal version.

[26] " ... enfin voiant que j'étois résolu de ne rien offrir (cequi aurroit été une espéce d'aveu) il change de Baterie (Batterie? — Tr.) & vient pleurer luy même dans mon appartement. m'assure qu'il connoit présentement la cause de son malheur; que les françois n'y entrent pour rien; & m'ayant allegué mille raisons superstitieuses, il me déclare qu'il part avec Bon augure, pour se venger sur l'énemi. il en a eu le dementi, il est revenu deux mois après avec la peur. mais c'est la ressource ordinaire des sauvages. l'entreprise seule est une sorte de consolation, & le succès fait oublier les plus grands malheur. — " (Washington version).

" ... enfin un petit présent pour couvrir les morts, le fait convenir que les françois sont innocents, qu'il connoit la cause de son malheur, & qu'il part pour se dédomager sur l'énemi, avec bon augure. cependant l'augure en e eu le démenti, car il est revenu trois mois après comme ils disent, *honteusement*. mais c'est la ressource ordinaire chez tous les sauvages, après une mortalité. l'enterprise seule est espéce de consolation, & s'ils réussissent les plus grands malheurs sont oubliés. — " (Montreal version).

SAVAGE WARFARE[1]

WAR is the greatest plague of all the Savages of the Upper Missouri. Neither in any place nor at any time do they enjoy perfect security. Near their village or camp, in their fields of maize, and even in the village itself, individuals are massacred by small parties; for it is seldom that the nation entire is attacked and still more seldom that such an attack is successful in one place or another. If necessity compels them to roam over the prairies, they can do it only by dragging their families in their train or they hunt in their neighborhood, keeping themselves constantly on guard. They make forts, in every part protected from the arrow, and I have seen in this circumstance Ricaras help their wives. What cannot panic terror do![2]

They all see the advantages of peace and seem to desire it; but, through inconsistency, or rather, through a passion, so much the more incorrigible since it has its origin in custom, war is necessary to them. The power, or the ascendency of a chief, as the influence of an individual, being usually measured by deeds, ambition (who would have believed it?) has also its effect upon these souls of mud. A young man, who has not fought, has no right to answer the insults of a warrior. He is admitted neither to an important feast nor to certain assemblies. He cannot wear certain glorious tokens with which he sees his friends ornamented. Even love is not favorable to him and a brave is the rival who wins most often in love affairs. A father, however reasonable and peaceable he may be, cannot see for long his son in this humiliating position and urges him to steal at least some horses. This plan is always made without prejudice to the assassination, if the opportunity presents itself, and, besides, as it is

---

[1] "de la guerre Sauvage" (Washington version); "de la guerre" (Montreal version).

[2] " ... & j'ai vu dans cette circonstance des ricaras aider leurs femmes, que ne peut pas la terreur panique!" (Washington version).

" ... j'ai vu les hommes mêmes travailler a ces ouvrages. que ne peut pas la terreur panique! ..." (Montreal version). It is worth noting that Alexander Henry tells in his journal of the self-sacrificing exertions of Indian men in defence of their women and children. See *Coventry Copy*, I, 360-64; Coues, *New Light* . . . . , I, 260.

a hostile move, the robbers often receive some check and, in one way or another, reprisals and war follow.

War has its own songs, which are sung for a long while day and night by that one who plans an expedition and by his partisans. Fasts, tears, feasts, mutilations, are used to excite pity and, especially, confidence, all these acts being of good omen. The young men are cajoled by liberality and, when the war chief thinks his party large enough, he announces his departure and, at first, goes only a short distance away to give time to those who should decide to follow him; and, in truth, for many days such and such a one is found to have left during the night to join the warriors.

The small parties succeed oftener than those which are large and which are less easily able to surprise the enemy. Surprise is so essential to the attack that, without it, the attack does not usually take place. On the contrary, however superior a party may be, all take to flight at the least sign of being discovered; for the war-chief dare not, by attacking, break this rule that sums up, so to speak, all the tactics and military art of the Savages. A victory, however complete it may be, must not be bought at the price of a single one of his warriors. It is necessary to conquer without running risks and, if it happens otherwise, it is rarely through deliberate planning; but often through circumstances that render flight more dangerous than fighting. In these cases, despair inspires this barbarous courage, called marvelous among the Savages. Why should a leader[3] overlook the means of saving his party entire, since, on returning to his village, even loaded with booty, if one person be missing, his family in tears demands him of him. He is loaded with reproaches instead of cries of joy and delight; he sees everywhere only grief and sorrow as after a general defeat. The warriors themselves, covered as he with earth and dust, look ashamed and vanquished. Besides, he loses much general confidence for new expeditions. A war chief, who has gained great victories, is listened to less than he who has never lost a man.[4]

[3] "partisant" (Both versions). The word should be retained, perhaps, because evidently used technically, as in the following excerpt from Perrin du Lac:

"Chez tous les Sauvages de l'Amérique septentrionale, sans exception, tout homme peut former un parti de guerre et se mettre à la tête; le chef d'une pareille expédition, se nomme *Partisan* ..." (*op. cit.*, p. 293).

[4] All this presents a most interesting resemblance to the old German *comitatus*.

It is in these circumstances that every kind of cruelty is inflicted upon the prisoners. Yet the barbarous custom of burning them appears everywhere abolished. But they are still sometimes killed and always, at least, they are jeered[5] at, beaten,[6] and bruised, until, protected by the crowd, they arrive at the lodge of grace, where the ones in power dispose of them, generally in the interests of the bereaved ones or of the relatives.

When, on the other hand, the party returns victorious and without loss, those who are on racers announce from afar, by particular cries, the meaning of which is known, the number of scalps, of prisoners, and of captured horses. The whole village with cries of joy answers this announcement, which is repeated many times as the war party approaches.[7] At length, the warriors appear, chant their victory, and come on at a slow pace. At once, the women pounce upon them, seize their arms, and disrobe them completely. The cries of joy, the feasts, and appropriate dances succeed one another for many days; the scalps are produced with ceremony and change owners several times a day. They are carried in triumph journey after journey and often to a friendly nation. All those who have had the honor of striking the enemy dead or alive, that is to say, for the first, second, third, and fourth stroke only, count this deed for themselves and then generally take a new name. They wear also the feather of the calumet bird or other honorable marks according to the number and the nature of their great deeds and the rank they had had while fighting. The stolen horses are also of suitable importance for the stake and the robber wears hair on his leggings and a string on his arm.

Out of twenty expeditions of war, fifteen are regularly given up. If a young man is wounded accidentally, if another inadvertently steps over the legs of a warrior, if a dream or other evil omen be told, despondency creeps over the army so that desertion reduces it to

---

5 "Baffoues" (Washington version). "invectivés," is substituted in the Montreal version.

6 "Batus," corrected, in revision, to "battus."

7 " ... tout le village répond par des cris d'applaudissement a cette annonce qui se réitere plusieurs fois toujours en approchant. ..." (Washington version).

" ... tout le village répond par des cris de joie. cette annonce se réitère trois fois, toujours en approchant par pauses. ..." (Montreal version).

nothing. It happens, sometimes, that all the men return to the village without being perceived.

The trader, not finding profit in war, the preparations for which cause hunting to be neglected, very easily changes the partisan's mind by some presents. But it often happens that hope of being stopped in this way induces a partisan to make preparations and the worst thing is that such a one, seeing his hope destroyed, does through spite that which he wished only to sham.[8]

DESCRIPTION OF SOME CEREMONIES[1]

THE first marriage of a daughter is generally one of convenience and her inclination is hardly consulted. Notwithstanding that, it is very rare for her not to conform to the wishes of her relatives. True, she knows that her bonds are not indissoluble and that, if needs be, she will readily find means to make a divorce for a new spouse desired. The daughter belongs by right to the father and to the paternal uncles; but the eldest son, having attained a certain age, makes himself master, ordinarily, as he encroaches upon all authority in the house. A young man begins by showing his intentions. He often bears the result of his hunt to the door of the lodge of that one whom he wishes to obtain. That being well received, he leads thither one or several horses loaded with presents suitable, in public opinion, to the rank and the worth of the future wife and leaves everything at the door. If all this is still accepted, he has no longer any doubt of his good fortune and a day or two afterwards the young woman, led by her relatives, goes to him in the evening with the presents, which take the place of a contract.[2] Everything ends by eating, as is said, with the stomach unbuttoned. The greatest and the true happiness of the Savages lies in gluttony. It is the subject of all their conversation, as it is the first object of their own interests, and, being incompatible with economy and cau-

---

[8] This paragraph is lacking in the Montreal version.

[1] "description de quelques ceremonies — du marriage" (Montreal version).

[2] "qui tienent lieu de contract" omitted from the Montreal version.

tion, exposes them so often to distress and famine. They would always have more provisions than would be needed to sustain them, if they were not prodigal in times of abundance. I have seen brought into the village of the Isle of the Ricaras,[3] comprising about two hundred people, more than a hundred boned cows, which certainly exceeded thirty thousand pounds[4] of meat, and the whole consumed in four days. The kettles boil day and night; the fire is surrounded with spits; hams are broiling on the coals; livers, kidneys,[5] and fat are eaten raw. All the men, mutual parasites, pass from one lodge to another where each one is proud of the desire to cram himself without discretion. In the short interval that these collations leave, feasts take place and courtesy compels honor being done to them. Then it is proper for each one to take at least his regular meal at his own lodge. The Ricaras, who at first often invited me, thought badly of me in that I would not conform to their custom. They did not realize that, in return for a couple of meals that I could take, I would have to provide more than a hundred a day.[6]

Whatever the fêtes, assemblies, and ceremonies may be, feasts are the foundation, the beginning, and the end of them. It appears even that the largest number are thought of only with this in view; for they are increased in time of distress. As the dogs are the most precious victims in the rite, the Savages have recourse, in famine, to this unique provision, which satisfies gluttony under the guise of religion or of ceremony. One cannot ask for an interview with a chief in order to consult him or tell him of some affairs and the chief himself cannot call a council of his principal men without the kettle seeming to preside. It serves sometimes to register[7] the votes; for

[3] " ... le 21 janvier 1804, j'ai vu apporter dans le village ou je résidois, ..." (Montreal version).

[4] "trente milliers de viande" (Washington version); "trente mille livres de viande" (Montreal version).

[5] " ... & les foies, les roignons (*rognons?* -Tr.), les graisses magnées cruees. tous les hommes, parasites mutuels, ..." (Washington version).
" ... les foies, les roignons, & une quantité de parties grasses mangées crües. = tous les hommes, parasites reciproques, ..." (Montreal version).

[6] These last two sentences, reflecting somewhat upon himself, Tabeau refrained from putting into his revised version, the paragraph concerned being made to end thus: "qui sont ordinairement fêves, citrouilles, ou mahy. = je crains que ceci paroisse éxagéré, & pourtant rien n'est plus vrai.= "

[7] "receuillir" in both versions.

one who does not acquiesce in the result of the deliberations, often manifests his opposition merely by refusing to eat.

The pipe precedes and crowns all the feasts and is everywhere of indispensable etiquette. In the Upper Missouri it takes the place of a bond and a contract for political affairs, also for ornament in assemblies and for an emblem in ceremonies. It is sometimes even a sacred vessel, which the profane (that is to say those who have failed in chastity since the watch[8]) do not touch. It is true that it is necessary to believe in the good faith of the people and that that faith is extremely uncertain. However it may be, I have not been able to keep from laughing in these respectable assemblies on seeing decrepit old men refuse to smoke certainly through vanity and I have said to myself, O Vanity! where do you take up your abode?[9]

FEAST OF THE FIRST BIRD[10]

The first little bird killed with an arrow by the son of a Savage, who wishes to become a man of importance, is dried entire with the plumage and carefully preserved until the father has amassed enough goods to cover the expenses, which the celebration of the first bird exacts. He then gives a great feast where it is to his credit, if there are many guests. He first distributes presents to the guests, reserving always the largest lot for that one for whom he designs the bird. This person is always a person of consideration and a medicine man. When the guests receive the plates of food, the sorcerer receives the bird with his portion. He is obliged to swallow it, head first, without rumpling it or touching it with his teeth.[11]

---

[8] The parenthetical expression in the Montreal version is, "(c'est a dire ceux qui ont manqué a la chasteté depuis 24 heures)."

[9] " ... en voiante des vieillards décrépis se priver de fumer certainement par amour propre & je disois en moy même. o vanité! ou vas-tu te nicher?" (Washington version).

" ... en voiants de vieux octogenaires décrépis, (sans doute pour en doner a garder) se priver de fumé (r) & repousser modestement la pipe. o vanité, ou vas-tu te nicher?" (Montreal version).

[10] In the Montreal version, this section is preceded by a section, entitled, "Cérémonie pour laisser le deuil," which is followed by "élection des soldats du cerne" and that by "fête du premier oiseau-tué par un enfant."

[11] The only material change made in revision comes at the end, where the following is added: "seulement il s'aide quelquefois d'un petit bois. ="

ELECTION OF SOLDIERS OF THE CIRCLE

Four principal[12] soldiers begin their duties in the kitchen making all preparations for an ample feast. Then, with body blackened and shining with grease, with several crows on the croup, a crown of calumet bird feathers on the head, armed from top to toe, they rush into all the lodges of the camp and, when they find a man whom they deem worthy of being admitted, they touch him lightly on the wrist without saying a word. The candidate follows them to the lodge of the soldiers where the election is to be held. Thirty or forty having assembled thus, the soldiers arrange them in a circle and, having laid aside their arms, they stand within, on each side of the door. They proceed, then, to the ceremony.

An old medicine man, whose head is crowned with a piece of the skin of a white cow the exact shape of an episcopal mitre, holding himself majestically and mysteriously, is seated at the farther end of the lodge, near to a kind of altar in the form of a half-moon. A sacred pipe, richly ornamented and reverentially placed upon a buffalo robe, the flesh-side uppermost, is on his right and holds the place of honor. About two feet in front of the pipe are twenty-four little trees, painted red, planted in a half-circle, half an inch apart, and, in the center, are three or four lighted coals, the fire of which is continually renewed with dry, sweet-smelling grass. Through the smoke of this fire, the venerable high priest passes the pipe many times, holding it mysteriously between the thumb and the left index finger and presenting the shank with the right hand to the sun, the earth, and the four cardinal points. While he does this, he mutters between his teeth and ends with a longer prayer, which, happily for the reader — to whom I perceive I am sparing no detail — I do not understand. Finally, after many grimaces, he lights the sacred pipe and, after inhaling the smoke three times, passes the pipe to his left-hand neighbor, who does likewise. Thus the pipe goes around the circle. After it is empty, it is passed four times around the assembly. Many do not touch it, as they are impure or profane.

Two large mastiffs, cut into pieces, boil, in the meantime, in great kettles and grind one's teeth. There is also a number of dishes al-

---

[12] "principaux" becomes *anciens* in the Montreal version.

ready filled with the best food the camp can furnish. As this food must be eaten first, one of the leading old men approaches, lays his hands on it, and blesses it. A beadle then distributes it. The food disappears in an instant and is very soon followed by the two dogs and the broth. During this repast, the high priest takes from the altar four grains of maize, offers them to the four cardinal points, and gives them with as many mouthfuls of meat to the four counsellors, his neighbors, who eat them meditatively. The ceremony ends there[13] and the soldiers of the circle are named. Mr. Loisel and three of his men received this honor among the Bois Brulés; but we had occasion to judge that it was only for the form and in the hope that they would supply an ample share to the lodge of the soldiers, continually maintained at public expense. Our men were many times at the circle and, far from enjoying their privileges, they did not even enjoy the common right and always came back without meat.

CEREMONY FOR ASSUAGING GRIEF

The ceremony for assuaging grief is one of the most curious, the most solemn, and the most expensive of the ceremonies. I attended one among the Bois Brulés, where the Partisan, always generous, distinguished himself largely at the cost of the store. Two large lodges of leather, raised very high, are extended with valences of dressed skin and form a room a hundred feet in circumference.[14] There is only one door, or rather hole, by which one can enter and that only by stooping. A single opening at the top, contrived for letting out the smoke, admits a feeble light; but, at night, a great fire of faggots or of dry branches gives sufficient illumination. In the center, a stake

[13] In the Montreal version, the section, with one slight addition, closes here:
"la ceremonie se termine par des chants & des danses. ⸗" leaving out the very significant detail respecting Régis Loisel and three of his men, upon whom the Bois Brulés — for what Tabeau intimates was decidedly some purpose of their own — had bestowed a rather unusual honor. It occurred, without doubt, on the occasion of Loisel's earlier visit to the Upper Missouri.

[14] " ... j'y ai assisté chez les Bois brulés, ou le partisant toujours genereaux s'est signale en grand partie aux depends du magasin. deux vaste loges ..." (Washington version).

" ... j'y ai assisté chez les bois brulés, ou le partisant dont j'ai tant parlé, généreux a son ordinaire, s'est signalé en grande partie aux dépends de m^r loisel. ⸗ deux vastes loges ..." (Montreal version).

painted red is planted, at the foot of which lies an old buffalo skull, the dried-up horns of which are also made red. On the right side of this Pagoda,[15] is a small, covered kettle, upon which are little bunches of swan's down, red with vermilion as it, and, on the left side, is a small tree, broken at the top and also decorated with swan's down. On the left, are seen six images of men and of women whose features of leather, rudely imitated, are the exact color of the savage dead. The clothes of both men and women are scarlet; the coats of the men are decorated in false gold, with a blue collar ornamented with silver; and the garments of the women are trimmed in the same way. All have a wide girdle of porcupine, beautifully worked. Each man is crowned with some feathers of the calumet bird and holds in his hand a spear and a pipe; and each woman has upon her head her collar of portage, richly ornamented, and bears upon her shoulders a little bundle of merchandise. Near their feet, hidden under their long robes, they have a pair of shoes of beautifully worked porcupine. At the farther end of the lodge a skin of a white cow, the hair uppermost, is stretched out upon leaves of wormwood and covered with diverse merchandise and trifles. In front, some sweet-smelling grass, tied in sheaves and made mysterious with little bunches of fine buffalo wool are put into a little dish and shared with the four cardinal points. Here also four arrow trees are set up, at the top of which are four ears of maize. Ten or a dozen full kettles and a great many dishes are on the right side of the lodge. Each person, on entering, may eat what he wishes. The high priest, wearing the same ornaments as at the election of the soldiers and bearing himself with yet more dignity, is between all the dishes and the skin of the white cow. Before him a piece of painted, undressed leather has upon it a number of trifles, such as vermilion, glass beads, little bells, and, especially, all the adjuncts of charlatanism. A little in advance, two spears and two knives are stuck into the ground and support, moreover, a medicine pipe.

This lodge was maintained thus and frequented day and night

[15] " ... sont aussi rougies. au coté droit de cette Bagode, est une petite chaudiere couverte, ..." (Washington version).

" ... sont aussi rougies & enjolivées. au coté droit de ce dieu penate est une petite chaudiére couverte, ..." (Montreal version).

for forty-eight hours and there was no cessation of the cries and lamentations. The last evening, Mr. Loisel, Mr. Dorion, and I were
invited.[16] The gathering was composed of the high priest, the relatives of the dead on his left hand and a large number of guests. To
the left of the door on entering, was the orchestra, composed of five
singers who held in their hands a kind of Biscayan tambourine, to
which little bells are attached. The time is beaten upon a roll of undressed skin lying at their feet. The lugubrious music was very long;
but the officiating priest never ceased a moment to talk with his gods
and to address the dead, always presenting the pipe and blessing the
dishes a hundred times over. Finally, the music ceasing for a moment,
the old man grows angry, raises his voice, and ends by howling and
weeping bitterly. The bereaved ones do the same and the entire assembly chimes in, so that one could not hear God thunder. At length
each one, exhausted, coughs. Then the oldest scullion takes a cloven
stick, which serves him for pincers, and seizes two coals. He bears
one to the feet of the high priest and the other to the feet of the first
singer. Then, his companions assisting him, he bears[17] to them also
two large dishes laden with forced meat balls. Some of these are
broken and the pieces thrown upon the coals. The priest, meanwhile, repeats his benedictions. Then the sacred pipe is lighted and,
after going the round of the circle, is returned to the high priest. On
receiving it, he speaks some words which cause the howling and the
hubbub to begin again.

At last, eating is thought of and faces are wreathed in smiles.
Then the old scullion takes once more his plate of forced meat balls
and goes around accompanied by a young girl, nine or ten years old,
who puts a meat ball into the mouth of each one present. The other
dishes and the kettles are distributed in silence; but, in a flash, all
disappears. The stomach being well-filled, the singers continue for
the remainder of the night and the women, outside the lodge, give
the accompaniments.

[16] " ... la derniere soirée on a invité mm. loisel, mm. dorion son interprete, &
moy. ..." (Washington version).

" ... la derniére soirée on a invité m^r loisel, m^r dorion & moy. ..." (Montreal
version).

This was undoubtedly Pierre Dorion, senior.

[17] The Montreal version adds, "dont j'ai parlé ailleurs."

At daybreak, all the merchandise and all the garments of the images are distributed among the relatives of the dead who redden themselves and abandon grief. In order to obtain this kind of consolation, each Savage, from whom death has taken a dear one, does not fail, before burying the body, to send a packet of his hair to some prominent person, whom he considers generous. This courtesy binds him, who is the recipient of it, to the payment of the expenses of the feast that I have just described. His relatives are assessed in order to aid him and the trader can scarcely claim exemption. The Partisan who had, a year before, received this mark of esteem performed his duty with much honor.

CEREMONY FOR PIERCING CHILDREN'S EARS[18]

Since all the circumstances may not be available for the ceremony for piercing children's ears, it often happens that the children are already large when the occasion does present itself. In order to give the feast a certain distinction, a Savage ordinarily waits for an important event, such as when an enemy is fortunate enough to arrive at the lodge of grace without being perceived or when he comes to the village as the deputy of his nation. In either case, he is an important person and he is selected to pierce the ears, an operation as lucrative as it is honorable; for he is loaded with presents.

In default of these circumstances, which rarely occur, an influential father, sensitive for the honor of his children, maintains at first at his expense the medicine lodge and keeps open house there a very long time, aided by his relatives during this period. He amasses what wealth he can and, when he judges his funds sufficient, he gives a great feast, for which the dogs are not spared. Before the repast and while smoking at the ceremony he distributes the presents and that one among his guests whom he honors as his choice is revealed by the importance of many presents, over and above the common share.

Another invites, in the same case, some important man in a

18 The account in the revised, or Montreal, edition is very much reduced, the reference to Kakawita and to the entire subject of adoption, extraneous anyway, being wholly eliminated.

strange village to come and dance the pipe upon the head of his children. The offer being accepted, the dancer comes with all his retinue and all possible pomp and, on arriving, gives the presents which he brings. The father has prepared a large lodge to which his children, richly dressed, are brought and, when the dance of the pipe begins, he throws at intervals some articles at the feet of the dancers, who, in their turn, please the spectators with them. The latter give back the things and the same objects circulate back and forth for four-and-twenty hours. If some persons, strange to the two nations, meet by chance at this kind of fête, they acquire everything without good manners requiring them to make any return. The ceremony ends with the bringing in of the children to the operator, who, after having pierced their ears, is rewarded according to the importance of the children. The solemnity and the liberality are, however, essential to this ceremony, as such a one during his whole life can receive the humiliating reproach of having had his ears pierced without anyone knowing in what manner. It is to recall, so to speak, the meanness of his birth.

The adoption of children is conducted in almost the same way. The same ceremonial in the dance of the pipe and the same passing back and forth of presents enrich only the strange spectators. The Ricaras of the island, invited by those of the other villages, danced the pipe dance naked when it was nineteen degrees below zero in an open country. These children, brought forth naked and bathed a very long time in icy water by their adopted fathers ceased to breathe and these imbeciles attributed their silence to a premature courage. Kakawita had the honor of adopting a young marriageable girl. As she was very pretty and well built, it was noticeable how the rascal prolonged his operations and was lavish in stroking the stomach and the womb. The presents were considerable. The Sioux, who always dupe the Ricaras, did not fail to represent themselves as strangers and they alone profited. The hope of gain had induced me and many Frenchmen to contribute to the ornament of the pipe; but I confess it was folly to speculate upon the gratitude of the Ricaras.

The bearer of the pipe is considered chief of the feast and he has the right afterwards, all his life, to wear a picture of it on his dress.

The dress of some important Ricara is all streaked with pictures of a pipe.

CEREMONY OF THE BLESSING OF THE GRAIN[19]

This ceremony is performed every year among the agricultural people of the Missouri and the Ricaras believe the harvest will fail if it is omitted. It has for its object the abundance of grain and fruit. Vows are made especially to the sun, the moon, Venus, the thunder, and the elements. Everything breathes gaiety at this festival, which is celebrated for three days by dances and particularly by abundant feasts. As it is held in a time of want the fête is fatal to the dogs. The gathering is held day and night in the lodge of the principal chief. At the farther end of the lodge, an altar, eighteen to twenty[20] inches high, has upon it six great gourds, vermilioned, and, in front, three bent bows, four arrows, decorated with white feathers in the manner of leaves of corn, are separated by a pipe crowned with leaves, a green branch, and a piece of dried meat. Six young men, nude during the ceremony, which is performed twice a day, stand with their backs to the altar, while the oldest man of the village mutters and makes a long prayer. At the close of it they hastily

---

[19] "Cérémonie de la Bénédiction des grains" (Washington version); "Ceremonie des semailles" (Montreal version).

[20] " ... on a dressé au fond un autel élevé de dix huit a vingt pouces, sur lequ'el sont six grosses calbasses vermillonées & audevant trois arcs tendus enjolivés & posés horisontalement sur des pivots. en face des arcs quatre fléches garnies de plumages Blancs en forme de feuilles de mahy, sont séparées par une pipe couronnée de verdure, un rameau vert & un morceau de viande séche. six jeunes hommes nuds pendant l'office qui se fait deux fois par jour, sont debout le dos tourné a l'autel, tandis que le plus ancien du village marmote & fait une longue priere, a la fin du laqu'elle ils saisissent Brusquement la pipe, la viande & le rameau & traversants l'assemblée a toute course, vont les offrir hors de la loge aux dieux, aux vents & au missouri. ..." (Washington version).

" ... au fond est un autel élevé de dix huit a vingt pieds orné de tous les ustenciles d'agriculture & de tout ce qui y a quelques rapport ainsi qu'aux moissons. six jeunes hommes absolument nuds pendant l'office, sont débout le dos tourné a l'autel, tandis que le plus ancien du village marmote quelques priéres, a la fin des qu'elles ils saisissent brusquement une pipe, quelques epies de mahy & des rameaux sur l'autel, & traversant l'assemblée a toute course, ils vont les offrir hors de la loge, aux dieux que j'ai nomé, aux vents & au missouri. ..." (Montreal version).

seize the pipe, the meat, and the branch and, walking the entire length of the assembly, they go outside the lodge to offer them to the gods, the winds, and the Missouri. Re-entering, they light the pipe which, in place of passing around from one to another, is carried from one end to the other, always the entire length of the lodge. The noise of twenty or thirty runners does not at all trouble the orator, who goes steadily along without being heard by anybody. When the pipe is exhausted, each one takes his place and a naked sacristan, who, in this fête to nature, seems to have been chosen so as to show her prodigality, places, before the bows, six pickaxes made from the shoulder-blades of cows and as many little baskets of osier, very well made. To these, he adds six crowns of woven straw. The assembly smokes tranquilly while this is going on and, during the silence,[21] a Ricara informs me that the crowns of straw are directed to the snakes, worms, locusts, and other insects. They are besought not to prey upon the corn, beans, and so forth. The pickaxes invite the cows to make their shoulders useful to agriculture and their flesh to sustain the women in their labors.[22] The baskets indicate the abundance which will fill them; the branches are offered particularly to the moon, to Venus, and to the stars so as to gain their favorable influence, and to the elements that they may do no harm to the harvest.

About two hours later, four women, in full dress, seat themselves, each one near to a post of the lodge. Each holds in her hand an artificial bird, which four warriors advance to seize while uttering peculiar cries. All do not know how to make these cries; for three criers were hooted and only one applauded. Then a number of other birds are brought in, the cry or song, of which each one tries to imitate. In doing this, the Savages, in general, succeed admirably.

21 " ... & pendant ce silence un ricara m'informe que ... & autres insectes. ..." (Washington version).

" ... pendant ce moment de silence, un ancien m'informe que ... & a tous insectes. ..." (Montreal version).

22 " ... que les pioches invitent les vaches a apporter leurs épaules utiles a l'agriculture & leur chaire pour soutenir les femmes dans leurs traveaux que les paniers. ..." (Washington version).

" ... que les pioches invitent les vaches a apporter leurs épaules, utiles instruments; que les paniers. ..." (Montreal version).

One rightly expects that all has ended with a great feast and with cries of dogs beaten to death.[23]

23 " ... & par les cris des chiens assommés." (Washington version). " ... & par les cris des chiens assomés pour y fournir." (Montreal version). So abrupt an ending supports the view that the Washington version was a preliminary, or rough, draft.

APPENDICES

APPENDICES

I. SPELLING OF THE NAME TABEAU

I have adhered to *Tabeau* as the spelling of the narrator's surname, choosing it in preference to all others; because, considering all things, it was the most constant in the original sources and seems now to be the standardized form, notwithstanding that there is reason to think Tabeau himself had a liking for a slightly longer, *Tabeaux,* the form that appears in the title to the Montreal version, in the signature to the letter of transmittal, and in a few other personal signatures of late date, the signature to the "Donation"[1] being a solitary and notable exception. The variants of the name have been many; e.g., *Tabaut,* which was, perhaps, the one that the founder of the family in the New World used, *Tabault, Tabaux, Tabeaux, Tabeau, Thabaut, Tabat, Taboe, Tabbo, Tabbow, Tabo, Tabau, Tabaud,* etc. The last three are especially to be found in the church records of Chateauguay;[2] but were more or less popular wherever the family appeared. The three before them are peculiar, in a measure, to the Lewis and Clark journals, where they are not to be taken too seriously; inasmuch as the American explorers were notoriously erratic in their spelling of even commonplace English words. It is worthy of note that, on an occasion when they receive written communications from Tabeau, they spelt his name in what I have taken to be the preferred way with him and doubtless as they saw it there before them:

[28 February 1805]

"Mr. Gravelin two frenchmen & two Inds arrive from the Ricara Nation with Letters from Mr Anty Tabeaux . . . .";[3] but they had short memories for the written word and, within a week, were spelling phonetically again.[4]

The family itself was long in arriving at a standardized spelling of its name. The greatest variety occurs in the trade licenses. A license, No. 20 of 1774[5], was issued to *J. Bte Tabaux* and Jean Calvet, the former probably Pierre-Antoine's father; but No. 18 of 1776[6] was for *Baptiste Tabault,* who, I am inclined to think, was his brother. The trade returns[7]

---

[1] See Appendix IX.

[2] See Transcripts, *Registres St. Joachim de Chateauguay,* Dominion Archives, Ottawa.

[3] *Original Journals, op. cit.,* I, 267. [4] *Ibid.,* p. 269.

[5] See Appendix III. [6] *Ibid.* [7] Dominion Archives, Ottawa.

for the years of the American Revolution give the name, *Tabau*, occasionally; but *Tabeau* much more often and that seems to have been the form that signatures took then and subsequently, until the close of the century. An interesting exception occurs in the *Registre Ste. Anne, Mackinac, 1695-1790*[8]; *for* "Baptiste Tabeaux" signed, in 1786, as an elector of church wardens. The succeeding year, however, "B[te] Tabeau" and "P[re] Tabeau" signed a similar document. Alas, for consistency! A promissory note given by Jacques Ponde to A. & P. Chouteau, dated March 5, 1800, was witnessed by "P. (A?) Tabeaux."[9]

There is yet the evidence of the *Militia Rolls* of Lower Canada to consider, which is negative until about 1800, when the name "Jean B[te] Tabeau Pere" appears as that of a *Captaine*. The next year its form is "Jean B[te] Tabau" and the next, "Jean B[te] Tabaut." In a book containing lists of officers, there are the following records:

p. 22. "J. B[te] Tabault, pere — Jan. 15, 1800" — Captain
p. 23. "J. B[te] Tabault, fils — Jan. 17, 1800" — Lieutenant.[10]

One name used by Lewis and Clark to designate Loisel's agent at the Arikaras was palpably wrong.[11] It was "Tiebeau," a modification of Thibaut, which must, in all its guises, *Thibeau, Thiebau, Tibaut, Tibau, Tibault, Thibauld*, etc., be rigidly distinguished from *Tabeau* and its equally numerous variants.[12] Contrariwise, Elliott Coues says, "One Tabault was on the Assiniboine in 1793. Basil Thifault [*sic*] appears as voyageur N. W. Co., Fort des Prairies. 1804. These two names are the same, and may indicate the same person . . . ."[13] According to Dionne, the Tabeau family originated in Gers[14] and the Thibault in Bas-Languedoc in the Department of Herault.[15] Thwaites says that the name *Thibaut* was a common one "among the voyageurs of the early Northwest. In 1790 there were five heads of families in the Illinois by the name of Thibaut (Thebalt, Thibeau, Thiebau, Tibault, Tibeau)."[16]

[8] *Ibid.*
[9] *Auguste Chouteau Papers*, MHS.
[10] Dominion Archives, Ottawa.
[11] *Original Journals, op. cit.*, I, 283.
[12] Marshall, Thomas Maitland, *The Life and Letters of Frederick Bates*, Index.
[13] *New Light on the Early History of the Greater Northwest*, II, 554, n. 10.
[14] *Les Canadiens Français: Origine des Familles*, pp. 562-63.
[15] *Idem*, p. 570.
[16] *British Régime in Wisconsin*, Wisconsin Historical Society *Collections*, XVIII, 264, n. 62. See also Alvord, C. W., *Kaskaskia Records*, Illinois Historical *Collections*, V, 418, 419, 442.

II. TABEAU GENEALOGICAL CHART

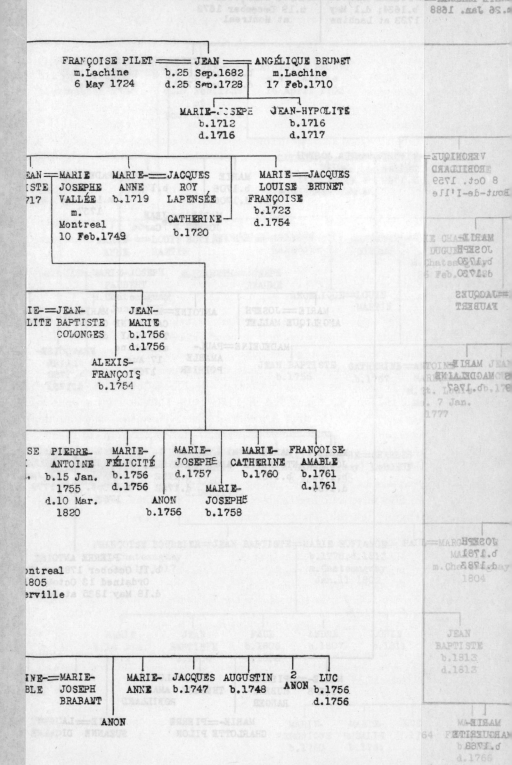

FRANÇOISE PILET====JEAN====ANGÉLIQUE BRUNET
m.Lachine   b.25 Sep.1682   m.Lachine
6 May 1724   d.25 Sep.1728   17 Feb.1710

                    MARIE-JOSEPH   JEAN-HYPOLITE
                    b.1712   b.1716
                    d.1716   d.1717

JEAN==MARIE   MARIE-====JACQUES   MARIE====JACQUES
ISTE JOSEPHE ANNE   ROY   LOUISE   BRUNET
717   VALLÉE   b.1719   LAPENSÉE   FRANÇOISE
      m.   CATHERINE-   b.1723
      Montreal   b.1720   d.1754
      10 Feb.1749

IE-==JEAN-   JEAN-
LITE BAPTISTE MARIE
      COLONGES b.1756
                d.1756
      ALEXIS-
      FRANÇOIS
      b.1754

SE PIERRE-   MARIE-   MARIE-   MARIE-   FRANÇOISE-
    ANTOINE   FÉLICITÉ   JOSEPHE   CATHERINE   AMABLE
    b.15 Jan. b.1756   d.1757   b.1760   b.1761
    1755   d.1756   d.1761
    d.10 Mar.   ANON   MARIE-
    1820   b.1756 JOSEPHE
                                  b.1758

ontreal
1805
erville

INE-==MARIE-   MARIE-   JACQUES AUGUSTIN   LUC
BLE   JOSEPH   ANNE   b.1747   b.1748   ANON b.1756
      BRABANT   2   d.1756
      ANON

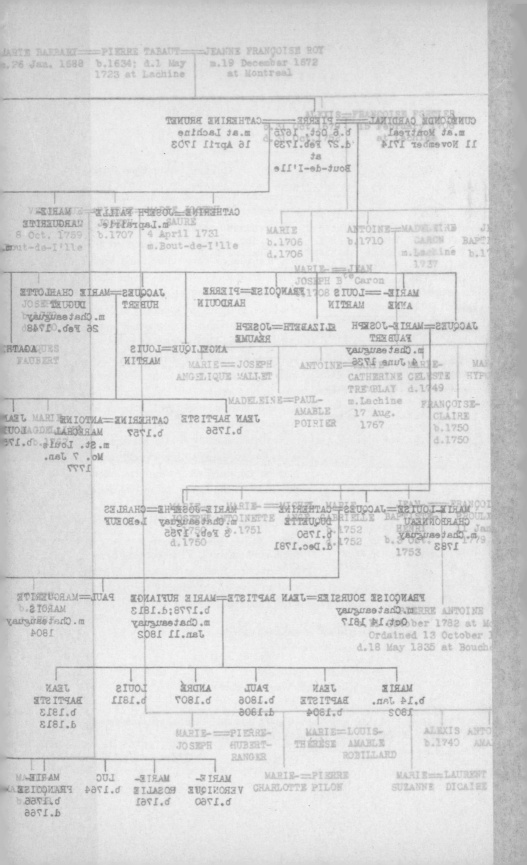

APPENDICES

III. TABEAU TRADE LICENSES[1]

1. 1769, License to J. B. Tabaux — No. 35

DUPLICATE 29" Apr^l 1769

By His Excellency Guy Carleton, Captain-General and Governor in Chief in and over the Province of Quebec, Vice-Admiral of the same, and Brigadier-General of His Majesty's Forces, &c. &c.

In OBEDIENCE to His Majesty's Commands, this License is granted to J^n. B^te. Tabaux to pass unmolested with One Canoe manned with Seven Men (whose Names, Occupations with Places of Abode, and also the Quantity of Merchandize on board, are reported upon Oath and specified in the Margin) to Michilimackinac and from thence to such Markets or Parts as he shall find most advantageous for the disposal of the said Merchandize, with Liberty to dispose of any such Goods or Effects as he shall occasionally find a Market for in his Passage to Michilimackinac aforesaid he taking Care to endorse upon this Licence the Quantity and Quality of the Goods to be disposed of and shewing the same to the Commanding Officer of the next Fort.

PROVIDED always, That nothing herein contained shall be construed to extend to give any Authority to the said J B^te Tabaux ...

BATTOE OR CANOE-MEN'S NAMES, OCCUPATIONS AND PLACES OF ABODE

Francois S^tCire of Batiscan
Aug^n Laderoute, Husbandman, Cedars

P^reDumay	"	Montreal
J. B^tAnge	"	LaChine
~~Chas Charlebois~~	"	~~St. Anne~~
		[sic]
Jos. Gray	"	Montreal
Jos. Chattel	"	Cote S^t. Paul
Pierre Cardinal	"	ditto

Quantity and Quality of Merchandise, viz.
One hundred & thirty Six Gallons of Rum and Brandy
_ _ _ _ _ _ _ _ _ _ _ _ _ _ _ _ _ _ Gallons of Wine
Three Fusils
fifty Pounds of Gun-Powder
One & a half Hundred Weight of Shot
and Balls.

[1] The originals of these trade licenses, given here almost entire, are to be found among the *Trade Records* of the Dominion Archives at Ottawa.

And Seven bales, Six kegs &
boxes of other   Merchandise
in all amounting to Two hundred
Pounds — lawful Money
of the said Province, or thereabouts,
upon Oath of Jean B^te Tabaux

Sworn before me, at Montreal
this fifth May 1769
          de
     Jonas Saulles
          Agent

By His Excellency's Command,
    Geo. Allsopp D Sec^y

These Securities being given, this Licence to
be in force for Twelve Months, otherwise to be
null and void to all Intents and Purposes

Given under my Hand and Seal at Arms, at
the Castle of Saint-Lewis, in the City of
Quebec, this twenty-ninth Day of April
One Thousand Seven Hundred and Sixty-nine-
                              Guy Carleton

I Jean B^te Tabaux do sincerely promise and swear, That I will be
faithful and bear true Allegiance to His Majesty King George the Third,
and him will maintain and defend, to the utmost of my Power So help
me Gd.   J tabaux[2]

(Third Page)[3]

Know all Men by these Presents, That I Jean Baptiste Tabaux of the
City of Montreal Merchant, am held and firmly bound, unto our Sov-
ereign Lord the King, in the full Sum of four hundred pounds — current
Money of this Province ....

The Condition of this Obligation is such, That whereas the Above-
bounden Jean B^te Tabaux has obtained a Licence dated ...

baptiz tabaux

[2] Then follows the oath submitted to the engagés and their marks. They could
evidently not sign their names and Tabaux could barely write his. The scratch that
stands for his initials is indecipherable.

[3] Other pages follow, a fourth, a fifth, a sixth, and a loose. The first three constituted a part of the form, in French, and only the third of them was filled out
partly. The loose page was obviously filled out by Tabaux in making application.
This is dated 22 April 1769. On its reverse side is Tabaux's surety's signature, that
of Joseph Perinault of Montreal. Tabaux's name is here, B^teTabo, and the date, 24
April. On the outside of the document is this briefing:

"No. 35
Mr. Tabaux
Delivered 5th May
1769
J. B^teTabaux
1 Canoe Michilimackinac."

APPENDICES

2. 1774, License to J. B. Tabaux — No. 20

Etat des marchandises de traite pour deux canotees, destinees pour La Baye ou les Limites, sous les ordres de Jean Baptiste Tabaux et Jean Calvet pour hyverner.

Savoir

Marchandises Seches

Consistant en quarante Ballots six Caisses et deux Cassettes montant a Mille Livres argent courant de la Province.

Engagés

Engagés	Ammunition
François Sanssouci	Ammunition
Augustin Dupont	3300 de Poudre a Tirer
Pierre La Franboise	3500 de Plomb & Balles
Louis La Framboise	2 Caisses conten. 10
André Saguina	Fusils chaque.
Raphael Dupuis	20 Barils d'Eaudevie
Louis Dubeau	20 Barils de vin.
Etienne Rouleau	Habitans de la Chine
Antoine Medor	
Jacques Robidou	
Fras Bisson	
Jean La Deroute	
Jean Marchand	
Paul La Lambe	
Pierre Cardinal	

Vivres

Douze Cens baris pezant de Biscuit
Cinq Cens Cinquante baris pesant de Lard
Huit Minots de Pois   Montreal le 6 avril 1774.

3. 1776, License to Baptiste tabault — No. 18

pour une cannottée   Michillimakinac
pour Baptiste tabault Bourgeois

400 lbs de poudre
400   de plomb a balle
 8 fusils
15 Barils de Boisson
& pour £300 de la province de Marchandise seiche

Le guide pascal pommainville de Ste Genevieve

Joseph Pilon
Jean Brisebois } de la pointe claire
Amable St Denis
paul Lenthier

Antoine tabault } de la chine
Jaques St Denis

Joseph Lafleure } de la prairie
Philipe Roy

A Montreal Le 12 juillet 1776.

Pierre Foretier & Jean Orillat

IV. LOISEL-VALLÉ LETTER

St. Louis, 13th. October, 1797.

Mr. François Vallé

Sir —

On unloading the boat, we found in the chests the five plates which you missed. I have sent them on, affixed Rabi, in order to return them to you. On leaving your house, I forgot the treaty of alliance and of friendship between the French Republic and His Catholic Majesty. It is a bit interesting for here no one has had a sight of it. As I promised it to Mr. Zenon, I pray you to send it to him immediately. You will oblige him. My assurances of respect to your family.

Your servant

Regs. Loisel

[The original of this letter is in the *Captain François Vallé Collection,* MHS.]

226

APPENDICES

V. PETITION OF RÉGIS LOISEL, MARCH 20,[1] 1800, AND ACCOMPANYING DOCUMENTS

To Mr. Charles Dehault Delassus, Lieutenant Colonel of the stationary regiment of Louisiana, and Lieutenant Governor of Upper Louisiana, &c.

SIR: Regis Loisel has the honor to submit that, having made considerable sacrifices in the Upper Missouri Company, in aiding to the discovery of Indian nations in that quarter, in order to increase commerce hereafter, as also to inculcate to those different nations favorable sentiments towards the Government, and have them devoted to the service of his Majesty, so as to be able to put a stop to the contraband trade of foreigners who scattering themselves among those Indians, employ all imaginable means to make them adopt principles contrary to the attachment they owe to the Government. The petitioner has also furnished, with zeal, presents, in order to gain the friendship of those different nations, for the purpose to disabuse them of the errors insinuated to them, and to obtain a free passage through their lands, and a durable peace. The petitioner, intending to continue on his own account the commerce which his partners have abandoned in that quarter, hopes that you will be pleased to grant to him, for the convenience of his trade, permission to form an establishment in Upper Missouri, where he will build a fort, about seven leagues higher up than the great bend, (grand detour), distant about four hundred leagues from this town, and which shall be situated on the said Missouri, between the river known under the name of Riviere du vieux Anglais (river of the old Englishman,) which empties itself into the said Missouri, on the right side of it, in descending the stream, and lower down than Cedar island, and the river known under the name of Riviere de la Cote de Medecine, (river of the medicine bluff,) which is on the left side in descending the stream, and higher up than Cedar island; which island is at equal distance from each of the two rivers above named.[2] That place being the most convenient for his op-

---

[1] This Loisel *Petition* and the documents here accompanying it are to be found in connection with the *Report* from the Commissioner of the General Land Office, Twenty-fourth Congress, first session, American State Papers, *Public Lands,* VIII, 117-18. They appear there under the caption, "Class 2, No. 6" of the numerous contested Missouri Land Cases.

[2] For the position of Loisel's Isle of Cedars in its relation to other marks of geographical identification, see the so-called Lewis and Clark itinerary map, *The Geographical Review,* I, opposite p. 344.

erations, as well in the upper as in the lower Missouri, and it being indispensable to secure to himself the timber in an indisputable manner, he
is obliged to have recourse to your goodness, praying that you will be
pleased to grant to him a title of concession in full property for him, his
heirs or assigns, for the extent of land situated along the banks of the
said Missouri, and comprised between the river called the Old Englishman's, and the one called the Medicine bluff, here above mentioned, by
the depth of one league in the interior, on each side of the Missouri, and
including the island known by the name of Cedar island, as also other
small timbered islands. In granting his demand, he shall never cease to
render thanks to your goodness.

REGIS LOISEL

St. Louis of Illinois, *March 20, 1800.*

In the spring following the death of Loisel, the United States Congress made provision for the creation of a Board to adjudicate claims under alleged grant from Spain. The possessory right of Loisel to the Isle
of Cedars and other property was among the first cases brought before it,
the plaintiff being Clamorgan who posed as Loisel's assignee. The above
petition was offered in evidence of title, likewise what was presumably a
provisional concession made by Delassus in answer to Loisel's prayer. The
text, as offered, is here given together with the certification of the Sur-
veyor-General and fragments of testimony, the most interesting part of
which is that furnished by Tabeau, who was apparently an adverse witness.

[a]   St. Louis of Illinois, *March 25, 1800*
Whereas it is notorious that the petitioner has made great losses, when
in the company he mentions, and as he continues his voyages of discoveries conformably to the desire of the Government, which are the cause
of great expenses to him; and it being necessary, for the commerce of
peltries with the Indians, that forts should be constructed among those
remote nations, as much to impress them with respect, as to have places
of deposit for the goods and other articles which merchants carry to them,
and particularly for those of the petitioner; for these reasons I do grant
to him and his successors the land which he solicits, in the same place
where he asks, provided it is not to the prejudice of any body; and the
said land being very far from this post, he is not obliged to have it sur-
veyed at present; but however, he must apply to the Intendant General,
in order to obtain the title in form from said Intendant, because to him

belongs, by order of his Majesty, the granting of all classes of lands belonging to the royal domain.

CARLOS DEHAULT DELASSUS

[b]

At the request of Mr. James Clamorgan, I do certify to have copied the part of the course of the river Missouri, comprised in the above part, from a chart of the said river, which I have in my possession, and to have drawn the plat of the land granted to Mr. Regis Loisel, deceased, by the Lieutenant Governor, Don Charles Dehault Delassus, under date of March 25, 1800, as near as possible conformable to the tenor of said title. The said land extends, on its front, 4¾ French leagues of 30 to the degree, or thereabouts, and on its depth 5½ of those same leagues, which will give a total superficie of the said land to about 14 leagues. The said grant is situated at about 1,200 miles from the mouth of the said river, and between the 107th and 106th degrees of the longitude of London, and 44 degrees of latitude. In testimony whereof, I have delivered the present (plat) to the party interested, to serve him to prove his claim, where needed.

ANTOINE SOULARD
Surveyor General Territory Louisiana.

St. Louis, November 20, 1805.

July 27, 1833.   Truly translated.

JULIUS DE MUN

[c]

No.	Name of original claimant	Arpens	Nature and date of claim	By whom granted	By whom surveyed date and situation
6	Regis Loisel	44,800	Concession, 25th March 1800.	Charles Dehalt Delassus	On the Missouri about 1,200 miles from its mouth.

[d]

Evidence with reference to minutes and records

August 22, 1806. The Board met, pursuant to adjournment.

Present: the honorable John B. C. Lucas, Clement B. Penrose, and James L. Donaldson.

The same, (Jacques Clamorgan,) assignee of Regis Loisel, claiming a tract of land or island on the Missouri. Produces a concession for the same from Charles D. Delassus, dated the 25th March, 1800, and a figurative plan of the same, dated the 20th November, 1805.

Antoine Tabeau, being duly sworn, says that the said land is situate

229

up the Missouri; that, in the year 1802, he, the witness, went up the said river with the said Regis Loisel, who built a four-bastion fort of cedar, the whole at his own expense, and without any assistance from Government; that the year following, to wit, in 1803, they again went up together, when the said Loisel ascended with witness about sixty-five leagues higher up; made a garden and a large field; and further, that he, the witness, never heard of said Loisel having a concession for the land.

Auguste Chouteau, being duly sworn, says that the aforesaid fort was begun in 1800.

The Board reject this claim, and require further proof. See book No. 1, Page 484.

September 14, 1810. Board met. Present: John B. C. Lucas, Clement B. Penrose, and Frederick Bates, commissioners.

Jacques Clamorgan, assignee of Regis Loisel, claiming one hundred and fifty-one thousand and sixty-two arpens eighty-five perches of land. See book No. 1, page 484. It is the opinion of the Board that this claim ought not to be confirmed. See book No. 4, page 500.

July 8, 1833. L. F. Linn, Esq,. appeared, pursuant to adjournment.

Regis Loisel, by Jacques Clamorgan's representatives, claiming 44,800 arpens of land, situate Cedar island, on the Missouri. See record-book C. page 172; minutes, No. 1, page 484; No. 4, page 500.

Produces a paper purporting to be an original concession from Carlos Dehault Delassus, dated March 25, 1800, also, a plat certified by Antoine Soulard, and dated November 20, 1805; also, a copy of an adjudication of the said land to Jacques Clamorgan, certified by M. P. Le Duc, the 7th of October, 1805; also, the affidavit of Antoine Tabeau and Pierre Dorion, taken before Charles Gratiot, judge court of common pleas.

M. P. Le Duc, being duly sworn, says that the signature to the decree of concession is in the proper handwriting of Carlos Dehault Delassus; that the signature to said plat and certificate is in the proper handwriting of Antoine Soulard; and that the signature to the adjudication is in the deponent's own handwriting. See book No. 6, page 222.

November 17, 1834. The Board met, pursuant to adjournment. Present: F. R. Conway, J. H. Relfe, J. S. Mayfield, commissioners.

Regis Loisel, claiming 44,800 arpens of land. See book No. 6, page 222. The Board do not take cognizance of this claim, it being out of their jurisdiction. See book No. 7, page 68.

JAMES S. MAYFIELD,
JAMES H. RELFE,
F. R. CONWAY

APPENDICES

VI. LOISEL-HENEY TRADE AGREEMENT

July 6, 1801[1]

*Convention for Trade among the nations of the Upper Missouri,
drawn up according to the articles hereafter stipulated between S^r. Regis
Loisel, merchant, living at St. Louis, of the one part and S^r. Hugh Heney,
now in this place,*[2] *of the other part to wit*:

ARTICLE I.

There shall be between the two parties an alliance in which S^r. Loisel
shall have two-thirds' interest and S^r. Heney one-third. In this proportion they shall share in the expenses, losses, as well as in the profits which
shall result from their entire trade. This alliance shall last for two entire
consecutive years, beginning from this day and ending on a like day,
1803. In case there should remain to the said company at the end of the
term of two years, merchandise, unsold, that one of the two parties who
shall remain at the said post on his private affair shall be obliged to guard
it in order to give to the said society that which it cost as given above.

ARTICLE II.

Seeing that the above said parties put, neither the one nor the other
any capital into the present company, now belonging to them, they will
make use of the ways that Mr. Auguste Chouteau, merchant of this city,
offers them so as to begin the trading they propose to do.[3]

ARTICLE III.

The merchandise necessary for the trade of the above said partners for
the two years only and for no longer shall be asked for through a mem-
oire signed by the said parties or by one alone authorized by the other
under the signature of Loisel or Heney.

---

[1] The original of the *Loisel-Heney Trade Agreement*, or *Convention*, is among
the *Col. Auguste Chouteau Papers*, MHS. The translation from the French here giv-
en was made by Dr. Rose Abel Wright.

[2] This would suggest that Heney had only recently come to St. Louis; but the
"Monsieur Héné," who, according to the complaint of Clamorgan, suffered spolia-
tion at the hands of British traders when at the head of an expedition, which Doctor
Nasatir thinks probably left St. Louis in June, 1800 (*Anglo-Spanish Rivalry on the
Upper Missouri*, Mississippi Valley Historical *Review*, XVI, 526) could certainly have
been no other than he.

[3] The precise connection between Colonel Chouteau and the newly-organized
company, if company it can be called, being left unincorporated, is matter for conjecture. The implication here is that it was pretty close and that view is strengthened
by such circumstances as that Loisel-Heney papers are among the *Auguste Chouteau*,
MHS, and that Chouteau figured as one of the deceased Loisel's assignees.

ARTICLE IV.

All the merchandise, peltries and other effects pertaining to or being for the account of the said company shall be marked L.H.

ARTICLE V.

Neither of the parties may take from the capital of the concern any stock or any sum to be considered as a deduction in the way of future profits in the affairs of the present company.

ARTICLE VI.

Each partner shall have the right to take from the stores of the present company that which he shall need for his personal use at the price of the equipment and, if he wishes to take something over and above for himself, it shall be posted and counted at the same price as for the engagees.

ARTICLE VII.

There shall be kept books of account for receiving and paying out so that each partner may know the balance of the trade of the said company. This balance will be made each year at a time most convenient.

ARTICLE VIII.

All the employing of engagees, clerks, interpreters, just as every other kind of agreement made by S^r. Loisel and in his own private name, relative to the present expedition and treaty are charged and accounted for the benefit of the said company.

ARTICLE IX.

Neither of the partners shall be responsible to the other for debts incurred before or during the term of the present company in his own name and private.

ARTICLE X.

At the expiration of the two years which this present treaty shall last, liquidation shall be made by the above named partners in order that all that shall have been contracted for be lost or not lost.

ARTICLE XI.

In case of the dissolution of the present company there shall be found a deficit in the affairs by some unforeseen event, then each partner shall give reciprocal security for the balance of that which the said company should have had until its complete liquidation.

ARTICLE XII.

In the event of the death of one of the partners before the complete sale of all the merchandise asked and bought for the account of the present company, the survivor shall close by turning it to the profit and loss account and shall be obliged to render account to the heirs or representative of the deceased when it shall be required, to remit to them the part and portion of profit which would have resulted from all the trading of their company.

Thus conceded and agreed upon between the said Sr Regis Loisel of the one part and the Sr Hugh Heney of the other part who pledge themselves respectively to execute each of the articles before stipulated in their form and tenure in pledge of which the said parties named below have signed in the presence of witnesses also signed below at St. Louis this sixth of July 1801 in duplicate and in good faith. *Art. 8, a word scratched out is nothing.*[4]

Reg^s Loisel

temoin   Aug^{te} Chouteau   H. Heney

The actual trade partnership probably did come to an end at the termination of the period stipulated, notwithstanding that the two Tabeau narratives, taken together, indicate a continued relationship between Loisel and Heney and, after Loisel departed, between Heney and Loisel's "agent and man of affairs." Commercially-speaking, however, the erstwhile inn-keeper of Montreal remains a man of mystery. Supposing him to have been Clamorgan's "Monsieur Héné, we are perplexed at the ease and completeness with which he became an employee of his one-time despoilers. Lewis and Clark received Heney at Fort Mandan as if he were then thoroughly well identified with the North West Company establishment on the Assiniboine. He made his appearance, December 16, 1804, "with a letter from M^r. Charles Chaboillez one of the C^o ..."[5] and, from Larocque's Journal, it is plain to see that he was with Chaboillez the preceding month.[6] According to Patrick Gass, Heney's object in crossing over to the Missouri was to find out what he could about the American expedition and "to gain information with respect to the change of government;" but he brought with him a tender of service from Chaboillez[7] and probably made one of his own, which Lewis and Clark saw fit, in the course of time, to take advantage of.[8] What they wanted was to induce Heney to prevail "on some of the most influential Chiefs" of the Sioux to visit the city of Washington and to accompany them thither

[4] "Art. 8 un mot Raye nul."

[5] *Original Journals, op. cit.,* I, 237-38.

[6] See Entry, November 11, 1804, Photostat, *Masson Collection,* Dominion Archives, Ottawa.

[7] Coues, *History of the Lewis and Clark Expedition,* I, 212.

[8] See Letter from Clark to Heney, dated, *"Camp on the River Roche jhone East of the Rocky Mountains, July* 20th. *1806," Original Journals, op. cit.,* V, 282-86.

himself. Since these chiefs were to be selected from the bands, "who usually resort the borders of Missouri," it seems a little odd that the proposal was not made to Tabeau, who was apparently regarding himself as an American citizen. The explanation, no doubt, is to be found in the fact that Heney, now working under the Union Jack, was *persona grata* with the Dacotahs.

The subsequent career of Hugh Heney was far from bright. By 1812, when he begins to figure in the *Selkirk Papers*, he was a deserter from the North West Company and connected with its rival, the Hudson's Bay.[9] For a time he was the local officer in charge of affairs at Red River[10] and his conduct, on various occasions, much complained of.[11]

[9] See Report of Archibald Mason, *Selkirk Papers*, II, 161, Dominion Archives, Ottawa.

[10] Bryce, George, *The Remarkable History of the Hudson's Bay Company including that of the French Traders of North-Western Canada and of the North-West, XY, and Astor Fur Companies*, p. 286.

[11] William Auld to Miles MacDonell, dated York Factory, July 8, 1812, *Selkirk Papers*, II, 78-79; William Auld to William Hillier, January 28, 1813, *idem*, pp. 209-13; Charles Sweeney to Miles MacDonell, dated Fort Dair, March 16, 1813, *idem*, p. 321; "McDonell Affidavit," dated April 23, 1813, *idem*, pp. 241-42; W. Hillier to Miles MacDonell, dated Fort William, May 3, 1813, *idem*, p. 255; Cox, I. J., *Early Explorations of Louisiana*, p. 33.

APPENDICES

VII. MEMORIAL[1] OF RÉGIS LOISEL, MAY 28, 1804, AND RELATED DOCUMENTS

To Don Carlos de Hault de Lassus, Colonel of the Infantry Regiment of Luisiana and its dependencies, etc.

In accordance with the instructions which Your Excellency was pleased to honor me on the 15th of April of last year 1803, I must inform you of what I have been able to learn on my last voyage for the trade and explorations of the Upper Misury, with relation to the Indian tribes whom I have frequented, their political status, commerce, etc.

I shall say nothing, Sir Lieutenant-Governor, of the customs of those tribes, which differ but little if any from those of other savages.[2] But I shall inform Your Excellency in writing of the geographical location of the districts which are of interest to the Government. Your Excellency will see therefrom and very distinctly how exposed the domains of His Majesty are to the undertakings of the foreigners who have for a long time been introducing themselves into the upper Misury, bribing the tribes by holding large assemblies among them in which they reveal propositions most harmful to our Government by taking away the richest furs.

They accompany all their steps with presents, which are the prime mover and the delight of those tribes, who will do whatever one may ask of them, by virtue of the merchandise. The presents or gifts incite them to peace or war, and decide the preference of their affection toward one or the other government. The gifts, in a word, are the great mainspring which moves them with the greatest facility.

Not having taken two years on my voyage, as I had promised myself, I have not had time to acquire all the information that I had proposed to

---

[1] Loisel's *Memorial* and the two related documents that follow here are included among those published in Houck's *Spanish Régime in Missouri*, II, 355-64. The Memorial, under the descriptive but not wholly satisfactory title, "The Boundary of Louisiana on the Upper Missouri and Mississippi under the Cession," covers pages 359-64, the end of the series; but it is placed here at the beginning as both a logical and a chronological arrangement would demand. Parentheses and brackets are as in Houck.

[2] Since Tabeau's narrative deals so fully with this particular matter, the customs of the tribes, and since there is some ground for thinking that it was prepared originally as a report, it may well have been that this task had been deputed to him, he being Loisel's "agent and man of affairs" and, perchance, better qualified than was Loisel for it.

myself, because of having been detained in the Island of Cedros[3] by the Sioux tribe, who kept me in sight all through the past winter. That, besides having caused me a great loss, has made it necessary for me to descend the river in order to adjust my business. I would have again ascended however, had it not been for the change which the Government has experienced, in order to satisfy the intentions of our Government and satisfy the confidence that it has reposed in me. I have sent M. Sabeau,[4] my agent and man of affairs, with seven more under his orders and my express orders with instructions to continue the undertaking in my name.

Nevertheless, I have discovered, Sir Lieutenant-Governor, that one may travel by water in a certain manner, from Hudson Bay to the chain

[3] To give this once very interesting place a modern signification, the following passage from Quaife may be quoted to advantage:

". . . . The M.R.C. (Missouri River Commission) map shows two islands near the boundary between Lyman and Stanley counties, the first called Cedar or Dorion Island, and the second Dorion Island No. 2. The latter was the site of Loisel's fort . . . . Two or three miles above the island a stream comes in from the south which is still known as Loiselle Creek" (Wisconsin Historical Society *Collections*, XXII, 135, n. 3). For discrepancies, consequent upon an attempt to bring the island within the limits of present-day nomenclature, compare Quaife, *idem*, p. 22, with Thwaites, *Early Western Travels*, V, 184, n. 105.

[4] Tabeau? The error, for such I am convinced it is, must have been made in translating from the French original — assuming that Loisel, ex-French-Canadian, wrote in French — to the Spanish or in transcribing from the latter; for the sentence in the *Houck Transcripts*, MHS reads, "No haviendo empleado dos anos en mi viage ... Mr. Sabeau, mi agente y hombre de conocimientos . . . ." Curiously enough, other instances of the sort can be shown to be not uncommon. In the *Mackinac Register*, as published, there is an entry of date July 23, 1786 to the effect that two of the vestrymen of the Church of Ste. Anne de Michilimakina, E[ne] Campion & B[te] Labeau (Tabeau?), elected two other men to serve as church wardens (Wisconsin Historical Society *Collections*, XVIII, 493). In the copy at Ottawa, Ontario of the *Frobisher Letter Book, 1787-1788*, the original of which is at McGill University, there is a letter from Joseph Frobisher to Isaac Todd, dated Montreal, 30 October 1788 (see p. 78) alluding to the finding of the body of Charles Paterson by two men, Campion and Tabace [Tabeau?]. Jean-Baptiste Tabeau was, at the time, Étienne Campion's partner. Similarly, in Dr. Burpee's valuable article on the Beaver Club (Canadian Historical Association *Report*, 1924, pp. 73-92), the elections for 1787 are indicated as having included a certain Jean Baptiste Jabeau, whereas Dr. Fauteaux of the Bibliothiqué St. Sulpice at Montreal, under whose direction a list of such elections has been made from the original records, insists that the man elected was Tabeau and that no such name as Jabeau is to be found in Lower Canada. The name Labault is to be found, seemingly, otherwise an entry in the *Militia Records* at Ottawa might be taken as yet another instance of error. It is an entry for 1798 as follows: "John B[te] labault-Montreal — Capitaine." What strengthens the case for error is the fact that "labault" is the only name on the page with a small initial letter.

of mountains in Mexico which surrounds Santa Fe, with the exception of a small portage overland of one-half league, in order to cross the small tongue or isthmus which separates the river *Bois Blanc* [*i.e.*, White Wood — the James or Dakota] from the River Qui Parle [*i.e.*, Who Speaks — the Sheyenne], which empties into the Colorada [*i.e.*, Red River of the North], which in turn empties into Lake Ouanipik [*i.e.*, Winipeg].

I must tell your Excellency at this point of the chief known tributaries that flow into the Misury. The Rio Chato (Riviere Platte) [*i.e.*, Platte River], which empties into the Misury at a distance of two hundred leagues from the Misisipi must not be passed by in silence. It rises west of Santa Fe, and flows between two mountains bordering the Neuve Reyno de Mexico in order to discharge its waters into the Misury under the well-known name of Rio Chato. It is impossible to open navigation with the Mexican territory by means of its channel, but there is no necessity for it, for transportation overland is easy and the distance but slight, and the road which is open so far as the savages are concerned, assures the American of the ease of penetrating without any trouble. In order to stop that, no other means present themselves than the resistance of the tribes. It is important that they be not allowed to be bribed by a new people of whom they know nothing more than the name; for they will always respect the word that Your Excellency has passed them, so long as they do not abandon themselves to a new master entirely. Let the Government cultivate their affection by the means by which men of all sorts may not be separated if they are employed suitably, and one may then immediately count on their fidelity. Benefits diffused and received for the sake of friendship and confidence, however slight that be, exceed in merit those which are scattered by fear and distrust although abundantly and profusely. Such is the political situation and general opinion of the tribes whom I have visited and with whom I have talked.

Ascending the Misury one hundred and thirty leagues above the mouth of the Rio Chato (Riviére Platte) one comes to the Rio Qui Corre [*i.e.*, River which runs — the Niobrara?]. Its direction is the same, and it rises in the first mountains known under the name of Costa Negra [*i.e.*, Black Hills]. That name was doubtless given those mountains because of the color of the earth. Under that earth are hidden precious minerals, as is declared by the tribes who frequent them. They are so abundant that they are found in nuggets, scattered here and there both in various places upon the Rio Chato and upon this river [Que Corre].

Although my purpose has been to fix my attention upon the rivers which empty into the Misuri, and rise on the side of the Spanish possessions or in Mexico, I must not fail to inform Your Excellency of the River Bois Blanc, which is also called the River Jacques [*i.e.,* James]. Its mouth is on the north side of the Misury fifteen leagues above the Rio Que Corre (Riviére Qui Court), of which we have just spoken.

This river, which is about two hundred leagues in length, and runs north northwest, rises very near the other which is called Rio Que Habla (Riviére Que Parle). The latter flows into another river called Colorado, and empties at the north into Lake Oanipik. Consequently, in order to reach the Misury by way of these last three rivers, one need make an overland portage of only one-half league.

The waters of Lake Oanipik communicate with Hudson Bay by means of the small river called York [*i.e.,* Nelson] which unites them. That allows one to believe that communication by water would be very possible from Hudson Bay to the Gulf of Mexico by means of a small portage one-half league in length between the river Que Habla and the river Jacques, and a second one at the costas [*i.e.,* hills or mountains] of Santa Fe.

Hudson Bay communicates with Lake Oanipik by means of York River. The said lake communicates also with the Colorado River, which unites with the River Que Habla, whose waters it receives. Here there is a small portage in order to reach the River Jacques which empties into the Misury. Thence ascending the Rio Chato or the River Que Corre, one may reach the mountains of Santa Fe, where are found the branches of the Rio del Norte [*i.e.,* Rio Grande, that forms the boundary between Mexico and Texas], which empties into the Gulf of Mexico.

Reascending the Misury to a distance of 450 leagues from San Luis, one comes to the River Chayennes, or as it is also called, the Courche or Braso. It offers the same means of communication with Nuevo Mexico to the west by crossing the Costa Negra of which we have spoken above. It rises in the chain of mountains in which are found settlements of Nuevo Mexico.

Continuing to ascend the Misury, one comes to the River of Rocas Paxizas (Roches Jaunes) [*i.e.,* Yellowstone], which leads also to the western region, and rises in the mountains of Neuvo Mexico, which extend farthest to the west.

Upon the banks of all these rivers as well as upon the banks of all that empty into them, are found an infinite number of different wandering tribes, who are as ready for war as for peace, and have their boundaries at the mountain chain of Nuevo Mexico; and [others who] are settled in fixed villages. The latter are the Ricaras, the Mandanas, the Ven-

238

trudos or Gros Ventres, and the Souliers (Zapatos), and they are located on the Misury. The wandering tribes are the Chayennes, Cayuguhas, Caninambiches, Catacas, Otomies, Chahuines, Sioux, Bois Brule, Sahonis, Onkpapas, Okendanes, Sintones, Zuktones, Zuktones, Zuktoananes, Huapitones, and Minikahuhup. There are also other tribes whom I have not visited, and whom I know only by name, who are also wandering. Such are the Cuerbos Serpientes, Ventrudos Volantes, Change de Venille, Salzis, Pieds Ganes, and Pieds Negros, all very numerous.

At the present time when the United States of America have negotiated for this province of Luisiana, their undertakings are so much more to be feared, for they believe that their boundaries ought to be considered as the sources of the various rivers which empty by different branches into the Misisipi, although many of those rivers take their rise in the midst of Spanish settlements. The Americans are enterprising and ambitious, and there is no doubt but that they will avail themselves of any means in their power to win the minds of the savage tribes, and will endeavor to erase by cunning arguments the fine impressions of our Government that they have received. In spite of the deep-rooted affection of the Indians toward us, it is quite easy to bribe them, by means of presents, as I have remarked, and I am of the opinion that the Government ought to watch over this so important matter. We have examples that these barbarous nations have fallen upon various Spanish settlements which they have devastated after having murdered a portion of their inhabitants, and carried the remainder off as slaves. The Spanish Government has kept them from making such raids for many years by winning and captivating their goodwill by making enormous expenditures, so that today they venerate His Majesty's banner, and the name of their great Spanish Father. But if with the lapse of time they hear no more talk of it, they will forget about it, and the Americans will captivate their minds with much less difficulty, and will make use of the Indians for their ambitious designs. Already do they talk of making the Mexican pesos descend the Misury by proposing to establish contraband trade with that kingdom. With that object in mind they are proposing to establish great merchandise magazines on the frontiers. Some men have already set out in order to prepare the way and to assure communication from the side of Santa Fe. I shall not dwell further on the consequences which Your Excellency can judge for yourself. I Have privately undertaken the continuation of the explorations that were commenced by the Company of the Misury. I have made great sacrifices in the presents which I have had to make to the savages in the name of the Government, especially on this last journey, in order to cover the foreign flags and medals, as Your Excellency had ordered me, by making gifts to the chiefs. In this way I have succeeded with the Chayennes, Caninambiches, Sioux, Sabines, or Sahonas, and Ricaras. There is no one here who knows as much as I do of the distant tribes among whom I have penetrated farthest. In view of this exposition, and as I am desirous of following Your Excellency's banners, since it is probable that the Government intends to employ some trustworthy person to restrain these tribes, and dissuade them from heeding all the persuasions and prejudicial impressions with which the Americans will endeavor to imbue them against the Government, and perhaps against the Spanish settlements, whether by trade or by arms, I offer myself voluntarily, promising my good services as a faithful vassal, and the one best fitted for the undertaking, if the Government desires to honor me with its confidence, by giving me some employment on the frontier, such as that of agent of the tribes, with the object of preserving their friendship with us and avoiding the result of the persuasions of the Americans, etc., etc., etc.

San Luis de Ylinoa, May 28, 1804   Régis Loisel
Addressed:[5] "The marquis of Casa-Calvo (rubric)."

[*The Marquis of Casa-Calvo to Don Pedro Ceballos*[6]]
Your Excellency:

Colonel Carlos de Hault de Lassus, ex-Lieutenant-Governor of the settlements of Ylinoa in Upper Luisiana, under date of August 10, secretly informed me of the results of his observations on the movements and conversations of the Americans in respect to the acquisition which they have made of that province.

He shows me clearly that the general idea of that nation is that their boundaries will pass through the very kingdom of Nuevo Mexico, and they carry their lines to the Bravo [*i.e.,* Rio Grande] River, penetrating by several points and following various small streams, showing only too clearly that they are making vast calculations, in consideration of the

[5] Loisel's Memorial was, in the first instance, addressed undoubtedly to Delassus, who communicated it to the Marquis of Casa-Calvo and he, in his turn, to Don Pedro Ceballos and, through him, to Godoy, "the Prince of the Peace."

[6] This, one of the two covering letters that Houck published with Loisel's Memorial (see pp. 356-58) is, in a political aspect, even more important than it itself is, since it indicates the extent of Spanish apprehensions and the means taken to allay them. It reveals the trust reposed in Loisel and the confidence placed in his judgment. The other of the two covering letters is in Houck, *op. cit.,* p. 355.

[7] Evidently the Lewis and Clark expedition, which was semi-military.

profits that they will make from the lands and the working of the mines. They are planning to send a troop[7] to the headwaters of the Missouri, for which object, and through others, officials, whom they are sending into Ylinoa, they are informing themselves in an efficacious manner and with continued eagerness from the Indians, hunters, and traders, in regard to the shortest paths by which to penetrate to Santa Fe and to other places of the Nuevo Reyno [*i.e.,* New Kingdom]. The traders Jeannot Metoyer[8] and Bautista Labarde,[9] who were to be joined among the tribes by the trader called Joseph Gerbais,[10] went as early as the month of July by the said Misury River for that purpose, leaving San Luis with merchandise and boats. All three are to work in concert, and have been equipped and supplied by Evan Morrison,[11] a wealthy inhabitant of Kaskaskias, an American post on the east bank of Misisipi. Gervais, who knows the road well, will guide them and show them the way into the Nuevo Reyno.

Last year the same man conducted the Panis tribe to make peace with the Governor of Santa Fe or with the Commandant-General — a voyage which it appears has been repeated this spring. When returning he must have met Metoyer and Lalande [*sc.* Labarde]. With the same intention, and in order to facilitate the undertaking Lorenzo Deroche[12] and Santiago d'Eglisse[13] have gone to the upper waters of the Misury. The latter was employed by the Company of the Explorations of the Misury, and since he has not returned this year it is inferred that he has penetrated into Nuevo Mexico.

The American Captain of Ylinoa, Mr. Stoddar, and [Mr.] Brush, in conference with the Osages Indians, have incited them to take the warpath and pillage the silver convoys which ply between different points, as they succeeded in doing some years ago.

[8] "The Metoyer family resided near Natchitoches" (Houck, *op. cit.,* p. 356, n. 1).

[9] The name was probably La Barbe, although Captain Pike, who came across the man, when on his Mexican expedition, called him, Baptiste Lalande. For evidence of this and for the alleged pecuniary claims against Lalande that Dr. John H. Robinson made the pretext for his own trip to Mexico, see Coues, Elliott, *Expeditions of Zebulon Montgomery Pike,* pp. xlix, 250 n., 264, 499, n. 4, 602-3, n. 5, 604, 623-24. The claim had been transferred to Robinson, who is believed to have been a spy, by William Morrison of Kaskaskia.

[10] Gervais? A Kaskaskia family of this name found its way to Ste. Geneviève (Houck, *op. cit.,* p. 356, n. 4).

[11] William Morrison.

[12] Laurent Durocher?

[13] For references to articles dealing with Jacques D'Eglise, the person evidently meant here, see Historical Introduction.

The said Lieutenant-Governor advises that those posts abounded, at the time of his writing, in all sorts of the finest drygoods, and although there were more than three fourths above the ordinary consumption, more were being brought in daily, with the idea of sending them to the Mexican frontiers. He is of the opinion that unless the most efficacious measures and the most exact precautions are taken in order to restrain the contraband, in a short time the silver will go from the Nuevo Reyno de Mexico by the Misury instead of the furs which are the only product of that river.

On the same occasion he remits me the memorial whose translation accompanies this letter. This document, while it at the same time enforces and confirms whatever has been said in regard to the navigation of the Misury, its proximity to Nuevo Mexico, and the fatal consequences that must be feared from the ambition of our neighbors, proves the urgency and the absolute necessity of not yielding even one foot of the west bank of the Misisipi, although it be necessary to have recourse to arms for that purpose. Any other means, even delay in preventing by real force those dangerous neighbors from entering our possessions will occasion their inevitable loss.

The water communication from Hudson Bay to the Gulf of Mexico, as soon as it is known and frequented, can increase the British and American commerce to the extreme of power, and they will meet their greatest support and encouragement at the passage of the inland rivers. Because of the treasures that they will tear from the very bosom of Spain, they will totally ruin our commerce. What is even more to be feared, I believe, is that they will alienate the affection of the Indians [from us], and may, perhaps, cause other inconveniences of the greatest consideration. At the bank, then, of the Misisipi must be established and raised solidly the dike that will restrain the rapidity of the current. If what I have shown happens, that dike ought to be procured at all cost. It will be easier now, however, by means of the most exact and continual vigilance of our Governors and Commandants to cut off the communication of the English who may penetrate by way of Hudson Bay, and of the Americans who may penetrate into the Misury by other currents than that bay.

The author of the memorial, Regis Loisel, proposes a method which is one of the most adaptable, and I am even so bold as to pronounce it one of the most adequate. Loisel has been an inhabitant of Ylinoa for some time, and both by his written statement and by the verbal conferences which I have held with him in order to instruct myself thoroughly of the matter, he advises me that he understands thoroughly and that he knows practically about 500 leagues of the course of the Misury. He is active, young, and enterprising — and I consider him suitable, and consequently, faithful, in the discharge of his promises. With these qualities, and since he possesses a knowledge of the English and French languages, at the same that he preserves the good-will of the tribes by means of trade, he can easily destroy the projects of the English and Americans, if he be employed on the frontier as agent of the Indian tribes, and if he also be given liberty to select one or two other men to help him, who shall receive a fixed salary.

I must beg Your Excellency to keep in mind numbers 1-15, with the exception of the 4th, 6th, and 7th, which are so closely connected with the present irrefragable testimony, which urges more and more the arguments and reasons in those settlements wherefore the Americans should not be permitted under any consideration to retain possession of the west bank of the Misisipi; and why this river should constitute the line of division between Spain and the United States, from its source to its discharge into the Gulf of Mexico, even if we should not succeed in regaining the island of Nuevo Orleans on the said west bank, which I have also proposed, and which I ever conceive as the most advisable thing.

I entreat Your Excellency to please bring this to the superior notice of His Majesty, in order that he may opportunely give the orders that are deemed most advisable for the preservation of those vast dominions in the imminent risks to which I believe them exposed. May God preserve Your Excellency many years.

Nuevo Orleans, September 30, 1804. Your Excellency,

The Marquis of Casa-Calvo

Addressed: "His Excellency, Don Pedro Ceballos."

[*The Marquis of Casa-Calvo to the Prince of the Peace*]
Most Excellent Sir:
Sir

The adjoined copies are transcrips of the representation and document that I am sending on this date through the Minister of State. As Your Excellency will see I am reflecting upon the information communicated by Colonel Don Carlos de Hault de Lassus, former Lieutenant-Governor of the settlements of Ylinoa; and discussing the memorial presented by Regis Loissel. I set forth the imminent danger to which the interior provinces are exposed, if the Americans retain the west bank of the Misisipi.

243

It is evident, General, that these dangers must be feared to the proportion that the easy and continuous communication by water from Hudson Bay to the Gulf of Mexico, without other obstacle than the sole portage of one-half league overland near the upper part of the Misury, is demonstrated in the memorial. Consequently, I propose the remedy that has appeared most suitable to me and even adequate, and that is the employment on the frontier of Nuevo Mexico of the author of the memorial as agent of the Indian tribes, with two subordinates to aid him in restraining the entrance of English and Americans.

I inform Your Excellency of this for your superior consideration.

May God preserve Your Excellency for many years, Nueva Orleans, September 30, 1804.

The Marquis of Casa-Calvo (rubric)

Your Excellency

Addressed: "His Excellency, the Prince of Peace."

APPENDICES

VIII. LE CERNE OU CHASSE EN COMMUN[1]

[*An extract from Tabeau's revised, or Montreal version*]

Dans l'opinion des titons & des ricaras, le boeuf, le cerf & l'ours sont des especes de génies qui se plaisent sous cette forme & qui mene [ent] cette vie ambulataire par bonté pour les sauvages & pour fournir a leur subsistance. aussi n'y fait-on la grande chasse qu'avec un respect relilig- ieux [*sic*] & elle est sujéte a des loix que persone n'oseroit enfreindre. c'est surtout le cas ou les soldats sont séveres dans l'éxécution de leur charge, & tout délinquant peut s'attendre a perdre ses armes que l'on brise, a voir sa loge de cuir taillée en lambeaux, quelques fois ses cheveaux tuées & luy même bien bâtoné. en effet, ces loix sont absolument nécessaires, sur- tout chez les nations ambulantes, qui ne pourroient subsister, si chaque particulier avoit le droit, pour se procurer une vache de metre [mettre] en fuitte tout un troupeau & détruire ainsi la base de la subsistance généralle. aussi prend-on toutre les peines & toutes les précautions possibles pour n'en être pas privé.

Un certain nombre de jeunes gens sont toujours en découvertes & font des courses circulaires a 7 & 8 lieuës de distance du camp ou du village; & celui qui découvre un troupeau est obligé de venir en avertir, sans lui doner la chasse, ni même se faire voir. on doit s'en rapporter aveuglement a la déclaration du découvreur, & il est de foi que le moindre doute sur la vérité de son rapport chasse infailliblement la vache. il arrive pourtant assez souvent chez les ricaras, les plus grands menteurs du monde, que tout le village, dupe de l'imposture court en vain des journées entierres. mais ce qui est le plus singulier, c'est que celui qui les trompe est per- suadé luy-même que sur sa parole la vache s'est rendue a l'endroit qu'il a désigné, & ne la trouvant pas, il a toujours des raisons plausibles qui satisfont tout le monde & le persuade souvent luy même.

Quand la saison & les grands froids annoncent que le passage de la vache n'est pas éloigné, on se prépare a la chasse, on fait l'élection des soldats & on employe mille moyens superstitieux pour l'engager a hâter la marche. on la fait appeler par des têtes de boeuf rangées aux environs du camp, sur les faites des maisons & dans chaque loge; ces têtes vermil- lonnées & entourées de sacrifices regardent le levant & le couchant &

---

[1] This excerpt from Tabeau's revised, or Montreal, version, is given here *in extenso;* because it is a section that, in its entirety, is without a counterpart in the Wash- ington version. For its availability I am indebted, as noted already in my Preface, to Professor Benoît Brouillette.

montrent quelques herbes séches qu'elles ruminent. on danse, on festine, on immole des chiens &c. — les engagés ces capitaines lewis & clark ont été témoins & acteurs chez les mandanes, dans une cérémonie singuliere a ce sujet. les vieillards s'assemblent sur le soir dans la loge de médecine & font annoncer par les harangueurs que la vache n'est pas fort éloignée mais qu'elle attend pour arriver que les braves fassent quelques grand sacrifice en son honeur. aussitot ces bons maris amenent leurs plus jolies femmes (car ils en ont plusieurs) a ce nouveau temple de paphos, enveloppées dans une simple couverture; un maitre de cérémonie les range autour de la loge d'un coté & les époux de l'autre. = les vieillards nuds beuglent, mugissent, grattent la terre, la frappent de leurs têtes & imitent en tout le taureau en saison. pendant cet bel éxercice on allume un petit feu au centre de la loge, sur le qu'el on brule quelques herbes odoriferentes, a la fumée des qu'elles les actrices vont se parfumer, sans beaucoup observer la décence. elles défilent ensuitte devant un nombre compté sur le leur de jeunes garçons assis en rang. chaque mari a mis entre les mains du jeune homme qu'il luy a plu, une baguette conuë [connue] de son épouse & qu'elle saisit en passant comme pour la ravir; mais le cavalier résistant, elle l'entraine sans beaucoup d'effort hors de la loge, & toutes les autres en fesant [faisant] autant, toute la compagnie se trouve dans un instant par couple dans la prairie, ou les vieillards beuglents toujours & se tenants a une certaine distance, semblent accuser leur foiblesse & témoigner leur désespoir; au retour a la loge, les maris font leurs très humbles remerciments. la cérémonie continuë ainsi toute la nuit, les acteurs changeants cependant de parteneuses a chaque scene. comme la vache étoit proche en effet, elle est arrivé le lendemain & les mandanes ont cru tout devoir aux soldats amériquains qui, pour attirer la vache, se sont portés avec un zéle infatigable.

l'automne & le printemps, saisons du passage annuel de la vache, on ne va pas a sa rencontre & seroit-on dans la plus grande disette, on la laisse approcher & même passer les premiers troupeaux, persuadés qu'ils servent de guides aux autres qui suivront tous la même passer les premiers troupeaux, persuadés qu'ils servent de guides aux autres qui suivront tous la même route. quand les soldats jugent qu'elle est suffisamment engagée, ils font haranguer & ordonent le cerne. cette chasse se fait en société & voici comme on y proccéde: on se rend en plus grand nombre qu'il est possible a un lieu Désigné par les soldats a une certaine distance des animaux. les meilleurs archers, les cavaliers & les coureurs ont leurs postes assignés & les vieillards commencent la cérémonie. on fait d'abord fumer le ceil, la terre, les quatre points cardinaux & on présente ensuitte tous les tuyaux des pipes a la vache & pendant qu'elle est supposée fumer, les vieillards mugissent & font a peu près les mêmes folies qu'a la fête chez les mandanes. le partisan du cerne (car il y en a un comme a la guerre) adresse ensuitte le discour au troupeau: "O vous autres vaches, vous apprenez tous les jours dans les entretiens de vos anciens que vous estes notre unique ressource; ayez donc pitié de nous aujourdhui. vous sçavez que nous avons faim. vous voyez que nos cheveaux sont maigres; que nos coureurs sont foibles & ne pourroient pas vous joindre, si vous fuyez de toutes vos forces. = & vous, terre, vents, roches grands peres des sauvages, aidez nous aujourdhui. donez de l'esprit a la vache: dites luy qu'elle ne soit pas folle & qu'elle ne fasse point de mal a nos jeunes gens." = Après ce morceau d'éloquence, il done le signal & l'on part en formant la marche de maniére a envelopper le troupeau qu'on veut attaquer; le cercle se resserre insensiblement jusqu'a ce qu'é-tants assez près ou ne pouvants avancer davantage sans être apperçus, les soldats détachent quelques jeunes gens audessus du vent, pour lancer les animeaux. aussitot que l'odeur leur parvient, ils prennent la fuitte, & se voïants environés, ils ne font plus que tournoyer & se gêner réciproque-ment. les cavaliers & les coureurs beaucoup plus légers leur ferment par-tout le passage & les ramenent au centre ou la flèche & le fusil en détrui-sent quelque fois jusqu'a deux & trois cents. enfin, pressées de toute parts, ces pauvres bêtes semblent prendre un parti désesperé & forcent dans un même endroit les rangs a s'ouvrir. = Pendant la melée les chasseurs sont assez hardis pour pénétrer dans le milieu du troupeau & y choisir les vaches les plus grasses mais ils prétendent connoitre au regard celles qui sont mal intentionnées & se donent bien de garde de les attaquer, s'ils ne voient pas moyen d'éviter leurs fureurs. se qui est certain, c'est que les accidents sont fort rares. il est vrai que la fléche décochée par un bon archer, passant de parc en parc & tombant encore loin au delà de l'animal, ne luy laisse pas grande vigueur. le nomé *kakawita* ricara & deux ou trois autres ont plusieurs fois transpercés deux vaches. = le plus grand nombre tel que les vieillards & les jeunes garçons sont sans armes, mais ayants aidé de leur persone a fermer le passage aux animeaux & contribué au succès, ils ont le même droit au partage qui se fait aussi conformé-ment a des régles fixes. Dès que les fuyards sont échappés on ne les poursuit guères & chacun au contraire se hâte de courir à la proie afin de toucher des premiers a une vache grasse, que la loi partage entre les cinq premieres persones qui la touchent. le premier arrivé a pour sa part moitié de la bosse, la panse, le veau, si la vache est pleine (morceau re-cherché de préference) & une épaule. le second prend aussi moitié de bosse, une épaule, un des flancs, la fressure, &c. = ainsi du 3éme, 4éme, & 5éme dont les parts respectives sont marquées. il arrive pourtant assez souvent des difficultés, soit sur l'instant de l'arrivée, soit que l'on profite de la circonstance pour satisfaire un ressentiment secret, ce qui est parfaitement dans le caracthere ricara. les soldats indépendant de leur droit commun ont encore le privilége de réclamer une certaine quantité de bosses & en certaines circonstances toutes les langues. tout particulier qui annonce le dessein de faire quelque grande cérémonie, tel que nomer [nommer] un enfant &c. peut choisir la vache qui luy plait, sans que persone prétende au partage, quand elle seroit déja divisée.

APPENDICES

IX. TABEAU'S DONATION, OR DEED OF GIFT, MARCH, 1819[1]

The beneficiary under this donation, or deed of gift, and the person to whom Pierre-Antoine Tabeau entrusted himself for the remainder of his days was the nephew and namesake, to whom it had been left to become what Tabeau himself might have been had he continued in the way he started. This younger Pierre-Antoine Tabeau was the son of Jean-Baptiste-Henri and Elizabeth née Proulx.[2] He had been ordained, October 13, 1805, although some two years before the Reverend Mr. Roux, Vicar-General of Montreal, had had some anxious fears lest he fall by the wayside.[3] He is best remembered for his missionary work in and around Fort William. On the occasion of one of his journeys to that place he travelled in the company of Dr. John L. Bigsby, who, in *The Shoe and Canoe,* has conveyed to his readers a very pleasing idea of "M Tabeau the curé of Boucherville, a stout, rosy, happy-looking priest of middle age, of unaffected and even polished manners, fond of music, and reasonably so of good living." "He was," says Dr. Bigsby, "a good man, and had nothing of the livid complexion and gloomy pugnacity of many of the Roman Catholic clergy in England."[4] With so likeable a man to care for him,[5] the old trader, Tabeau, must have been well content. He was in good hands for the short term of life that remained to him. He was weary and ailing when he made his "donation" and he died a year thereafter.[6]

---

[1] A certified copy of this legal document was procured, through the kindness of E.-Z. Massicotte, Archivist, Old Court House, Montreal, from the archives of the judiciary district of Montreal.

[2] See Tabeau Genealogical Chart, Appendix II.

[3] Morice, A.-G., *Histoire de l'Église Catholique dans l'Ouest Canadien,* I, 115, n. 8.

[4] See I, 127, 130, 134, 148, 159, etc.

[5] For additional information about Father Tabeau, who died at Boucherville, May 18, 1835, and, concerning whom it is much less difficult to get information than concerning his uncle, see, among other things, *Bulletin des Recherches Historiques,* VI, 75; VIII, 81; XIII, 7, 14; *Le Pantheon Canadien,* p. 268; *Archives de Québec* (1927-28), pp. 235, 256, 277, 279, 296, 310; (1928-29), pp. 90, 99, 115, 116, 123, 125, 126, 127, 128, 129; *Répertoire Général du Clergé Canadien,* p. 170; Allaire, L'Abbé J-B.-A., *Dictionnaire Biographique du Clergé Canadien-Français,* p. 505; *Morice, Le R. P.A.-G., Dictionnaire Historique des Canadiens et des Métis Français de L'Ouest,* p. 281. From the *Militia Records* of Lower Canada, I am led to infer that Father Tabeau had a brother, another Jean-Baptiste.

[6] He died at Lachine, March 10, 1820, aged 65 years.

1819, 4 mars

Cession de Jouissance par le Sr Pierre Antoine Tabeau à Messire Ant. Tabeau.

Pardevant Les notaires publics pour la Province du Bas Canada residants à Montréal Soussignés

Fut présent le Sieur Pierre Antoine Tabeau Cidevant marchand demeurant en la paroisse Saint Michel de La Chine, d'une part

Et messire Antoine Tabeau prêtre et Curé de la paroisse de la Sainte famille de Boucherville dans le District de Montréal d'autre part

Lesquelles parties ont déclaré que le dit Messire Antoine Tabeau seroit propriétaire des biens ci après désignés savoir lod'une terre Située en la dite paroisse de La Chine de la contenance de trois arpents de front Sur vingt huit arpents de profondeur prenant pardevant du Fleuve Saint Laurent, parderriere a un terrain non concedé Joignant d'un coté au nordest au dit Messire Antoine Tabeau et dautre Côté a Dame veuve Nicolas Robert.

2o D'un emplacement situé en la Cité de Montréal rue Notre Dame de la Contenance de trente pieds de front sur la profondeur qui peut se trouver entre les rues notre Dame et Saint Jacques par lesquelles rues ce terrain se trouve borné en front et en profondeur Joint d'un Coté au Nordest a Michel Fournier et au Sudouest au Sr Horatio Gates avec Une maison dessus Construite.

3o de la somme de deux mille huit Cent Livres de vingt Sols constituée sur un terrain Située en la cité de Montréal la propriété du Sr Eustache Prévost par lequel la dite rente est due au denier vingt.

4o d'Une autre somme de Quinze Cent Livres de vingt Sols due aussi a Constitution de rente au denier vingt par Jean Baptiste Rodier de la Cité de Montreal et Constituée sur un terrain que ce dernier possede au dit Lieu Le tout les parties disent bien Connoitre

Que le dit Pierre Antoine Tabeau auroit la jouissance de moitié des dits biens pendant sa vie durante en vertu des Testaments du Sr Jean Baptiste Tabeau et Marie Anne Vallée son épouse, ses pere et mere par acte passés devant   ... (un blanc)

Laquelle jouissance le dit Pierre Antoine Tabeau a offert au dit Messire Antoine Tabeau son neveu a Compter du premier jour de février dernier Jusqu'au décès de lui dit Pierre Antoine Tabeau moyennant la pension et aux conditions ci après exprimées ce que le dit messire Antoine Tabeau a accepté, en Conséquence le dit Pierre Antoine Tabeau a Cedé et abandonné au dit Messire Antoine Tabeau a ce present et acceptant la dite jouissance a Compter dud't premier Février dernier Laquelle demeurera des lors comme a tousjours réunie et Consolidée au fond et Propriété des dits biens, dememe que sils en eussent Jamais été grevés.

Cet cession ou abandon est fait lo-en considération que le dit Sr. Pierre Antoine Tabeau Conservera la jouissance sa vie durante de moitié de la maison batie sur la terre susdésignée, quil occupe actuellement et du jardin tel quil est enclos et duquel il est en possession, avec cette Condition expresse que le dit Pierre Antoine Tabeau ne pourra louer, ni donner la dite jouissance a qui que ce puisse être sans la permission expresse et par écrit dudit Antoine Tabeau a peine de nullité.

Enfin moyennant la Somme de Soixante Six Livres Courrant par an a Compter du premier fevrier dernier Jusqu'au jour du décés du dit Pierre Antoine Tabeau, Que le dit Messire Antoine Tabeau promet payer audit Sr Pierre Antoine Tabeau par payements de deux Livres quinze chelins par chaque demi mois.

Pour sureté du payement de laquelle dite rente et des conditions de cet acte les parties ont hypothequés leurs biens et Elu leur domiciles en leur demeures respectives auxquels lieux & par ainsi Promettant obligeant Fait & passé a Montréal demeure du dit Sr Pierre Antoine Tabeau L'an Mil huit Cent dix neuf le quatre mars apres midi et les parties ont Signé avec Les notaires apres lecture faite

P. Tabeau

Ant. Tabeau Pt

F. G. Lepallieur

N. B. Doucet

Copie conforme de la minute trouvée dans l'étude de Me N. B. Doucet en son vivant notaire en Bas-Canada, ou Province de Québec, déposée dans les archives de la Cour Supérieure district de Montréal.

Montréal, le 14 décembre 1937

E. Z. Massicotte

D.P.C.S.

INDEX

INDEX

INDEX

INDEX

INDEX

271

Tabeau, Pierre Antoine, 1755–1820.

Tabeau's narrative of Loisel's expedition to the upper Missouri, edited by Annie Heloise Abel, translated from the French by Rose Abel Wright. Norman, University of Oklahoma press, 1939.

xi p., 2 l., 3–272 p. 2 facsim. (incl. front.) fold. geneal. tab. 23½ cm.

"First edition."

1. Loisel, Régis, d. 1804. 2. Missouri river. 3. Arikara Indians. 4. Indians of North America—Northwestern states. I. Abel, Annie Heloise, 1873–   ed. II. Wright, Rose (Abel) 1876–   tr.

F598.T14   917.78   39—19289